# CHINA'S NEW ENTERPRISE BANKRUPTCY LAW

*A methodical exposition of the modern law of Chinese insolvency, this text brings together expertise from academia and practice in order to provide a conceptual basis for the workings of the modern law as well as an incredibly detailed analysis of its provisions with additional information about the participants in the insolvency process.*

Paul Omar, University of Sussex, UK

# Markets and the Law



Markets and the Law is concerned with the way the law interacts with the market through regulation, self-regulation and the impact of private law regimes. It looks at the impact of regional and international organizations (e.g. EC and WTO) and many of the works adopt a comparative approach and/or appeal to an international audience. Examples of subjects covered include trade laws, intellectual property, sales law, insurance, consumer law, banking, financial markets, labour law, environmental law and social regulation affecting the market as well as competition law. The series includes texts covering a broad area, monographs on focused issues, and collections of essays dealing with particular themes.

*Other titles in the series*

**Product Liability Law in Transition**
**A Central European Perspective**
Magdalena Tulibacka
ISBN 978 0 7546 4710 2

**The Yearbook of Consumer Law 2009**
Edited by Deborah Parry, Annette Nordhausen, Geraint Howells and Christian Twigg-Flesner
ISBN 978 0 7546 7574 7

**Statutory Priorities in Corporate Insolvency Law**
**An Analysis of Preferred Creditor Status**
Christopher F. Symes
ISBN 978 0 7546 7519 8

# China's New Enterprise Bankruptcy Law

## Context, Interpretation and Application

*Edited by*

REBECCA PARRY
*Nottingham Trent University, UK*

YONGQIAN XU
*Dacheng Law Firm, China*

HAIZHENG ZHANG
*Beijing Foreign Studies University, China*

Routledge
Taylor & Francis Group
LONDON AND NEW YORK

First published 2010 by Ashgate Publishing

2 Park Square, Milton Park, Abingdon, Oxfordshire OX14 4RN
52 Vanderbilt Avenue, New York, NY 10017

*Routledge is an imprint of the Taylor & Francis Group, an informa business*

First issued in paperback 2020



**British Library Cataloguing in Publication Data**
China's new enterprise bankruptcy law : context,
interpretation and application. -- (Markets and the law)
1. Bankruptcy--China.
I. Series II. Parry, Rebecca. III. Xu, Yongqian, 1967-
IV. Zhang, Haizheng.
346.5'1078-dc22

**Library of Congress Cataloging-in-Publication Data**
Parry, Rebecca.
China's new enterprise bankruptcy law : context, interpretation, and application / by Rebecca Parry, Yongqian Xu, and Haizheng Zhang.
p. cm. -- (Markets and the law)
Includes bibliographical references and index.
ISBN 978-0-7546-7637-9 (hardback)
1. Bankruptcy--China. 2. Corporate governance--Law and legislation--China. 3. Business failures--Law and legislation--China. I. Xu, Yongqian, 1967- II. Zhang, Haizheng, 1982- III. Title.

KNQ1942.P37 2009
346.5107'8--dc22

2009031356

ISBN 978-0-7546-7637-9 (hbk)
ISBN 978-0-367-60293-2 (pbk)

# Contents

# List of Tables and Figure

**Tables**



**Figure**

# List of Abbreviations

**AMCs** – Asset Management Companies
**Appointment Regulations** – 'Regulations of the Supreme People's Court on the Appointment of Administrators for Hearings on Cases of Enterprise Bankruptcy'
**CAS** – Chinese Accounting Standards
**CBRC** – China Banking Regulatory Commission
**CCP** – Chinese Communist Party
**CIRC** – China Insurance Regulatory Commission
**CPAs** – Certified Public Accountants
**CPL** – Civil Procedure Law of the PRC
**CSOP** – Capital Structure Optimization Programme
**CSRC** – China Securities Regulatory Commission
**EBL 1986** – Enterprise Bankruptcy Law 1986 (For Trial Implementation)
**EBL 2006** – Enterprise Bankruptcy Law 2006
**GAAP** – General Accepted Accounting Principles
**GITIC** – Guangdong International Trust Investment Corporation
**HKSE** – Hong Kong Stock Exchange
**IFRS** – International Financial Reporting Standards
**MOFTEC** – Ministry of Foreign Trade and Economic Co-operation (replaced by Ministry of Commerce since 2003)
**NBLG** – National Bankruptcy Liaison Group
**NDRC** – State Development Planning Commission
**NPC** – National People's Congress
**NPLs** – Non-performing loans
**OECD** – Organization for Economic Co-operation and Development
**PRC** – People's Republic of China
**Regulations 2002** – 'The Regulation on Several Issues Concerning Hearing Enterprise Bankruptcy Cases'
**Remuneration Regulations** – 'Regulations of the Supreme People's Court on the Determination of Remuneration for Administrators in the Hearing of Enterprise Bankruptcy Cases'
**SASAC** – State-owned Assets Supervision and Administration Commission of the State Council
**SETC** – State Economic and Trade Commission
**SEZ** – Special Economic Zone
**SOEs** – State-owned enterprises
**SPC** – Supreme People's Court

**UNCITRAL** – United Nations Commission on International Trade Law
**WTO** – World Trade Organization

# Notes on Contributors

**Rebecca Parry** is a Professor at Nottingham Trent University. She has published widely in the area of insolvency law and has a particular interest in international developments in this area. She obtained her PhD from the University of Manchester.

**Yongqian Xu** is the Director of the Supervisory Committee of Dacheng Law Firm, a qualified lawyer, legal advisor, insolvency practitioner and senior partner. He also works as the vice-director of the civil law committee of the China Bar Association. He is a member of the Commercial Law Institute of the China Law Society and visiting professor at Beijing Technology and Business University and the Training Centre of China Entrepreneurial Confederation. He has published several works about Chinese bankruptcy law. Mr Xu is currently producing an insolvency guideline for the Chinese qualified insolvency practitioners under the authorization of Ministry of Justice of PRC.

**Haizheng Zhang** is a Lecturer in the Law School of Beijing Foreign Studies University. He holds a PhD from the University of Leicester and he has a strong research interest in corporate insolvency and rescue law. He has published both English and Chinese language articles on China's bankruptcy law.

**Qingxiu Bu** is a Lecturer in Law at Queen's University Belfast. He was formerly a lecturer at Cardiff University. He holds a PhD from the University of Birmingham. He has a strong interest in Chinese company law.

**Xin Ge**, LLM, was called to the Chinese Bar, and is now a professional consultant in DS Avocats Beijing Office (<http://www.dsavocats.com>). DS Avocats is a leading French law firm, in Europe and among European law firms in Asia.

**Jingxia Shi** is a Professor of Law at China University of International Business and Economics. She holds a PhD from Wuhan University. She is a leading expert in corporate insolvency law in China and has been involved in the legislative process. She was a drafter of the new bankruptcy law and has been invited by the International Insolvency Institute and American Bankruptcy Institute on many occasions to introduce this new law. She is currently doing research at Yale University.

**Xiaohe Tan** is a Senior Accountant and Certified Public Accountant (CPA) of China. She used to act as a financial manager and was in charge of auditing work in a large state-owned enterprise affiliated to the State Council. She gained her BSc in London and is a member of the Association of Chartered Certified Accountants (ACCA). She is working as a senior auditor at Bond Partners LLP in London (<http://www.bondpartners.co.uk>).

**Roman Tomasic** is the Chair in Company Law at the Durham Law School. He has a particular interest in corporate governance, comparative corporate law and the use of socio-legal research methods. He holds an MA and LLB from the University of Sydney, an SJD from the University of Wisconsin-Madison and a PhD (in Sociology) from the University of New South Wales. Prior to moving to Durham, Professor Tomasic was a Research Professor in the School of Law at Victoria University in Melbourne, Australia. He has held visiting positions at the Wisconsin Law School and at the City University of Hong Kong and has held continuing law teaching positions at Kuring-Gai College (now the University of Technology, Sydney), the University of Canberra, and Victoria University in Melbourne.

**Bin Wang,** LLM, of Liaoning University, is a Lecturer at Shenyang Normal University with rich experience in bankruptcy law and is an experienced lawyer in Liaoning Yingtai Law Office.

**Jianhua Xiao** is a Professor and PhD supervisor of China University of Political Science and Law, from which he holds his Master and PhD degrees. He also acts as the Dean of Law School of Tianjing University of Finance and Economics, Visiting Professor of Hebei University and Visiting Scholar of the Law School of Northwestern University in the US from 2003-2004. He is a prominent expert in civil procedural laws and bankruptcy laws.

**Bingkun Ye** is a Judge of the 2nd Civil Division and the head of the Bankruptcy Tribunal in Xiamen Intermediate Peoples Court, Fujian Province. He has extensive experience of insolvency proceedings under both the old and the new bankruptcy regimes. He holds the degrees of LL.B (CUP&L), LLM (Xiamen Univ.), and LLM with Distinction (University of Leicester).

**Weiwei Zheng** is a PhD candidate at the Law School of Jilin University, one of the best universities in China. She holds the degrees of LLM from the University of Leicester and LLB from Jilin University. She has strong research interest in private international law and insolvency law.

# Preface

Recent years have seen many significant legal reforms in China, including judicial reforms, accession to the WTO and a whole raft of new legislation. The enactment of the Enterprise Bankruptcy Law 2006 may be regarded as one of the most notable developments at this time, for two main reasons. First, this law represents a tremendous breakthrough in view of the historical incompatibility of bankruptcy laws with Chinese culture and ideology: not only were bankruptcy laws absent from China for many years under the planned economy, they are to some extent incompatible with Confucianism, which exerts a tremendous influence on Chinese law and society. While experimental bankruptcy laws had previously been developed following the launch of the Reform and Opening up Policy in 1978, these laws were so controversial that they were restrictive in a way in which the new law is not. Secondly the enactment of the new bankruptcy law is remarkable since the developing Chinese socialist market economy was hitherto considered to be insufficiently ready for the introduction of bankruptcy laws that did not contain tight controls. These concerns led to the reform process which preceded the new law becoming rather protracted.

The context for the enactment of the new bankruptcy laws is the development of a legal infrastructure to support the emerging Chinese market economy which has been established under a process of economic transition in the past three decades. The national economy has risen particularly dramatically in recent years and foreign capital has increasingly been attracted into the Chinese market. Through inbound and outbound investment, China now stands as one of the most influential countries in the global economy. Its flagging state-owned enterprises have been reformed and the private sector has risen dramatically in scale and importance. Alongside these developments there has been a shift away from the traditional socialist ideology and as a result people's mindsets are no longer completely closed to the legal concepts and institutions of Western jurisdictions. In order to maintain economic order, China has enacted a series of laws in accordance with the requirements of a market economy, and the new bankruptcy law was one of them.

The new Chinese bankruptcy law inspired and encouraged the editors to produce an English text which aims to systematically and comprehensively describe and analyse the Chinese bankruptcy legal framework, including theoretical, substantive and procedural issues, particularly concentrating on its notable features, including the new office of the insolvency administrator, the revised corporate rescue procedures, the new creditor's committee and cross-border insolvency provisions. In addition to the law itself, the book also identifies relevant regulations and judicial interpretations.

As editors, we are grateful to all the authors for their efforts, their scholarship and their contributions to this book and, in particular, for delivering their chapters in accordance with our timescales. We have found the work of the authors to be insightful and informative.

The book in part draws upon work done by Haizheng Zhang towards his PhD at the University of Leicester, awarded in 2008. He would like to thank his examiners, Professor David Milman and Ian Snaith for their support and encouragement. He would like to thank his supervisors Professor Cosmo Graham and Professor Rebecca Parry for their comments on drafts of the thesis and Dr Camilla Baasch Andersen and Mrs Jane Sowler, Research Degrees Administrator, for their support and encouragement. He is grateful to Professor Jingxia Shi, a drafter of the new bankruptcy law, who provided a lot of useful articles and information. He would also like to thank his wife and family for their continuous belief and support.

Rebecca Parry thanks her partner Jonathan and her family for their support. She would also like to thank the British Academy and the Society of Legal Scholars for funding to enable her to present a paper at XVI Biennial Conference of the European Association of Chinese Studies, Ljubljana, in August 2006 in the very early stages of this project. Versions of some of the material from this book and related projects were also presented at the European Association of Chinese Studies conference in Lund, 9 August 2008; the INSOL International Annual Regional Conference, Shanghai, 16 September 2008; and at the Joint INSOL Europe Academic Forum/Sussex Law School conference held at the University of Sussex, 26-27 March 2009. We thank the audience participants at all of these conferences for their insightful questions and comments.

We would both like to thank Professor Adrian Walters, Professor David Burdette, Gary Wilson, Richard Sheldon QC, Joe Bannister and Dr Paul Omar for their encouragement of this project. Thanks are also due to the anonymous referee who gave us very insightful comments on the formulation of the structure of this book in its initial stage. We would like to thank Alison Kirk, Carolyn Court, David Shervington and Bibi Stoute of Ashgate, as well as proofreader Albert Stewart for their contributions to the publication of this book.

We welcome the comments of readers from all over the world. The opinions of the Chinese and the international legal communities can play significant roles in enabling the Chinese legal reformers to reconsider the new bankruptcy law, to identify its potential problems and to formulate solutions to enable the new law to reach its full effectiveness. We sincerely hope that this book will become a bridge which may connect the Chinese bankruptcy legal reformers and international insolvency professionals.

Rebecca Parry
Haizheng Zhang
Nottingham and Beijing, 2009

# PART I
# China's Bankruptcy Legal Framework

# Chapter 1
# Introduction

Rebecca Parry and Haizheng Zhang

This book presents an analysis of the new Enterprise Bankruptcy Law 2006 of the People's Republic of China, presenting a detailed discussion of key features of the law and its context. This context is important, since the concept of bankruptcy is by no means a straightforward one in China, ideologically, socially and politically. The enactment of this law was a complex and difficult task which took many years of efforts. The new law therefore represents a significant milestone but the economic, social and political context of the law is likely to continue to impact upon its operation for many years to come.

This introductory chapter will provide a background to the concept of bankruptcy in China, highlighting the role of legal culture, the early history of bankruptcy laws in China, the social and economic impact of the Mao era, the previous bankruptcy law and the passage of the 2006 Law. The new law will then be briefly introduced before an overview of the book and its structure will be provided.

## Impact of Traditional Legal Culture

Chinese traditional legal culture has had a significant historical impact, both on the understanding of the concept of bankruptcy, and on the bankruptcy legislation itself. This legal culture can clearly be divided into three stages. In the ancient Chinese empire, it was built upon the Confucian theory which was involved in every aspect of people's lives including politics, the economy, law, culture and morality. When the Chinese Communist Party (CCP) took control over the new China in 1949, people were living under the strong influence of Maoism which was formulated through the combination of Marxist theory and unique Chinese perspectives. In contemporary China, the legal culture and ideology have been developing towards a rule of law since the government carried out the economic reform and opening up policy in 1978.[1] This chapter will consider each of these phases and their impact on the development of bankruptcy laws at the time.

1 See in particular Lubman (1999) and Peerenboom (2002).

## Confucianism

Confucianism emphasized the natural harmony of the society that motivated the approach of collectivism and opposed individual rights which were deemed to be contrary to the natural order.[2] There was no autonomy for individuals who only assumed obligations to the community. Under Confucian theory, the ancient legal system was comprised by propriety (*li*) and law (*fa*). It was noteworthy that propriety was preferred as a means of conflict resolution, rather than law.[3] Confucius advocated that 'If people are guided by *fa*, and order among them is enforced by means of punishment, they will try to evade the punishment, but have no sense of shame, but if they are guided by virtue, and order among them is enforced by *li*, they will have the sense of shame and also be reformed'.[4] In this conception, law played a less important role than morality in dispute resolution between individuals. In addition, the disputants might have felt shamed and embarrassed at having to resolve their conflict through judicial process. Out-of-court means of reconciliation were preferably adopted.[5] Viewed through Western eyes, the Chinese ancient legal culture was not individualist. The most significant point was that Confucianism had been adopted by the ruling class since the Han Dynasty as the principal guideline which strongly influenced the ruling strategy of each emperor, the enforcement of laws and people's patterns of thought in the feudal society.[6] A conception that a 'son should repay the debts of his father' was deduced from Confucian theory which had a negative impact on the legislation of bankruptcy law.[7] Since the debts could pass from one generation to another, it is submitted that there was no need for the enactment of bankruptcy laws for insolvent individuals because the creditors could enforce their debts by claiming against the debtor's children who had the ability to repay. It can be perceived that the Confucian theory had a far-reaching influence on the ideology and legal construction. Just as Friedrich Hirth said 'for even at the present day, after the lapse of more than two thousand years, the moral, social and political life about one-third of mankind continues to be under the full influence of his (Confucius's) mind'.[8]

## Early Bankruptcy Laws, 1906-49

Influenced by Confucian ideologies, bankruptcy laws were absent from China for much of its history. Such laws only appeared in the last few years of Imperial

2 Hoecke and Warrington (1998), p. 506.
3 Lee and Lai (1978), p. 1308.
4 Confucian Analects, bk. II, ch. III. as quoted in Lee and Lai (1978), p. 1310.
5 Hoecke and Warrington (1998), p. 506.
6 Zhang (2007), pp. 72-3.
7 Tang (2005), para. 1.07.
8 Ibid. at para. 1.02.

China and accordingly there were no bankruptcy laws for several decades following the emergence of modern business enterprises in Imperial China in the 1840s.[9] Besides the ideological factors, noted above, a possible further factor that may have lain behind this comparatively late development may have been the nature of business at this time. It has been noted that 'family businesses' were at this time prevalent[10] and so the nature of business may not have given rise to a need for such laws. This is, however, a point of some debate, as the scale of such businesses may have been rather more significant than their family nature suggests. A strong contention is that the 'kinship' which marked the family business out was in effect a smokescreen, 'a finely wrought legal fiction that legitimated the existence of private enterprises by profit-seeking individuals in a state in which Confucianism was the official orthodoxy'.[11] These 'family businesses' were in fact 'clan corporations'[12] or 'patricorporations'[13] which in fact performed similar functions to modern corporations.[14] It seems clear however that the development of modern commercial *law* in China only took place towards the end of the Qing dynasty.[15]

The first company law, *Da Qing Gong Si Lu*, was enacted in 1904 and the first bankruptcy law, *Pochan Lu*, followed soon after, in 1906. However, this first bankruptcy law was only short lived, due to protests by merchants and implementation difficulties, and it was abolished by Emperor Guan Xu in 1908.[16] The Qing dynasty fell in 1912 and during the era of the Republic of China, which lasted until 1949, a time of legal instability followed, in particular during the period from 1912 to 1928, when the Republic was ruled by warlord factions. Several versions of bankruptcy laws were enacted during the period from 1915, when a new bankruptcy law was enacted by the Northern Warlords Government by referring to the bankruptcy laws of Germany and Japan.[17] This bankruptcy law included substantive rights, procedures and responsibilities and contained as many as 337 articles. However, owing to a lack of legal skills and legislative lacunae, this law did not come into force.[18] Subsequently, in the 'Nanjing Decade' established by the Kuomintang from 1928, significant efforts were made towards the modernization of the legal system, and a new bankruptcy law was enacted in 1935 on the basis

9 It is contended that this emergence began when China was forced to enter the world of globalized trade following the Opium Wars of the 1840s: Gu Minkang (2006), p. 5.

10 Weber (1978), p. 727.

11 Ruskola (2000), pp. 1617-18.

12 Ruskola (2000).

13 Gates (1996).

14 See Gates (1996), pp. 31-3 and sources cited therein.

15 See for example Rowe (1984), p. 145 noting that tea guild merchants in nineteenth century Hankou preferred to 'rely upon private compulsion to guarantee prompt and fair payment'.

16 Li (2001).

17 Gu (2006), p. 278.

18 Wang (2007), p. 28.

of the 'Provisional Regulation on the Disposal of the Debts of Merchants' which was issued in 1933. This bankruptcy law included corporate liquidation and composition procedures which drew upon the advanced experiences of Western jurisdictions.[19] However, like all laws enacted by the Kuomintang, these laws were abolished following the founding of the People's Republic of China in 1949.[20]

## Establishment of the People's Republic of China

When the new China was founded in 1949, the people became the 'real masters' of the state under the leadership of the Chinese Communist Party, 'CCP', which developed the traditional Marxist theory on the basis of the peculiar characteristics of China. In terms of legal culture in the Maoist era, law was treated as a tool of the ruling class and all the legal rules were politicized, whether criminal or civil law.[21] In the West, private law in particular is utilized to facilitate the exchange of private property rights and transactions, while in the Maoist China, private law, which mainly referred to civil law, was 'far from the autonomous and semiautonomous institutions that bear similar labels in the west'.[22] The legal system under Mao emphasized the functions of extra-judicial mediation as a fundamental means of dispute resolution. One major distinction between mediation under Mao and reconciliation under Confucius was that the former was strongly marked by its political colour. In that era, the ideological debate was intense and sensitive, and it was important that a line was drawn between capitalism and socialism. It can be generalized that the Maoist legal framework focused on the collectivist approach and neglected the protection of individual rights. Fundamentally, this system led to a serious problem, equalitarianism, which may be metaphorically termed as 'eating from the big pot' (giving an equal claim to state and enterprise largesse).[23] It largely influenced people's attitudes and incentives to produce and innovate, and impeded the enhancement of productivity.

In the 1950s the Chinese Communist Party swiftly and successfully accomplished the 'socialist transformation' in which all the private enterprises and factories were transferred to public ownership. Replacing capitalism was

19 Ibid.

20 See further Li (2001). The 1935 law survives as the framework of the bankruptcy law of Taiwan.

21 Lubman (1999), pp. 88-9.

22 Ibid. at 91.

23 'Eating from the big pot' was a vivid description of equalitarianism. Literally, it meant that people who worked in a state-owned enterprise or a rural collective shared food from the same pot. In essence, it criticized people's backward thought in pursuit of equality of living standards. Under this thought, people who worked or did not work and people who worked well or worked badly enjoyed the same treatment and social distribution. It eroded people's attitudes and creativity. From Western people's eyes, the Chinese equalitarianism in the Maoist era was unbelievable. Wong (2004), p. 156.

the tenet of this political and economic campaign, the result of which was that all the private property in enterprises and businesses was owned by the state.[24] The completely public ownership and state-owned property structure paved the way for the construction of a highly centralized planned economic system and a socialist institutional framework which formulated the almighty and unshakable leadership of the Communist Party on the nationalized economy and the operation of enterprises. The deployment of resources and the transactions between enterprises was arranged in accordance with the order of the central or local government, rather than the market forces of supply and demand.[25] It has therefore been observed that 'politically, conceptually and ideologically, it was impossible at the time to bankrupt any ailing or failing business enterprise. Any and all failing enterprises would have the support and back up of the State'.[26]

In the first decade since 'liberation' in 1949, Communist China experienced the increasing development of the economy and the full construction of socialism. Then a large-scale economic campaign, which was launched by the central government in 1958 named the 'Great Leap Forward', caused a significant setback in the economy.[27] The partial pursuit of incredibly high goals and a 'catch up strategy' (*ganchao zhanlue*) in heavy industry and the production of steel caused an imbalance in the industrial structure and chaos for the economic order.[28] The subsequent Cultural Revolution, which invoked political campaigns, mass mobilization and class struggle at the national level from 1966 to 1976, resulted in a deterioration of the national economy. Many state-owned enterprises fell into financial difficulties or reached the brink of bankruptcy during these events. Because the state-owned enterprises could not be wound up at that time, the state adopted a compulsory administrative approach to deal with the distressed enterprises, which was called a programme of 'closures, stoppages, mergers and transfers' (*guan ting bing zhuan*). Administrative orders of closure or provisional stoppage could be imposed on ailing enterprises or factories which consumed excessive natural resources, caused extremely high costs or produced products that were inferior in quality. Where a weak enterprise severely lacked equipment or technologies, the government could bring about through a merger an amalgamation with a strong enterprise doing the same business. Where an enterprise which operated under a wrong productive strategy, or where the product of the enterprise could not be readily sold, the enterprise could be ordered to change its strategy or to transfer to another area. Workers who were made redundant under the 'closures, stoppages, mergers and transfers' programme were reallocated to the rural commune to contribute to the rural economy.[29] It should be noted that even

24 Article 10, Chinese Constitution 1954.
25 Wong (2004), p. 153.
26 Tang (2005), para. 3.04.
27 Yang (2006), pp. 45-7.
28 Vogel (2005), pp. 753-5.
29 Xie (2005), pp. 30-31.

though this centralized programme was only a temporary administrative process to handle ailing enterprises, it did play a significant role in closing completely failing enterprises and rehabilitating financially distressed enterprises which could still be rescued. As a result, the programme played a role of enhancing the efficiency of the operation of enterprises in the era of the planned command economy where there was no bankruptcy legislation.[30]

## Development of a Socialist Market Economy

China has been in the process of establishing a socialist market economy since the CCP initiated the economic reform and opening up policy in 1978. The development of the economy required an efficient and well-functioning legal system to facilitate commercial transactions and protect the order of the market. In a bold step the government bravely introduced market-oriented mechanisms and borrowed Western legal institutions to promote the legal reforms and to change people's traditional views and attitudes towards legal rules. The CCP was determined to transfer the focus from the class struggle to the national economy.

### *Impact of Marxism*

One problem that seemingly stood in the way of economic development was that traditional Marxism viewed the market mechanism and legal concepts such as private property, companies and bankruptcies as unique characteristics of capitalist society. A key contribution to the resolution of this problem was made by a former party veteran, Chen Yun, who came up with a notable metaphor, known as 'bird in a cage' theory:[31]

> In this metaphor, the market is the bird and the plan is the cage. The cage can be enlarged to give greater freedom to the bird, but without the cage, the bird will fly away – which is analogous to disorder in the market.[32]

This theory ingeniously resolved the ideological argument and influenced people's attitudes towards the Western advanced legal institutions. It may however be observed that the concepts of 'planning' by the state and the 'competitive market' are not fundamental distinctions between capitalism and socialism but merely economic tools. A capitalist economy cannot operate well without macroeconomic regulation in fiscal policy, and, accordingly, capitalist governments still play some significant roles in order to avoid economic recession, inflation, high unemployment and to safeguard the order of the market economy. Equally, a socialist economy

30 Tang (2005), para. 3.04.

31 Vogel (2005), p. 759.

32 Bell, Khor and Kochhar (1993), p. 2.

is unlikely to be prosperous without a market base.[33] This viewpoint effectively harmonized the 'planning' and 'market' in the Chinese economy and motivated the reforms of marketization, legal construction and individuals' patterns of thought which paved the way for the acceptance and establishment of a bankruptcy legal framework.

### *Enactment of the EBL 1986*

Historically, the legal concept of bankruptcy was among those categorized into the domain of capitalism which was ideologically resisted by the Chinese people in the Maoist era. Since all the enterprises and their property were completely owned by the State, the bankrupting of enterprises would indirectly mean the insolvency of the State, which was unlikely to be understood and accepted by the people whose families were working in the SOEs from one generation to another. The ideological mindset that Western bankruptcy law theory and Communism could not co-exist dominated in the era of the traditional planned economy.

The launching by the central government of its opening up policy in 1978 was a striking and bold achievement and since then China has been placed on a track of economic structural transition. The economic reform led to a relaxation of the government's control over the SOEs, which to some degree were conferred operational and managerial autonomy. As the door gradually opened to the outside world, China bravely introduced market-orientated competitive mechanisms and closely related legal concepts which encouraged the swift and continuous growth of its economy, even though they were traditionally identified as capitalist characteristics. With the deepening of the reform, the Chinese leadership became released from the previous constraint of ideological debate and came to view the market and related legal institutions such as bankruptcy as economic tools to resolve economic problems in the Communist context. Economic development therefore overrode ideology. In the words of the former party leader Deng Xiaoping, 'it did not matter if the cat was black or white; it was a good cat if it caught the mouse'.[34]

The importation of market-orientated rules intensified competition among enterprises, and was one of a number of measures that urged poorly operated enterprises to improve their management and reduce costs, and to redeploy their limited resources. In this sense, the winding up of any insolvent enterprise that had no hope of a turnaround was a necessary part of the reform of marketization, since competitive market forces would enable uneconomic and inefficient enterprises to be exposed.[35] The planned economy had not been conducive to the economic efficiency and profitability of state-owned enterprises. Although the exact scale of the problem at the time was not known with precision, official statistics indicated

33 Guo (2003), p. 553.

34 Vogel (2005), p. 756.

35 Xiao (1989), p. 58.

that around 20 to 25 per cent of SOEs sustained losses each year and there were many such enterprises that made losses year upon year.[36]

The role that might be played by bankruptcy laws in the economic transformation of China, was not merely as a means to remove failing enterprises from the market but also as a spur to improved levels of performance. This idea was enthusiastically promoted by Cao Siyuan,[37] an economist and lobbyist who at one time held a position at the State Council's Technology and Economic Research Centre. He had become enthusiastic about promoting the need for a bankruptcy law while a graduate student and in 1979, soon after graduation, he produced a paper, 'On Reforming the State-Ownership System', that was subsequently expanded and which set out the case for reform. The contention was that the potential for bankruptcy might shock failing enterprises into a 'sense of crisis'[38] and as a result this might raise their productivity. This was, however, only one of a number of necessary measures and, to the same end, SOEs would be exposed to competition; the level of state interference in the market would be scaled down; and enterprises would be responsible for their own profits and losses. Managers would be held accountable for mismanagement and corruption and the threat of unemployment would encourage higher standards among employees.[39]

Bankruptcy therefore came to be considered in principle to be an effective approach to deal with the problems of financially ailing and loss-making enterprises by the government in the early stages of the economic reform, even though the government was reluctant to bankrupt distressed enterprises due to the concerns of large-scale unemployment and the threat to the nature of Communism.[40] On 27 February 1984, an article named 'A Discussion on the Bankruptcy of Long-term Loss-making Enterprises' was published in an official journal, and for the first time at the national level discussed the legal concept of bankruptcy, of which most citizens had never heard before.[41] Cao Siyuan's lobbying led in late 1984 to the establishment of a Bankruptcy Law Committee by the State Council and he was appointed to head up a Bankruptcy Law Drafting team. The process of drafting began in early 1985 and a working group was given the task of drafting, investigation and research.[42]

By late 1984 it had therefore become clear that the introduction of bankruptcy laws was needed. However in view of the scale of such an undertaking, the central government firstly selected three significant industrial cities, respectively Shenyang,

36 Zheng (1986), p. 685.

37 For an introduction to whom see Keyser (1998), pp. 4-7. A detailed account of the efforts taken to influence the enactment of a bankruptcy law are detailed in Cao (1998).

38 Cao (1998), p. 25.

39 Cao (1998).

40 Tang (2005), para. 5.01.

41 Chang (1987), p. 336.

42 Zheng (1986), p. 694.

Wuhan and Chongqing,[43] to formulate a bankruptcy system on a trial basis at the beginning of 1985. The local governments of the three cities were delegated to produce local bankruptcy regulatory rules. Shenyang issued its local bankruptcy regulation known as 'Bankruptcy of Urban Collective Industrial Enterprises' on 9 February 1985, which only applied to the collective enterprises owned by the Shenyang city.[44] It is noteworthy that the government's efforts gradually changed the people's patterns of thoughts and attitudes of hostility to bankruptcy.

As part of the process of changing the mindsets of the people, steps were taken from mid-1984 to provide empirical evidence of the potential for bankruptcy laws to act as a stimulus to improved performance by companies.[45] Eight failing companies in the test cities were issued with warning notices and were ordered to go through reorganization.[46] The first of these was the No. 3 Radio Factory in Wuhan, which had been losing money on a significant scale for three years. This firm was warned by the Mayor of Wuhan that unless it became profitable in 12 months it would be closed. In response to this warning the company was shocked into reviewing its business. It conducted market research, as a result of which it adjusted its factory production structure, discontinued some lines and opened others. The warning acted as a remarkable trigger for improved productivity and the firm soon became profitable.[47] Similar experiments were carried out in Shenyang.[48] Although the experiment in that city involved the issuing of warning notices to only three companies, one of which failed,[49] it was considered to have had effects more widely in improving working practices and productivity in the city.[50] This experiment provided valuable evidence that bankruptcy laws could be employed beneficially to shock companies into improving their efficiency and profitability in a manner that did not have devastating consequences for the economy or for society.[51] In the third participating city, Chongqing, the experiment

43 The trial also extended to the northern industrial city of Taiyuan, although to a more limited extent: Zheng (1986), p. 688.

44 Xiao (1989), p. 59. For detailed discussion of typical bankruptcy cases which happened in the three cities at the initial stage, see Tang (2005), para. 5.02; *People's Daily*, 10 November 1986.

45 Cao (1998), p. 19 notes the failure of a similar ultimatum at a loss-making machinery factory prior to the introduction of bankruptcy laws.

46 Zheng (1986), p. 688, reporting that seven of the eight companies returned to productivity as a result of the warning having been issued.

47 For further details see Cao (1998), pp. 33-7.

48 See Cao (1998), pp. 38-44.

49 Shenyang Explosion-Prevention Devices Factory, which had been loss making for ten years, failed to gain the capacity to repay its debts, in spite of some improvements. It therefore became the first company to become bankrupt in China since the commencement of the reform process. See further Cao (1998), p. 43.

50 Cao (1998).

51 Zheng (1986), p. 683 provides an overview of debates that appeared in newspaper articles during 1985 and 1986.

was initially less ambitions, since it was carried out in relation to rural enterprises, although it was subsequently extended, with effective results, to a medium sized SOE.[52]

Building upon the momentum of these experiments, Cao wrote newspaper and journal articles and conducted public opinion polls in support of the proposed law. Eventually, after much lobbying, progress was made with the enactment of the Chinese General Principles of Civil Law 1986 which for the first time mentioned the term 'bankruptcy' in a national law,[53] and introduced the concept of a 'legal person' and the notion of corporate property rights which paved the way for the promulgation of a bankruptcy law. By early 1986, following further lobbying and propaganda but also significant opposition, a draft bankruptcy law was taking shape. The idea of introducing a bankruptcy law was widely supported by Chinese economists and lawyers at a conference held in Shenyang in June 1986. Eventually the draft law was put before the Standing Committee of the National People's Congress. After much debate and investigation as to the feasibility of such laws,[54] the law, consisting of only 42 articles, gained approval in November 1986. The approval of this law, after two years of efforts by the State Council, was a notable achievement.[55] However, since it was considered that insufficient experience of the operation of bankruptcy laws had yet been gained, the law was enacted with the qualification that it was for 'trial implementation'. In addition the application of the law was restricted to state-owned enterprises.[56]

*Enactment of Additional Bankruptcy Laws to Supplement the 1986 Law*

The restriction of the scope of the 1986 Law to state-owned enterprises meant that there was no unified bankruptcy law dealing with the insolvencies of all types of enterprises prior to the promulgation and implementation of the new Enterprise Bankruptcy Law 2006. With the deepening of the economic reforms and the emerging establishment of a market economy, the 1986 Law was followed by a series of additional measures, which caused the legal framework to become very complicated and cumbersome.[57] First of all, Chapter XIX of the Civil Procedure

52 See Cao (1998), pp. 46-7.

53 Article 45, General Principles of Civil Law 1986; Harmer (1996), p. 2569.

54 See generally Zheng (1986), pp. 695-6.

55 For further discussion of the 1986 law, see: Chen (2000), p. 49; Chang (1987), p. 333. The English version of the 1986 bankruptcy law is available at <http://www.chinacourt.org>, and Boshkoff and Song (1987), p. 359.

56 It had earlier been contemplated that the law might extend also to foreign investment enterprises. See Zheng (1986), pp. 697-9 regarding the approach that was ultimately taken to such enterprises.

57 Metaphorically, China's old bankruptcy legal system was described as 'an onion' with different layers of laws and regulatory rules which applied to different types of enterprises and in specific situations. It was inevitable that ambiguities and conflicts of laws would arise. See Tomasic (2006), p. 95.

Law 1991 regulated the reconciliation and liquidation of non-SOEs with legal person status. In addition, disparate insolvency provisions were enacted in relevant national laws and regulations to specifically deal with the bankruptcies of various types of foreign investment enterprises.[58] Further measures of importance were two judicial interpretations that had been promulgated by the Supreme People's Court, respectively in 1991 and 2002, both of which were of far-reaching influence on the hearing of bankruptcy cases.[59] The 1991 Interpretation aimed to overcome the loopholes and imprecision of the EBL 1986, and the 2002 Interpretation clarified the ambiguities of insolvency provisions in various national laws and attempted to avoid the potential conflicts of bankruptcy procedures.[60] Furthermore, some national laws also involved bankruptcy provisions. For example, the Company Law stipulates the dissolution and liquidation of companies including limited liability companies and joint stock companies, both of which have separate corporate personality,[61] and the Commercial Bank Law also articulated particular rules regulating the winding up of commercial banks and the distribution of bankruptcy estates.[62] Finally, it is notable that bankruptcy regulatory rules were enacted by the local legislatures of 'special economic zones'.[63] For example, the Shenzhen Enterprise Bankruptcy Regulations, were enacted by the local congress on 10 November 1993 under the delegated power of the Standing Committee of NPC and may be regarded as a typical example. These local bankruptcy regulations comprised an important component of the Chinese bankruptcy legal framework, and they applied in local areas as long as they did not conflict with the principles of the national laws.[64] The effect of accumulation of all these laws was that the

58 For more details, see Tomasic (2006), p. 97.

59 Although in China's legal structure, judicial interpretations issued by the SPC are placed at a lower level than national laws enacted by the NPC, in practice, judicial interpretations almost have the same legal effect as the national laws.

60 'The Opinion of the Supreme People's Court on Several Issues in the Implementation of PRC Enterprise Bankruptcy Law (Trial Implementation)', (the 1991 Opinion); 'The Regulation on Several Issues Concerning Hearing Enterprise Bankruptcy Cases', (Regulation 2002); Tang (2005), paras 5.26, 5.27 and 5.29; Lam and Wong (2003), p. 82.

61 Articles 188 and 191, PRC Company Law 2005.

62 Article 71, PRC Commercial Bank Law 2003.

63 These special areas include Shenzhen, Zhuhai, Shantou, Xiamen and Hainan which were the earliest cities to engage in market-oriented economic practices, ahead of other areas of mainland China. These areas were deemed as the 'windows' of the reform and opening up policy. In these areas, foreign investors can enjoy special economic and tax policies and the local governments to some degree have autonomy.

64 Harmer (1996), p. 2571; Zhang and Booth (2001), p. 1. According to Article 136 of EBL 2006, the new law replaces the 1986 law, but it does not stipulate that the new law replaces the previous judicial interpretations and other regulations. As long as those regulations do not conflict with the rules, principles and spirits of the new, they should still be applicable.

bankruptcy legal structure as a whole was scrappy in nature, embracing a wide range of measures for different types of enterprises and geographical regions.

*Weaknesses of the pre-2006 Bankruptcy Legal Framework*

From the perspective of judicial practice, the old bankruptcy legislations were not effectively used for a number of reasons. The most significant problems related to debt-laden SOEs, which could not be simply liquidated since they were the main social welfare providers of the employees. It was feared that the insolvent winding up of SOEs would cause social instability because the social security system was not adequate to provide a social safety net for redundant employees. In addition, it was anticipated that the bankruptcy of SOEs would give rise to an accumulation of non-performing loans of state banks which had been required to advance policy loans to SOEs under government instruction. The above two factors led the government to be highly active in bankruptcy-related matters respecting SOEs, practices that continue even today. Rather than using the bankruptcy legislations to deal with struggling SOEs, the preference was to apply government policies under the planned bankruptcy programme. The problems of uneconomic SOEs and the administrative response to them are considered in detail in Chapter 15.

*Enactment of the EBL 2006*

With the development of the market reform, China was in need of an effective bankruptcy law which accorded with its socialist market economy. The process of bankruptcy law reform commenced in 1994 and lasted for 12 years. The way towards the passage of the legislation was paved by the economic transition, the reform of SOEs, development of the social security system and progress of the Chinese judicial reform. However, it was notable that the reform process was prolonged by lingering fears over uneconomic SOEs. There were a number of factors that led to these fears eventually being overcome.

One factor that contributed to the eventual passage of the new bankruptcy law was external pressure from the international economic environment. Although China has made great achievements on its economic transition to becoming a market economy, China's full market economy status is still not recognized by the US and EU, both of which are the two largest trade partners of China.[65] The inefficiency and ineffectiveness of China's old bankruptcy law constituted one of the reasons upon which the EU refused to recognize China as having a full market economy.[66] Undoubtedly, this non-recognition may have a bad impact on

65 See EU-China News (2004).

66 At the 9th Annual EU-China Business Summit held in September 2006 in Helsinki, the EU Commission once again rejected the China's petition for full market economy status, giving four reasons, one of which was the ineffectiveness and inconsistency of China's bankruptcy law.

China's export interests, put China in a disadvantageous position in trade disputes and will have eroded its international image and reputation.[67] To some degree, the non-recognition urged the Chinese legislature to push forward the bankruptcy law reform and accelerated the legislative process, particularly after the EU first refused China's petition for full market economy status in 2003.

Although China was left relatively unscathed by the Asian Financial Crisis that began in 1997, since the controls that were exerted in China over the flow of capital meant that the crisis did not have the devastating effect on China that it had on other jurisdictions, the crisis drew attention to the dangers of having undeveloped insolvency laws and acted as a spur to bankruptcy reform. Such laws can both prevent financial difficulties and also reduce the duration of a crisis. Furthermore, a modernized bankruptcy law which is in line with international standards and principles may assist China to build an appealing investment environment, which could eliminate the concerns of investors and ensure an increase in the flow of foreign capital into the Chinese market.[68]

In spite of the attractions of the new law, the reform process was long and difficult. During the legislative process, the draft of the new bankruptcy law was revised many times and, as discussed further in Chapter 2, the Chinese reformers travelled extensively to gain experience of insolvency systems elsewhere in the world and consulted widely with foreign insolvency law experts in order to devise a suitable set of laws for China and to follow international standards. The final draft eventually passed the deliberation of the Standing Committee of the National People's Congress on 27 August 2006, and the Enterprise Bankruptcy Law 2006 came into force on 1 June 2007.

### *Overview of the EBL 2006*

The features of the EBL 2006 will be discussed in detail in subsequent chapters in this volume and so only a brief overview of the main achievements of the law will be noted here. The new law is a law which contains identifiable influences of German, Australian and United States laws in particular but which has been carefully drafted to take account of the particular circumstances in China. It represents a breakthrough and a modernization of Chinese bankruptcy law in several aspects, including the following:

- The law is significantly expanded, running to 136 Articles, which although short in comparison to the laws of some jurisdictions, is very much more detailed than the 43 provisions of the EBL 1986.

---

67 Shi (2007), p. 653.

68 See European Bank for Restructuring and Development (2000), p. 43; La Porta et al. (1997) regarding the link between effective bankruptcy laws and the attraction of foreign direct investment. See also Tabb and Curtis Campbell (2006); and vom Eigen (2006) regarding the position in China.

- The conditions for opening insolvency proceedings are less stringent than under the EBL 1986: see further pp. 74-8.
- The EBL 2006 applies to both SOEs and non-SOEs with legal person status.
- Government intervention is significantly scaled down, with only a limited remaining scope for the liquidation group to administer proceedings, although it is likely that the state will continue to exert influence behind the scenes via the courts.
- A new office of 'administrator' has been established to oversee bankruptcy proceedings, a significant development in the transition from state control: see further Chapters 5 and 6.
- The new law emphasizes the reorganization of insolvent companies and, although the default position is that such proceedings will be managed by an administrator, it contains provision for the proceedings to be converted to debtor in possession proceedings: see further pp. 215-16.
- Creditors' committees appear in the legislation for the first time: see further Chapter 10.
- A more extensive list of transaction avoidance powers is included: see further Chapter 8.
- The new law contains the first provision as to the bankruptcy of financial institutions in insolvency law: see Chapter 16.
- It includes the first provision as to cross border insolvencies: see Chapter 17.
- A more detailed overview of the new law, in light of international standards, is provided by Professor Roman Tomasic in Chapter 2 of this volume.

## Overview of this Book

The aim of the book is to provide a comprehensive overview of this important new piece of legislation by systematically and comprehensively introducing the Chinese bankruptcy legal framework, including theoretical, substantive and procedural issues, drawing upon comparisons with the laws in other jurisdictions where appropriate. In addition, this book will analyse typical cases which have been, or are being, heard since the new bankruptcy law was implemented. The book will draw a clear picture of the newly reformed Chinese bankruptcy legal structure.

The authors in the contribution team include authors with legislative and judicial experience, practising lawyers and accountants with experience of handling insolvency cases and also academic authors with specialist interests in Chinese bankruptcy law. Each chapter is devoted to a particular aspect of the new law and, given the multi-authored nature of the text, some small points of overlap may be found between chapters from time to time. We have tried to minimize these areas of overlap during the editing process and those that remain are considered important to the development of arguments and ideas in the chapters concerned.

The authors will analyse Chinese bankruptcy-related issues in the following four parts. Part I, with three chapters, will identify the historical development of China's bankruptcy legal framework, the background to the enactment of the law, the corporate governance structure and the general principles of the new bankruptcy law. Part II, from Chapter 4 to Chapter 14, will discuss the detailed contents of the new law, including substantive issues such as the powers and duties of the administrator, and the key procedures of liquidation, reorganization and reconciliation. Part III will examine the bankruptcies of SOEs and financial institutions, and these issues will be explored in two separate chapters. Part IV will focus on cross-border insolvencies which is a notable feature in China's new bankruptcy law.

The law is stated according to sources available to the authors on 1 February 2009. Throughout the text the abbreviation 'EBL 2006' will be used to refer to the Enterprise Bankruptcy Law 2006 and 'EBL 1986' will be used to refer to the previous law, the Enterprise Bankruptcy Law (for Trial Implementation) 1986.

## References


Bell, M., Khor, H. and Kochhar, K. (1993), *China at the Threshold of a Market Economy* (Washington, D.C.: International Monetary Fund).

Boshkoff, D. and Song, Y. (1987), 'China's New Bankruptcy Law: A Translation and Brief Introduction' 61 *American Bankruptcy Law Journal* 359.

Chang, T. (1987), 'The Making of the Chinese Bankruptcy Law: A Study in the Chinese Legislative Process' 28 *Harvard International Law Journal* 333.

Chen, F. (2000), 'Chinese Bankruptcy Law: Milestones and Challenges' 31 *St. Mary's Law Journal* 49.

EU-China News (2004), 'Market Economy Status Report Encourages Further Progress', No. 4, 2004, available at <http://www.delchn.cec.eu.int/newsletters/200404/018.htm>, last accessed 1 March 2009.

European Bank for Restructuring and Development (2000), *Law in Transition* (Spring) 43.

Gates, H. (1996), *China's Motor: A Thousand Years of Petty Capitalism* (Ithaca: Cornell University Press).

Gu, M. (2006), *Understanding Chinese Company Law* (Hong Kong: Hong Kong University Press).

Guo, S. (2003), 'The Ownership Reform in China: What Direction and How Far?' 12 *Journal of Contemporary China* 553.

Harmer, R. (1996), 'Insolvency Law and Reform in the People's Republic of China' 64 *Fordham Law Review* 2563.

Hoecke, M. and Warrington, M. (1998), 'Legal Cultures, Legal Paradigms and Legal Doctrine: Towards a New Model for Comparative Law' 47 *International and Comparative Law Quarterly* 495.

Keyser, C.H. (1998), 'Guest Editor's Introduction' 31(1) *Chinese Law and Government* 3.

Lam, J. and Wong, J. (2003), 'FIE Bankruptcy Legal Framework Clarified by the New Judicial Rules in the People's Republic of China' 18 *Journal of International Banking Law and Regulation* 82.

La Porta, R., Lopez de Silanes, F., Shleifer, A. and Vishny, R.W. (1997), 'Legal Determinants of External Finance' 53 *Journal of Finance* 1131.

Lee, L. and Lai, W. (1978), 'The Chinese Conceptions of Law: Confucian, Legalist, and Buddhist' 29 *Hastings Law Journal* 1307.

Li, S. (2001), 'Bankruptcy Law in China: Lessons of the Past Twelve Years' 5(1) *Harvard Asia Quarterly* <http://www.asiaquarterly.com/content/view/95/40/>, last accessed 1 March 2009.

Lubman, S. (1999), *Bird in a Cage: Legal Reform in China after Mao* (Stanford: Stanford University Press).

Peerenboom, R. (2002), *China's Long March toward Rule of Law* (Cambridge: Cambridge University Press).

Rowe, R. (1984), *Hankow: Commerce and Society in a Chinese City, 1789-1889* (Stanford: Stanford University Press).

Ruskola, T. (2000), 'Conceptualizing Corporations and Kinship: Comparative Law and Development Theory in a Chinese Perspective' 52 *Stanford Law Review* 599.

Shi, J. (2007), 'Twelve Years to Sharper One Sword: The 2006 Enterprise Bankruptcy Law and China's Transition to a Market Economy' 16 *Norton Journal of Bankruptcy Law and Practice* 645.

Siyuan, C. (1998), 'The Storm Over Bankruptcy' 31(1) *Chinese Law and Government* 12.

Tabb, C.J. and Curtis Campbell, A. (2006), 'The Importance of Bankruptcy Law to Economic Development and Implications for China' 22 *Insolvency Law and Practice* 98.

Tang, A. (2005), *Insolvency in China and Hong Kong: A Practitioner's Perspective* (Hong Kong: Sweet & Maxwell Asia).

Tomasic, R. and Wang, M. (2006), 'The Long March Towards China's New Bankruptcy Law', in Tomasic, R. (ed) *Insolvency Law in East Asia* (Aldershot: Ashgate).

Vogel, E. (2005), 'Chen Yun: his Life' 14 *Journal of Contemporary China* 741.

vom Eigen, A. (2006), 'China's New Bankruptcy Law Encourages Investment' 25 *American Bankruptcy Institute Journal* 8.

Weber, M. (1978), G. Roth and C. Wittich (eds), *Economy and Society* (Berkeley: University of California Press).

Wong, L. (2004), 'Market Reform, Globalization and Social Justice in China' 13 *Journal of Contemporary China* 151.

Xiao, Z. (1989), 'China's Bankruptcy Law: Socialist in Characteristics, Capitalist in Methods' 10 *Company Lawyer* 58.

Xie, J. (2005), *Theory of Chinese Bankruptcy Legal System* (People's Court Press, Beijing) (in Chinese).
Yang, G. (2006), 'An Institutional Analysis of China's State Power Structure and its Operation' 15 *Journal of Contemporary China* 43.
Zhang, J. (2007), *Chinese Legal History* (Beijing: Higher Education Press) (in Chinese).
Zhang, X. and Booth, C. (2001), 'Chinese Bankruptcy Law in an Emerging Market Economy: The Shenzhen Experience' 15 *Columbia Journal of Asian Law* 1.
Zheng, H.R. (1986), 'Bankruptcy Law of the People's Republic of China: Principle, Procedure and Practice' 19 *Vanderbilt Journal of Transnational Law* 683.
Wang, X. (2007), *Bankruptcy Law*, 2nd edn (Beijing: Renmin University Press) (in Chinese).

## Chapter 2

# The Conceptual Structure of China's New Corporate Bankruptcy Law

Roman Tomasic

### Introduction

The passage of China's new corporate bankruptcy law on 27 August 2006 stands as a landmark in the legislative history of China's reform efforts in the area of economic law.[1] In 1994 this legislation was first put onto the national legislative program in China,[2] and numerous drafts were then produced prior to the enactment of the 2006 Law by the National People's Congress of the People's Republic of China (PRC).[3] Not only has it had a lengthy legislative history,[4] it was also one of the last remaining building blocks in the framework of China's economic laws and now sits beside other important new PRC economic and civil laws, such as the Contract Law, the Company Law, the Securities Law, the Anti-Monopoly Law and the Property Law.

It has long been argued that the existence of a comprehensive corporate insolvency law is a key element of any well-developed market-based legal system. Although the 2006 Enterprise Bankruptcy Law is not China's first bankruptcy law, with earlier regional and national laws being enacted by the People's Republic of China,[5] the new bankruptcy law brings China much closer to having a broadly-based corporate bankruptcy statute than at any time previously.

The 2006 Law replaced the much more limited 1986 Enterprise Bankruptcy Law (For Trial Implementation). That earlier law had had a considerable impact upon state-owned Enterprises (SOEs). As Professor Li Shuguang pointed out a few years before the passage of the 2006 Enterprise Bankruptcy Law:[6]

> Many Chinese and foreign scholars as well as members of the business community share the common misconception that there are only few enterprise

---

1 See further Tomasic and Wang (2006).

2 Shi (2002), p. 46.

3 For a discussion of an earlier version of this legislation, see Tomasic (1998).

4 See further Tomasic and Wang (2005).

5 See generally China Chapter 2 in Tomasic and Little (1997); and pp. 4-5 of this volume.

6 Li (2004).

> bankruptcies in China. In reality, since the [1986] Bankruptcy Law came into effect in November 1988, the law has been invoked to close more than 16,000 enterprises. After a slow start, the rate of bankruptcies has accelerated rapidly, particularly in the last several years ... Bankruptcy has not been limited to ailing state firms, but rather has applied to all types of enterprises. In 1994, only 395 of the total 1,624 bankrupt enterprises were state firms. Among the 5,396 bankruptcies in 1997, 3,060-plus were SOEs (675 in the 111 experimental cities); the rest were private, collectively owned or Sino foreign joint ventures.

The spectre of large-scale bankruptcy of China's indebted SOEs had been a concern for government in China and efforts were therefore made to moderate the use of the 1986 bankruptcy law; as Professor Li explained:[7]

> Aware of the problems associated with bankruptcies, the government has adopted a policy of promoting mergers over bankruptcies. This new policy accounted for the sharp decrease in the number of bankruptcies in the experimental cities in 1997 compared to 1996. While this approach may prove to be a palliative in the short term, in the long run, it raises the question of who will merge with a bankrupt SOE. In addition, in the area of SOE bankruptcies, there are further obstacles such as an imperfect legal system, excessive administrative intervention, disordered guarantee arrangements, fraudulent bankruptcies, low benefits of liquidation, a shortage of bankruptcy professionals, local protectionism, and difficulties in selling assets for cash. ... Recognizing the inefficiency of this approach, which results in mere shifting of problems from one enterprise to another, I proposed in 1998 that bankruptcy be adopted as the preferred solution for insolvent SOEs. Only bankruptcy, rather than merger, can provide a complete cure. Indeed, in 2000, the central government began a new policy of 'more bankruptcies, less mergers'.

Of course, it needs to be said that China's Enterprise Bankruptcy Law of 2006 has yet to be fully implemented as its practical meaning will depend upon the availability of a range of qualified insolvency practitioners and experienced insolvency law judges. This partly explains why in 2007, only 3,817 bankruptcy cases were accepted by PRC courts.[8] The challenges facing the implementation of this new law will inevitably define the nature and impact of this law.

Whilst the new legislation does not deal with personal bankruptcy, its focus is upon enterprise legal persons, whether incorporated or not. The Law provides for a number of important remedies in addition to liquidation, such as court sanctioned corporate reorganizations and compromises with creditors. In so doing, it brings China closer to the more debtor-friendly corporate rescue philosophies found in

7 Li (2004) supra.

8 Quoted by Tang (2006).

other insolvency laws; it also comes closer to the emerging global norms that are applicable to corporate insolvencies.[9] But it also seeks to ensure that the interests of creditors, particularly employees of the debtor enterprise, are fairly treated. The new law has provided the mechanism of corporate rescue or reorganization as an alternative to liquidation and in so doing has provided greater flexibility in the administration of corporate insolvencies.

Inevitably, like all laws, this new law should be understood by reference to the social context in which it has emerged. Not surprisingly, there will be 'Chinese characteristics' in this law, just as China's form of capitalism has been described as having Chinese characteristics.[10] This is in keeping with broader debates concerning the 'varieties of capitalism' that can be identified.[11] China's culture and political processes will have an important effect on the shape of its markets as has also occurred in other parts of the world.[12] This is related to the argument that pre-existing legal patterns in China will affect how its new bankruptcy law operates; this argument emphasizes the importance of 'path dependency' in the development of laws in different nations.[13] It is clear that many cultural factors have shaped Chinese attitudes to debt and bankruptcy.[14] A large body of scholarly writing on enterprise reform and corporate governance in China has now emerged; however, we have yet to see a similar body of writing in regard to China's insolvency laws. This is attributable to the fact that wider official concern about the importance of this area only began to be felt in the decade after the Asian financial crisis in the late 1990s.

## The Evolution of International Insolvency Law Principles

American and European authors have written at length on the principles underlying corporate insolvency laws.[15] Each has produced their own lists of key principles, and these lists have tended to share a number of common features. For example, ten broad insolvency principles were identified by the influential English legal scholar, Professor Roy Goode, in his *Principles of Corporate Insolvency Law*, in the following terms:[16]

1. corporate insolvency law recognizes rights accrued under the general law prior to liquidation;

9 See further Tomasic (2007).
10 Huang (2008).
11 See further Hall and Soskice (2001).
12 See further Roe (1994).
13 See generally in regard to path dependency literature: Gordon and Roe (2004),
14 See further Tomasic and Little (1997).
15 See for example, Jackson (1986). Also see Wood (1995).
16 Goode (2007), pp. 69-81.

2. only the assets of the debtor company are to be available for distribution to creditors;
3. security interests as well as other real rights that were created prior to insolvency proceedings should not be affected by the liquidation;
4. the liquidator gains possession of the company's assets subject to all limitations and defences;
5. the pursuit of personal rights against the company is converted into a right to prove for the dividend in the liquidation;
6. with the commencement of liquidation, the company ceases to be the beneficial owner of its assets (as they are held on trust for the discharge of its liabilities);
7. no creditor has any interest in any specific asset of the bankrupt company;
8. liquidation accelerates creditors' right to payment;
9. unsecured creditors rank *pari passu*;
10. members of a company are not as such liable for its debts.

Over the last decade we have also seen the emergence of an international template or palette of measures which constitute a well developed body of insolvency laws; this has been orchestrated by various multilateral bodies, such as the World Bank and the Asian Development Bank,[17] culminating with the efforts of UNCITRAL to draft a broadly based legislative guide on insolvency law.[18] This had been preceded by regional efforts to prepare core insolvency principles or practice guides, such as has been seen in the work of the Asian Development Bank in East Asia.[19] Other regional banks, such as the European Bank for Reconstruction and Development, have also undertaken similar efforts. However, unlike many other Asian countries, China has been more able to resist pressure from multilateral bodies seeking to impose externally derived legal models. Instead, we have seen an internal debate between domestic Chinese elites being especially important in shaping insolvency laws in China.[20]

These international efforts were reflected in debates that were occurring within China itself. These debates were to shape what is now the Enterprise Bankruptcy Law of 2006. One of the key forums in which these debates took place was the Finance and Economics Committee of the National People's Congress; this was supported by efforts of foreign aid bodies, and particularly by the German international aid body, GTZ.[21] Towards the end of the domestic debate, other Chinese institutions such as the Legislation Committee of the State Council, also

17 See further Halliday and Carruthers (2009). Also see Carruthers and Halliday (2006), and Block-Lieb and Halliday (2004).

18 UNCITRAL (2005).

19 See for example, Harmer (2000).

20 This may be compared with the role of local elites in law reform efforts in other transitional economies. See further Dezalay and Garth (2002).

21 See further Gebhardt and Zhu (eds) (2004).

played significant roles in shaping the consensus upon which the new law is now based. China's law makers were well aware of the international debates that had been underway regarding the transformation of bankruptcy laws since the early 1980s culminating with the work of the OECD and the Forum for Asian Insolvency Reform (FAIR) leading to a major international conference of FAIR held in Beijing in April 2006; this was co-sponsored by the Development Research Centre of the PRC State Council.[22] The involvement of the State Council engaged the highest levels of government in China in the domestic bankruptcy reform debate.

There have clearly been many domestic and international influences that have had an effect upon the shape of the 2006 Enterprise Bankruptcy Law. The actual meaning of this Law will of course evolve over time as efforts are made to implement its provisions. However, at this point in time, it is appropriate to seek to evaluate this new law and to assess how its provisions reflect insolvency law ideas found in other parts of the world. This may be seen as an effort to identify its key principles or assumptions. The identification of such principles or assumptions has been central to the enactment of other new corporate insolvency laws in other parts of the world and is reflected in the UNCITRAL Legislative Guide on Insolvency Laws (hereinafter 'Legislative Guide') that was approved by the United Nations in 2005.

To assist insolvency law reformers around the world, the UNCITRAL Legislative Guide set out nine key objectives of insolvency law; these were in the following terms:

1. the provision of certainty in the market to promote economic stability and growth;
2. the maximization of the value of assets;
3. striking a balance between liquidation and reorganization;
4. ensuring the equitable treatment of similarly situated creditors;
5. provision for timely, efficient and impartial resolution of the insolvency;
6. preservation of the insolvency estate to allow equitable distribution to creditors;
7. ensuring a transparent and predictable insolvency law that contains incentives for gathering and dispensing information;
8. the recognition of existing creditor rights and establishment of clear rules for ranking of priority claims; and
9. the establishment of a framework for cross-border insolvency.

These objectives are further discussed in greater detail in the body of the Legislative Guide, and reference should be made to these discussions for a further elaboration of these principles. To varying degrees these earlier efforts to set out national,

22 For papers from these OECD sponsored meetings see further <http://www.oecd.org/document/63/0,3343,-en_2649_34845_38141887_1_1_1_1,00.htm>.

regional and global standards for insolvency law making have had an influence upon insolvency law reformers in China.[23]

This chapter will seek to identify the key principles or assumptions that are reflected in the form of the 2006 Enterprise Bankruptcy law and to contrast these with parallel ideas reflected in international standards, such as the Legislative Guide. This may serve as something of a base line against which to evaluate subsequent efforts to implement this law. What is clear from the following discussion is that China's Enterprise Bankruptcy Law in different ways seeks to achieve most, and perhaps all, of the global insolvency law objectives listed above.

## The Objectives of China's Corporate Bankruptcy Law

On the eve of the passage of the new 2006 Enterprise Bankruptcy Law there was a realization that there were serious inadequacies with the existing bankruptcy laws in China and that the time had come for a change. As Professor Li Shuguang, a member of the legislative drafting group for the Enterprise Bankruptcy Law, had pointed out:[24]

> The existing [1986] Bankruptcy Law is hard to implement. Much of its content does not adequately address the complex economic realities of China. SOE bankruptcy procedures are vague and those governing non-SOE bankruptcies are deficient. There is no legal basis for filing bankruptcy for a natural person, partnership, or corporation. Since there is no reorganization procedure for insolvent enterprises, it is difficult to determine where the responsibility of the managers of the bankrupt enterprises lies. In addition, there are conflicts and inconsistencies between the Bankruptcy Law and existing government policies.

Based upon his review of China's experience over the preceding 12 years, Professor Li went on to persuasively argue the case for a new Chinese bankruptcy law:[25]

> Some scholars argue that bankruptcy law is not suitable for the national conditions in China. Nevertheless, twelve years of practice with bankruptcy law, combined with the deepening of the SOE reform and the development of the market economy, have persuaded many Chinese of the country's need for a new bankruptcy law. Bankruptcies have become an inevitable economic reality. Recently, many scholars and entrepreneurs, particularly creditors, have advocated the replacement of the existing bankruptcy law with a new bankruptcy law that is more suitable for the new market economy. The original bankruptcy law is out of date with current realities. First, a large number of companies not

23 See for example, Wang (1998).

24 Li (2004) above.

25 Li (2004) above.

> owned by the government have been established under the rules of the new market economy in the twenty years since economic reforms began. These companies expect to operate within a legal framework more suited for a market economy. Clearly, the original bankruptcy law cannot apply to these companies. Second, even for money-losing SOEs that still carry the inertia of the planned economic system, the inevitable transition to market economy has made the existing bankruptcy law inadequate.

It is clear that the 2006 Enterprise Bankruptcy Law was aimed at remedying many problems in the pre-existing Law. Of course the passage of a law will not necessarily bring about changes overnight, but its passage was an important signal suggesting that the central government was more serious about adopting new approaches to bankruptcy and market failure.

However, it should not be forgotten that in the past the government itself may have been the cause of many bankruptcy problems that arose, especially in regard to SOEs. As Professor Li pointed out:[26]

> The Chinese government plays a special role in enterprise bankruptcies in China. The government's role is both dominant and multi-faceted in SOE bankruptcies. It initiates these bankruptcies, yet at the same time, is the policymaker, the leader, and the direct operator in them. The government not only controls their number, scale, and speed, but also decides what industries and trades are covered under the bankruptcy law.

The objectives or principles underlying the new Law are important statements of national policy; these can be discerned from a number of sources. The most obvious of these are the terms of the legislation itself; the legislative history of this Law may also reveal important principles and assumptions. As no living body of law is static, the interpretation of this law, especially by the Supreme People's Court, is likely to give further shape to broadly based principles found within the legislation. However, at this point in time, the focus here is limited to the legislation itself. More work will need to be undertaken at a later time on its actual implementation.

The principles underlying China's Enterprise Bankruptcy Law may be found in a number of provisions within the legislation. These principles are most evident in the 'General Provisions' found in Chapter 1 of the Law, but they are also to be found in later chapters. The General Provisions proclaim a number of general principles in a summary fashion and many of these are subsequently expanded upon in later chapters. Thus, Article 1 provides for five broad purposes of the Law. In many ways they echo objectives found in the UNCITRAL Legislative Guide. These new Chinese bankruptcy principles might be described as the 'Article 1 principles':

---

26 Li (2004) above.

1. providing a legal procedure for the regulation of enterprise bankruptcy;
2. ensuring the fair settlement of claims and debts in regard to the enterprise;
3. protecting the lawful interests of creditors;
4. protecting the lawful interests of debtors; and
5. maintaining an orderly (socialist) market economy.

These are fairly conventional goals for any corporate insolvency law, but with a slight Chinese variation. Inherent within these principles is an overriding commitment to the use of legal mechanisms for the handling of corporate insolvency proceedings. To this extent, this is a conscious decision to use the rule of law, rather than administrative mechanisms for dealing with enterprise insolvency.[27]

The general principles in Article 1 of the Enterprise Bankruptcy Law are supplemented by five further principles found in Articles 2 to 6 of Chapter 1 which might be seen as flowing from these five specific objectives. These might be described as second order principles and may be termed as follows:

1. the insolvency principle;
2. the rescue principle;
3. the judicialization principle;
4. the extra-territoriality principle; and
5. the employee protection principle.

Each of these five second order principles found in Chapter 1 of the Law can be briefly discussed.

### *Insolvency Principle*

An insolvency test is laid down in Article 2 which is built upon inability to pay debts that are due; this test may be generally described as the *insolvency principle.* This test provides a procedural mechanism with which to commence insolvency proceedings. Further procedural rules are to be found in the Civil Procedure Law which is applied to bankruptcy cases by Article 4.

### *Rescue Principle*

The inclusion of the rescue procedure in the Law provides for some procedural flexibility, as Article 2 contemplates the use of liquidations and/or reorganization procedures and thereby assumes that corporate rescue may be a viable alternative to liquidation; this may be described as the *rescue principle*; this is articulated more fully in Chapter 8. The rescue principle has dominated insolvency law

27 In relation to progress in the development of the rule of law in China see Peerenboom (2002).

reform since the passage of the 1978 US Bankruptcy Reform Act[28] and the 1986 UK Insolvency Act.[29] In many ways, the most distinctive feature of the new 2006 Enterprise Bankruptcy Law is its provision of a formal set of procedures for the reorganization of companies or enterprises in distress.[30]

*Judicialization Principle*

Article 3 of the Law provides for judicial oversight of enterprise bankruptcy proceedings; this suggests a rule of law approach to insolvency, although considerable reliance is placed by the courts upon the use of suitably qualified insolvency administrators to implement its rulings; this may be described as the *judicialization principle.* Court supervision and control of corporate insolvency and reorganization proceedings is not always essential, as a country may have a well developed pool of independent insolvency practitioners who may be trusted to manage reorganizations, with courts only having a residual function, as occurs with voluntary administrations in Australia.[31] However, the absence of a tradition of insolvency administration in China means that an authoritative national institution, such as the PRC courts, must play a much greater role in such proceedings. Courts in China are assuming an increasingly important role in the handling of corporate insolvency cases as is evident from judicial statements made by various Chinese judges.[32] However, despite the improvements made in recent years in the capacities of Chinese courts,[33] criticisms have been made of their capacity to act with any degree of independence.[34] As Professor Li Shuguang has observed in regard to SOE bankruptcies:[35]

> The courts' role in SOE bankruptcies is derived from the power of the government and is thus limited in many aspects. Since the government appoints judges and allocates budgets for courts, Chinese courts are hardly independent of the government. Chinese courts are divided into four levels: the Supreme Court, High Court, Intermediate Court and Local Court. Unlike the American system, in which bankruptcy courts have exclusive jurisdiction over bankruptcy cases, there is no unified provision in China specifying which court (i.e. the

28 See further Baird (1993).

29 See further Fletcher (2009).

30 See further Parry and Zhang (2008).

31 See further Part 5.3A of the Corporations Act 2001 (Aust) for the provisions regarding the Deed of Company Arrangement procedure; For an overview of this procedure see: Murray (2005).

32 See further Song (2006).

33 See generally Liebman (2008).

34 For an insider's review by a member of the Supreme People's Court of China of the development of the Chinese court system and its response to economic development see Xi Xiaoming, (2006).

35 Li (2004).

> court of which level) has jurisdiction over bankruptcy cases. Most of these cases are conducted by the Economic Trial Branch of Local Courts and Intermediate Courts. Absent approval by the government, courts are often hesitant to accept and hear bankruptcy cases. Judges are supposed to apply the existing bankruptcy law when handling these cases. They are, however, restrained by bankruptcy policies of governments of different levels, which at times conflict with the bankruptcy law. Moreover, the majority of Chinese judges are not experienced in dealing with bankruptcy cases. …

However, in some parts of China, such as Shenzhen, there has been more experience with bankruptcy matters because Shenzhen had established a bankruptcy court and insolvency legislation since 1994.[36] In any event, it has been widely recognized that efforts will need to be made to further strengthen judicial expertise in the handling of insolvency cases in China.[37]

*Extra-territoriality Principle*

The Law also adopts an *extra-territoriality principle* in Article 5 which applies the law to a debtor's property located outside the PRC, as well as setting up a procedure for the handling of claims made by foreign insolvency administrators against property located within China's territorial boundaries. See further Chapter 17. This is likely to become an increasingly important principle given the internationalization of business transactions affecting China. It is however a principle that will depend heavily upon the quality and experience of Chinese judges, or in the absence of that experience, upon the quality of the advice that courts are able to draw upon in making their decisions.

*Employee Protection Principle*

Finally, the Law seeks to 'guarantee the legitimate rights and interests of employees of the enterprise' (Article 6). This *employee protection principle* is supplemented by more detailed provisions in later Chapters of the Law setting priorities between various unsecured creditors and giving employee claims a higher priority than normal unsecured claims, such as those of trade creditors.

## Additional Principles

Chapter 1 of the Law thus sets out ten primary insolvency related principles that are built upon in later provisions of the Law. These additional principles can be

---

36 See further Zhang and Booth (2001). Also see Tomasic and Little (1997), pp. 32-3 and 41-3.

37 See further Wang (2001).

implied from the terms and procedures found in subsequent Chapters of the Law. For example, the judicialization principle in Article 3 is linked to another important principle, namely, the expeditious handling of insolvency proceedings. This may be seen as another important principle.

In addition to the above ten Chapter 1 principles, at least ten further implied principles or objectives can be identified from Chapters 2 to 12 of the 2006 Enterprise Bankruptcy Law. These principles, each of which will be considered further below, are as follows:

1. the expeditious processing of bankruptcy cases;
2. the efficient proceedings principle;
3. the qualified insolvency administrator principle;
4. the creditor participation principle;
5. the antecedent transactions principle;
6. the priorities principle;
7. the shareholder subordination principle;
8. the *pari passu* or equality principle;
9. the protection of secured creditors;
10. the director liability and the sanctioning of fraud principle.

### *The Expeditious Processing of Bankruptcy Cases Principle*

The Law imposes strict time lines for the processing of corporate insolvency applications, as set out in Articles 10-14. As effective insolvency proceedings require expeditious handling of insolvency applications, strict time lines are imposed on the court. Thus, in a creditor's bankruptcy petition, the court has five days from the date of its receipt of the application to notify the debtor that it has received a bankruptcy application; the debtor has seven days in which to object and if an objection is made, the court then has ten days in which to decide whether or not to accept the application. In the case of a debtor's petition, the court normally has 15 days in which to decide whether to accept a bankruptcy application, although in 'special circumstances', this period may be extended for a further 15 days (Art. 10). Once an application has been accepted by the court, it has a further 25 days in which to notify known creditors and to announce its decision (Art. 14). A concern for 'timeliness' is found in other parts of the Enterprise Bankruptcy Law, such as in Article 69 (concerned with creditors' committees) and in Article 111 (concerned with the realization and distribution of assets).

### *The Efficient Proceedings Principle*

A related principle is that after the commencement of insolvency proceedings, the insolvency administrator should be able to undertake his or her responsibilities without time-consuming distractions. For this reason, it is common to impose a moratorium or constraint on other legal proceedings during the course of the insolvency administration. This philosophy is in part reflected in Article 20 which suspends existing civil actions or arbitrations involving the debtor company, and in Article 21 which limits new civil proceedings against the debtor unless these are filed with the court that has accepted the bankruptcy application. But, these provisions fall short of providing a full moratorium on legal proceedings during the course of the insolvency administration.

*The Qualified Insolvency Administrator Principle*

Effective insolvency proceedings depend upon the availability of suitably qualified insolvency practitioners to assist the court in the handling of cases that have been accepted by the courts. It will be difficult for China to build a corps of qualified insolvency practitioners overnight; unfortunately, these did not emerge under the 1986 Bankruptcy Law; as Professor Li observed in 2004:[38]

> Professional services for handling bankruptcy cases are uncommon and rudimentary in China. The majority of Chinese liquidation professionals lack experience in handling complicated bankruptcies, resulting in low efficiency and high cost for their work. Only a few law firms and accounting firms have been involved in bankruptcy cases. Moreover, there is no trustee system for handling bankruptcies.

Thus, Article 13 provides that once the court has accepted a bankruptcy application it is required to 'designate an administrator' to manage the insolvency administration. The administrator is required to perform their duties in accordance with the Law and is obliged to report to the court and be subject to the supervision of the creditor' committee (Art. 23). Usually that person will be drawn from a government department or from a law firm, a certified public accountancy firm or from a bankruptcy liquidation firm. Although the administrator has very wide duties in an insolvency, the Enterprise Bankruptcy Act itself does not lay down any detailed rules regarding the qualifications of such a person, apart from excluding various categories of persons from being appointed as an insolvency administrator, such as a person with a criminal record, a person whose professional qualifications have been revoked, a person with an interest in the case or such person that the court may deem it to be improper to appoint (Art. 24). However, the Supreme People's Court Regulations, which are discussed in Chapter 6, do set out more detailed rules in regard to this important matter.

38 Li (2004).

*The Creditor Participation Principle*

Another important principle that is reflected in corporate insolvency statutes is the principle that creditors should be given an opportunity to participate in the insolvency proceedings. This principle is important as insolvency proceedings are usually brought by creditors and they naturally have a significant interest in the manner in which the administration of the insolvency is conducted. This principle is expressed in a number of ways in the PRC Enterprise Bankruptcy Law, such as in the procedure allowing creditors to prove their debts (Art. 49); also, the provision for the holding of meetings of creditors gives a wide range of functions and powers to creditors, including the supervision of the administrator and voting on and adopting plans made by the administrator (Art. 61).

Creditors' meetings can potentially play an important role in insolvency administration as the resolutions passed by these meetings are binding on all creditors (Art. 64). Furthermore, a creditors' committee may be established and given a wide range of functions, such as those set out in Article 68; these include the supervision of the management and disposition of the debtor's property and the supervision of the distribution of this property. The administrator is required to report to the creditors' committee and Article 69 requires that this be done in a timely manner. In the absence of a creditors' committee, the administrator is required to report to the People's Court (Art. 69). In practice, although there are good theoretical reasons why creditors should participate in insolvency procedures,[39] in reality they do not do so very much in China or Hong Kong.[40]

*The Antecedent Transactions Principle*

It is common for corporate insolvency statutes to have specific rules for the handling of antecedent transactions which are deemed to have been entered into to avoid the effects of later bankruptcy proceedings. Thus, Article 31 gives the administrator the right to request the court to nullify certain questionable transactions that were entered into in the 12 months prior to the court's acceptance of the bankruptcy application. See Chapter 8 of this volume where these laws are discussed. This important principle could be linked to the last two principles, the director liability principle and the principle regarding the handling of fraudulent actions.

*The Priorities Principle*

In any insolvency there will be a variety of claims made against the debtor's property. It is therefore necessary to have a priorities regime that ranks different claims by class. This principle is reflected in Articles 41 to 43 which list the order in which debts are to be paid. Firstly, the costs of the insolvency proceedings,

---

39 Tomasic (2006).

40 Tang (2006).

including the expenses of the insolvency administrator, have priority and may be paid at any time (Arts 41 and 43); secondly, priority is given to the payment of all expenses and debts incurred 'for the common good of creditors' (Arts 42 and 43).

In a bankruptcy liquidation, similar priorities are set out in Article 113. Thus, after the payment of the expenses of the bankruptcy and debts incurred for the common good of creditors, the priority order in which bankrupt property is to be distributed, as set by Article 113, is firstly, the payment of wages and related employee expenses; secondly, social insurance premiums that the bankrupt enterprise has failed to pay, and finally, 'common bankruptcy claims'. The concern for the interests of employees of bankrupt enterprises has been an important issue in the internal Chinese debates leading up to the passage of the Enterprise Bankruptcy Law.[41] A sense of these debates concerning the priorities of employees in an insolvency can be gained from the following passage from a paper prepared by Li Guoqiang, a senior officer of the State Council's Development Research Centre:[42]

> There are a number of arguments that support the priority of workers' claims; it is people oriented; it conforms to the spirit of the Constitution; failure to pay wages and social security premiums due violates laws such as the Labour Law; it does not conflict with Security Law; it supports social stability; and banks are more capable of identifying and bearing risks than workers. At the same time, there are arguments against the priority of workers' claims: wages and social security premiums in arrears should be regulated in accordance with the Labour Law; the Bankruptcy Law can not violate the principle of priority of security interests; some enterprises are more likely to infringe upon the rights and interests of workers; banks will be forced to increase interest rates and will be reluctant to lend, resulting in an eventual loss of employment opportunities; and workers' priority will cause an increase in bad loans and, in turn, increase financial risks. The essence of the controversy is how to balance the interest relation among creditors based on the national conditions of China in order to properly protect the rights and interests of creditors, and to establish and develop an efficient and fiduciary economic order.

### *The Shareholder Subordination Principle*

A basic principle of company law is that the company is a separate legal person and therefore that the liability of shareholders is limited to any amount that remains unpaid on their shares. This is impliedly recognized by Article 35 of the Enterprise Bankruptcy Law which allows the administrator to make calls upon shareholders to contribute any remaining capital contribution that they have agreed to make to

41 See further Wang (2006).

42 Li (2006).

the company. In a liquidation of a company the shareholders would normally stand in line after the unsecured creditors. It is commonly accepted that shareholders would be entitled to receive any residue that remained after the payment of the costs of the insolvency and of claims by secured and unsecured creditors.

This principle does not seem to be directly recognized by the EBL 2006 as Article 118 contemplates that any residual assets would only be distributed to creditors. This may need to be clarified so as to confirm the well established principle that shareholders are not liable for any debts of the company and that they are entitled to any residue that may remain after the distribution of assets to creditors.[43] There may also be situations where a shareholder might be allowed to claim as a creditor if they can show that they invested in the company upon the basis of misleading information provided by the company.[44] In the context of a reorganization under Chapter 8 of the Law, shareholders are prohibited by Article 77 from claiming a distribution of any profits from their investment in the company.

### *The* Pari Passu *or Equality Principle*

Professor Goode has suggested in his ninth principle that 'unsecured creditors rank *pari passu*'.[45] The *pari passu* principle provides that where there are insufficient assets to pay all of the debts of a particular class of creditors, then each creditor in that class is to be paid equally in proportion to the level of their debt. Thus, Article 43 refers to the payment on a '*pro rata* basis' of the debts of the insolvency proceedings and incurred for the common good of creditors. Earlier, we saw that Article 6 in the General Provisions in Chapter 1 also provided for the protection of the legitimate rights and interests of employees. The *pari passu* principle is also reflected in Article 113 which deals with the payment of priorities in the liquidation of a bankrupt enterprise. Where the assets are not sufficient to satisfy all demands, they are to be distributed amongst members of the group of creditors on 'a *pro rata* basis'. In practice, the *pari passu* principle is more often offended against than complied with in many insolvency rules. This is because statutory priorities for employee claims, for example, operate to undermine this principle. The principle is also to be balanced against other principles, such as freedom of contract, which allows a debtor to give advantages to particular creditors, such as by providing security for the debt.[46]

---

43 This principle can be traced back at least to the celebrated decision of *Salomon v Salomon & Co* [1897] AC 22. Professor Goode (2005), pp. 79-81, also discusses this principle.

44 See for example, Hargovan and Harris (2007); also see Hargovan and Harris (2006).

45 Goode (2007), p. 77.

46 It is beyond our scope here to provide a detailed discussion of the *pari passu* principle, but the interested reader is referred to the lengthy discussion of this matter in the UNCITRAL Legislative Guide, pp. 116-61.

### *The Protection of Secured Creditors*

The protection of secured creditors is widely regarded as a basic insolvency principle. Professor Goode lists this as the third in his list of insolvency objectives and the UNCITRAL Legislative Guide lists as its eighth objective 'the recognition of existing creditor rights and establishment of clear rules for ranking of priority claims'. There has been a heated academic debate about the alleged unfair advantages enjoyed by secured creditors over other creditors, especially involuntary creditors. This debate is well described in the UNCITRAL Legislative Guide and space prevents a further review of it here. Whilst it is true that the well advised lender will ensure that they obtain some security over an asset of the debtor, other creditors are not in as advantageous a position. Nevertheless, the importance of the protection of secured creditors has been recognized in the 2006 Law.

In the situation of a reorganization under the 2006 Enterprise Bankruptcy Act, during the reorganization period, Article 75 provides that secured creditors are prevented from being able to exercise their legal rights as secured creditors; however, secured creditors are permitted to apply to the court to be allowed to exercise their rights if they can show that a 'marked depreciation of value of the security' may arise. Any draft reorganization plan must classify creditor claims into different classes (Art. 81). Where meetings of creditors are to be held to consider a draft reorganization plan, Article 82 requires that separate meetings of secured creditors must be organized. In regard to a compromise under Chapter 9, secured creditors may exercise their rights as secured creditors as soon as the court has approved a proposed compromise (Art. 96). Finally, in a bankruptcy liquidation, Article 109 proclaims that a 'creditor secured by the specific property of the bankrupt shall enjoy the priority in being repaid with the specific property'. Where the security is insufficient to repay the amount that is owed as a secured creditor, that creditor must then claim any remaining amount due to them as if they were an unsecured creditor.

### *The Director Liability and Sanctioning of Fraudulent Actions Principle*

Insolvency laws have long contained provisions which are aimed at attaching liability to the former controllers of a company who may have acted illegally and who might be able to contribute to the pool of funds available for distribution by the administrator. Although this is categorized as an implied principle, it is of such importance that evidence of it can also be found in the General provisions in Chapter 1; thus, Article 6 states that the people's court which accepts a bankruptcy case may also 'investigate the business managers of the bankruptcy enterprise for their legal obligations'. Article 125 of the Law creates a civil liability for a director, supervisor or senior manager of the bankrupt enterprise who failed to comply with his or her legal obligations and failed 'to be honest and hardworking' and where this conduct 'leads to bankruptcy of the enterprise'. This article also disqualifies a director, who is found to have breached this provision, from serving as a director, supervisor or senior manager of any enterprise during the three years after the termination of the bankruptcy. This provision may be compared with other insolvent trading provisions found in other countries.[47] See Chapter 14.

The Enterprise Bankruptcy Act also contains a series of sanctions to ensure that certain key principles are complied with. As we have seen, Article 6 provides that when the court hears a bankruptcy matter, it is obliged to investigate whether any managers of the business acted in breach of their legal liabilities. As a means to ensure an effective bankruptcy administration, various persons are prohibited from serving as a bankruptcy administrator (Art. 24); this includes persons convicted of an offence, persons whose qualification certificate has been revoked, persons with a conflict of interest and such persons as may be deemed by the court to be improperly appointed. See further Chapter 6 of this volume. The Law also declares certain actions to be void; these include the concealment or transfer of property to avoid the repayment of debts and the fabrication of debts (Art. 33). Probably the most important liability provision is found in Article 125 which, in part, states that:

> Where a director, supervisor or senior manager, going against his obligations, fails to be honest and hardworking, which leads to bankruptcy of the enterprise where he works, he shall bear civil liability according to law.

What is missing in these provisions is a suitable insolvent trading provision which holds directors to be personally liable if they consciously allow the company to trade even though they know that it will not be able to pay its debts when they fall due. Such mechanism are an import trigger to ensure that directors do not allow insolvent enterprises to continue to trade to the detriment of creditors.[48] Without such sanctions as these, it is likely to be difficult to find evidence that connects the dishonest and the bankruptcy of the enterprise so as to satisfy the requirements of Article 125. An insolvency administrator should also be able to bring proceedings against former directors of an insolvent company where it can be shown that they failed in their duty of care and diligence towards the company. Perhaps this may be implied from the use of the phrase 'honest and hardworking' in Article 125. At the

47 See the insolvent trading provisions in s. 588G of the Australian Corporations Act 2001 and the provisions in ss 216 and 217, Insolvency Act 1986 dealing with the use of phoenix companies by directors or shadow directors in the UK. Both the Australian and UK provisions impose a personal liability upon directors of insolvent companies who have breached these provisions. The UK Insolvency Act 2006 also prohibits 'fraudulent trading' (in s. 213) as well as the more useful prohibition of 'wrongful trading' on the part of directors (in s. 214) making them personally liable for their actions leading up to the liquidation of the company.

48 Examples of such provisions might include the 'fraudulent trading' provisions found in s. 993 of the UK Companies Act 2006; the 'wrongful trading' provisions found in s. 214 of the UK Insolvency Act 2006; and the insolvent trading provisions found in s. 588G of the Australian Corporations Act 2001.

very least, this should imply a disqualification regime for incompetent or careless directors. A more detailed director disqualification regime is therefore essential if this principle is to be made effective. The legal responsibilities provisions in Chapter 12 of the PRC Companies Law of 2005 also do not impose personal liabilities upon directors of failed companies; instead, their principal focus is upon the failures of companies and not of their directors. However, Article 148 of the Companies Law states that directors and senior managers have 'duties of loyalty and diligence to the company' whilst Article 149(8) proscribes acts of directors that are committed in breach of the 'duty of loyalty to the company'. Moreover, Article 150 does provide an important avenue for actions for damages being taken against corporate officers when it states that:

> Where a director, supervisor or senior manager violates laws, administrative regulations or the company's articles of association in performance of his duties for the company, and thus causes losses to the company, he shall be liable for compensation.

There is however a need for further refinement of legal rules in regard to directors' duties in the context of insolvent corporate enterprises in China.[49]

## Conclusions

Efforts to distil principles or objectives from legislative instruments such as the PRC's 2006 Enterprise Bankruptcy Law are to some degree impressionistic. Given the drafting style adopted, the language of the statute is sometime opaque and as such it will be left to the Supreme People's Court to issue more detailed guidelines or instructions as to how to interpret this new law.[50] It may be that more principles or objectives are read into the Law or that some 'principles' identified here are reduced to being nothing more than flexible norms or expectations.

Moreover, some principles may well sound impressive when read in the statute, but what will be more important will be how these principles are implemented; this will determine the real meaning and significance of these principles. Furthermore, the nature of enforcement actions that may be taken to enforce the principles that are evident from a reading of the Law, will be important in settling the importance of each of these various principles.

All of this may take some time to accomplish and as such this chapter is only the start of a journey of discovery and not the end of the road. However, the enactment of the legislation is an important landmark on this road. It may well be

49 See further for a discussion of these corporate governance issues: Feinerman (2008), pp. 46-57.

50 See for example the Regulations discussed in Chapter 6 of this volume.

a long journey before the full significance of the new law is both understood and accepted in China.

## References

Baird, D.G. (1993), *The Elements of Bankruptcy* (New York: Foundation Press).

Block-Lieb, S. and Halliday, T.C. (2004), 'Harmonization and Modernization in UNCITRAL's Legislative Guide on Insolvency' 42 *Texas International Law Journal* 475.

Carruthers, B.G. and Halliday, T.C. (2006), 'Negotiating Globalization: Global Scripts and Intermediation in the Construction of Asian Insolvency Regimes' 31 *Law and Social Inquiry* 521.

Dezalay, Y. and Garth, B. (2002), *The Internationalization of Palace Wars: Lawyers, Economists, and the Contest to Transform Latin American States* (Chicago: University of Chicago Press).

Feinerman, J.V. (2008), 'New Hope for Corporate Governance in China?', in Clarke D.C. (ed.), *China's Legal System: New Development, New Challenges* (Cambridge: Cambridge University Press).

Fletcher, I.F. (2009), *The Law of Insolvency*, 4th edition (London: Sweet & Maxwell).

Gebhardt, I. and Zhu, S. (eds) (2004), *The Bankruptcy Law of the People's Republic of China – Materials on the drafting process 2000* (Beijing: CITIC Publishing House).

Gordon, J.N. and Roe, M.J. (eds) (2004), *Convergence and Persistence in Corporate Governance* (Oxford: Oxford University Press).

Goode, R. (2005), *Principles of Corporate Insolvency Law* (3rd rev. ed.) (London: Sweet & Maxwell).

Goode, R. (2007), *Principles of Corporate Insolvency Law* (London: Thomson/ Sweet & Maxwell).

Hall, P. and Soskice, D. (eds) (2001), *Varieties of Capitalism: The Institutional Foundations of Comparative Advantage* (Oxford: Oxford University Press).

Halliday, T.C. and Carruthers B.G. (2009), *Law's Global Markets – International Organizations and Bankruptcy Law after the Asian Financial Crisis* (Stanford: Stanford University Press).

Hargovan, A. and Harris, J. (2006), 'Sons of Gwalia: Policy Issues Raised by the Subordination of Shareholder Claims' 7(1) *Insolvency Law Bulletin* 1.

Hargovan, A. and Harris, J. (2007), 'Sons of Gwalia and Statutory Debt Subordination: An Appraisal of the North American Experience' 20 *Australian Journal of Corporate Law* 265.

Harmer, R.W. (2000), 'Insolvency Law Reforms in the Asian and Pacific Region: Report of the Office of the General Counsel on TA 5795-REG: Insolvency Law Reforms' (1-86) in *Asian Development Bank, Law and Policy Reform at the Asian Development Bank* (Manila: ADB).

Huang, Y. (2008), *Capitalism with Chinese Characteristics: Entrepreneurship and the State* (New York: Cambridge University Press).

Jackson, T.H. (1986), *The Logic and Limits of Bankruptcy Law* (Cambridge: Harvard University Press).

Li, G. (2006), 'The Establishment of Limited Priority of Workers' Claims in the Enterprise Bankruptcy Law of China', written after the Fifth Forum for Asian Insolvency Reform (FAIR) which was held on 27-28 April 2006 in Beijing, China available at: <http://www.oecd.org/dataoecd/-42/44/38184516.pdf>, last accessed 27 May 2009.

Li, S. (2004), 'Bankruptcy Law in China: Lessons of the Past Twelve Years' V *Harvard Asia Quarterly*, available at: <http://www.leggicinesi.it/dottrina/LiShuguang_Bankruptcy.pdf>, last accessed 27 May 2009.

Liebman, B.J. (2008), 'China's Courts: Restricted Reform' in Clarke D.C. (ed.), *China's Legal System: New Developments, New Challenges* (Cambridge: Cambridge University Press).

Murray, M. (2005), *Keay's Insolvency – Personal and Corporate Law and Practice* (Sydney: Thomson/LawBook Co).

Parry, R. and Zhang, H. (2008), 'China's New Corporate Rescue Laws: Perspectives and Principles' 8 *Journal of Corporate Law Studies* 113.

Peerenboom, R. (2002), *China's Long March toward Rule of Law* (Cambridge: Cambridge University Press).

Roe, M. (1994), *Strong Managers, Weak Owners – The Political Roots of American Corporate Finance* (Princeton: Princeton University Press).

Shi, J. (2002), 'Recent Developments in Chinese Cross-Border Insolvencies' 15 *Australian Jnl of Corp Law* 35.

Song, Xiaoming, (2006) 'The Court's Role in Enterprise Bankruptcy Proceedings and Restructuring in China', paper written after the Fifth Forum for Asian Insolvency Reform (FAIR) which was held on 27-28 April 2006 in Beijing, China and available at: <http://www.oecd.org/dataoecd/42/60/-38184314.pdf>, last accessed 27 May 2009.

Tang, A.C.W. (2006), 'Creditor Participation in China and Hong Kong, China', written for the Fifth Forum for Asian Insolvency Reform (FAIR) which was held on 27-28 April 2006 in Beijing, China, available at: <http://www.oecd.org/dataoecd/41/45/38182753.pdf>, last accessed 27 May 2009.

Tang, L. (2009), 'New Issues in Chinese Enterprise Bankruptcy Law' 34 *Eurofenix: The Journal of INSOL Europe* 22-3.

Tomasic, R. (1998), 'Insolvency Law Principles and the Draft Bankruptcy Law of the People's of China' 9 *Australian Jnl of Corporate Law* 211.

Tomasic, R. (ed.) (2006), *Insolvency Law in East Asia* (Aldershot: Ashgate Publishing).

Tomasic, R. (2006), 'Creditor Participation in Insolvency Proceedings – Towards the Adoption of International Standards' 14 *Insolvency Law Journal* 173-87.

Tomasic, R. (2007), 'Insolvency Law Reform in Asia and Emerging Global Insolvency Norms' 15 *Insolvency Law Journal* 229.

Tomasic, R. and Little, P. (1997), *Insolvency Law and Practice in Asia* (Hong Kong: FT Law & Tax).

Tomasic, R. and Wang, M. (2005), 'Reforming China's Corporate Bankruptcy Laws' 18(3) *Australian Jnl of Corporate Law* 220.

Tomasic, R. and Wang, M. (2006), 'The Long March Towards China's New Bankruptcy Law' in UNCITRAL (2005), *Legislative Guide on Insolvency Law* (New York: United Nations) available at: <http://www.uncitral.org/uncitral/en/uncitral_texts/insolvency/2004Guide.html>, last accessed 27 May 2009.

Wang, W. (1998), 'Adopting Corporate Rescue Regimes in China – A Comparative Survey' 9 *Australian Journal of Corporate Law* 234.

Wang, W. (2001), 'Strengthening Judicial Expertise in Bankruptcy Proceedings in China', paper presented Forum for Asian Insolvency Reform, Bali, 7-8 February 2001 available at: <http://www.oecd.org/dataoecd/8/24/1874188.pdf>, last accessed 27 May 2009.

Wang, W. (2006), 'The order of payment of workers' claims and securities interests under China's new Bankruptcy Law', paper presented at Fifth Forum for Asian Insolvency Reform (FAIR) which was held on 27-28 April 2006 in Beijing, China, available at: <http://www.oecd.org/dataoecd/-41/40/38182499.pdf>, last accessed 27 May 2009.

Wang, H. (2006), 'An International Comparison of Insolvency Laws', paper prepared after the Fifth Forum for Asian Insolvency Reform (FAIR) which was held on 27-28 April 2006 in Beijing, China, available at: <http://www.oecd.org/dataoecd/41/41/38182541.pdf>, last accessed 27 May 2009.

Wood, P. (1995), *Principles of International Insolvency* (London: Sweet & Maxwell).

Xiaoming, X. (2006), 'Economic Development and the Role of the Judiciary', paper presented at the 50th Anniversary Celebrations of the Supreme Court of Pakistan and available at: <http://www.supremecourt.gov.pk/web/subsites/scp50/Articles/5/4.pdf>, last accessed 27 May 2009.

Zhang, X. and Booth, C.D. (2001), 'Chinese Bankruptcy Law in an emerging market economy: the Shenzhen Experience' 15 *Columbia Journal of Asian Law* 2.

Chapter 3

# Corporate Governance, Accounting Procedures and Prevention of Insolvency

Qingxiu Bu

## Introduction

In a time of global financial crisis, bankruptcy prevention and corporate governance are at the forefront of the public consciousness, with a hypothesis that there is a fundamental link between these two concepts. A business failure is commonly accompanied by poor corporate governance within the organization. The failure to adopt an effective corporate governance model often leads to a sterile, inactive board of directors and may hasten a firm's demise. Conversely, attention to corporate governance concerns can greatly benefit firms in staving off bankruptcy, or in emerging from bankruptcy.[1] Board independence and equity ownership, along with the principle of good corporate governance, can create an environment in which management is effectively monitored and bankruptcy generally is avoided.[2] Following a recent spate of global corporate abuses such as Enron, WorldCom and Parlamat, China has experienced its own corporate governance scandals resulting in the destruction of investor confidence. The exposure to such Enron-like corporate collapses has acted as a global wake-up call for states to undertake corporate governance reforms within an urgent timescale. Enhancing investor confidence must be achieved through meaningful transparency, effective oversight and strong governance, while effective bankruptcy legislation may also be regarded as a cornerstone of good corporate governance. However if corporate governance is to realize its full potential any reforms must work effectively in combination with company law and other legislations.

This broader context to effective insolvency prevention will be considered in this chapter. The chapter will begin by defining 'corporate governance'. Attention will be paid to differing approaches to ownership and board structure, since these matters provide an important context for the consideration of corporate governance issues. Another important contextual factor that one may note, as a direct result of the overwhelming dominance of state ownership in China, is a lack of independence among board directors. The introduction of the 'independent director' institution in China is intended to alleviate the weakness of the

1 Elson, Helmsand and Moncus (2002), p. 1932.

2 Ibid.

supervisory board and to hold the board accountable for the company's interests. In addition, the problem of transparency, posing challenges to proper accounting procedures, calls for improvements to ensure accurate and timely disclosure of all material matters. China has recently enacted some new laws to commit itself to the values of accountability, transparency and responsible ownership. One of the fundamental aims of these reforms is to streamline corporate governance and accounting procedures in firms, so as to prevent financial difficulties which may result in insolvencies. It remains to be seen whether the EBL 2006 can efficiently assist in the maintenance of sound corporate governance, in combination with other relevant legislations.

Particular consideration must be given to the prevention of business failure in the context of bankruptcy, such as through reorganization and composition: see further Chapters 11 and 12. Since most state owned enterprises (SOEs) are usually obliged to carry out public functions, China has made considerable efforts to rescue those problematic companies in the form of a new reorganization process and a compromise procedure: see further Chapter 15. The Enterprise Bankruptcy Law of the People's Republic of China (EBL 2006)[3] introduces a reorganization scheme similar to the United States Chapter 11, which allows some troubled companies to avoid bankruptcy and further to recover their businesses.

A paradoxical issue is to be highlighted, namely, how, through a sound corporate governance regime, such as through applying healthy accounting procedures, may China avoid needless bankruptcies, and how may the efficient application of the newly-established bankruptcy law improve corporate governance. The interactive and interwoven relations between the governance and prevention of insolvencies will be considered in this chapter.

## Corporate Governance and Its Constraints

Corporate governance is a mechanism under which corporations are operated and controlled, seeking to mitigate financial, ethical and operational irregularities. Directors may be deterred from manipulating their position to gain benefits at the expense of the company or of non-controlling shareholders. Minority shareholders or creditors may pursue appropriate remedies with reliance on a sound corporate governance system. There are many different views of the concept of corporate governance, one of which was developed by the Organization for Economic Co-operation and Development (OECD):[4]

> Corporate governance is the system by which business corporations are directed and controlled. The corporate governance structure specifies the distribution of

3 The Standing Committee of the 10th National People's Congress (NPC), China's highest legislative body, adopted the PRC Enterprise Bankruptcy Law on 27 August 2006.

4 OECD (2004).

> rights and responsibilities among different participants in the corporation, such as the board, managers, shareholders and other stakeholders, and spells out the rules and procedures for making decisions on corporate affairs. By doing this, it also provides the structure through which the company objectives are set, and the means of attaining those objectives and monitoring performance.

The principles represent an objective initiative to develop the core elements of a good corporate governance regime.[5] With an aim to strike a sensible balance between maintaining efficient management and deterring malfeasance, many governments have adopted these principles as a benchmark to design, evaluate and improve their relevant laws and regulations. The ultimate objective is to achieve higher-level transparency, accountability and responsibility and to enhance investor confidence under a healthy and well-functioning corporate governance framework. In the specific context of insolvency issues, a sound corporate governance regime can serve as a catalyst to accelerate the quality of accounting procedures and avoid unnecessary insolvencies *inter alia* by detecting and preventing fraudulent activities and by ensuring that companies in difficulties, or on the edge of difficulties, obtain help at a sufficiently early stage.

### *Corporate Governance in China: Overview*

China's transition from a state-planned into a market-orientated economy commenced three decades ago, however corporate governance has been gaining prominence only during the last few years.[6] More significantly, China's entry into the World Trade Organization (WTO) has served as a catalyst in disciplining listed companies and accelerating the pace of building a more comprehensive and systematic corporate governance regime. With the onset of the recent financial crisis, once again attention has been focused on the adequacy of insolvency prevention and accounting procedures in China.

The basic principles are put into practice with a combination of laws and regulations, including the new Company Law and Securities Law. As one of the most important legal pillars, the much anticipated EBL 2006 came into effect on 1 June 2007, superseding the PRC State Enterprise Bankruptcy Law (for Trial Implementation), which was promulgated in 1986.[7] The new law with its 136 articles contained in 12 chapters appears to emulate insolvency schemes that may be found in jurisdictions with sophisticated credit economies.[8] The EBL 2006 seems to promote and facilitate US-style corporate rescue procedures, of which a

5 Feinerman (2007), p. 612.

6 Tai (2004), pp. 439-58.

7 PRC Enterprise Bankruptcy Law (Trial Implementation) was adopted by the Standing Committee of the NPC on 2 December 1986 and was superseded on 1 June 2007.

8 Falke (2007), p. 74.

key aim is to enable the debtor to continue its operation. If properly implemented, the new bankruptcy law can promote sustainable economic development in China by encouraging investors and creditors to further invest and expand the provision of credit.

*Impediments to Sound Corporate Governance*

As the corporate governance standard is heavily influenced by cultural, political and legal factors, some impediments may be identified as potential limitations on the effectiveness of China's current corporate governance regime to efficiently accelerate the implementation of laws for the prevention of further business failures. It appears that the system suffers from cultural considerations which differ from Western concepts of good business practice. Although it is difficult to quantify and measure cultural barriers, they can often be intransigent.[9] The impact of the new laws and regulations may be undermined in particular by the inherent goal of harmony in relationships which has been fostered in China for thousands of years. The long-standing traditional Chinese culture places considerable emphasis on the nurturing and maintenance of interpersonal relationships, and Chinese business is conducted on this basis.[10] There is a strong preference for the resolution of disputes through conciliation rather than litigation. Such cultural conditioning may make a Western vision of corporate governance practice difficult to implement.

Recent legislations have however brought China more closely into alignment with international practice. For example, to a large extent, the Chinese securities market has adopted an infrastructure – accounting, legal and regulatory – typically found in the West. The provisions should, if vigorously enforced, improve the standard of corporate governance in China. However, the proof of a judicial system's effectiveness largely depends upon its implementation and enforcement. As Feinerman observed:[11]

> Much has been accomplished in establishing the basic features of corporate governance; however, there still much to do with effectiveness of enforcement.

China's lack of an effective enforcement infrastructure, such as an independent judicial system, constitutes another intrinsic barrier to good governance. Therefore although the new law, on paper, has good potential, it is unlikely to be fully effective in the short term.

9 Peerenboom (2001).

10 Mayeda (2006). See also p. 4 where the impact of traditional Chinese culture on insolvency laws is considered.

11 Feinerman (2007), p. 619.

## Concentrated State Ownership

The current corporate governance mechanisms are likely to remain imperfect in the context of dominant state ownership and political control over managers.[12] The real power in Chinese companies is exercised through the state, which has an overwhelming majority of shares in most SOEs, exercising its control through a holding company, which is the entity that holds all of the Chinese state's shares.[13] Although it is officially recognized that 'the non-public sectors constitute an important component of the socialist market economy',[14] the state remains as controlling shareholder of many listed companies under a highly concentrated structure, with, in particular, the Blue Chips being still overwhelmingly state-owned.[15] A 2007 annual report from Shanghai Stock Exchange showed that 65 per cent of the listed companies are state enterprises.[16] Although the total market capitalization of Chinese listed companies has reached 146-67 per cent of China's GDP, more than two-thirds of this comes from state-owned, non-tradable shares.[17] In other words, this prohibits more than two thirds of shares technically listed on the market from actually trading.[18]

The State-owned Assets Supervision and Administration Commission of the State Council (SASAC) is a Commission of the State Council which wields considerable power over the SOEs. It ensures that the State's interests are represented in the activities of China's listed companies. This means that it is involved in the appointment and removal of directors and top executives, which means that the top executives' careers are not closely tied with the businesses' success or failure but rather with the pursuit of a political relationship with government officials.[19]

The predominant state ownership is in conflict with the classical principle that encourages the separation of ownership and management. The problem has evolved from the once centrally-controlled economy. Politics has skewed the corporate governance process, which has created a culture of dependency on the state, one aspect of which results in a lack of accountability. In this vein, the effective control of corporate governance would rest in State entities which may have an agenda conflicting with the interests of private shareholders/creditors desiring profits.[20] Creditors cannot afford to ignore that their goal (i.e. profit) will often conflict

---

12 'World Bank Releases Report on China's Reform of State Ownership' (26 May 2002) <www.china.org.cn> accessed on 16 March 2009.

13 Dallas and Scott (2006), p. 144.

14 PRC Constitution Law Article 11 (1999 Amendment).

15 The SASAC holds the China Government's shareholding in all China's listed companies (other than those in the finance sector). In 2008, total assets were over US$1.56 trillion.

16 Liu (2008).

17 Xie (2007).

18 Kister (2007), p. 363.

19 Li, Wang and Deng (2008), p. 623.

20 Clarke (2006), p. 228.

with the government's goals (e.g. development).[21] Corporate governance may not be able to solve the problem unless the State makes fundamental changes to bring about a more market-orientated system. It would be advisable for the State Council to strike a balance between limiting the exception of SOEs for 'policy bankruptcy'[22] in a transparent and foreseeable manner.

## Two-tier Board

In this part, the supervisory board and the independent director, two corporate governance mechanisms that are intended to act as controls on managerial power will be considered. It must firstly be explained that Chinese companies adopt a two-tier board system for their internal governance i.e. companies have a board of directors and a supervisory board.[23] This structure resembles the German model, where the management board shall abide by the articles of association and perform their duties *bona fide* in the best interests of the company and the supervisory board shall assume a monitoring role. An active supervisory board can hypothetically prevent the management from engaging in conduct that may possibly lead to bankruptcy. The Company Law 2005 seems to place emphasis on strengthening the power of the supervisory board, and providing it with broad new authorities. However, given the overwhelming dominance of the state's influence on the board of directors, the supervisory board may not yet be able to play an effective monitoring role. Moreover the quasi two-tier board may lead to redundancy and inefficiency in corporate governance. A further governance mechanism which has been introduced, the independent director, may not offer much to improve the situation.

### *Ineffective Supervisory Board*

It is essential for a firm to implement a corporate governance model that is capable of effectively monitoring its operations. The supervisory board seems, *prima facie*, capable of playing a strategically critical role, with a primary function of detecting and preventing directors' violations of laws and regulations as well as duties of loyalties, due diligence and care. A supervisor is entitled to effectively

21 Pace (2006), p. 585.

22 Failure of SOEs could lead to mass unemployment and perhaps political unrest as China generally does not have national unemployment insurance or welfare programmes for its citizens. Employees have taken priority over secured creditors in the sale of SOE assets and the government has met the shortfall. However this conduct is due to be phased out. See further Chapter 15.

23 Company Law 2005 Article 123; The CSRC *Guidelines for Articles of Association of Chinese Listed Companies 2006* also stipulates that senior managers and employees' representatives must not account for more than half of the directors.

inspect and protect the interests of the company, and among other things,[24] is empowered to initiate an action against wrongdoing directors.[25] Nevertheless, the supervisory board has consistently failed to effectively perform the monitoring role envisaged for it for varying reasons, such as the vague conferral of statutory powers, their lack of professional qualifications and impotent enforcement system against wrongdoing behaviours. A particularly notable factor is the dominance of state-tied controlling shareholders. With the state as the dominant shareholder, the two-tier boards are both controlled by insiders, which has restricted the exertion of supervisory strength over the management. In addition, a significant proportion of supervisors are employees who are subordinate to directors of the company. Therefore, regardless of its intended watchdog position, the supervisory board appears to play no genuinely important role in China's corporate governance regime.

It is also notable that the absence of a clear statutory framework for the regulation of corporate behaviours has led to frequent abuses of power by directors and supervisors. Insiders in control of the company may seek personal gains without regard to shareholders' interests, e.g. through excessively increasing their compensation. The Supervisory Board is not generally qualified enough to prevent such conduct, lacking sufficient knowledge and experience to effectively supervise the Board of Directors. These difficulties make the monitoring role of the supervisory board weak and illusory.[26] Although an aim of the Company Law 2005 was to reinforce supervision by the board of supervisors, it neither actually equips the board with any significant powers nor provides structurally for its independence from its supervisees.[27]

The supervisory board also has little say in major corporate decisions, due to its vaguely-defined monitoring role overseeing the board of directors. Unlike its counterpart in Germany, the Chinese Supervisory Board has neither strategic decision-making power nor a power to appoint or dismiss management board members, as substantial power vests in the general meeting. Although the CSRC has endeavoured to strengthen the shareholder's meeting's functions,[28] this meeting still cannot be relied upon as a potent and effective supervisory institution. To a large extent, it plays a nominal and limited role in China's corporate governance regime at the current stage.[29]

Against such a supervision infrastructure, the supervisory board cannot be perceived to give effect to efficient supervision of the directors through minimizing

24 Company Law 2005 Article 54.

25 Company Law 2005 Article 152.

26 Schipani and Liu (2002), p. 69; Ho (2003), p. 88.

27 Article 52, Company Law 2005 merely provides that no director or senior manager can concurrently work as a supervisor.

28 CSRC (2006).

29 Hu (2002).

insider control problems which have penetrated throughout the whole corporate governance system.

*Independent Directors*

An independence mechanism is designed to motivate and enable the board of directors to monitor the management of the corporation, so as to prevent a controlling shareholder from using their control to harm other shareholders and the corporation itself. An independent director assumes the responsibilities of monitoring and evaluation of management. As observed by Clarke:[30]

> the need for non-management directors on the board to serve as a check on management is in the interests of shareholders.

The concept of the independent director was first adopted in a Guiding Opinion issued by the China Securities Regulatory Commission (CSRC) on 26 December 1997.[31] The independent directors are expected to:[32]

> bear the duties of good faith and due diligence toward the listed company and all [its] shareholders. They shall ... protect the overall interests of the company, and shall be especially concerned with protecting the interests of minority shareholders from being infringed.

To strengthen supervision and alleviate the prevalent irregularities, independent directors should constitute at least one-third of the board directors and at least one such director must be an accounting professional.[33] However, the independent

30 Clarke (2006), pp. 154-5.

31 CSRC operates as the Chinese Government's corporate regulator through promulgating the corporate governance code, regulations, and regular reports on corporate governance reform and performance in China. CSRC also liaises closely with the management of the stock exchanges in Shanghai and Shenzhen, and with those foreign exchanges which list Chinese stock. As a regulatory body, it primarily aims to protect investors and simultaneously seeks to maintain tight control over directors' behaviour. CSRC has powers analogous to the SEC in the United States.

32 Article 112, 'Guiding Opinions for Listed Companies' Articles of Incorporation'. The CSRC was established in 1992 overseeing all the securities business activities in China, and it is also commonly recognized as the most active authority formulating and enforcing various rules and procedures related to regulated listed companies' activities. See Shen and Jia (2005), p. 230.

33 See 'Guideline for Introducing Independent Directors to the Boards of Directors of Listed Companies' which was issued by CSRC and the State Economic and Trade Commission (SETC), part of which was merged into a newly created State Development Planning Commission (NDRC), on 16 August 2001; Article 49 of the 'Corporate Governance Guidelines for Listed Companies' issued by the CSRC (2002), providing that

director did not gain a statutory footing until the introduction of the Company Law 2005.[34]

To avoid disturbing the independent directors from acting independently and objectively, they are prohibited from directly or indirectly holding more than 1 per cent of the company's total shares,[35] and are forbidden from acting in this capacity where they have any relationship with a large shareholder that would impair their independence.[36]

The integration of an independent director system into the supervision framework seems to combine the merits of both German and common law solutions to make up for the weaknesses of the supervisory board in a culture where, to a fair extent, independent thought is not a hallmark. Realistically, however, it is almost impossible for the selection process of independent directors to avoid influence by controlling shareholders or management, since *Guanxi*[37] pervades throughout the intertwined web of social and business settings. Given coherent cultural and legal traditions and concentrated ownership, companies with truly independent boards remain rare and independent directors play a less meaningful role in corporate governance than envisaged. The independent directors are too close to the management so that effective monitoring is rendered impossible. The lack of independence usually leads to inefficacy of directors' exercising their powers. In reality, the independent directors are selected by controlling shareholders who often appoint those with some connections and thus will side with them. Usually as the largest shareholder, the State's motives may not always align with those of the other investors. In the absence of legal specification, the government uses its position as the largest shareholder to designate top executives and to control the company.

### *Supervisory Gap*

Apparently, companies' supervisory functions remain to be adequately addressed under the current situation. Neither the independent directors nor the board of supervisors have the motivation to monitor the management in a state-dominated company, due largely to the lack of well-equipped supervision mechanisms. The insufficiency of monitoring tends to engender the insiders' discretion with

---

an independent director should be separate from the company which appoints him and its major shareholders; and the Listing Rules of the HKEx (rule 3.10, para. 1) requiring that 'every board of directors of a listed issuer must include at least three independent non-executive directors'. In Taiwan, Rule 9(12) of the 'Listing Review Rules' requires directors and supervisors to act independently and for companies to have at least one independent director as a condition of listing.

34 Article 123, Company Law 2005.

35 Article 3(2), 'Guideline for Introducing Independent Directors to the Boards of Directors of Listed Companies'.

36 Article 1(1), 'Guideline for Introducing Independent Directors to the Boards of Directors of Listed Companies'.

37 Vanhonacker (2004), pp. 18-19.

corresponding detriment to the proper safeguarding of creditors' rights and interests. The supposedly impartial role of independent directors, if able to reach its full potential, might serve as a complement to the supervisory board, after all, the creation of the former was a direct response of the CSRC to the virtual failures of the latter.[38] Although it appears that the independent directors system has played a more effective role than the supervisory board, it is still too early to assess to what extent the overlapping institutions will improve the supervision framework, due to limited judicial tests.[39]

## Liabilities and Investor/Creditors' Protection

Directors, supervisors and other senior management personnel shall bear obligations of fidelity and diligence to the company. They may be subject to personal liability for any loss or damage caused to the company due to their wrongful act during the performance of their duties, varying from civil, administrative and even criminal liabilities. Dominant as the criminal and administrative penalties are, a general trend of resorting to private enforcement against wrongdoers is on a steadily increasing track. The EBL 2006 provides relevant provisions that apply in combination with the recently-enacted Company Law, Securities Law and Criminal Law to impose liability on managerial members,[40] who may be exposed to civil, administrative and even criminal liabilities for their violation of fiduciary duties under the interwoven legal framework.[41] See also Chapter 14 of this volume. The threat of such liabilities can act as an important governance tool, encouraging directors to achieve good standards of performance, and so such liabilities can play a part in the prevention of financial difficulties.[42]

### *Administrative and Criminal Liabilities*

Traditional breaches of managerial duties are usually subject to administrative or criminal liability in China, in particular, where they arise in the management

38 Kang, Shi and Brown (2008), p. 30.

39 Gu (2003); Wang (2007).

40 The Company Law of the People's Republic of China and the Securities Law of the People's Republic of China were amended at the 18th Session of the Standing Committee of the 10th National People's Congress (NPC) on 27 October 2005, and became effective as of 1 January 2006.

41 Article 125, EBL 2006.

42 Coffee (2006), 1552-3 (arguing that civil liability does constitute a meaningful deterrent to misconduct); Black (2008), 171. The *World Com* case may serve a perfect example of possible deterrent effects. There Bernard J. Ebbers, the founder and former chief executive of World Com, was convicted of fraud, and reached an agreement with the SEC surrendering nearly all of his personal fortune (about $40 million) to investors who lost billions when the company went bankrupt.

of SOEs. The Company Law 2005 expands the breadth of the directors' criminal liabilities. For instance, a new crime of 'false bankruptcy' is introduced to penalize fraud perpetrated by companies through the concealment of assets or fictitious debts. The wrongdoer may be subject to a monetary penalty of a maximum of RMB 200,000 (£20,000) or such penalty in combination with a custodial sentence of up to five years if such false bankruptcy harms the interests of creditors.[43]

In response to the recent development in the Company Law 2005, the Criminal Law of the People's Republic of China (the Criminal Law first enacted in 1979 and revised for the sixth time in 2006, hereafter 'Criminal Law Amendment Six 2006') has been amended to stipulate relevant criminal liabilities for violation of the statutory duties by directors, supervisors and senior staff.[44] These management personnel are expressly identified in the provision that effectively establishes the legal basis under which criminal prosecution may be undertaken.[45] The Criminal Law Amendment Six 2006 contains updated supplemental provisions regarding the crimes which violate the financial orders or corporate governance of the companies. These violations now correspond to and result in such crimes as the manipulation or looting of a listed company, fraudulent bankruptcy and so on.[46] The Law provides for shareholders that abuse a company's independent legal status and limited liability status to evade debts, and who thereby materially damage the interests of the company's creditors, to bear joint and several liabilities for the company's debts. This provision, however, does not clearly specify the circumstances under which the corporate veil can be pierced.[47] In consequence, rarely have wrongdoers been subject to criminal punishment, regardless of increasing fraud and financial fakery being exposed, due largely to ineffective implementation.

With the legal infrastructural improvement growing significantly, there is a gradual shift from criminal and administrative penalties to private enforcement of a wrongdoer's civil liabilities. These alternative monitoring mechanisms represent endeavour to come into alignment with the commonly-established practice in other developed jurisdictions.[48] Such a shift under China's transition to a market-orientated economy makes profound sense in that it accelerates the creation of a disincentive system to deter wrongdoers from abusing their positions and, as a result, it can play a part in insolvency prevention.

---

43 Article 216, Company Law.

44 The Criminal Law of the People's Republic of China, as amended at the 22nd Session of the Standing Committee of the 10th National People's Congress (the NPC being the highest legislative body in China) on 29 June 2006, came into effect on the same day.

45 Article 217. Securities Law of the People's Republic of China.

46 Article 129, EBL 2006.

47 Deacons (2006).

48 UK Companies Act 2006 Article 260 (3); New Zealand Companies Act 1993, ss 165-8; Australian Corporations Act 2001, Part 2F.1A; Australian Civil Liability Act 2003.

*Civil Liabilities*

Breaches of fiduciary duties may constitute a cause of action giving rise to civil liabilities for directors, supervisors and senior managers who commit breaches of their obligations of loyalty or due diligence, which in a serious case may cause the enterprise to become bankrupt. There remains a controversial issue as to whether the concept of fiduciary duties exists in China, since they are neither well-defined nor expressly recognized in China's jurisdictions. However such laws can arguably play a part in effective governance. For example, Tomasic and Andrews have attributed the rampant insider trading which has been witnessed in China to two fundamental factors, i.e. the lack of a concept for fiduciary duties and inefficient enforcement.[49] However the concept of fiduciary duties, developed in common law jurisdictions, may not compatibly fit in well with the Chinese civil law tradition, with neither precedents nor an explicit statutory definition in place.

The development of fiduciary duties may not however be necessary. Arguably, the existing Chinese duties of loyalty, due diligence and care serve an equivalently functioning role which may be inferred from Articles 59, 61 and 63 of the Company Law 2005:

1. directors shall faithfully perform their duties, maintain the interests of the company and not take any advantage of their position to seek personal gains;[50]
2. the directors shall not operate on their own, or operate for others, the same category of business as the company they are serving, or engage in activities which damage the interests of the company;[51] and
3. directors shall be liable to pay compensation where they violate laws, rules, regulations or the articles of association in performance of their duties and thus cause damages to the company.[52]

These statutory requirements appear to pay more attention to the standards of conduct and competence by imposing 'a duty of loyalty and due diligence'.[53] The duty of loyalty requires that board members subordinate their own personal interests in the event of a conflict of interest between the company and themselves. The duty of due diligence requires that a board member exercises reasonable care in the management of the company and fulfils his or her duties in accordance with all relevant laws and regulations. Apparently, Article 59 emphasizes a director's duty to exercise power for proper purposes, while

49 Andrews and Tomasic (2006), p. 309.

50 Article 59, Company Law 2005.

51 Article 61, Company Law 2005.

52 Article 63, Company Law 2005.

53 UK Companies Act 2006, s. 148 provides mandatory duties of loyalty and diligence for all board members.

Article 62 especially targets conflicts of interest, both of which are commonly well-established in the Western corporate law,[54] although Chinese directors may not be fully aware of the essence and the necessity of precluding conflicts of interest while exercising their powers. These provisions, to some extent, manifest concepts akin to directors' fiduciary duties enshrined in common law jurisdictions. However an issue arises as to whether the duty of loyalty equates to something as high as a fiduciary duty. The same as well goes to judicial operation, where the judges are likely to fail to observe the fiduciary duty without applicable civil law specifications.[55]

Furthermore, certain activities are strictly forbidden. Directors and senior management are prohibited from involvement in self-dealing, usurpation of corporate opportunities as well as ordinary misappropriation.[56] Any director shall be required to compensate the company for damages where detriment to the company's interests is caused. Such detriment is presently prevalent in China. To avoid conflicts of interests, directors are also required to abstain from voting on issues that are related to their own interests, although what constitutes a relevant connected relationship is yet to be explicitly defined.[57]

The statutory principles reflect a shift from criminal and administrative penalties to private enforcement which is commonly used in other developed jurisdictions. More significantly, both management and minority shareholders are well-advised of their specific rights and obligations which, to a certain extent, facilitates the accessibility of minority shareholders' remedies and at the same time serves a substitutive deterrence role in place of the public authority.

The Company Law 2005 also establishes a new insolvency regime to provide a more orderly and well-structured approach to deal with failing companies and seeks to provide better protection for investors as well creditors. Shareholders are entitled to appeal to the supervisory board to resolve what they deem as misconduct by the managers and directors, and the same entitlement can be used in respect of misbehaviours by members of the supervisory board.[58] In addition, this law confers on shareholders a power to initiate a court action if any director or senior manager injures shareholders' interests by violating any laws, administrative regulations, or any provisions of the articles of incorporation.[59] After unsuccessfully requesting

54 UK Companies Act 2006, ss 170-77; Australian Corporation Act, ss 180-83; New Zealand's Companies Act 1993, ss 131-7.

55 Kang, Shi and Brown (2008), p. 31.

56 Article 149, Company Law 2005; Feinerman (2007), p. 601.

57 Article 125, Company Law 2005 regulates how an interested director must abstain from voting and the voting procedures for the resolution of transactions between or among affiliated parties. Interested directors and non-interested directors of a listed company are subject to statutory duties to abstain from voting on affiliated party transactions. The 2006 CSRC 'Guidelines for Articles of Association of Chinese Listed Companies' reinforce the regulations that shareholders cannot vote on transactions in which they are involved.

58 Article 152, Company Law 2005.

59 Article 153, Company Law 2005.

the company's board of directors or supervisory board to take action, shareholders may commence litigation against directors, supervisors or senior executives who have committed fraudulent acts breaching their duty of loyalty.[60] In light of these statutory provisions, it might be considered that minority shareholders have sufficient means of protection. However, the would-be claimants, as a matter of Chinese civil procedure, need to be responsible for litigation costs and they bear the burden of proof.[61] To meet the threshold of *locus standi*, a minority shareholder must hold no less than 1 per cent of the company's shares for more than six months and must notify the company of the intention to sue in advance.[62] These demanding *ex ante* requirements may be justified on the basis that they maintain a basic principle that it is for the board of directors, rather than the shareholders to manage the company, and further that they shield the directors or supervisors from frivolous disruptions caused by litigious shareholders. On the other hand, the procedural barriers, to a great extent, constitute *de facto* barriers and discourage meritorious would-be claimants from pursuing their statutory remedies. The potential for the statutory provisions to both impose liability on errant directors and to deter wrongful conduct on the part of other directors may be undermined as a result. It is unrealistic to expect that the current legal system can protect the interest of individual investors without overcoming procedural and substantial hurdles. In this regard, the protection of investors and creditors remains weak, due to the lack of clear civil remedies provided in circumstances where their legal interests have been violated.

The director liability mechanisms become increasingly significant in a bankruptcy context. As discussed further in Chapter 14, the EBL 2006 has transplanted the concepts of directorial liability for trading during insolvency and directors' disqualification orders found in other jurisdictions.[63] Theoretically, these provisions of the EBL 2006 may provide creditors and investors with more certainty, transparency and protection. However uncertainty remains as to how the Supreme People's Court will tackle the existing gaps of the EBL 2006 in its expected judicial interpretation.[64]

### *Implications*

The increasing liabilities provided under the new law may be considered to demonstrate, at least on paper, that China's capital market has become more

60 Article 152, Company Law 2005.

61 Article 107, PRC Civil Procedure Law provides that any party filing a civil lawsuit shall pay court costs according to the rules; Article 2 of the 'Provisions on Evidence for Civil Litigation' issued by the Supreme Court.

62 Article 152, Company Law 2005.

63 See e.g. UK Insolvency Act 1986, ss 213 and 214 and the Company Directors Disqualification Act 1986.

64 Falke (2007), p. 74.

market-oriented. Interestingly, the duties of loyalty, due diligence and care, to a great extent, manifest the concept of fiduciary duty that is well-established in common law jurisdictions, and breaches of these duties may provide a cause of action for minority shareholders to seek judicial recourse. Any board member who encroaches on a company's lawful rights and interests and who causes losses is very likely to be held accountable for damages towards the company or shareholders. They are exposed to dramatically increased risks of being sued and in consequence the potential for liabilities may have some deterrent effects. The extent to which the regime will realize its potential however largely depends upon whether efficient and consistent implementation can be achieved. Although the whole enforcement system is far from mature, the current legal framework, at least, provides a statutory basis on which a minority shareholder may access judicial assistance for further remedies that are to be analysed below. Concerns reasonably arise as to how effective, efficient and consistent the implementation of the law may turn out to be in reality.

## Accounting Procedures, Transparency and Information Disclosure

To promote sound corporate governance and prevent unnecessary insolvencies, it is desirable for relevant accounting standards to be updated and modified as well as for their application and enforcement to be improved. Adequate and timely information disclosure is a vital component of proper accounting procedures.

### *Accounting Procedures*

China's accounting procedures are quite different from those of its Western counterparts, especially in the accounting rules, quality of data, and other factors that may affect the performance of firms. False financial reporting has been proliferating due to the lack of audit independence and qualified auditors. The requirement, discussed in Chapter 4, of both cash flow insolvency and the balance sheet insolvency for a voluntary proceeding under the new law[65] could be problematic given the lack of transparency and uniformity of accounting standards and the practice of maintaining two sets of books and records for non-public companies in China.[66] The majority of China's certified public accountants (CPAs) lack sufficient qualifications in international accounting practices, and this makes it realistically difficult for them to cope adequately with corporate fraud.

To prevent irregularities, the Ministry of Finance has since the 1990s attempted to establish standard accounting practices across diverse types of enterprise.[67] China announced a commitment to converge Chinese Accounting Standards

65 Article 2, EBL 2006.

66 Eaton (2006).

67 PricewaterhouseCoopers (2006).

(CAS) with International Financial Reporting Standards (IFRS) in November 2005, a move which represents a significant step toward a single set of globally accepted accounting standards. In addition, to protect the legal interests of the company as well as its investors and creditors, SOEs are subject to an annual audit by registered Chinese certified public accounting firms.[68] The primary objective of auditing is to carry out inspection of the financial records of a business to ascertain their accuracy and legality. However, it has been found that the endeavour has been frequently resisted by some SOEs that prefer small local auditors which may be helpful in gaining regulatory approval resulting from their political connections and influence.[69] Notably, the local auditors, who have greater economic dependence on local SOEs, and are subject to more political influence from local governments than non-local auditors, are inclined to report favourably on the SOEs, so as to meet the regulator's requirements.[70]

To combat fraud, the supervision of auditors needs to be strengthened, even extending as far as the provision of means to revoke an auditor's licence on grounds of their involvement in fraudulent behaviour. Uncertainty remains as to how far the process of convergence may go towards the amendment of existing standards through the integration of the IFRS principles into CAS under the unique circumstances in China. In principle, it is required by the Ministry of Finance that 'central-level SOEs would comply with the new regulations by 2008 and the scope would be expanded to include all large and mid-scale enterprises a year later'.[71]

The role and value of the audit committee have been firmly established as an integral component of corporate governance. Many measures have been taken to regulate the accounting standards, for instance, only the shareholders' meeting can appoint accounting firms.[72] Chinese law does not clarify the status of internal auditors. The supervisory board may engage outside accountants at the company's expense to investigate irregularities.[73] Although the Company Law 2005 requires that the appointment and termination of the company's auditor be reviewed and determined by a board meeting or general meeting in accordance with the company's Articles of Association,[74] in reality, total subjection to a general manager substantially weakens an auditor's monitoring power.

---

68 Article 2 PRC Audit Law 2006.

69 Wang, Wong and Xia (2008), p. 134.

70 Chan, Lin and Mo (2006).

71 Central People's Government of the People's Republic of China (2007).

72 Article 170, Company Law 2005. A shareholders' general meeting acts as the company's highest authority, where a company plans to hire or dismiss any accounting firm to undertake the auditing of the company, a resolution shall be made by the shareholders' meeting or shareholders' assembly or the board of directors according to the provisions of the articles of association: CSRC 'Guidelines for Articles of Association of Chinese Listed Companies' (2006).

73 Article 55, Company Law 2005.

74 Article 170, Company Law 2005.

### *Transparency and Information Disclosure*

The correlation between information disclosure and investor protection cannot be overestimated. Shareholders are entitled to receive adequate, timely and complete information as well as regular disclosure of audited annual reports, apart from which disclosure of corporate practices should be made and information on *de facto* and *de jure* controlling shareholders should also be included. Investors rely on publicly disclosed information to make their investment decisions, and to monitor board and management performance. However, there is insufficient publicly available information as to China's compliance with matters such as the *Principles and Guidelines for Effective Insolvency and Creditor Rights Systems* developed by the World Bank.[75] Instead, the low standards of transparency and information disclosure represent a pervasive problem, with false and inaccurate financial reports being prevalent. Information asymmetry arises from the concentration of ownership of a company,[76] which discourages minority shareholders from engaging in long-term investment.[77] Furthermore, there remains suspicion as to whether the Chinese media could serve as an independent source for accurate information disclosure.[78]

Since the key issue of corporate governance is transparency or information disclosure, the law has improved provisions on continuous disclosure, strengthened reporting and auditing regulation, and includes measures to combat fraudulent disclosure.[79] However, there is scope for much pessimism in terms of their enforcement mechanisms. The Criminal Law Amendment Six 2006 expands the penalties related to failure to discharge legal disclosure obligations. It constitutes a crime for a person to provide a financial report with fabricated information, or with material information being concealed, thus harming its shareholders. The persons who are directly in charge of such conduct shall be liable to a monetary penalty of a maximum of RMB 200,000 (£20,000) or such penalty in combination with a custodial sentence of up to three years.[80] However, the provision does not explicitly define under which circumstances the wrongdoer should be subject to such criminal liabilities and this vagueness may give rise to enforcement difficulties.

---

75 Fremond and Capaul (2002).

76 Fama and Jensen (1983) 325.

77 Kang, Shi and Brown (2008), p. 27.

78 Liebman (2005), p. 157.

79 Article 124, Company Law 2005; Article 63, Securities Law 2006; 'Regulations on Information Disclosure of Listed Companies' issued by the CSRC on 30 January 2007.

80 Criminal Law Articles 160-62; Criminal Law 2006 (sixth amendment) Article 5; Zhang (2007), p. 767.

The Company Law 2005 expands the statutory rights of minority shareholders, who are entitled to examine the company's account books,[81] but it neither imposes disclosure obligations on directors nor stipulates any specific liabilities for them in the event of any failure to disclose material information in an accurate and timely manner. In addition, China's Securities Law prohibits persons[82] who are capable of accessing inside information from using it to trade securities.[83] However, enforcement remains considerably limited as the CSRC, as a primary supervision organ, lacks specific legally binding powers for the regulation of corporate governance, such as compulsory disclosure. Furthermore, the effectiveness of implementation has been undermined partly by the CSRC's limited personnel resources for the enforcement of the law and rules.[84]

The Supreme People's Court (SPC) made considerable progress in building a framework, which potentially enables investors to initiate litigation against directors and management for losses due to false financial disclosure.[85] However, the SPC has failed to provide effective procedural and substantive auxiliary provisions to apply the Notice. Therefore, would-be claimants attempting to pursue actions are confronted with serious obstacles, such as the narrowly defined causal link between a false statement and a shareholder's actual loss. The intentional elements and causal relationship needed to give rise to a successful damages claim remain to be determined by the courts.

*Cross-listing*

Companies attempting to be listed overseas or even in Hong Kong are supposed to abide by the listing rules of the target jurisdiction. When Chinese companies are cross-listed, compliance with the regulations of the foreign exchanges has been an essential factor in the development of corporate governance. For instance, the HKSE has enacted the Code of Governance Practices which sets out the principles of sound governance for companies listed in Hong Kong. It should in principle raise PRC issuers' corporate governance standards in line with international standards and best practices. As Coffee said,

81 Company Law 2005 Articles 98, 34(1); notably, there is a significant difference between the rights of shareholders of limited liability companies (LLCs) and companies limited by shares (CLSs) to obtain information about the operations and accounts of the company. Investors in a LLC may in addition review the company's accounting records upon request and are thus granted a continuing right to access in-depth financial information which is not available to shareholders of a CLS.

82 Article 68, Securities Law 2006 lists those who are considered 'persons with knowledge of inside information'.

83 Article 67, Securities Law 2006.

84 Clarke (2003), p. 507.

85 The *Notice on Relevant Issues Concerning Accepting Civil Tort Dispute Cases Caused by False Statement on the Securities Market* was issued by the Supreme People's Court on 15 January 2002; Xi (2006), p. 496.

> Listing on a developed foreign stock exchange imposes higher disclosure requirements and a more stringent regulatory environment.[86]

Listed companies overseas are keen to raise their corporate governance standards to better position themselves in competition with their counterparts in the host jurisdiction. An appropriate mechanism must be in place to enhance investor confidence to seek outbound investment. In this vein, the Sarbanes-Oxley Act 2002 may have a far-reaching impact on China's accounting practices, in view of Chinese companies listed on the New York Exchange and NASDAQ. The Act will help to build up a healthy model for China's corporate governance. Based on the globalization of Chinese listed companies, the practice of cross-listing has pushed them towards international standards of accounting procedures. The host countries' regulatory effect on Chinese companies' corporate governance has gradually translated into better transparency and accountability back home on China's stock market. After all, Chinese cross-listed companies are under pressure to compete with their Hong Kong and American counterparts for investors in the host jurisdictions. Some observers have doubted whether corporate governance in mainland China can converge towards global standards through encouraging local companies to list in the United States or other developed markets.[87] As Black has observed:[88]

> Those firms have escaped from their weak home country institutions through foreign listings; without the help of local enforcement and institutions, such escape is only partial.

Cross-listing may serve as a catalyst to accelerate China's accounting and disclosure levels. It still remains uncertain however, to what extent, the host jurisdictions' more sophisticated systems could be compatible with China's existing governance regime.

## Insolvency Prevention

The traditional understanding of bankruptcy means the termination of the life of a company. However modern bankruptcy laws place particular focus on reviving struggling but viable companies. There are a number of innovations in the EBL 2006 which reflect a new emphasis on corporate rescue and insolvency prevention. It provides 'much clearer procedures for insolvent enterprises to restructure or exit the market by means of restructuring, composition or bankruptcy'.[89] This

86 Coffee (2002).
87 Tang (2007), p. 617.
88 Black (2001), p. 855.
89 PricewaterhouseCoopers (2007).

approach will be conducive to the avoidance of the social ramifications resulting from liquidation, such as unemployment and loss of social wealth.

*Reorganization*

The traditional bankruptcy reorganization has focused primarily on business and financial restructuring, but has ignored the equally important considerations of corporate governance reform. In a reorganization, if the successful revival of a company is to be achieved, the appropriate course of action may necessitate the restructuring of its corporate governance structure to incorporate, *inter alia*, both the election of independent outside directors and the use of equity ownership to incentivize these directors to effectively monitor management. A harmonized mechanism may make great sense to the realization of the debtor's fresh start. With an aim to provide debtors with an opportunity for rehabilitation, the EBL 2006 has introduced an alternative avenue for enterprises that are in financial difficulties and can still be rescued and revived through a court-driven process of reorganization.[90] See further Chapter 11. Several important features of the new law are meant to support an effective reorganization mechanism. An application may be made on the basis that the debtor is insolvent and its assets are insufficient to discharge all of its debts, or that it clearly lacks capacity to discharge them, or that the company is obviously likely to reach such a state of affairs.[91] The debtor or a shareholder representing one tenth or more of the debtor's registered capital may apply to the court for a reorganization proceeding.[92] When a creditor has already petitioned for the bankruptcy of a debtor, the debtor or a shareholder holding one tenth or more of the registered capital may also file an application to restructure the debtor.[93] The restructuring period lasts from the day that the court approves the restructuring until the termination of the proceedings.[94]

While the EBL 2006 places the responsibility for preparing the restructuring plan on either the debtor or administrator,[95] the debtor is responsible for the implementation of the plan once it has been approved by the court.[96] In the interests of transparency, the EBL 2006 requires that an independent administrator should be appointed upon acceptance of the bankruptcy petition,[97] although a debtor may apply to remain in possession during the reorganization.[98]

90 Young (2007), p. 61.
91 Article, 2 EBL 2006.
92 Article 70, EBL 2006.
93 Article 70, EBL 2006.
94 Article 72, EBL 2006.
95 Article 71, EBL 2006.
96 Article 89, EBL 2006.
97 Article 24, EBL 2006 enables the reorganization of not only SOEs but also any troubled enterprise legal persons.
98 Article 73, EBL 2006.

The administrator's role is to then supervise the implementation of the plan. Once appointed, the administrator appears to assume a general fiduciary role, owing duties to both creditors and the debtor, breaches of which may result in civil and criminal sanctions.[99] The EBL 2006 does not provide guidance or criteria for the courts to use in deciding whether the debtor should remain in possession or whether an independent administrator should be in control of the restructuring process. Another major concern remains upon how to effectively operate the bankruptcy administrator system, largely because many issues need to be ascertained if a proper enforcement system is to be established.[100]

To relieve the problem, The EBL 2006 calls for the convening of a creditors' meeting and the related creation of a creditors' committee, which are given broad powers to, among other things, 'supervise the management and disposal of the debtor's assets'.[101] The debtor or bankruptcy administrator is required to explain to the creditors' committee any matter within its scope of responsibilities. Additionally, the debtor's management staff may be fined in the event that they fail to co-operate with the court at the creditors' meeting.[102]

The method of reorganization enables debtors to make use of the automatic stay to weed out failing businesses and concentrate on better-quality business. The provisions, are consistent in principle with the methods employed in most modern insolvency regimes internationally, which, to a large extent, are akin to the English administration regime as well as to the Chapter 11 under the US Bankruptcy Code, although they are closest in nature to the German reorganization system. Positively, the reorganization regime enables debtors to be rescued and revived, in contrast to the forced liquidation bankruptcy of the past.[103] At least, the reorganization serves to avoid unemployment or loss of social wealth as a result of bankruptcy liquidation. However, despite reasonably modern mechanisms for corporate rescue, the EBL 2006 contains a number of procedural ambiguities which may render it toothless during enforcement procedures. It may be abused in that the process might well lend itself to long delays and strategic applications by the debtor in an attempt to prevent a creditor from bankrupting the debtor.

### *Composition*

As another court-driven approach, the debtor may apply to the court for composition whereby the debtor proposes a compromise settlement of its debts with creditors, which provides another avenue for the rescue of enterprises in financial difficulty:

---

99 Article 130, EBL 2006; Chua (2005).

100 See Chapter 6 of this volume in which Supreme People's Court Regulations, which provide some further details in relation to the system of administrators, are discussed.

101 Article 67, EBL 2006. The committee should have no more than nine members, including one representative of either employees or trade union. See further Chapter 10.

102 Articles 126 and 127, EBL 2006.

103 Article 70, EBL 2006; Bendapudi (2008), p. 219.

see Chapter 12. Although the composition is not normally used in practice, it can potentially play a positive role in resolving bankruptcies due to its consistency with Chinese Civil Procedure Law.[104]

### Immature Judicial System

Chinese judicial resources are rooted in an immature credit-based economy. China's administrative and regulatory framework and its judicial system are still in their infancy, which renders a more unpredictable legal regime. Although the EBL 2006 complies with international standards, its successful application will mainly depend on its application and enforcement by the judiciary. While China enjoys perhaps the world's oldest great culture, the re-establishment of modern legal development has been in process for only three decades, during which period China's society and economy have experienced many significant changes. The existing laws and regulations obviously lag behind China's rapid development. Due to a lack of consistency in relevant laws and regulations, unexpected obstacles and problems will be encountered. The challenges are embodied in the lack of necessary legal mechanisms, judicial independence, professional expertise and weak enforcement.

The role of an independent court would certainly have improved the likelihood that the interests of creditors would be considered. China lacks the Western traditional spirit of the rule of law and in particular lacks a tradition of judicial independence. The courts have historically preserved and enforced the interests of the State, which is enshrined in the new law. For instance, the EBL 2006 provides that any employee's entitlements which accrued before the promulgation of the new law on 27 August 2006 and which remain outstanding will, after implementation of the new law, have a priority claim over the debtor's assets,[105] in spite of other guarantee provisions for secured creditors' priority.[106] Although it appears to be a transitional measure, the compromise may reflect China's intent to prioritize the maintenance of social stability and minimization of the ramifications of bankruptcies as top of the State's interests while designing and applying the EBL 2006.

The legal environment in China differs from other jurisdictions in view of their different legal and philosophical backgrounds, i.e. Hong Kong Law is rooted in British tradition, while Taiwan's law is itself a hybrid since it was originally based on both German and Japanese Law and came under US influence.[107]

The stresses associated with providing adequate legal-system capacity present a formidable challenge which impedes the provision of effective civil remedies.

---

104 Article 9, Civil Procedure Law of the People's Republic of China.

105 Article 132, EBL 2006.

106 Articles 109 and 113; PricewaterhouseCoopers (2007).

107 Siems (2007), p. 66.

The key challenge that China is facing in implementing the promising new law turns not on the EBL 2006 itself but rather on the competence and experience of both the courts and administrators who will be key in carrying out bankruptcies, reorganizations and compositions. The lack of expertise in the courts poses a formidable problem, on which the EBL 2006 places substantial responsibility and discretionary authority. There is no specialized bankruptcy court for insolvency matters. A lack of consistency and the paucity of trained insolvency professionals lead to uncertainty about outcomes. The court system is inexperienced in dealing with cases that involve creditors' rights concerns, particularly in China's underdeveloped areas, where judges generally lack adequate knowledge and experience. Since bankruptcy cases are often more complicated than other types of cases and need more professional knowledge, the courts lack confidence in dealing with bankruptcy cases and they may even be inclined not to accept bankruptcy applications, which may deny many distressed enterprises the protection of proper bankruptcy procedures.

## Conclusion

Corporate governance emerges as a crucial consideration for modern enterprises and the importance of its relationship with corporate bankruptcy cannot be overestimated. The recently enacted legislations discussed in this chapter represent a catalyst for change in China's business landscape, paving the way for true corporate and economic reform. Specifically, the EBL 2006 widens alternatives for debtors, creditors and shareholders to deal with problematic businesses. The introduction of reorganization practices has, at least theoretically, brought Chinese law into greater alignment with modern global procedures. The intertwined legal framework provides that those managerial members, who commit a breach of their obligations of loyalty or due diligence causing the enterprise to go bankrupt, shall bear administrative, criminal or civil liability. A framework is therefore in place for the encouragement of high standards among directors, both through the provision of specific duties and through the provisions of legal consequences for them in the event of wrongdoing.

The provisions, if properly and vigorously implemented, should improve the standard of corporate governance in China. The possible legal consequences may incentivize directors to operate their businesses with due care, both by endeavouring to overcome financial difficulties and detecting and preventing fraudulent transactions. More specifically, the litigation risks leading to possible investigation and legal punishment may have deterrent effects on directors who might otherwise be tempted to take advantage of their positions, causing them to modify their conduct in carrying out their managerial functions.

However, to judge whether the current legal framework is of great value depends on its ability to solve real world problems. The continuing uncertainty in the judicial system still presents serious challenges in relation to the handling of a modern corporate governance system. Investors as well as creditors have been provided with remedies to only a limited extent. The current corporate governance regime, with a unique and local Chinese application, cannot at the moment therefore efficiently serve as a shield for the prevention of insolvencies. Given cultural and legal traditions and an extremely uneven ownership structure, modern relevant Chinese corporate governance law is very much in its infancy. It should be rationally acknowledged however that the current progress has only been achieved within three decades. In the transition towards building the world's fastest growing capital market, the establishment of efficiently-functioning corporate governance systems remains a mammoth task.

## References


Andrews, N. and Tomasic, R. (2006), 'Directing China's Top 100 Listed Companies: Corporate Governance in an Emerging Market Economy' 2(3) *The Corporate Governance Law Review* 245-309.

Bendapudi, R. (2008), 'People's Republic of China Bankruptcy Law' 6 *Santa Clara Journal of International Law* 205.

Black, B.S. (2001), 'The Legal and Institutional Preconditions for Strong Securities Markets' 48 *UCLA Law Review* 781.

Black, B.S. and others (2008), 'Legal Liability of Directors and Company Officials Part 2: Court Procedures, Indemnification and Insurance, and Administrative and Criminal Liability' 1 *Columbia Business Law Review* 1.

Central People's Government of the People's Republic of China (2007), 'New Accounting Standards to be Adopted by Large, Mid-Scale Companies in 2009' (12 July) <http://english.gov.cn/2007-07/12/content_682474.htm>, last accessed 13 April 2009.

Chan, K.H., Lin, K. and Mo, P.L. (2006), 'A Political-Economic Analysis of Auditor Reporting and Auditor Switches' 11(1) *Review of Accounting Studies* 21, 48.

Chua, E.J. (2005), 'China's Central Government Sets Short Timetable for Bankruptcy Law Reform' *Journal of International Banking Law and Regulation* 610.

Clarke, D.C. (2003), 'Corporate Governance in China: An Overview' 14(4) *China Economic Review* 494.

Clarke, D.C. (2006), 'The Independent Director in Chinese Corporate Governance' 31(1) *The Delaware Journal of Corporate Law* 125.

Coffee, J.C. (2002), 'Racing towards the Top? The Impact of Cross-Listing and Stock Market Competition on International Corporate Governance' 102 *Columbia Law Review* 1757.

Coffee, J.C. (2006), 'Reforming the Securities Class Action: An Essay on Deterrence and its Implementation' 106 *Columbia Law Review* 1534.

CSRC (2006), 'Notice of the China Securities Regulatory Commission on Promulgating the Rules for the Shareholders' Meeting of Listed Companies' 16 March.

Dallas, G.S. and Scott, H.S. (2006), 'Mandating Corporate Behaviour: Can One Set of Rules Fit All?' 2 *Corporate Governance Law Review* 117.

Deacons, C. (2006), 'China: Company Law Amended' <http://www.hg.org/articles/article_1184.html>, last accessed 18 April 2009.

Eaton, D.L. et al. (2006), 'China's New Enterprise Bankruptcy Law' <http://www.kirkland.com/siteFiles/kirkexp/publications/2272/Document1/Chinas_New_Enterprise_Bankruptcy_Law.pdf>, last accessed 8 December 2008.

Elson, C.M., Helms, P.M. and Moncus, J.R. (2002), 'Corporate Governance Reform and Re-emergence from Bankruptcy: Putting the Structure back in Restructuring' 55 *Vanderbilt Law Review* 1917.

Falke, M. (2007), 'China's New Law on Enterprise Bankruptcy: A Story with A Happy End?' 16 *International Insolvency Review* 63.

Fama E.F. and Jensen, M.C. (1983), 'Separation of Ownership and Control' 26(2) *Journal of Law and Economics* 301.

Feinerman, J.V. (2007), 'New Hope for Corporate Governance in China' 191 *The China Quarterly* 590.

Fremond, O. and Capaul, M. (2002), 'The State of Corporate Governance: Experience from Country Assessments' World Bank Policy Research Working Paper 2858, June 2002) <http://ssrn.com/-abstract=636222>, last accessed 18 April 2009.

Gu, M. (2003), 'Will an Independent Director Perform Better than a Supervisor?' 6 *Journal of Chinese and Comparative Law* 59.

Ho, S.M. (2003), 'Corporate Governance in China' in Ho, S.M. (ed.) *The Practitioner's Guide to Corporate Governance in Asia* (Hong Kong: ISI Publication).

Hu, A. and Hu, G. (2002), '*Corporate Governance in China in the Transitional Era: A Review and A Foresight*', Paper Submitted to 'Comparative Corporate Governance: Changing Profiles of National Diversity' and 'Corporate Governance in Perspective: Diversity or Convergence' Academic Conference, Tokyo, Japan December 2002 <http://www.rieti.go.jp/jp/events/03010801/pdf/Hu.pdf>, last accessed 21 May 2009.

Kang, Y., Shi, L. and Brown, E.D. (2008), *Chinese Corporate Governance: History and Institutional Framework* (RAND Corporation).

Kister, S.P. (2007), 'China's Share-Structure Reform: An Opportunity to Move beyond Practical Solutions to Political Problems' 45(1) *Columbia Journal of Transnational Law* 312.

Li, H., Wang Z. and Deng, X. (2008), 'Ownership, Independent Directors, Agency Costs and Financial Distress: Evidence from Chinese Listed Companies' 8 *Corporate Governance: The International Journal of Business in Society* 622.

Liebman, B. (2005), 'Watchdog or Demagogue? The Media in the Chinese Legal System' 105 *Columbia Law Review* 1.

Liu, S. (2008), 'An Analysis of the Actual Company Controllers from the 2007 Annual Reports' *Shanghai Security Times* (6 June).

Mayeda, G. (2006), 'Appreciate the Difference: The Role of different Domestic Norms in Law and Development Reform: Lessons from China and Japan' 51 *McGill Law Journal* 547.

OECD (2004), *OECD Principles of Corporate Governance* <http://www.oecd.org/dataoecd/32/18/-31557724.pdf>, last accessed 18 April 2009.

Pace, V.A. (2006), 'The Bankruptcy of the Zhu Kuan Group: A Case Study of Cross-Border Insolvency Litigation against a Chinese State-Owned Enterprise' 27(2) *University of Pennsylvania Journal of International Economic Law* 517.

Peerenboom, R. (2001), 'Globalisation, Path Dependency and Lists of Law: Administrative Reform and Rule Law in the People's Republic of China' 19 *Berkeley Journal of International Law* 161.

PricewaterhouseCoopers (2006), 'PRC Accounting Standards Convergence Commentary: Best or Worst of Times?' <http://www.pwchk.com/webmedia/doc/1142231497844_hkfrs_news_mar2006.pdf>, last accessed 14 April 2009.

PricewaterhouseCoopers (2007), 'China's New Enterprise Bankruptcy Law' <http://www.pwccn.com/webmedia/doc/633286452859584640_cn_enterprise_bankruptcy.pdf>, last accessed 18 March 2009.

Schipani, C.A. and Liu, J. (2002), 'Corporate Governance in China: Then and Now' 1 *Columbia Business Law Review* 1.

Shen, S. and Jia, J. (2005), 'Will the Independent Director Institution Work in China?' 27 *Loyola of Los Angeles International and Comparative Law Review* 223.

Siems, M. (2007), 'Legal Origins: Reconciling Law and Finance and Comparative Law' 52 *McGill Law Journal* 55.

Tai, K. (2004), 'Corporate Governance in China' in G.S. Dallas (ed.) *Governance & Risk – an Analytical Handbook for Investors, Managers, Directors and Stakeholders* (New York: McGraw-Hill).

Tang, X. (2007), 'Commentary on New Hope for Corporate Governance in China' 191 *The China Quarterly* 613.

Vanhonacker, W.R. (2004), 'When Good Guanxi Turns Bad' 82(4) *Harvard Business Review* 18.

Wang, J.Y. (2007), 'The Strange Role of Independent Directors in a Two-tier Board Structure of China's Listed Companies' 3 *Compliance and Regulatory Journal* 47.

Wang, Q., Wong, T.J. and Xia L. (2008), 'State Ownership, the Institutional Environment, and Auditor Choice: Evidence from China' 46 *Journal of Accounting and Economics* 112.

Xi, C. (2004), 'Case Note: Private Enforcement of Securities Law in China: *Daqing Lianyi Co v Zhong Weida and Others* Heilongjiang High Court' (2006) 1(2) *Journal of Comparative Law* 492.

Xi, C. (2006), 'Private Enforcement of Securities Law in China: *Daqing Lianyi Co v Zhong Weida and Others* (2004) Heilongjiang High Court' 1 *Journal of Comparative Law* 492-6.

Xie, G.Z. (2007), 'Capital Bubble Might Burst but Have Limited Impact upon the Economy' *Southern Metropolitan News* (5 November).

Young, T. (2007), 'Enterprising Reform' 26(7) *International Financial Law Review* 60.

Zhang, Z. (2007), 'Legal Deterrence: the Foundation of Corporate Governance – Evidence from China' 15(5) *Corporate Governance: An International Review* 741.

# PART II
# Contents of the New Law

# Chapter 4
# Bankruptcy Petition and Acceptance

Haizheng Zhang and Xiaohe Tan

## Introduction

Bankruptcy petition and acceptance procedures determine the initiation of bankruptcy proceedings. A company cannot be placed into bankruptcy procedures without a court order under application. The new bankruptcy law[1] improves the opening procedure, and provides insolvent companies with easy and convenient access to bankruptcy proceedings. It applies to all types of companies and does not provide special treatment for state-owned enterprises (SOEs). The scope of application is enlarged to include financial institutions, which were not regulated under the previous bankruptcy legal framework. It also applies to partnerships, in connection with the newly revised Partnership Law 2006, but it does not apply to partners in the partnership because there is currently no personal insolvency legislation. Another notable feature is the revised insolvency conditions which remove some cumbersome requirements that were stipulated in the 1986 law.[2] The new tests of whether an enterprise is insolvent not only enable the applicant to trigger the bankruptcy procedure more efficiently, but also provide the court with a reasonable standard by which to assess whether the company is insolvent and whether to declare its bankruptcy. This chapter will emphasize the detailed procedures of petition and acceptance, and explore the underlying principles and spirit of the new law from the perspective of a comparative analysis.

## The Previous Scope of Application

The system of bankruptcy laws which operated in China previously was fragmented according to business type. The old EBL 1986 applied only to SOEs, whereas the bankruptcies of non-SOEs with legal person status were regulated by Chapter 19 of the old Civil Procedure Law 1991. In addition, public utilities companies and enterprises which had significant influence on the national economy and people's daily life were subject to special provision under the EBL 1986. If a creditor applied for liquidation of a utility company or an enterprise which could be categorized into the above types, the court would refuse to declare bankruptcy and

1 Enterprise Bankruptcy Law 2006, hereafter 'EBL 2006'.

2 Enterprise Bankruptcy Law (for Trial Implementation) 1986, hereafter 'EBL 1986'.

normally the government advanced finance to pay the debts of such enterprise.[3] During the legislative process which led to the enactment of the EBL 2006, in order to avoid potential social instability which might be caused by the redundant workers and the effect of non-performing loans on state banks, the government took administrative measures to deal with the bankruptcies of debt-laden SOEs under the planned bankruptcy programme.[4] However, with the development of the economic transition and market reforms, the planned bankruptcy programme was merely an expedient, of particular importance when the social security system was inadequate. All the bankruptcy legal reformers in the drafting group had reached a consensus that the more the government was involved in the bankruptcy process of SOEs, the more negative effects this would have on the bankruptcy legal framework. China is establishing a market economy, and undue administrative intervention might be not compatible with a free market.[5] See further Chapter 15.

## Scope of Application under the EBL 2006

In contrast to the position under previous law, a notable feature of the new law is that the scope of application covers all enterprises with separate corporate personality.[6] The new law provides a legal ground which equally applies to the SOEs and non-SOEs. No special entitlements are given to the SOEs, and utilities companies are included. Since the utilities companies have a monopoly over their provision of necessities in people's lives, such as water, gas and electricity, they are unlikely to be placed into bankruptcy proceedings even where they are insolvent.

### *Financial Institutions*

Financial institutions, including commercial banks, insurance companies and companies doing the business of securities, also fall within the scope of application of the new law.[7] The regulatory and supervisory organizations under the State Council, normally the China Banking Regulatory Commission (CBRC), the China Securities Regulatory Commission (CSRC) and the China Insurance Regulatory Commission (CIRC) shall present an application to the court for the reorganization or bankrupt liquidation of the financial institutions.[8] In the circumstances where the regulatory and supervisory commissions under the State Council take over a financial institution, or take it under custody when it is carrying huge business

3 Article 3(1), EBL 1986.

4 The issues regarding planned bankruptcy will be examined in Chapter 15 of this book.

5 Shi (2007), p. 656.

6 Article 2, EBL 2006.

7 See further Chapter 16.

8 Article 134, EBL 2006.

risk, the regulatory and supervisory commissions can apply to the court for a stay on the civil action and execution procedures against the financial institution.[9] The new bankruptcy law authorizes the State Council to produce relevant regulations in relation to the bankruptcy-related issues concerning financial institutions in accordance with the principles of the new law.[10] Obviously, Article 134 of the new bankruptcy law is evidence of remarkable progress in relation to bankruptcy-related issues concerning financial organizations because under the old bankruptcy legal framework, the bankruptcy of such organizations was a legislative lacuna.[11]

*Personal Insolvencies*

The new bankruptcy law uniformly applies to all the enterprises with legal person status. However, it notably excludes applications in relation to non-legal-person business entities, which normally include partnerships and sole proprietorships.[12] Separate provision which is made in other legislation for the liquidation of partnerships is discussed below. The position in relation to sole proprietorships is also considered further below.

The principles of limited liability and separate corporate personality do not apply to partnerships and sole proprietorships. In consequence, in a partnership, all the partners shall take unlimited liability for the debts of the partnership, and they also assume joint and several liability. In a sole proprietorship, the sole investor shall be liable to pay all the debts of the enterprise with his own personal property. The bankruptcy of a partnership or sole proprietorship may cause the personal insolvency of the partners or sole proprietor.

Historically, the concept of personal insolvency law has been non-existent in China, and there was no such experience in the Chinese short history of bankruptcy law.[13] Whether the EBL 2006 shall apply to non-legal-person enterprises was one of the hotly-debated issues during the legislative process. The majority of the reformers in the drafting group supported the idea of expanding the scope of the new law to the business entities without legal person status.[14] The early draft law of 1994 envisaged that the scope of new bankruptcy law should cover all the profit-making enterprises, and this principle was also reflected in the draft of 2002 which explicitly included partnerships and their individual partners, and sole proprietorships and their sole investors.[15] However, the draft of October 2004 fundamentally changed direction and limited the scope of application to

9 Article 134(1), EBL 2006.

10 Article 134(2), EBL 2006.

11 The bankruptcies of financial institutions will be further explored in Chapter 16 of this book.

12 Wang (2007), p. 4.

13 See pp. 4-14 regarding the history of Chinese insolvency laws.

14 Shi (2007), p. 667.

15 Article 3 of the 2002 draft.

enterprises with separate legal personality. It was considered that the bankruptcies of non-legal-person business entities should be regulated under other related laws. Ultimately, the EBL 2006 adopted the approach of the October 2004 draft and it only applies to legal-person enterprises. However, it did not completely preclude the bankruptcies of partnerships and sole proprietorships. Article 135 of the new law anticipates that other laws might be enacted to formulate insolvency procedures for non-legal-person enterprises, and Article 135 provides that, in doing so, such laws can refer to the liquidation proceedings of the EBL 2006. This article therefore provides a legal ground for the insolvent liquidation of non-legal-person entities, such as individual entrepreneurs, if in future provisions for the bankruptcy of such entities are enacted in other laws.

*Partnerships*

The amended Partnership Enterprise Law 2006 mentions the insolvent liquidation of partnerships. In the circumstances where a partnership is unable to repay its debts, any creditor is entitled to petition to the court for insolvent liquidation or to request the common partners to make payments.[16] The common partners shall still assume joint and several liability for the debts of the partnership, even though the partnership is declared bankrupt.[17] According to the amended Partnership Enterprise Law 2006, the creditor is entitled to apply for bankrupt liquidation of the partnership, and this petition right is only conferred on the creditor rather than the debtor.[18]

*Sole Traders*

Sole proprietorships are explicitly excluded from the scope of the new bankruptcy law, since they are not conferred separate legal personality. Because there is no connection between the EBL 2006 and the Sole Proprietorship Enterprise Law, the bankrupt liquidation of a sole proprietorship cannot be carried out under the new bankruptcy law. In relation to the sole traders with small businesses, the bankruptcy-related issues have not yet been resolved because of the legislative lacuna in the area of personal insolvency.

*Consumer Bankruptcies*

Should the new bankruptcy law apply to non-entrepreneurial individuals? The legislative answer was no. Even though some reformers in the drafting group supported the idea of expanding the scope to consumers, clearly this was not the

16 Article 92, Partnership Enterprise Law (amended in 2006).

17 The common partners are different from the partners who only bear limited liability. Article 2, Partnership Enterprise Law (amended in 2006).

18 Booth (2008), p. 290.

common view during the legislative process.[19] Historically, personal insolvency in China was under the influence of the mindset that the 'son should repay the debts of his father'. Since the creditors could realize their claims by forcing the progeny of the debtor to make payments, there was no need for bankruptcy law to apply to individuals. In England and the United States, by contrast, personal insolvency cases account for the majority of bankruptcy petitions.[20] People in these countries might be surprised to see that there is no personal insolvency legislation in the new bankruptcy legal framework of China, which is establishing a socialist market economy. During the legislative process, the main focus of the reform was to produce provisions regulating the liquidation and reorganization of enterprises, and consumer bankruptcy was never put on the table. With the progress of the economic reform, the Chinese financial market is developing consumer financing and credit card business. Although the new law explicitly excludes the bankruptcy of consumers, a personal insolvency law is arguably needed because an emerging financial credit system is being established.[21] People will in time be accepting of the conception 'consumer bankruptcy' and will understand the significance of personal insolvency law.[22]

## Who is Entitled to Apply for Bankruptcy?

Under the previous EBL 1986, any creditor of the insolvent enterprise could present a petition for bankruptcy to the court if the enterprise failed to pay a debt which was due. The creditor was required to provide information regarding the unpaid debt, whether the debt was secured or not, and to prove that the debtor was unable to pay off this debt.[23] If the debtor was a non-SOE with legal person status, the debtor was entitled to apply to the court for bankruptcy when it was in

---

19 Booth (2008), p. 292.

20 Recent statistics indicate that in the United States the number of business bankruptcies represents less than 4 per cent of the total number of bankruptcies, a proportion far lower than the number of non business bankruptcies. According to US Bankruptcy Court statistics for the 12-month period ending 31 December 2008, there were 43,546 business bankruptcies filed under Chapters 7, 11, 12 and 13 in the period, whereas 107,4225 non-business bankruptcies were filed under Chapters 7, 11 and 13: see US Bankruptcy Courts (2009). Official statistics are collected differently in the UK, and so no exact comparison can be made with the US position. However, in 2008, corporate insolvencies accounted for just short of 17 per cent of insolvency filings: see Policy Directorate (2009). Although personal insolvencies therefore account for the majority of insolvency filings, the proportion of consumer filings is not known.

21 See Zhang (2003).

22 See UNCITRAL (2005), pp. 38-40 regarding international approaches to personal insolvencies. See also Niemi-Kiesiläinen et al. (2003) for an interesting collection of papers and Efrat (2002).

23 Article 7, EBL 1986.

a position of serious loss and was unable to pay off its debts.[24] If the debtor was a SOE, the debtor could not apply for bankruptcy without the consent of the superior government department of the debtor. In other words, the government was involved in deciding whether SOEs could be placed into bankruptcy proceedings.[25]

Under the EBL 2006, the conditions which must be met if a bankruptcy application is to be made vary depending on who is making the application and what procedure is being applied for. Where a creditor applies for the bankruptcy liquidation or reorganization of a debtor, the debtor must be unable to pay debts falling due.[26]

The debtor is entitled to apply for bankruptcy liquidation, reconciliation or reorganization if one of the conditions stipulated in Article 2 is satisfied.[27] Those conditions are respectively that (1) the debtor is unable to pay its due debts and the value of the assets is less than the value of its liabilities; or (2) the debtor is unable to pay its due debts and the debtor obviously lacks the capability of paying off all the debts. An application for reorganization may also be made if the enterprise is obviously likely to become insolvent.[28]

If the financial institutions, including commercial banks, insurance companies and companies doing the business of securities, fall within the conditions of Article 2, above, the CBRC, CIRC and CSRC under the State Council can apply for its bankrupt liquidation or reorganization.[29]

If a company is dissolved, a liquidation group should be organized to deal with the company's property and books recording financial information, produce a liquidation proposal and report to the general meeting of shareholders or the court for confirmation. If the liquidation group realizes that the company's property is not sufficient to pay off its debts, the liquidation group shall apply to the court for its bankruptcy.[30]

## What Materials Should the Applicant Submit?

To apply for bankruptcy, the applicant should submit the application and relevant evidence to the court.[31] The application materials should include the following matters:[32]

---

24 Article 199, Civil Procedure Law 1991.
25 Article 8, EBL 1986.
26 Article 7(2), EBL 2006.
27 Article 7(1), EBL 2006.
28 Article 2, EBL 2006.
29 Article 134, EBL 2006.
30 Article 184, Company Law 2005.
31 Article 8(1), EBL 2006
32 Article 8(2), EBL 2006.

1. the basic situations of the applicant and the debtor;
2. the purpose of the application;
3. facts and reasons of the application; and
4. other matters which the court thinks necessary.

If the applicant is a creditor, the creditor needs to prove that the debtor is unable to pay the due debt to him. To what extent will a court be satisfied with a claim by a creditor that the debtor is unable to pay its debts? Since creditors do not have access to the financial information of the debtor, it will be unreasonable to require the creditor to prove balance sheet insolvency. A creditor can most appropriately prove the cash flow failure of the debtor based on their contract with the debtor and can also on this basis prove that the situation of the debt not having been paid has lasted for a relatively long period, three months or half a year. Since there is no explicit requirement as to the amount of the claim in the new law, theoretically any creditor is entitled to trigger the bankruptcy procedure. However, in a particular case the court may assess the percentage of the value of this claim in the value of the total debts. The precise approach to be taken by the courts in assessing the solvency of a debtor, is a legislative lacuna which may present difficulties for the judges. It may be argued that, if the value of the creditor's claim is very small, the court may dismiss the application and suggest that the creditor pursues his claim before the court by other civil procedures.[33]

Although the Chinese law is presently vague about the conditions that a creditor must meet, an alternative approach is taken under English insolvency law, which has provided a good example of how to addresses the tests of a company's inability to pay debts. It is stipulated that if '(a) [the company] neglects to pay, secure or compound to the reasonable satisfaction of the creditor a debt exceeding £750 within three weeks of a written demand in the prescribed form; or (b) execution or other process on a judgment against the company is returned unsatisfied, wholly or in part'; the court may adjudicate the company's inability to pay debts.[34] It is submitted that the Chinese legislature or the Supreme People's Court could follow this example, and design its own rules and standards on the basis of economic and legal reality.

If the debtor files a bankruptcy application, in addition to the materials mentioned above, the debtor should provide a report regarding the status of its assets (value, security and location), a detailed list of all the debts and credits, financial and accounting information, a scheme for the rearrangement of the affected employees, as well as the situation of payment of employees' wages and social insurance premiums.[35]

---

33 This point has been explained by Prof. Shuguang Li, a drafter of the new bankruptcy law, at a conference which was organized by the Research Center of Bankruptcy Law and Restructuring of Renmin University and Beijing Weiheng Law Firm on 27 August 2007.

34 S. 123(1), Insolvency Act 1986; Goode (2005), para. 4.08.

35 Article 8(3), EBL 2006.

## Withdrawal of the Bankruptcy Application

The applicant may withdraw the bankruptcy application before the case is accepted by the court.[36] Generally, there are four possible approaches which might have been taken regarding the withdrawal of an application and that were considered by the drafters, based on approaches in other jurisdictions. The first possible approach is that the withdrawal is restricted. The applicant is entitled to withdraw before the court finally accepts the application, however, the withdrawal needs the permission of the court. The withdrawal process will not be effective without the court's sanction. The second approach is that the withdrawal of an application does not require a court order. The applicant may withdraw the bankruptcy petition at any time before the petition is accepted by the court. The third approach is that normally the application can be withdrawn before it is accepted by the court but in some circumstances which are prescribed by the court, the withdrawal cannot be done without a court order. The final possible approach is that the withdrawal of an application depends on who is the applicant. If the applicant is the debtor, withdrawing the application needs the court's permission. If the applicant is a creditor, the withdrawal can be done freely. Such a difference will confer special treatments on the creditor applicant.[37]

The new law adopts the first approach, which emphasizes the permission of the court. It follows the principle of Article 11 of the Judicial Interpretation which was issued by the Supreme People's Court on 8 July 2002.This Interpretation prescribed that the applicant is allowed to withdraw an insolvency application under the court order. The applicant needs to pay for all the expenses which are incurred after the filing of the application prior to the withdrawal of the application.

## Insolvency Tests: Cash Flow Insolvency and Balance Sheet Insolvency

The purpose of bankruptcy law is to liquidate insolvent companies which cannot be rescued, and to give companies which are financially troubled but economically viable a second chance through corporate rescue procedures. The key questions are, in what circumstances can a company can be put into bankruptcy proceedings, and under what conditions can the court make a bankruptcy declaration? An effective bankruptcy law should provide the insolvent debtor with an easy, convenient and quick access to bankruptcy proceedings.[38]

Insolvency in China, as in many other countries, can be defined in two ways: balance sheet insolvency and cash flow insolvency. The new bankruptcy

36 Article 9, EBL 2006.

37 Wang (2007), p. 24.

38 Shi (2007), p. 660.

**Table 4.1 Company A balance sheet**

| Assets | | Shareholders' interests | |
|---|---|---|---|
| Fixed assets | 5,000 | Capital | 5,000 |
| Debtors | 5,000 | Profit and Loss | (25,000) |
| Cash | 0 | | |
| *Liabilities* | | | |
| Loans | (20,000) | | |
| Creditors | (10,000) | | |
| Total | (20,000) | Total | (20,000) |

**Table 4.2 Company B balance sheet**

| Assets | | Shareholders' interests | |
|---|---|---|---|
| Fixed assets | 2,000 | Capital | 5,000 |
| Debtors | 3,000 | Profit and Loss | (25,000) |
| Cash | 5,000 | | |
| *Liabilities* | | | |
| Loans | (20,000) | | |
| Creditors | (10,000) | | |
| Total | (20,000) | Total | (20,000) |

law provides that the court can declare bankruptcy if one of the following two conditions is satisfied:[39]

1. that the debtor is unable to pay its debts falling due and the debtor's assets are insufficient to meet all of its liabilities; or
2. that the debtor is unable to pay its due debts and the debtor obviously lacks the ability to repay all the debts.

In other words, the first condition indicates that both cash flow insolvency and balance sheet insolvency should be met before a bankruptcy declaration can be made. The second condition is a little bit easier to establish. If the debtor falls into liquidity failure and loses the capability to meet all of its debts, the court can make the order of bankruptcy without the presence of balance sheet insolvency.[40]

39 Article 2, EBL 2006.
40 Wang (2007), pp. 5-7.

**Table 4.3 Company C balance sheet**

| Assets | | Shareholders' interests | |
|---|---|---|---|
| Fixed assets | 100,000 | Capital | 10,000 |
| Debtors | 5,000 | Profit and Loss | (40,000) |
| Cash | 0 | | |
| *Liabilities* | | | |
| Loans | (40,000) | | |
| Creditors | (15,000) | | |
| Total | (50,000) | Total | (50,000) |

Balance sheet insolvency means that an entity has negative net assets. For example, if a company's balance sheet shows total assets of US$10,000 and total liabilities of US$30,000, we can conclude that this company has a negative net asset value of US$20,000. A negative asset value does not necessarily mean that a company is facing an insolvency problem. The following examples, shown in Tables 4.1 and 4.2 above, relate to two companies who both have negative asset values. Negative balances are shown in parenthesis.

Company A, as we can see from its balance sheet, is a loss maker which has run out of cash. It has a cash flow problem. Company B has made the same loss as Company A but still has $5,000 cash. This means that it has the ability to continue to pay its debts, although it is absolutely vital for Company B to start making a profit out of its business and for it to carefully manage its cash flow at this point. Otherwise Company B can end up in the position of Company A, facing cash flow insolvency. The risk for creditors and loan providers of Company B is that they will not normally be given the most update company financial information. This means that they will not be able to see the true situation of Company B until Company B has failed to pay them. This is why some banks in China require financial statements on a monthly basis when they provide loans.

Cash flow insolvency can be defined as the situation where an entity fails to pay its debts as they fall due. An entity could be cash flow insolvent but balance sheet solvent. This point can be illustrated by reference to the balance sheet of Company C, shown in Table 4.3.

In this case, Company C is running a profitable business. However the company has invested all its profit and has run out of cash. It has poor cash flow management. In fact business cash flow management is a very critical element which determines the success or failure of a business.

There are some connections between balance sheet insolvency and cash flow insolvency. In general, when a business is continually making a loss it will become balance sheet insolvent once it has accumulated a loss higher than its capital, where, in effect, its business eats up all its capital. If no new capital is invested,

**Table 4.4 Company C balance sheet revised**

| Assets | | Shareholders' interests | |
|---|---|---|---|
| Fixed assets | 40,000 | Capital | 10,000 |
| Debtors | 5,000 | Profit and Loss | (20,000) |
| Cash | 0 | | |
| *Liabilities* | | | |
| Loans | (40,000) | | |
| Creditors | (15,000) | | |
| Total | (10,000) | Total | (10,000) |

sooner or later it will become cash flow insolvent. On the other hand, poor cash flow management will cost a business but does not necessarily cause balance sheet insolvency.

In practice, balance sheet insolvency is not as straightforward as cash flow insolvency. Let us look at the example of Company C. The cash flow insolvency of this company is evident. But when you look at the balance sheet itself there is one item, 'long-term investment' that we need to discuss further. Let us assume that long-term investment here is not an investment in subsidiaries. The tricky question is what is the company accounting booking policy for this item? The IFRS (International Financial Reporting Standard) requires that a fair value should be used in this case. Some countries following GAAP (General Accepted Accounting Principles) will use the historical cost. In China public companies adopt the IFRS and other companies are still more likely to use the historical cost for this item, particularly when it is a project investment and there is no generally accepted market price for this type of project. Let us assume that the above Company C balance sheet is using historical costs. Now if we use a fair value of $40,000 for long-term investment, the Company C balance sheet will be as shown in Table 4.4.

When we look at the Company C balance sheet now we can see that the company is both balance sheet insolvent and cash flow insolvent, while previously the balance sheet indicated that it was cash flow insolvent only. The establishment of a true picture of a company's finances is very important when we come to rescue a company or to attempt to reconstruct company debts.

The EBL 2006 provides new insolvency tests which largely improve upon the old provision in the outdated EBL 1986. Under the old legislation, a SOE could not be declared bankrupt until three conditions were met.[41] First, it was necessary for the SOE to have incurred serious losses. However, the law failed to explain the standard of serious loss. Second, it was required that the serious loss should have

41 Article 3, EBL 1986.

resulted from poor management rather than other reasons, for example a mistake of state policy or unpredictable market factors. Third, it had to be established that the SOE was unable to pay its due debts. The Judicial Interpretation issued by the Supreme People's Court in 2002 explained that terms of 'inability to pay due debts' must have three elements: (1) the debt must have become due; (2) the debtor must obviously lack the ability to pay the debt; (3) the situation of the debt not having been paid must have lasted for a long time.[42] It can be observed that the old law imposed some conditions which impeded the initiation of bankruptcy proceedings, notably the requirement for the difficulties to have been caused by mismanagement and the requirement that the debtor's losses must have been serious. The Civil Procedure Law 1991 changed the insolvency tests which applied to enterprises with legal person status other than SOEs. It was provided that the debtor or a creditor could apply to the court for bankruptcy when the debtor was in a position of serious loss and unable to pay its due debts.[43] The EBL 1986 and the Civil Procedure Law 1991 therefore stipulated different conditions for different types of enterprises, reflecting the different treatment that the state gave to SOEs and non-SOEs.[44]

The new EBL 2006 removes the conditions of 'serious loss' and 'mismanagement' and provides insolvency tests which uniformly apply to all the enterprises with separate legal personality. Both cash flow insolvency and balance sheet insolvency are required when the court makes a bankruptcy declaration. If a company is in cash flow insolvency and the company obviously lacks the capability to pay its due debts, the court can also declare bankruptcy.[45]

## The Acceptance of a Bankruptcy Case

If the application is made by a creditor, the court shall notify the debtor within five days after receiving the application. If the debtor has objections to the application, the debtor should apply to the court for the dismissal of the petition within seven days after receiving the court's notification. This is a significant power for the debtor who may provide evidence to attest that the insolvency requirements are not made out and that it is able to pay off its debts. However, the raising of objections should be done within the seven day period. If the debtor raises the objections after the prescribed period, the court will ignore the debtor's objections. The court shall make a decision on the application within ten days after the expiration of the period for raising objections.[46] The court shall decide whether to accept the application or not within 15 days after it receives the bankruptcy petition. This

42 Article 31, Regulation 2002.
43 Article 199, Civil Procedure Law 1991.
44 Tang (2006), p. 4.
45 Article 2, EBL 2006.
46 Article 10(1), EBL 2006.

period can be extended by another 15 days in special circumstances under the approval of the court in upper level.[47]

If the bankruptcy application is filed by a creditor and the court accepts it, the notice of acceptance should be sent to the debtor within five days. The debtor is required to submit a report regarding the status of its assets (value, security and location), a detailed list of all the debts and credits, relevant financial and accounting information, and the situation of payment of employees' wages and social insurance.[48] If the debtor can provide a healthy balance sheet, or someone who is willing to guarantee the applicant's claim, the court may dismiss the application of the creditor. The court will declare the bankruptcy of the debtor if the debtor is both cash flow insolvent and balance sheet insolvent. The debtor will also be wound up if the court thinks that the debtor is unable to repay its due debts and that the debtor apparently lacks the ability to pay off all the debts.

The court may refuse the bankruptcy application if it thinks that the financial situation of the debtor does not satisfy the above conditions. The adjudication of refusal should be sent to the applicant within five days after the adjudication and it should specify the reasons why the application is not accepted. If the applicant objects to the court's adjudication, the applicant is entitled to appeal to the superior court within ten days of receiving the adjudication.[49] If the court accepts a bankruptcy application but then finds that the debtor does not meet the insolvency conditions as prescribed in Article 2, the court can also reject the application prior to making the declaration of bankruptcy.[50]

The court shall designate an administrator in its opening order.[51] The court shall, within 25 days from the date when it accepts the bankruptcy application, notify those creditors who are known and make a public announcement.[52] The following matters should be stipulated in the notice and announcement: (1) the names of the applicant and the respondent; (2) the time when the court accepts the application; (3) the period, place and points of attention in relation to the filing of claims; (4) the name of the administrator and where the administrator undertakes his business; (5) stipulations that the debtors of the debtor shall pay their debts to the administrator, and that the asset-holders of the debtor shall deliver the assets to the administrator; (6) the time and place of the first creditors' meeting; and (7) other matters to be notified if the court thinks necessary.[53]

The court order of acceptance will lead to the suspension of the powers of directors in the management board and supervisors in the supervisory board. After

47 Article 10(2), EBL 2006.
48 Article 11(2), EBL 2006.
49 Article 12(1), EBL 2006.
50 Article 12(2), EBL 2006.
51 Article 13, EBL 2006.
52 Article 14, EBL 2006.
53 Article 14, EBL 2006.

the notice of acceptance is delivered to the debtor, the legal representative of the debtor should perform the following duties: (1) properly protecting the assets, seals, accounting books and documents under his possession and management; (2) carrying on his work as required by the court and administrator and answering queries; (3) attending the creditors' meeting and answering the queries of creditors. In addition the representative will be subject to two restrictions, under which he is (4) not allowed to leave the place where he is living without court's permission; and (5) not allowed to take a post of director, supervisor or senior management staff of another company.[54] Under the court's confirmation, the member of management staff who is in charge of the debtor's finance department or business affairs should also undertake the above functions.[55]

A number of additional effects of the court's acceptance of the bankruptcy application are specified in the legislation. Firstly, as discussed further at pp. 152-154, any repayment made by the debtor to an individual creditor will be invalid.[56] Secondly, the debtor's debtor shall make payment to the administrator as required under contract, a tort claim or any other legal reasons after the court accepts the bankruptcy application.[57] In addition, a third party who holds the debtor's property under a lease agreement or other legal reason should deliver the property to the administrator. If the debtor's debtor or property holder fails to perform this duty and causes harm to the debtor, the obligation to make payment or delivery of property will not be discharged.[58] Thirdly, the administrator will have the power to decide whether to rescind or to continue to perform any contract which has been concluded prior to the acceptance of the application, and which has not been fully performed by both parties concerned.[59] The administrator shall inform the counterparty of his decision. If the administrator fails to inform the counterparty of this decision within two months from the day of acceptance, or the administrator fails to reply to an urgent request which is made by the counterparty, the contract shall be deemed to be rescinded. Where the administrator decides to continue the unfinished contract, the counterparty shall continue to perform according to the contract terms. However, the counterparty is entitled to request that the administrator provides security. If the administrator fails to provide a guarantee to secure the debt, the contract shall be deemed to have been rescinded.

---

54 No legislative indication is given as to whether a director must resign from existing additional directorships, however it may be inferred that the legislative intention was for this to be so.

55 Article 15, EBL 2006.

56 Article 16, EBL 2006.

57 Article 17, EBL 2006.

58 Article 17, EBL 2006; Wang (2007), p. 47.

59 Article 18, EBL 2006.

## Automatic Stay

After the court accepts an application for bankruptcy, there is an automatic stay on the debtor's property:[60]

- All judicial measures which are being taken against the debtor for the purpose of preserving the debtor's property should be stayed. Civil execution procedures should be suspended.[61] Preserving the debtor's property under a court order is intended to prevent the debtor from transferring his property when a civil litigation suit has not finished. It aims to protect the debtor's property from unlawful transfer and to maintain the creditor's interests. When a company is placed into bankruptcy proceedings, the preserving order should be removed and the relevant property should be under the control of the administrator. All the property will be distributed to creditors in accordance with the scheme of priorities established under the law.[62]
- Any civil action or arbitration against the debtor which is in the process of trial shall be suspended after the bankruptcy application is accepted by the court. The civil action or arbitration can be resumed after the administrator takes over the debtor's property.[63]
- Once a bankruptcy application is accepted by a court, any civil litigation against the debtor which is initiated after the commencement of bankruptcy proceedings should be handled by the same court.[64]

## Conclusion

The new Enterprise Bankruptcy Law 2006 equally applies to both SOEs and non-SOEs. The planned bankruptcy programme, which was intended to provide special entitlements for SOEs and their employees, was terminated at the end of 2008. The bankruptcy of financial institutions falls within the scope of the new law, and is discussed in Chapter 16, but personal insolvency remains a legislative lacuna. The new tests of insolvency set out under the EBL 2006 remove the unreasonable requirements of the old law, avoid government involvement and follow internationally accepted standards.[65] The petition and acceptance procedures provide an efficient triggering mechanism. As a result, the door could be effectively opened for insolvent companies, and judges should be able to make an adjudication efficiently under the new opening proceedings.

---

60 Wang (2007), p. 55.
61 Article 19, EBL 2006.
62 Wang (2007), 56.
63 Article 20, EBL 2006.
64 Article 21, EBL 2006; for more details, see Wang (2007), p. 60.
65 See further UNCITRAL (2005), pp. 45-8.

## References

Booth, C. (2008), 'The 2006 PRC Enterprise Bankruptcy Law: The Wait Is Finally Over' 20 *Singapore Academy of Law Journal* 275.

Boshkoff, D. and Song, Y. (1987), 'China's New Bankruptcy Law: A Translation and Brief Introduction' 61 *American Bankruptcy Law Journal* 359.

Bufford, H. (2007), 'The New Chinese Bankruptcy Law: Text and Limited Comparative Analysis' 16 *Norton Journal of Bankruptcy Law and Practice* 697.

Efrat, R. (2002), 'Global Trends in Personal Bankruptcy' 76 *American Bankruptcy Law Journal* 81

Goode, R. (2005), *Principles of Corporate Insolvency Law* (3rd edn) (London: Sweet & Maxwell).

Niemi-Kiesiläinen, J., Ramsay, I. and Whitford W.C. (eds) (2003), *Consumer Bankruptcy in Global Perspective* (Oxford: Hart Publishing).

Policy Directorate (2009), 'Statistics Release: Insolvencies in the Fourth Quarter 2008' Reference <http://www.insolvency.gov.uk/otherinformation/statistics/200902/index.htm>, dated 6 February 2009, last accessed 27 May 2009.

Shi, J. (2007), 'Twelve Years to Sharper One Sword: The 2006 Enterprise Bankruptcy Law and China's Transition to a Market Economy' 16 *Norton Journal of Bankruptcy Law and Practice* 645.

Simmons, M. and Jiang, J. (2007), 'A New Insolvency Law in China' 4 *International Corporate Rescue* 10.

Tang, A. (2005), *Insolvency in China and Hong Kong: A Practitioner's Perspective* (Hong Kong: Sweet & Maxwell Asia).

Tang, W. (2006), *A Comparative Analysis between the New and Old Enterprise Bankruptcy Law and Case Materials* (Beijing: China Legal Publishing House) (in Chinese).

UNCITRAL (2005), *Legislative Guide on Insolvency Law* (New York: United Nations).

US Bankruptcy Courts (2009), 'Business and Nonbusiness Bankruptcy Cases Commenced, By Chapter of the Bankruptcy Code, During the Twelve Month Period Ended Dec. 31, 2008' <http://www.uscourts.gov/Press_Releases/2009/bankrupt_f2table_dec2008.xls>, last accessed 27 May 2009.

Wang, W. (2007), *The Interpretation and Substance of Bankruptcy Law* (Beijing: Law Press-China) (in Chinese).

Zhang, X.-C. (2003), 'Development of Consumer Credit in China and Concerns about the Underlying Legal Infrastructure' in Niemi- Kiesiläinen, J., Ramsay, I. and Whitford W.C. (eds) (2003), *Consumer Bankruptcy in Global Perspective* (Oxford: Hart Publishing).

# Chapter 5
# Bankruptcy Administrator: Status, Powers and Duties

Jianhua Xiao

## Introduction

The bankruptcy administrator is a new legal office established by the Enterprise Bankruptcy Law of the People's Republic of China (hereafter referred as to the 'EBL 2006'). The EBL 2006 not only devotes a whole chapter, Chapter 3, to the qualification, position, appointment,[1] authorities, supervision, remuneration and, where necessary, punishment of, or for, the administrator, but reference is also made to the bankruptcy administrator in many other chapters. This regime brings into effect not only a substantial reform of the liquidation group system which administered insolvency proceedings under the previous Enterprise Bankruptcy Law (For Trial Implementation) 1986, but it also establishes a system of bankruptcy administration that is comparable to other systems to be found internationally. The innovation of the establishment of an administrator system in the EBL 2006 therefore manifests a significant breakthrough in the Chinese bankruptcy law system and it has attracted much attention at home and abroad.

This chapter will consider the powers and duties of the administrator. The processes of the qualification, appointment and remuneration of administrators are dealt with in detail under Regulations issued by the Supreme People's Court and they will be addressed in detail in Chapter 6.

## Overview of the Office of the Bankruptcy Administrator

The administrator occupies the most important role in bankruptcy proceedings, since he is specifically responsible for managing various issues in a bankruptcy and undertaking critical functions and responsibilities: the administrator is in charge of the management and disposal of the debtor's estate; the making of decisions relating to internal management issues; and participation in lawsuits and other legal proceedings on behalf of the debtor. In contrast, other agencies or organizations

1 The process of administrator appointments is elaborated in the 'Regulations of the Supreme People's Court on the Appointment of Administrators for Hearings on Cases of Enterprise Bankruptcy'. See Chapter 6 for discussion of these laws.

who may be involved in bankruptcy proceedings only play a role of supervision or assistance. Except for the situation where the debtor has been permitted to manage its own property and operations in the reorganization procedure, in 'debtor in possession' proceedings,[2] the administrator will, in effect, virtually become the agency for the expression of the will of the insolvent enterprise, deciding everything for it.[3] Thus, the issue of whether the bankruptcy proceedings can be undertaken and terminated smoothly on a fair, equal and efficient basis will therefore closely depend on the activities of the bankruptcy administrator.

*Concept of the Administrator*

The term 'administrator' refers to the special agency that is responsible for the management and disposal of the estate, the debtor's business operations and the formulation and implementation of the bankruptcy plan.[4] An independent administrator may conduct the disposal, appraisal and distribution of the estate at its own discretion. Although a new concept for China under the EBL 2006 the office of administrator has long established equivalents in the bankruptcy legislations of many countries and regions, though these offices differ in name. In British law, several terms are used, with 'insolvency practitioner' and 'office holder' being the most general and other terms, such as 'administrator', 'administrative receiver', 'supervisor' and 'liquidator' are also used in relation to particular procedures. In Japanese Bankruptcy Law, the office holder is called a 'bankruptcy manager'; in US law, an 'insolvency trustee'; and in Taiwan, a 'bankruptcy administrator'. These different names, in a sense, show different considerations by the legislators regarding the legal status of these office holders.[5]

*Historical Origins* The bankruptcy administrator system can be traced back to ancient Rome, when the principle of creditors' self-help (or *Fehde*) was dominant. When a creditor won a lawsuit, he might realize his rights and interests by self-enforcement; and thus, bankruptcy proceedings were no different from individual mandatory enforcement proceedings. Moreover, the creditor might settle the debt by means of enforcement against the person of the debtor (all the freedom, fame, body and life of the debtor could be the object of enforcement, and creditors might even dismember the corpse of the debtor for the purpose of equal distribution). Later, the property enforcement system was established gradually and developed. The judge could grant the private right of *missio in bona* to the creditor upon request, allowing the latter to possess all the properties of the debtor. The *missio* would be announced and other creditors could participate in the management of the debtor's property

2 See Article 73, EBL 2006.

3 Peng and Zhou (2006), p. 66.

4 Li (2000), p. 150.

5 Xie (2005), pp. 257-8.

and gain distribution. This system is regarded as the origin of the bankruptcy system. However, such *missio* is only equivalent to the modern declaration of bankruptcy, while subsequent procedures such as the administration and distribution of the estate were handled by the creditors at their own discretion, under the principle of creditor's self-help. Meanwhile, law also provided that, 30 days after announcing that the debtor's property was occupied by the creditors, the creditors could, for the purpose of appraising the property, apply for the court to select a *Magister*, namely, a property administrator, from among them, who would act as a special manager for the auction of the property by way of a blanket auction. However, since a long time was required from the court's issuance of the *misso* to the appraisal and distribution of the property, a special person was needed to manage the debtor's property; hence, the *Magister* sometimes took on the responsibility of management. In this sense, the role of *Magister* has similarities to the role of the bankruptcy administrator; thus, the *Magister* in Roman law can be regarded as the origin of the bankruptcy administrator system.

After the age of the Roman Empire, the individual auction of the estate replaced the blanket auction. The procedures of individual auction were more complicated than those of blanket auction and required a longer time; therefore, a special administrator was required. Consequently, the legislation provided that a Curator, equivalent to modern bankruptcy administrator, should be selected. Later, the authority for handling bankruptcy cases was gradually vested in the courts. Nevertheless, after the declaration of bankruptcy, the management and liquidation of the estate was complex and onerous, attended by a number of both legal and non-legal issues, far beyond the capacity of the courts in terms of labour and material resources. Hence, it was still necessary to set up a special liquidation organization procedure. Such a system developed, it has continued and evolved and it has finally formed the modern bankruptcy administrator system.

From the perspective of international experiences, the administrator system is a mature feature in the bankruptcy laws of western developed countries. Arguably, the generation and development of the administrator system has been closely related to market economy status. Though governments in some countries, and state banks in others, bear the responsibility for handling the affairs of distressed companies, in a society of a mature market economy, the profession of administrators is highly free, open, professional and self regulated, exercising roles and functions in the development of the market economy and the handling process of bankruptcy cases.[6] A remarkable feature of the EBL 2006 is that it marks a transition of the Chinese system from tight state control to the establishment of a profession of administrators akin to those found in western developed countries.

6 He (2005), p. 85.

## Features of the Office of Administrator

The administrator undertakes the management and liquidation of the bankruptcy estate. The following four features of this office are particularly notable.

### *Neutral Position of the Bankruptcy Administrator*

The paramount objective of the bankruptcy system is to realize credits and protect the interests of creditors to the maximum extent, and to achieve the equitable distribution of the debtor's estate among all creditors, if there is more than one creditor. Meanwhile, the subject status of a legal person will be eliminated after its bankruptcy and any unsatisfied credits will be discharged. Thus, the modern bankruptcy system is not a system totally against the debtor, but it manifests a value orientation that protects the interests of the debtor and provides the opportunities for its rehabilitation. In the bankruptcy of an enterprise, the first victims are its staff and workers. In the circumstance where the insolvent enterprise has tax arrears, the state is also a party interested in bankruptcy proceedings. Besides, the legitimate rights and interests of creditors, recall right holders and the exclusion right holders shall also be protected.

Consequently, the subjects of interests involved in bankruptcy proceedings are various and their interests are always opposite. To realize the target value of 'protecting the legitimate rights and interests of creditors and debtors and maintaining the order of the socialist market economy',[7] the bankruptcy administrator shall handle bankruptcy issues in an objective and fair way, as conflicts of interest may affect his handling of the case, undoubtedly damaging the legitimate rights and interests of some stakeholders. Hence, it is required that the interests of the bankruptcy administrator are not to be affected by the changes to the substantive interests of the legal subjects in bankruptcy proceedings, where the bankruptcy administrator shall be neither the representative of creditors or state agencies, nor that of the debtor, but shall be a neutral organization.[8]

### *Professional Status*

Whether the disputes over credits and debts can be settled among the parties concerned in a timely manner totally depends on the efficiency of the administrator in carrying out his duties. However, in many bankruptcy proceedings, complex issues can arise. Proceedings generally including reorganization, composition and liquidation procedures, under which the administrator will be engaged, *inter alia*, in identification of the list of creditors; the management, liquidation, appraisal, disposal and distribution of the estate; as well as the occasional conduct of lawsuits; and related issues concerning substantive law and procedural law,

7 Article 1, EBL 2006.

8 Peng and Zhou (2006), p. 67.

plus a number of other legal and financial and accounting affairs can result in proceedings becoming highly technical. The bankruptcy administrator should therefore be professional and should be an organization specialized in the field: firstly, it shall be well versed in law and familiar with the relevant provisions of bankruptcy law; secondly, the administrator shall be acquainted with accounting business, and capable of the management of properties; thirdly, it shall be familiar with commercial transaction rules; and fourthly, it shall be engaged in such work on an ongoing basis and have corresponding experience in practice. Otherwise, the target value of improving economic operation efficiency through the operation of the bankruptcy law system could not be realized.[9] The system that has been established for ensuring the professionalism of administrators is discussed in Chapter 6.

### *Explicit Functions of the Bankruptcy Administrator*

The administrator is in charge of managing all the property of the debtor and undertaking the liquidation, assessment and appraisal of the estate. As a result, he has a wide range of functions, to be discussed further below.[10] The administrator is responsible for reporting to the court, and accepting the supervision of the creditors' meeting. If the administrator is selected by creditors, he shall accept the supervision of the court. In his management, the administrator shall also exercise a duty of care, besides carrying out his statutory functions.[11] When the administrator causes any loss to creditors, due to his intentional act or gross negligence, he shall bear civil liability for liquidated damages;[12] and if a crime is committed, criminal responsibilities shall also be prosecuted.[13]

*'Administrator centrism'* A paramount issue in bankruptcy proceedings is how to enhance the management of the debtor's property. When the court decides to commence bankruptcy proceedings, such proceedings will have a general preservation effect regarding the estate of the debtor, and there is no need for the court to take any individual civil preservation measures.[14]

The preservation effect of bankruptcy proceedings on the debtor's estate shall firstly be manifested as control on the occupation, use, gain and disposal of the debtor's property. Such control will not be realized automatically from the decision of the court to start bankruptcy proceedings. As the court is not a professional 'manager' of the debtor's property, it is impossible for it to fully achieve the objective of 'value maximization' of the control on the occupation,

9 Ibid.

10 Article 25, EBL 2006.

11 Article 27, EBL 2006; Wang (2007), p. 76.

12 Article 130, EBL 2006.

13 Article 131, EBL 2006.

14 See e.g. Article 16, EBL 2006, discussed further at pp. 152-4.

use, gain and disposal of the debtor's property and thus, generally, the court is not required to realize such control. The bankruptcy proceedings shall therefore resort to special institutional designs to realize its preservation effect on the debtor's estate. Accordingly, after bankruptcy proceedings commence, unless a decision permitting the proceedings to be 'debtor-in-possession' has been made by the court,[15] the issues in bankruptcy proceedings shall be managed by the administrator and the role of the court shall be defined as an arbitrator of disputes.[16] In other words, what may termed 'administrator centrism' is a key feature of the bankruptcy law system.

Under a system of 'administrator centrism' the routine aspects of bankruptcy proceedings shall be conducted by the administrator, who, upon the commencement of the bankruptcy proceedings, will take over the debtor's estate and undertake its liquidation, safekeeping, operation and necessary disposal, so as to better protect the interests of creditors. The approach of administrator centrism is designed to set up a system under judicial procedure for the effective preservation of the debtor's property. The administrator shall not only completely take over the debtor's property, but also shall potentially contribute to the appreciation of the debtor's property. He shall safeguard the interests of debtors and creditors. To take the administrator centrism as the standing point for the management of the debtor's property in Chinese bankruptcy proceedings is obviously conducive to strengthening the management and preservation of the debtor's property. Meanwhile, the adoption of the administrator centrism may reduce the responsibilities and burdens placed on the court correspondingly, enabling it to focus more on the relevant procedural issues in bankruptcy proceedings, rather than on the routine aspects that shall be undertaken by the administrator.

The establishment of a profession of bankruptcy administrators is a necessary requirement for the smooth progress of bankruptcy proceedings, and in the EBL 2006, the whole bankruptcy proceedings lays the operation foundation for administrator centrism. In particular, Articles 13, 23 and 25 of the EBL 2006, dealing with the administrator and his status in bankruptcy proceedings, arguably reflect an approach of administrator centrism.[17]

## Legal Status of the Administrator

The legal status of the bankruptcy administrator in bankruptcy proceedings determines the nature of its conducts and its responsibilities and the rights, obligations and may balance the relationships among creditors, the debtor and third party stakeholders. Thus, the discussion of the legal status of the bankruptcy administrator is both of theoretical value and is required in practice. This is a matter

15 Article 73, EBL 2006.

16 Zou (2006), pp. 121-2.

17 Ibid. at 122.

that has aroused particular debate in civil law systems, where various models have been presented. In contrast, it is an issue that has tended to be addressed expressly in the legislation of Anglo-American systems[18] and, accordingly, disputes have been rare.

The bankruptcy legislation of the Anglo-American law systems defines the administrator as a trustee, from which the following advantages naturally flow. Firstly, it can ensure the relatively independent legal status of the administrator in bankruptcy proceedings, conducive for the administrator to manage and handle the estate independently. Secondly, it clarifies the legal relationship between the administrator and third parties. A trustee in the trust relationship can act legally with third parties in his own name, the consequence of such acts being attributed to the trust property. The administrator plays the same role in bankruptcy proceedings.

### *Theories Regarding the Legal Status of Bankruptcy Administrators in Continental Law Systems*

Four main doctrines regarding the legal status of bankruptcy administrators have emerged in civil law systems, as follows:[19]

*Doctrine of agency* This doctrine is the earliest one on the legal status of the bankruptcy administrator. It holds that the bankruptcy administrator is an agent and exercises duties and authorities in bankruptcy proceedings in the name of others. The theoretical groundings of such doctrine are as follows: firstly, bankruptcy liquidation proceedings are common civil proceedings and fall in the non-litigation category in nature. Thus, it is considered to be impossible for the bankruptcy administrator to have any public right and this office is regarded as belonging to the category of private law. The legal relationship thereof is not different from that of a general civil agency relationship. As for the party in respect of whom it acts as agent, it depends on the interests that represents. Secondly, the results of either litigation acts or non-litigation acts of the bankruptcy administrator in bankruptcy proceedings are actually attributed to the insolvent party, and as such the phenomenon is closer to the agency relationship in civil law. Therefore, the

18 See United States Code, Title 11, § 323, providing that the trustee is an agent of the company; and the UK Insolvency Act 1986, under which it is expressly provided that an administrator acts as the agent of the company. See s. 14(5), applicable to administrators under the 1986 Act as originally enacted, and Sch. B1, para. 69, applicable following the reforms of the Enterprise Act 2002. See also s. 44 of this Act, applicable to administrative receivers. In summary, the UK and US bankruptcy laws shift the legal relationship of trust in property law to bankruptcy law where the trustee has an independent status beyond the court, the bankrupt and creditors, acts legally only in the name of trustee, and obtains the right in law to manage, appraise and distribute the estate for the interests of creditors in the name of the 'owner' of the estate. The lawsuit against the estate shall be filed and responded in its own name.

19 Ge (2004), pp. 76-7.

bankruptcy administrator falls undoubtedly in the category of agency.

This doctrine was more popular under early research on the bankruptcy administrator system, and was once the dominant doctrine among scholars in the countries of the continental law system. The reason for the doctrine of agency is very simple: the results of any act of the bankruptcy administrator in bankruptcy proceedings are attributed to the bankrupt or debtor, which is just the embodiment of an agency relationship in civil law.[20]

*Doctrine of title* This doctrine, which differs from the doctrine of agency, stems from a precedent dated 30 March 1892 in the collection of civil cases of the German Reichsgericht. It was held that bankruptcy proceedings were a general enforcement proceeding for the interests of all the creditors and that the bankruptcy administrator participates in bankruptcy proceedings on the basis of its title, on behalf of neither creditors nor the debtor, but as an 'enforcement agency in the nature of a public servant'.[21]

The doctrine can be further divided into the theory of title based on public law and the theory of title based on private law. The former holds that bankruptcy proceedings are general mandatory enforcement proceedings and that the administrator participates in bankruptcy proceedings due to his title, representing neither creditor nor debtor, and his functions in the management and appraisal of the estate are similar to those of enforcement agencies under public law. Thus, the administrator's title is based on public law.

The theory of title based on private law holds that, though the title of the bankruptcy administrator is entrusted by the state, the administrator does not work in the name of the state but in the name of private individuals; hence, the administrator's title is based on private law. The theory was once dominant in the academic circles of bankruptcy law in Japan. The scholars following this theory believe that the doctrine of title solves the hard question of for whom the administrator performs his functions, enabling the bankruptcy administrator to have a totally neutral legal status, and meanwhile, the specific responsibilities of the administrator provided for in the bankruptcy law reflect the theory.

*Doctrine of estate agency* This doctrine was advocated by Botticher, professor of civil procedural law in the German University of Hamburg in 1964, which was totally innovative. At present, this doctrine is the most popular doctrine among Japanese bankruptcy theorists.[22] It holds that the properties of the bankrupt become independent properties for the purpose of the bankruptcy liquidation due to the bankruptcy declaration, and those properties are personalized on the whole as the bankruptcy estate, and the administrator is the representative authority of such personalized property. Scholars of the continental law system further believe

20 Jiang (2005), p. 72.

21 Ge (2004), p. 76.

22 Qi (2004), p. 285.

that, although the Japanese Bankruptcy Law and the German Insolvency Law do not explicitly recognize the estate as an independent civil subject, reasonable interpretations of various legal relationships in bankruptcy law can be made only by recognizing the estate as an independent civil subject, either in theory or in practice.[23] As the estate is regarded an independent civil subject, the bankruptcy administrator shall be the representative authority of this subject.

Since the doctrine of estate agency originated in Germany, compared with the doctrine of agency, it has won more support from scholars of the continental law systems. These scholars believe that the biggest advantage of the doctrine is that it allows the bankruptcy administrator to be independent from the bankrupt and its creditors in terms of interests, hence ensuring the fair and reasonable progress of the bankruptcy proceedings. In addition, this approach may solve such theoretical problems as the subject attribution of the estate and the succession of credit and debt relations before the bankruptcy declaration.

*Doctrine of the corporate qualification of the administrative institution* This doctrine holds that the administrator shall be granted the corporate qualification, that is, the concept of the 'administrator' shall include the administrative institution and its executive. With respect to the administrator as an administrative institution, its corporate qualification and powers of management and disposal of the estate shall be recognized.

*Evaluation* Although the above-mentioned four doctrines have each, to some extent, explained the relevant issues in bankruptcy proceedings and are reasonable in some sense, the existence of a doctrine and the judgement about its reasonableness shall be based on its theoretical and practical values.

The essence of the 'doctrine of agency' stems from the principle of self-help in bankruptcy proceedings, emphasizing the position of the administrator as an 'agency of private rights'. Theoretically, it should be questioned as follows: firstly, if the bankruptcy administrator is an agent, he can only act legally in the name of his principal, but in jurisprudence and judicial practice, he has independent personality and acts legally and independently in his own name. Secondly, according to the theory of agency, the legal consequences of the acts done by the agent within authorized scope shall be attributed to the principal and the agent's acts shall not exceed his authorized scope, but in fact, the bankruptcy laws of all countries grant many rights to administrators and the exercise of these rights is sometimes to protect the interests of creditors and debtors in opposite positions. Therefore, no matter which party the administrator represents, the interests that he acts for may not be completely consistent.

---

23 For instance, Article 47 of the Japanese Bankruptcy Law provides for the 'right of claim against the estate'; Article 56 provides for the 'interests shared by the estate', and Article 143 provides for the 'loss incurred due to the estate'.

The 'doctrine of title' stems from the thought of 'public relief' in bankruptcy proceedings, emphasizing the position of the administrator as an 'authority of public rights', which is in relative accordance with the practical tendency of modern bankruptcy legislation. Though this doctrine can solve some problems, especially overcoming the defects of the doctrine of agency, it is also inconsistent in some aspects: firstly, the administrator is appointed by the court and his functions and responsibilities are provided for by law and the nature of his work is in the scope of liquidation; hence, it shall dissolve when bankruptcy proceedings terminate, which is different from the enforcement agency of the court or the civil servants of the state. Secondly, according to the general theories of bankruptcy law, the administrator participates in bankruptcy proceedings in his own name as a party in bankruptcy proceedings. The fact that the enforcement agency in bankruptcy proceedings may act as a party in the litigation of the subject matter of enforcement apparently departs from the theory of legal enforcement. Thirdly, according to the theory of bankruptcy law, bankruptcy creditors enjoy the statutory avoidance rights: see Chapter 8, but such right shall be exercised by the administrator in bankruptcy proceedings. It is an obvious paradox that the administrator, as enforcement agency, can exercise credit rights.

The 'doctrine of estate agency' breaks the traditional pattern of thinking, raising the estate, which is normally deemed as an object in the legal relations of bankruptcy, to the theoretical position of a subject, that is, the subjectification of the object. Although this doctrine has gained support from some scholars, it is seldom adopted by legislations of nations and is totally inconsistent with customary concepts. Besides, it is illogical to subjectify the object and give to it subjective legal objectives.[24]

As to the 'doctrine of corporate qualification of the administrative institution', on one hand, with respect to the argument that the management and disposal of the estate is realized by the administrator through suppressing the opinion of the bankrupt, as the subject of rights, bankruptcy is similar to enforcement, and this doctrine acknowledges the advantages of the doctrine of title. On the other hand, with respect to the reasonable explanation of the legal relationship as the consequence of the acts of the administrator, it acknowledges the advantages of the doctrine of estate agency. However, it fails to make a reasonable explanation of the neutral status of the administrator, who both represents the interests

24 However, the doctrine has at least the following reasonableness: firstly, it clarifies the legal relationships among subjects and objects in bankruptcy proceedings, which is conducive for the administrator to exercise his functions and responsibilities; secondly, as the estate may become the subject of rights, rather than the object of rights, the argument that the estate shall be owned by one owner cannot hold water; thirdly, the establishment of the estate subject system may get rid of some defects of the doctrine of title and solve the contradiction existing in the doctrine of title that the administrator cannot find the object it serves or act for itself.

of creditors and debtors in bankruptcy proceedings. Though this doctrine is manifested to some extent in the current Japanese bankruptcy law, there are still some disputes and it has not become dominant.

## From Bankruptcy Liquidation Group to Bankruptcy Administrator: Choice of Chinese Bankruptcy Legislation

As noted above, the administrative control of bankruptcy proceedings has undergone a significant transition with the passage of the EBL 2006 from state control to the establishment of the office of administrator, with a market-based office.

### *Position under Previous Law*

The EBL 1986 did not establish an administrator system and only provided in Article 24 that: 'the liquidation group shall be responsible for and report to the court'. Article 201 of the Civil Procedural Law provides that, 'the liquidation organization shall be responsible for and report to the court'. Article 249 of the 'Opinions of the Supreme People's Court on Some Issues Concerning the Application of the Civil Procedure Law of the People's Republic of China' and Article 51 of the 'The Regulation on Several Issues Concerning Hearing Enterprise Bankruptcy Cases' of 2002 also reiterate the above-mentioned provision. Under the EBL 1986, therefore, the liquidation group was defined as the receiver and enforcement organization of the insolvent enterprise, designated by and responsible to the court. Hence, the doctrine of title was adopted to define the liquidation group at that time.

Meanwhile, the composition of the previous liquidation group also conformed to the 'doctrine of title' approach discussed above. Article 48 of the 'Provisions of the Supreme People's Court on Some Issues Concerning the Trial of Enterprise Bankruptcy Cases' provides that:

> The members of the liquidation group may be selected from the competent superior department of the insolvent enterprise, liquidation intermediaries, accountants and lawyers, or designated from the governmental department of finance, administration for industry and commerce, planning commission, economy commission, and auditing department, taxation, appraisal, labor, social insurance, land administration, state asset administration and personnel. The branches (sub-branches) of the People's Bank of China may also assign persons to the liquidation group in accordance with the relevant provisions.

The liquidation group was therefore basically constituted by public servants, a feature which fully demonstrates its legal status.

### *Position under the New Law*

The promulgation of the EBL 2006 explicitly provides for the administrator system, and ultimately reflects a change from the doctrine of title approach of the EBL 1986 to the doctrine of 'creditor agency'. Article 13 of the EBL 2006 provides: 'The court shall designate an administrator when ruling on accepting an application for bankruptcy'. Article 61 enables the creditors' meeting to replace and supervise the administrator, which indicates the legal status of the administrator by legislation.

Essentially, the EBL 2006 pays greater attention to the protection of the interests of creditors. When a debtor goes bankrupt, its creditors are the most vulnerable. They are usually dispersed without organization and the amounts of their credits differ. Due to different rights and interests of creditors, it is impossible to maximize the interests of creditors in bankruptcy proceedings as intended if there is no professional and experienced administrator to represent their interests. Moreover, the interests of other stakeholders in bankruptcy proceedings are protected by corresponding legal rules and provisions; for example, the interests of employees are protected by labour law. The protection of the interests of creditors is the basic goal of bankruptcy law, which is demonstrated by the development history of bankruptcy law: the bankruptcy laws of most countries (whether Anglo-American law systems or continental law systems) provide that the administrator shall be selected and supervised by the creditors' meeting and his responsibilities are authorized by the creditors' meeting.[25]

### *Qualification and Appointment of Administrators*

This chapter considers the status, powers and duties of the administrator, in addition to the means of supervision of administrators. The processes of qualification and appointment of administrators are discussed in Chapter 6.

## **Supervision System of Bankruptcy Administrator**

With respect to the supervision over, and restriction of, the bankruptcy administrator, legislations adopt diversified supervision systems. Besides the court which exercises its right of supervision,[26] the creditors' meeting may

25 Li, available at http://www.jcrb.com/zyw/n317/ca277409.htm.

26 See e.g. para. 5 of Sch. B1 of the Insolvency Act 1986 (UK); Article 161 of Japanese Bankruptcy Law; and Article 58(1) of the German *Insolvenzrecht*.

have supervisory powers;[27] a special bankruptcy supervisor[28] may be established independent of the creditors' meeting and the bankruptcy administrator. In some jurisdictions an administrative agency may have supervisory powers,[29] to achieve balance, since the court has a heavy burden of tasks, while the supervisor is the representative of the interests of creditors.[30]

The EBL 2006 establishes a supervision system that is dominated by the representative agency of the creditors' meeting and supplemented by the supervision of the court. Article 23 provides that the administrator is to perform his functions and duties according to the provisions of the EBL 2006 and that he shall report his work to the court. In addition, it is provided that he shall accept the supervision of his functions by the creditors' meeting and the creditors' committee. The administrator must attend the creditors' meeting as a non-voting delegate, report the performance of his functions to the creditors' meeting and answer enquiries.[31]

To assist the creditors' committee with its monitoring role, Article 68 provides that when performing its duties and powers, the creditors' committee shall be entitled to require the administrator and the relevant personnel of the debtor to make explanations or to provide the relevant documents within the scope of their duties and powers. Where the administrator, or the relevant personnel of the debtor, violates the provisions of this Law and refuses to accept supervision, the creditors' committee shall be entitled to request the court to make a supervisory ruling.[32]

The creditors' committee must also be kept informed of various activities of the administrator. Under Article 69 of the EBL 2006 the administrator must make a report to the committee in a timely manner upon the occurrence of the following: (1) a transfer of the ownership of real estate such as land and housing; (2) a transfer of property rights, such as mining rights, tenure and intellectual property rights; (3) a transfer of all the stock or business operation of the company; (4) the granting of a loan; (5) the provision of property collateral; (6) a transfer of credits or marketable securities; (7) the performance of a contract, the performance of which has not been completed by the debtor and his counterparty; (8) a waiver

27 In general, the creditors' meeting of the continental law system only exercises limited right of supervision over the bankruptcy administrator indirectly by way of making a decision and applying to the court for replacing the bankruptcy administrator. The creditors' meeting of the Anglo-American law system is granted with a broader and effective right of supervision over the bankruptcy administrator.

28 Wang (2002), p. 67. The legislations of different countries have different names for the supervisor: in the US, New Zealand and Australia, it is called the examination commission; in Italy, France and Germany, it is called the creditors' committee; in Japan and South Korea, it is called the supervision commissioner or supervisor; and in Taiwan, it is called the inspector.

29 For instance, the US established the federal trustee system in 1978.

30 Xie (2005), p. 312.

31 Article 23(2), EBL 2006.

32 The Court shall make a ruling within five days upon such a request by the creditors' committee.

of rights; (9) a withdrawal of a guarantee; and (10) any other disposal of property that is of material impact on the interests of the creditors. Where no creditors' committee has been set up, the administrator is required to promptly report upon the above-mentioned acts to the court.

Thus, with respect to the supervision system in relation to bankruptcy administrators, the EBL 2006 adopts as its basis that 'the administrator shall be responsible for and report his work to court'[33] on one hand, and on the other hand defines the creditors' meeting and the creditors' committee as the bankruptcy supervisory organ, responsible for supervising the work of the bankruptcy administrator, which not only meets the trend of legislation internationally, but also effectively safeguards the justness of bankruptcy proceedings.

## Scope of Duties of the Bankruptcy Administrator

In accordance with Article 15 of the EBL 2006, from the date when the ruling of the court to accept the bankruptcy application is delivered to the debtor, until the date of the conclusion of the bankruptcy proceedings, the relevant personnel of the debtor (namely, the legal representative of the insolvent enterprise, and the financial management and other operation management of the insolvent enterprise through the decision of the court) shall bear obligations concerning the proper safekeeping of the occupied and managed property, as well as the materials including seals, accounting books and documents. Once the bankruptcy proceedings start, the debtor will lose the right to manage and dispose of its own property.[34] After the court appoints the administrator, the effect will be that the bankruptcy administrator takes over the debtor's estate, as well as materials including seals, accounting books and documents. The take-over by the bankruptcy administrator of the estate is in essence the take-over by the administrator of all the rights in relation to the estate, excluding the ownership, and thus the administrator becomes the actual controller of the estate in law.[35]

Under the framework of the 'administrator centrism', outlined above, the administrator is dominant in the whole bankruptcy proceedings, and is fully responsible for the smooth operation of the bankruptcy proceedings. Under the leadership of the court, the administrator fully exercises the rights of management of the property of the debtor, and takes specific responsibilities. The administrator is the special institution elected by law to be responsible for the management of the property of the debtor, and he holds an independent position in the bankruptcy proceedings. The administrator performs his duties independently by law within the scope of his functions and duties. The main duties and responsibilities of the administrator are set out below.

33 Article 23, EBL 2006.

34 See e.g. Article 16, EBL 2006.

35 Zou (1995), p. 236.

*Management of the Estate*

The bankruptcy administrator takes over the estate and becomes the actual controller of the estate in law.[36] In managing the estate the administrator will undertake the safekeeping, arrangement and disposal of the estate. Such duties are key to the smooth progress of the whole bankruptcy proceedings, and are therefore among the most important duties of the administrator.

*Safekeeping* Under the duty of safekeeping, the bankruptcy administrator shall fulfil the duty of care of a good manager and adopt active and proper measures to keep the property of the debtor, including safekeeping by distinguishing the way of existence of properties and by centralized sealing and storage and realizing perishable commodities and goods through auction proceedings without assessment. If necessary, the bankruptcy administrator may also engage assistant workers.[37]

*Arrangement* Through the process of arrangement of the property of the debtor the administrator will ascertain the real situation in respect of the property of the debtor and this process is an important premise to enable the administrator to draw up the distribution plan of the estate. The process of arrangement shall include the arrangement of 'positive' and 'negative' property: the term 'positive' property refers to tangible assets, intangible assets and credits; and the term 'negative' property refers to the debts of the debtor. When the administrator arranges the property of the debtor, he shall make a directory of the properties and list the categories, their original values, his assessments and the locations of properties falling within the estate.

Where the administrator finds that the estate is not sufficient to enable any distribution to be made, the administrator shall apply for the court to terminate the bankruptcy proceedings.[38] This is an important duty of the administrator. However, in the event that a third party is willing to provide funding, the proceedings may continue.[39]

The administrator has the power to conduct the following acts during the arrangement:

---

36 Xie (2005), p. 299. See for example, Section 1106 of the Bankruptcy Code of the United States.

37 Article 14, 'Regulations of the Supreme People's Court on the Determination of Remuneration for Administrators in the Hearing of Enterprise Bankruptcy Cases,' provides that the fees of such agents must be paid from the administrator's own remuneration; Xie (2005), p. 301.

38 See similarly Article 148 of the Bankruptcy Law of Taiwan and s. 207 of the German *Insolvenzordnung*.

39 See further pp. 129-30.

1. To make inquiries of the debtor, directors, managers and other relevant personnel of the company.[40]
2. To receive payments of property to the debtor from third parties.[41] Debtors of the debtor are required to make any payment to the administrator and any holder of the debtor's property must deliver this property to the administrator. Any intentional violation of this requirement, where payment is made to the debtor, rather than the administrator, shall result in the obligation of the debtor or the property holder not being discharged, where this has caused harm to creditors.[42]
3. The right to claim for a division of jointly owned property.[43]
4. If the debtor is a company, the bankruptcy administrator shall require its members to pay their subscribed contributions regardless of the period of capital contribution of its members or shareholders.[44] In other words, if the members of the debtor company have not made full capital contributions to the company's assets according to the incorporation contract, the administrator is entitled to request that the relevant members pay the remaining capital in ignorance of the period in the incorporation contract.[45]

*Disposal of the property of the debtor* The bankruptcy administrator enjoys the right of disposal of the property of the debtor. However the administrator is only able to, *inter alia*, transfer real estate rights, mining rights, fishery rights, copyrights, patent rights, inventory or business, movable property, credit rights and marketable securities if the permission of the creditors' committee or the court is acquired.[46] Once bankruptcy proceedings start, the insolvent debtor may not make payment to any specific creditor.[47]

*Continued Trading*

The administrator must decide whether to continue or close the debtor's business operation prior to the first creditors' meeting.[48] In some instances, continued trading of the insolvent business can increase the value of the estate of the debtor and protect the interests of creditors. Where this is the case, the administrator shall,

40 Para. 2 of Article 15, EBL 2006.

41 Para. 1 of Article 17, EBL 2006.

42 Article 17, EBL 2006.

43 For instance, Article 61 of Japanese Corporate Rehabilitation Law provides that 'in case of common properties of the company and other persons, at the beginning of the rehabilitation proceedings, the property administrator shall make the request of claiming for division even if there is an agreement that the property cannot be divided'.

44 Xie (2005), p. 302.

45 Article 35, EBL 2006.

46 Articles 26 and 69, EBL 2006.

47 Article 16, EBL 2006.

48 Article 25(5), EBL 2006.

within necessary scope, be entitled to keep undertakings of the debtor as ongoing concerns, provided that the permission of the creditors' meeting or the court is acquired.[49] Where the bankruptcy administrator exercises the right of business management, he may carry out the following related acts:

1. Deciding upon the discharge or continuous performance of bilateral contracts of the debtor.[50]
2. When the business of the enterprise is in need of loans to meet the demand of capital, the bankruptcy administrator may take loans with the permission of the creditors' committee or the court in the circumstance where the creditors' committee is not established.[51]

*Participation in the Relevant Lawsuit and Arbitration Activities*

After the declaration of bankruptcy, the bankrupt loses the right of management and disposal of properties, as well as rights to pursue lawsuits, and all the civil procedures related to the insolvent debtor shall suspend.[52] This restriction is aimed at preventing the debtor from maliciously giving up rights or making compromises adverse to the creditors. The bankruptcy administrator takes the place of the debtor in pursuing the lawsuit or arbitration that has been initiated by the bankrupt and he assumes the litigation position of the former debtor.

The debtor is entitled to apply for the composition procedure directly. If the debtor has been put into bankruptcy liquidation proceedings, he can also petition for composition before the bankruptcy declaration is made by the court.[53] Upon receipt of the composition application of the debtor, the court shall timely hand the matter over to the bankruptcy administrator, who will make the necessary investigation of the composition application of the debtor. Before deciding to hold the creditors' meeting to discuss the composition conditions of the debtor, the court shall ask for opinions from the bankruptcy administrator and hear the results of the bankruptcy administrator's investigations.[54]

*Drawing up and Proposal of the Bankruptcy Distribution Plan and Appraisal and Distribution of the Estate*

The appraisal and distribution of the estate is the core stage of the bankruptcy liquidation work. Appraisal is the premise of distribution and distribution is the

49 Xie (2005), p. 304.
50 Article 18, EBL 2006. See also e.g. Article 103 of the German *Insolvenzrecht*.
51 Article 69, EBL 2006; Xie (2005), p. 304.
52 Article 20, EBL 2006.
53 Article 95, EBL 2006.
54 Xie (2005), p. 305.

purpose of appraisal. Appraisal and distribution of the estate are therefore centrally important duties of the bankruptcy administrator.

Following the process of claims declaration,[55] the bankruptcy administrator shall investigate the situation of debts and make a list of creditors who have filed their claims.[56] The administrator shall also collect the property and ascertain the total amount of the estate available for distribution.[57]

While appraising the estate at the current rate, the bankruptcy administrator shall prepare the appraisal scheme in the principle of overall appraisal of the estate, which shall be implemented in a timely, rapid and proper manner upon discussion by and approval of the creditors' meeting. The distribution plan in respect of the estate shall also be formulated without undue delay[58] and shall be implemented only after discussion by and approval of the creditors' meeting and approval by the court.[59]

### *Bankruptcy Administrator's Duties under Article 25*

Article 25 of the EBL 2006 provides that the administrator shall fulfil the following duties.

*Taking over the debtor's property as well as materials including seals, books and documents of the debtor* Where the debtor makes the bankruptcy application, it shall submit to the court an explanation of the property status, debt list, credit list, related financial accounting report, pre-planning on personnel placement, payment of staff salaries and payment of social security expenditures.[60] Where it is a creditor that makes the application, the court shall deliver it to the debtor within five days of the date when adjudication is made.[61] The debtor shall submit to the court a specification of its properties, its debt list, credit list, related financial accounting reports, payment of staff salaries and payment of social security expenditures within 15 days of the date of the service of the ruling.[62]

Therefore, after appointing the administrator, the court shall hand over the property and materials including seals, books and documents of the debtor to the administrator, who takes the responsibility for specific operation of the bankruptcy affairs.

---

55 See further pp. 173-7.
56 Article 57, EBL 2006.
57 Xie (2005), p. 306.
58 Article 111, EBL 2006.
59 Article 115, EBL 2006.
60 Article 8(3), EBL 2006.
61 Article 11(2), EBL 2006.
62 Article 11(2), EBL 2006.

*Investigation of the property position of the debtor and preparation of the report on property position* Article 48 of the EBL 2006 provides that any creditor shall report his claim to the administrator within the deadline for doing so that is specified by the court.[63] Article 57 of the EBL 2006 provides that, after receiving the report documents of the creditor, the administrator shall register and make a filing of them and shall scrutinize the reported credit rights and prepare the list of credit rights. The list of credit rights and reported documents of credit rights shall be kept by the administrator for inspection by stakeholders.

One of the purposes of bankruptcy legislation is to fairly settle and arrange the debts and credits, for protection of the legitimate rights and interests of creditors and the debtor. Hence, the creditors of the debtor should report their credit rights by force of law, and the debtors of the debtor, or the holders of properties of the debtor, shall liquidate the debts or deliver the property to the administrator and streamline the relationship of credits and debts. In addition, the administrator has the right to take initiatives to investigate the actual property status of the debtor, complete an assessment of the estate to the fullest extent and prepare written reports to guarantee the progress of the consequential bankruptcy proceedings.

*Deciding the internal management affairs of the debtor* The progress of bankruptcy proceedings does not necessarily mean the termination of the undertakings of the debtor. The administrator shall perform its duty of care of a good manager in managing the internal affairs of the debtor in an effort to release the debtor from its difficult situation. Article 28 of the EBL 2006 provides that the administrator shall, with the permission of the court, employ necessary workers. In addition, Article 74 of the EBL 2006 provides that, where the administrator is responsible for the management of property and business, it has the right to employ the business and management personnel of the debtor who will be in charge of the business affairs.

*Deciding the daily expenses and other necessary expenditures of the debtor* The bankruptcy administrator is responsible for the conduct of the bankruptcy proceedings and thus he or she has the right to decide on all the expenditures of the debtor, so as to ensure the effective progress of the bankruptcy proceedings while taking over the property and managing the internal affairs of the debtor.

*Deciding to continue or stop the business of the debtor prior to the first creditors' meeting* Article 26 of the EBL 2006 provides that, prior to the first creditors' meeting, where the administrator decides to continue or stop the business of the debtor or conduct any acts in Article 69, set out above at p. 101, it shall acquire the permission of the court, that is, before the first creditors' meeting, the decision by the administrator on keeping or stopping the business of the debtor or disposing of the property with material impacts on the interest of the creditor requires the

63 See further Chapter 9 regarding the filing of claims.

permission of the court before execution.

After the court accepts the application for bankruptcy, the administrator shall have the right to discharge or keep on performing the contracts that are established but not fully performed by the debtor and the counterparties before the acceptance of the application for bankruptcy and he shall inform the counterparties of the same.[64] If the administrator fails to give notification to the counterparty within two months of receipt of the application for bankruptcy, or fails to reply within 30 days of receipt of the reminder from the counterparty, it shall be treated as discharge of the contract. Where the administrator decides to keep on performing the contract, the counterparty shall perform it, provided that the counterparty is entitled to claim a guarantee from the administrator. Where the administrator fails to provide a guarantee, it shall be treated as a discharge of the contract. This provision clarifies the specific duties of the administrator when keeping on or stopping the business of the debtor.

*Managing and disposal of the property of the debtor* The bankruptcy administrator shall manage and dispose of the property of the debtor in the principle of maximizing the value of the estate. Article 17 of the EBL 2006 provides that after the court accepts the application for bankruptcy, the debtor's debtors shall pay off their debts to the administrator and the holder of the debtor's property shall deliver the property to the administrator. The bankruptcy administrator shall have the right to actively take measures to arrange and keep safe the property to make preliminary preparations for possible appraisal and distribution of the estate.

In accordance with Article 39 of the EBL 2006, at the acceptance of the application for bankruptcy by the court, when the seller has already dispatched the subject matter of sales to the debtor as the buyer, for which the debtor has neither received such subject matter nor paid off the full price, the seller may take back the subject matter in transit. However, the administrator may pay off the full price and ask the seller to deliver the subject matter. The administrator may, according to the actual circumstances of the business of the debtor, dispose of the property for protecting the legitimate rights and interests of the debtor.

*Representing the debtor in lawsuits, arbitration proceedings and other legal proceedings* Upon entering bankruptcy proceedings, the debtor loses its rights of management and disposal of the property, as well as the rights to implement lawsuits, and the administrator takes the place of the debtor in continuing with the lawsuit, arbitration and other legal proceedings related to the debtor. Article 20 of the EBL 2006 provides that civil litigation or arbitration concerning the debtor that has started but has not yet ended shall be suspended after the court accepts the application for bankruptcy; and the litigation or arbitration shall continue after

64 Article 18, EBL 2006.

the administrator takes over the debtor's property. The administrator is also able to pursue transaction avoidance powers.[65]

Meanwhile, in order to perform the duties of the administrator, Article 122 of the EBL 2006 provides that in the case of a pending lawsuit or arbitration, the administrator still cannot terminate the execution of duties even though the process of revocation of registration has been completed.

*Proposing the convening of the creditors' meeting* The first creditors' meeting shall be called by the court, and shall be convened within 15 days after the expiration of the period for declaration of credits.[66] Subsequent creditors' meetings are convened at such times as the court deems necessary, and may also be convened upon a proposal to the chairman of the creditors' meeting by the administrator, the creditors' committee, or by creditors whose credits are confirmed to comprise more than one-fourth of the total amount of claims. Meanwhile, Article 63 of the EBL 2006 provides that the administrator shall notify the known creditors 15 days in advance of the convention of the creditors' meeting.

*Other duties that the people's court thinks the administrator shall perform, and the duties of the administrator otherwise specified in the EBL 2006* The duties of the administrator, as set out above, are a series of legal acts mainly concerning the management and disposal of the estate. In addition, the legislation contains a general and overarching duty, together with the eight specific duties of the administrator.

In accordance with the EBL 2006, further duties stem from the general duty as follows:

1. Applying to the court for the conclusion of the bankruptcy proceedings where the debtor's property is insufficient to pay off the expenses for bankruptcy.[67] The court shall make a ruling for the termination of the bankruptcy proceedings within 15 days after receiving such application of the administrator.
2. Preparing a draft reorganization plan in cases where reorganization proceedings are not being conducted on a debtor in possession basis.[68]
3. Timely drawing up the disposition of the estate and appraising and selling the estate at an appropriate time.[69] The disposition plan shall be submitted to the creditors' meeting for discussion and the administrator shall dispose of

65 Articles 31-3, EBL 2006. See further Chapter 8.
66 Article 62, EBL 2006.
67 Article 43(4), EBL 2006. See further pp. 129-130.
68 Article 80(2), EBL 2006.
69 Article 111, EBL 2006.

the estate in due time according to the disposal plan passed by the creditors' meeting or decided by the court.[70]

4. Implementing the distribution plan. Article 116 of the EBL 2006 provides that the administrator shall be responsible to carry out the plan of distribution of the bankruptcy estate upon its ruling and recognition by the court.
5. Request the court to rule on the conclusion of the bankruptcy proceedings. Article 120 of the EBL 2006 provides that if the bankrupt has no property to distribute, the administrator may apply to the court for termination of the bankruptcy proceedings.[71] Otherwise, following the final distribution of the bankruptcy property, the administrator shall timely submit to the court a distribution report of the estate and apply for the conclusion of bankruptcy proceedings.
6. Handle the registration of revocation. Article 121 of the EBL 2006 provides that the administrator shall, within ten days upon the conclusion of bankruptcy proceedings, handle the procedures for the revocation of registration of the bankrupt at the original registration authority by producing the ruling of the court on the conclusion of the proceedings.

## Rights and Obligations of the Administrator

A bankruptcy administrator who undertakes important duties is supposed to enjoy certain rights and shall undertake corresponding obligations in bankruptcy proceedings.

### *Rights of the Administrator*

The rights of the administrator mainly relate to remuneration. Paragraph 2 of Article 28 of the EBL 2006 provides that the remuneration of the administrator shall be determined by the court, and in case of any objection to the remuneration of the administrator, the creditors' meeting is entitled to submit such objection to the court. Meanwhile, paragraph 3 of Article 22 provides that the methods for the appointment of and for payment of the administrator shall be specified by the court. These provisions are considerably augmented by Regulations issued by the Supreme People's Court, discussed in Chapter 6.

### *Obligations of the Administrator*

The administrator shall be subject to general legal obligations to ensure standard and fair progress of the bankruptcy proceedings, in addition to the series of duties specified by law.

---

70 Article 65(1), EBL 2006.

71 See further p. 263.

*Duty of care* While the bankruptcy administrator performs functions, Article 27 of the EBL 2006 provides that he shall do so with due diligence and loyalty. If the administrator lacks such care, it may be regarded as a minor fault; if he or she lacks the care of an ordinary person, it is a gross fault. In either case, the bankruptcy administrator shall shoulder the liability for compensation if damages are caused to the creditors.

Article 130 of the EBL 2006 provides for the liabilities of an administrator who breaches his obligations: where the administrator fails to loyally execute its functions with due diligence according to the provisions of the EBL 2006, the court may impose a fine by force of law; and if losses are suffered by creditors, the debtor or a third party, the liabilities for liquidated damages shall be undertaken by force of law.

*Restrictions on individual transactions* An area in which the EBL 2006 is apparently lacking is in provision to prohibit the administrator from individual transactions with the insolvent enterprise, or from inducing a third party to have transactions with the insolvent enterprise. Such provision is a common feature of the laws of other jurisdictions[72] and is important for the purpose of guaranteeing the fair performance of the administrator's duties.

*Property guarantee system* To effectively prevent and crack down on bankruptcy crimes,[73] most countries have established a property guarantee system and corresponding legal liability system in bankruptcy proceedings. As discussed further at pp. 287-9, China is no exception. The property guarantee system generally applies at the time when the bankruptcy administrator is appointed, and requires the bankruptcy administrator to provide proper properties as guarantee before taking office. This system greatly stimulates the initiatives of the administrator to exercise the duty of care of a good manager in performing his functions. In addition, or alternatively, a civil liability system may apply under which the bankruptcy administrator is required to pay corresponding compensation for the actual loss caused to the bankruptcy estate intentionally or by negligence. In serious cases criminal liability may be warranted.

*Liability system* To effectively crack down on bankruptcy crimes, in modern times, the legislations of most nations have moved the relevant provisions on

72 Article 54(3) of Japanese Corporate Rehabilitation Law: 'without permission of the court, the administrator shall neither accept the products or properties of the bankruptcy corporation nor transfer its/his/her own products or properties to the bankruptcy corporation, or have other transactions between itself or a third party and the bankruptcy corporation'.

73 The term 'bankruptcy crime' generally refers to the behaviour of the bankrupt or others which prejudices the interests of the creditor and violates statutory obligations before the declaration of bankruptcy or during the bankruptcy proceedings and which shall be punished by the criminal law after the declaration of bankruptcy. Cited from Gu (1995), p. 313.

bankruptcy crimes from the Bankruptcy Law to Criminal Law, to increase the deterrent effect of such crimes and so aid in the effective prevention of crimes.[74] See Chapter 14 on bankruptcy crimes in China.

## References

Chen, R. (1986), *Bankruptcy Law* (Taipei: San Min Book Co., Ltd.)

Ge, X. (2004), 'Inquiring the Legal Position of the Bankruptcy Administrator' *Journal of Henan Judicial Policemen Vocational College* 2, 76.

Gu, P. (1995), *Bankruptcy Law Course* (Beijing: Law Press-China).

He, Z. (2005), 'Thinking on Bankruptcy Administrator System' *Guangxi Social Sciences* 5, 85.

Jiang, P. (2005), 'Research on the Legal Position of the Bankruptcy Administrator' *Journal of Nanjing Administrative Institute of Nanjing CPC Party School* 5, 72.

Li, S. 'Administrator System in the New Bankruptcy Law' *Court Daily*, source: http://www.jcrb.com/zyw/n317/ca277409.htm.

Peng, H. and Zhou, Y. (2006), 'Administrator System Established by the Enterprise Bankruptcy Law' *Zhuoyue Financing* 10, 67.

Qi, S. (2004), *Research on Bankruptcy Law* (Xiamen: Xiamen University Press).

Wang, W. (2007), *The Sum and Substance of Bankruptcy Law* (Beijing: Law Press-China).

Wang, Y. (2002), 'Research on Bankruptcy Administrator System' *Social Science Journal* 2, 66.

Xie, J. (2005), *Chinese Bankruptcy Law System* (Beijing: Court Press).

Zhang, H. (2009), 'A Notable Feature of China's New Bankruptcy Law: "Administrator"' 6 *International Corporate Rescue* 2, 98.

Zou, H. (1995), *Comparative Research on Bankruptcy Proceedings and Bankruptcy Law Substantive System* (Beijing: Law Press-China).

Zou, H. (2006), 'New Enterprise Bankruptcy Law and Administrator Centrism' *Journal of East China University of Political Science and Law* 6, 121.

74 Ibid. at 319.

# Chapter 6
# Administrator: Appointment and Remuneration

Rebecca Parry

## Introduction

The previous chapter provided an introduction to the role of the administrator, concentrating on the status, powers and duties of the administrator. These matters are dealt with primarily in the EBL 2006. However the EBL 2006 is not the only relevant law that we must consider in order to gain an understanding of the legislation relating to the administrator. In Chinese law a significant role is played also by Regulations issued by the Supreme People's Court, hereafter 'SPC'. Two important sets of Regulations have been issued relating to administrators. They deal with the processes for their appointment and with the level of their remuneration. These Regulations, and related issues concerning the appointment and remuneration of administrators, will be considered in this chapter.

## Administrator Appointments

The EBL 2006 brought about a major change in the governance of insolvency proceedings. The previous EBL 1986 was characterized by strong government control, under which the administration of cases involving SOEs was dealt with by a 'liquidation group', composed of government officials: see further p. 99.[1] Therefore there was little work available for private individuals and firms in the administration of such insolvency cases.[2] The EBL 2006 changes this position and, as a result, detailed rules regulating appointments to the new office of administrator were required. These rules are provided by the 'Regulations of the Supreme People's Court on the Appointment of Administrators for Hearings on Cases of Enterprise Bankruptcy',[3] hereafter the 'Appointment Regulations', which were passed by the SPC under the authority of Article 22 of the EBL 2006 on 4 April 2007. The Regulations were promulgated on 12 April 2007 and came into

1 For further discussion of the 'liquidation group', see Zhang (2009), pp. 98-100.

2 Li (2001).

3 For an English language translation of the Appointment Regulations see Wang (2009a).

force on 1 June 2007, on the same day as the EBL 2006. It will be noted that the time between the promulgation of these Regulations and their coming into force was relatively short, which did not give the courts a great deal of time to bring them into effect.[4]

The aim of the Appointment Regulations is to enable fair and impartial hearings in bankruptcy cases, to ensure that trials proceed smoothly in accordance with the law and to promote the improvement and development of the bankruptcy administrator system.[5] The courts have been required to establish local rosters of administrators and the administrators who are appointed in bankruptcy cases will normally be appointed from the rosters.[6] This system bears some similarity to the process in the US of the selection of a trustee from a panel established by the US Trustee.[7] As discussed further below, exceptions to the use of rosters arise in relation to important or complex cases.[8] Separate rosters are maintained for firms and for individual administrators.[9]

As noted above, the courts were not presented with much advance warning of the arrangements that they needed to put in place and the Regulations were issued at a time when the courts were under significant workloads. The rates at which the courts were able to respond to the Regulations differed between jurisdictions. In jurisdictions such as Yunnan and Chongqing, the court invited applications from potential administrators prior to the new law coming into force and several jurisdictions completed the process of assembling panels within three months of the law coming into force.[10] While it might have been more desirable for all courts to have had the rosters in place upon the law coming into force, as it turned out, the lack of notice does not seem to have caused any problems, since the numbers of cases that were brought in the first year since the EBL 2006 came into force was relatively low.[11]

### *Eligibility*

The conditions of eligibility for those wishing to act as an administrator are set out in the EBL 2006 and elaborated in the Appointment Regulations. Both individuals and organizations, such as specialist liquidation firms, law firms, accountancy firms, and other social intermediary institutions, are eligible for designation as

4 See Tang and Au (2007) for a survey of the progress made in different regions regarding the establishment of rosters of administrators.

5 Preamble, Appointment Regulations.

6 Article 1, Appointment Regulations.

7 This is done in circumstances where no trustee has been elected by creditors.

8 Article 15, Appointment Regulations.

9 Article 2, second paragraph, Appointment Regulations.

10 Tang and Au (2007), p. 50.

11 See the graph at p. 350.

administrators.[12] The ability for organizations to be designated as administrators may be surprising to those from some jurisdictions, such as the UK,[13] Australia[14] and Germany,[15] where it is necessary for the office holder to be a natural person,[16] holding appropriate qualification. The advantages of a requirement for an appointee to be a natural person are that the qualifications and experience of the person handling the case can be clearly ascertained and that the person in charge of the case is clearly identifiable. However other jurisdictions, such as the US, also enable suitable organizations to act as administrators.[17] An argument in favour of permitting organizations to act as administrators is that this may perhaps enable complex cases to be handled more effectively, since otherwise multiple administrators might have to be appointed. This would seem to be the reasoning of the Supreme People's Court in enabling organizations to be admitted to the rosters. Indeed, as discussed further below, the preference under the Chinese system is for organizations to handle all but the simplest cases.

A survey by the firm Grant Thornton in the early stages of establishment of rosters of administrators found that 40 to 60 per cent of the panel members were law firms, 20 to 40 per cent were accountancy firms and 5 to 20 per cent were bankruptcy liquidation firms.[18] These statistics are broadly reflected in the administrator roster of Beijing, where 100 organizations have been licensed to act as administrators, respectively 65 law firms, 33 accountancy firms and two liquidation firms.[19] The finding that the majority of authorized administrators are lawyers contrasts with the position in jurisdictions such as the UK and Australia, where administrators also occupy a key role, where the professions are dominated by accountants. The Chinese profession of administrators has emerged in a pattern similar to the profession in the US, where the profession is also dominated by lawyers.

An important issue in the authorization of organizations, as opposed to natural persons, to act as administrators must surely have been the identification of suitably qualified individuals within these organizations as being appropriate to handle insolvency cases. It is accordingly important for the qualifications and experience of individuals who will be working on insolvency cases on behalf of organizations to be adequate, in addition to the organization itself having sufficient resources and being appropriately regulated.[20] Naturally individuals who handle insolvency cases on behalf of organizations may wish to be authorized in their own right.

12 Article 24, EBL 2006.
13 S. 390(1), Insolvency Act 1986.
14 S. 154A, Bankruptcy Act 1966.
15 Article 56(1), *Insolvenzordnung*.
16 Zhang (2009), p. 100; Paulus (1998), p. 146.
17 US Code, Title 11, §321.
18 Tang and Au (2007).
19 See <http://china.findlaw.cn/law/viewnews-3510>.
20 UNCITRAL (2005), p. 177.

Accordingly, the Appointment Regulations also contain provision for employees of organizations which have been designated as eligible to act as administrators to themselves apply for admission to the roster of individual administrators where they have relevant professional expertise and vocational qualifications.[21]

The process of initial establishment and maintenance of the rosters is discussed further below.

*Appointment Priorities: Individual, Organizations and Liquidation Groups*

As noted above, the preference will normally be for a firm or other organization, rather than an individual or a liquidation group, to be appointed as administrator.[22] It is envisaged that individuals will only be appointed in cases where the issues concerning creditors' rights and debts are relatively straightforward and the estate is not widely dispersed.[23]

Liquidation groups, which handled the bankruptcies of SOEs under the previous law, may be appointed under the EBL 2006 in four circumstances:[24]

1. If a bankruptcy application was accepted and a liquidation group was established before the EBL 2006 came into force on 1 June 2007, in which case the court shall appoint the liquidation group to be administrator as long as the organization of the liquidation group is in accordance with the requirements of Art 19 of the Appointment Regulations.
2. During the remaining phase of planned bankruptcies, according to Art 133 of EBL 2006: see further p. 305 regarding this phase.
3. Where an enterprise is insolvent and the application for bankruptcy has been accepted according to the provisions in relevant laws. One example is Article 71 of the Commercial Bank Law 1995 (amended in 2003), which provides that if a commercial bank is unable to pay its due debts, the court may declare the bankruptcy of the bank with the consent of the Banking Regulatory and Supervisory Commission (BRSC) under the State Council. If the bank is declared to be bankrupt, the court shall organize a liquidation group, the members of which are drawn from the BRSC and other relevant government agencies to perform the duty of carrying out the liquidation.
4. If the court considers the establishment of a liquidation group to be appropriate, which might be the case if the debtors is of significant public importance.

The liquidation group is composed of members of relevant government departments, social intermediary agencies listed in the rosters of administrators, and financial

21 Article 3, Appointment Regulations.

22 Article 16, Appointment Regulations.

23 Article 17, Appointment Regulations.

24 Article 18, Appointment Regulations.

asset management companies. State banks and financial supervisory agencies may also send persons to participate in the liquidation group.[25]

*Disqualification*

A number of circumstances are specified in the EBL 2006 and the Appointment Regulations in which a person or organization will be ineligible for appointment. These circumstances apply either to prevent an individual or organization generally from acting as an administrator, or they relate only to the circumstances of a particular case and prevent appointment in that instance.

Firstly an individual or organization will be generally ineligible for appointment in the following circumstances, mainly relating either to misconduct or a failure to meet the conditions of qualification for an administrator:

- if they have been subject to a criminal penalty on account of an intentional crime;[26]
- if they have ever had their licence revoked;[27]
- if they have, within the last three years, been subject to administrative sanctions or disciplinary actions by administrative organs, regulatory institutions or self regulatory organizations on grounds of deliberate errors or gross negligence;[28]
- if they are currently under investigation for alleged violations of the law;[29]
- if they have, within the last three years, been removed from the roster on account of improper performance of duties or a refusal to follow the instructions of the court;[30]
- if they lack the professional capabilities necessary for acting as an administrator;[31]
- if they have insufficient resources to meet possible civil liabilities that may arise.[32]

The court should also not appoint an individual or organization to be an administrator in a particular case if such individual or organization is involved in a significant debt dispute, or an alleged violation of the law which is subject to an investigation by a court.[33] In addition, the court may find a person or organization ineligible for

25 Article 19, Appointment Regulations.
26 Article 24, EBL 2006.
27 Article 24, EBL 2006.
28 Article 9(1), Appointment Regulations.
29 Article 9(2), Appointment Regulations.
30 Article 9(3), Appointment Regulations.
31 Article 9(4), Appointment Regulations.
32 Article 9(5), Appointment Regulations.
33 Article 26, Appointment Regulations.

appointment where there are other circumstances that they consider capable of affecting the performance of the administrator's functions and duties.[34]

The grounds considered in the previous paragraph constitute general prohibitions from individuals and organizations acting as an administrator. In addition, a person or organization will be ineligible to act in a particular case if they have an interest in it,[35] since such an interest would have the potential to undermine the independence and objectivity of the administrator and could give rise to unfairness or bias.[36] Such an interest will be considered to be present where any of the following circumstances exist among members of the organization or the liquidation group to an extent that would affect their faithful performance of their duties as administrators:[37]

- outstanding claims against or liabilities to the debtor or to creditors;
- professional intermediary services, for example engagement as a legal adviser or accountancy consultant, other than 'one off' services, provided to the debtor within three years prior to the acceptance of the bankruptcy case by the court;
- a controlling shareholding, or *de facto* control, of the debtor or a creditor at present or within three years prior to the acceptance of the bankruptcy case by the court;
- the provision of services as a financial adviser or legal counsel to the debtor or a creditor within three years prior to the acceptance of the bankruptcy case by the court;
- any other circumstances which the court considers may affect the proper performance by the administrator of his duties.

These circumstances may also give rise to unsuitability to act as an administrator for a liquidation group, where one of the above circumstances is applicable to the government agencies which designate the members of the liquidation group; an intermediary agency, where one of the circumstances applies to the involved staff of the intermediary agency; or an individual professional, where one of the circumstances applies to him, where, in each case, this circumstance may affect their faithful performance of their duties as administrators.[38]

In addition, the following matters may be regarded as giving rise to a disqualifying interest where they are present in relation to the government agencies which designate the members of the liquidation group, the involved staff of the intermediary agency or the individual insolvency professional:[39]

34 Article 9(6), Appointment Regulations.
35 Article 24, paragraph 3, EBL 2006.
36 Finch (2009), pp. 192-3.
37 Article 23, Appointment Regulations.
38 Article 24(1), Appointment Regulations.
39 Article 24, Appointment Regulations.

- current service, or service within three years prior to the acceptance of the bankruptcy case by the court, as a director, supervisor or senior officer of the debtor or a creditor;
- a connection of marriage, or a parental relationship by blood, or a blood relationship within three generations, or a close relationship through marriage, with the controlling shareholder, director, supervisor or senior management officer of the debtor or a creditor;
- any other circumstance that the court considers may affect the proper performance by the administrator of his duties.

It may be that, following the commencement of the appointment process, an administrator discovers that it has an interest in the case. Should this be so, the administrator is required to submit an explanation of the circumstances and to ask that it be withdrawn from eligibility.[40] If the court believes that there is a conflict of interest, it should not appoint the individual or organization as administrator.

*Compilation of the Rosters*

The Appointment Regulations set out the conditions for the initial establishment of the rosters, and the subsequent addition and removal of persons and organizations to the roster. Although in some jurisdictions the process of qualification and authorization of administrators is undertaken by specialist bodies,[41] no such organizations have yet been established in China. It might have been considered too big a step to establish what is almost an entirely new profession and, at the same time, to establish new regulatory bodies to administer this profession. The role of authorizing administrators in China is therefore taken by the courts.

The Higher Courts were required to establish their own rosters and those of the intermediate courts in their jurisdiction, taking account of the number of bankruptcy cases in their jurisdiction and also on the number of eligible organizations, and professional persons.[42] In the case of a Higher Court which is not in a municipality administered directly by the central government,[43] it was necessary for the roster which was produced by such High Court to indicate the jurisdiction of which intermediate court the intermediary agencies and individual administrators would be subject.[44] It is notable that some areas of China have seen higher levels of market driven (as opposed to administratively controlled) insolvencies and, as a result, some areas will have higher numbers of persons and organizations with appropriate skills and qualifications. As a result, the courts were not required to

40 Article 25, Appointment Regulations.

41 UNCITRAL (2005), p. 175. See e.g. s. 391, Insolvency Act 1986 (UK) and the Insolvency Practitioners (Recognized Professional Bodies) Order 1986 (SI 1986/1764).

42 Article 2, Appointment Regulations.

43 Beijing, Chongqing, Shanghai and Tianjin.

44 Article 2, Appointment Regulations.

apply uniform criteria in assessing applications for designation as administrators, since they could take account of the actual circumstances of organizations and individuals in the region, in addition to their professional performances, abilities, professional levels, business size and experience of bankruptcy cases.[45]

The Chinese system bears some similarity to the system in the United States of America of appointment of trustees by the Attorney General. Like the Chinese courts, it is for the US Attorney General to decide the criteria for the appointment of trustees.[46] Relevant criteria used by the Attorney General include the qualification of the applicant; their honesty; impartiality; general competence and experience; and under Title 11, §322 the trustee must also qualify through the provision of a bond.[47] In some instances a trustee will be disqualified from appointment. Therefore we can identify in the US approach both positive factors in favour of qualification and negative factors which will either exclude a person from admission to the profession outright or which will restrict their involvement in a particular case.

The range of factors that have been taken into account in China do not however seem in all instances to be four square with the US approach. For example, in Beijing, Tang and Au[48] report that the selection panel allocated to each applicant a score out of 100 based on six criteria: the turnover of the business (20 points); the size of the firm by head count and by the number of qualified individuals (20 points); the level of practical experience of bankruptcy cases (30 points); the number of relevant liquidation reports issued (15 points); the number of relevant articles published (5 points); and the level of professional liability cover (10 points). It has been noted that the Beijing ranking may have placed insufficient emphasis on actual experience of bankruptcy cases.[49] To some extent the criteria established by the different courts may be regarded as transitional measures and, in time, it may be anticipated that the qualification requirements will change and that admission to the roster will require appropriate training and the acquisition of a qualification by means of a common entrance examination.[50]

The first rosters established by the courts had to be on public display for ten days to allow time for objection and for such objections to be reviewed by the courts.[51] If the court found an objection to be validly made it was required to remove an individual or organization from the roster. Following the period of public display the rosters were finalized, publicized and reported to the SPC.[52]

45 Article 10, Appointment Regulations.
46 For example, in the USA under US Code, Title 28, §586(d).
47 Blum (2006), p. 110.
48 Tang and Au (2007).
49 Booth (2008), p. 296.
50 Wang (2004).
51 Article 11, Appointment Regulations.
52 Article 12, Appointment Regulations.

A person or organization who wishes to be designated as an administrator must submit an application for review and approval by the local court with control of the roster.[53] Such an application must be supported by, *inter alia*, relevant licences and certificates and evidence of their business performance.[54] An organization who wishes to submit an application to a court in another locality may do so only where their application is submitted by through a branch agency that they have in the locality concerned.[55]

If a high court was unable to finish producing its full roster at once, the high court would be able to compile the roster in several stages, adding the organizations and individuals which have been qualified to the roster according to local circumstances.[56]

The roster may be adjusted by the court where necessary on account of the circumstances of bankruptcy case acceptances, the performances by administrators of their duties and changes in the qualifications of administrators.[57] The main circumstances in which adjustments to the roster are likely to be made are where an individual or organization that has been designated as administrator becomes ineligible through the disqualifying events noted above.[58]

*Appointment Process*

The normal rule is that a court, in accepting a bankruptcy case, will appoint an administrator drawn from the local roster.[59] As noted above, it is envisaged that the administrator who is appointed will be an organization,[60] rather than an individual, except where the case is relatively simple, in terms of the issues arising and where the estate is not dispersed.[61]

The preference is for the selection to be by random methods, such as the drawing of lots or the use of a 'cab rank' system, where a waiting list is maintained and the administrator to be appointed is taken from the top of the list.[62] Although these random means of appointment reduce the possibility of corruption and cronyism in appointments, it is notable that they may give rise to difficulties where e.g. an administrator that is appointed to a case is located in a different city far from the one where the administrator is based. This means of appointment also does not

53 Article 4, Appointment Regulations.

54 The information that must be submitted by persons and institutions intending to apply to act as an administrator are set out in Articles 6 to 8 of the Regulations.

55 Article 4, second paragraph, Appointment Regulations.

56 Article 13, Appointment Regulations.

57 Article 14, Appointment Regulations.

58 Article 14, second paragraph, Appointment Regulations.

59 Articles 16 and 17, Appointment Regulations.

60 Article 16, Appointment Regulations.

61 Article 17, Appointment Regulations.

62 Article 20, Appointment Regulations.

enable advantage to be taken of particular expertise that may make an individual or firm the most suitable for the case in hand.[63] In addition, some firms may be deterred from seeking work as administrators where the waiting list is long and the likelihood is that they will be appointed insufficiently frequently for this line of work to be worth their while.

Although the normal rule is for a random appointment from the local roster, in important or complex cases it may be necessary to cast the net more widely so that an administrator of appropriate experience and expertise can be appointed. Accordingly, it is provided that in a bankruptcy case which involves a financial institution, such as a commercial bank, a securities house, or insurance company; or a case that has major nationwide influence; or involves complex legal relationships; or a bankruptcy estate which is geographically dispersed, an appointment may be made from another roster in the same region or from a roster compiled by a court in another locality. In such cases, rather than the normal random mode of appointment, the court may instead make a public announcement, or hold a competition among organizations listed in the rosters of various regions.[64] A limit of three competing organizations will normally be set.[65] The administrator will be appointed from those competing by a selection panel, taking account of the professional standards, experience and size of the organizations and the initial offers of these organizations.[66] The panel must make a selection by majority verdict[67] and must identify one or two organizations that may act as a replacement administrator, should this become necessary.[68]

In the case of the insolvency of a financial institution such as a commercial bank, a securities company, or an insurance company, an additional administrator may be appointed from the roster upon the recommendation of the Financial Supervisory and Administrative Institutes.[69]

The court, in making an administrator appointment, should make its decision in writing and should provide a copy of this decision to the administrator; the person who initiated the bankruptcy application; the debtor; and the debtor's registered office.[70] Any materials produced by the court in making the appointment should be retained in the files concerning the bankruptcy case and the creditors' meeting or creditors' committee must be given access to the materials.[71]

63 Booth (2008), p. 296.
64 Article 21, Appointment Regulations.
65 Article 21, Appointment Regulations.
66 Article 21, third sentence, Appointment Regulations.
67 Article 21, third sentence, Appointment Regulations.
68 Article 21, fourth sentence, Appointment Regulations.
69 Article 22, Appointment Regulations.
70 Article 27, Appointment Regulations.
71 Article 30, Appointment Regulations.

A person or organization which is appointed as administrator should not normally refuse the appointment,[72] which should prevent unpopular cases from being declined. It is, however, an expectation that may operate a little harshly, given the random nature of many appointments, the onerous level of obligations that acting as an administrator will bring and the limited scope for resignation.[73] The administrator should also not in any way delegate its duties wholly or partly onto another social intermediary organization or individual.[74]

Upon being notified of its appointment, the administrator will have a seal carved for use in relation to relevant bankruptcy matters.[75] Upon the conclusion of the bankruptcy case the seal must be destroyed.

*Replacement of the Administrator*

The administrator may be replaced by the court upon the application of the creditors' committee, or upon the emergence of circumstances which affect the administrator's qualification. The administrator may also be replaced upon his resignation. In any case where the court decides to replace an administrator it must serve a written decision on the former administrator, the replacement administrator, the person who initiated the bankruptcy proceedings, the debtor and the debtor's registered office.[76] In addition, the replacement must be publicly notified.

The creditors' meeting is entitled to request the replacement of the administrator appointed by the court where the meeting considers that the administrator cannot perform its functions in an impartial way, or that it is not capable of performing its functions or duties.[77] To make such a request, the meeting must pass a resolution and submit an application to the court in writing.[78] The court must then notify the administrator to produce a written explanation.[79] The court must make a decision within ten days of receiving the explanation, although the Regulations do not specify a period within which the written explanation must be provided. If the court finds the reasons for the objection by the creditors' meeting to be untenable, it should, within ten days of receiving the administrator's explanation, dismiss the application.[80] The court should replace the administrator where it considers that the reasons for the application are tenable.[81]

---

72 Article 28, first sentence, Appointment Regulations.

73 See Articles 35 and 36, Appointment Regulations, discussed below.

74 Article 28, second sentence, Appointment Regulations.

75 Article 29, Appointment Regulations.

76 Article 38, Appointment Regulations.

77 Article 22, EBL 2006.

78 Article 31, Appointment Regulations.

79 Article 31, second sentence, Appointment Regulations.

80 Article 32, Appointment Regulations.

81 Article 32, second sentence, Appointment Regulations.

The court may replace the administrator upon its own initiative or upon an application by the creditors' committee where specified circumstances emerge. The following circumstances can result in the replacement of an organization which has been appointed as administrator:[82]

- the revocation or cancellation of the licence of the organization to practice, or of its business licence;
- circumstances that may give rise to the dissolution of the organization, or signs that the organization has become bankrupt, or that it has lost its capability to assume risks and liabilities;
- a conflict of interest;
- damage to the interests of creditors caused by deliberate or gross errors in the performance of the administrator's duties;
- investigation of the administrator by a relevant department for involvement in a significant debt dispute or an alleged violation of the law.

These circumstances also apply to the members of liquidation groups.

The following circumstances can result in the replacement of an individual who has been appointed as administrator, relating to their suitability, including their capability of meeting any liabilities that may arise as a result of their conduct:[83]

- his qualification to practice being revoked or cancelled;
- a conflict of interest;
- damage to the interests of creditors caused by deliberate or gross errors in the performance of the administrator's duties;
- the disappearance of the administrator;
- the death of the administrator;
- the administrator becoming incapable of meeting civil action liabilities;
- the expiry of the administrator's professional liability insurance;
- an inability for the administrator to perform his functions due to health reasons;
- investigation of the administrator by a relevant department for involvement in a significant debt dispute or an alleged violation of the law.

These circumstances are also applicable to involved staff of organizations and involved staff of members of liquidation groups.[84]

An administrator may resign from office where he has legitimate reason for doing so. In determining whether there is good reason for the resignation, the court will take account of the presence of circumstances noted above as enabling the

82 Article 33, Appointment Regulations.

83 Article 34, Appointment Regulations.

84 Article 34, Appointment Regulations.

administrator to be removed.[85] In the absence of such reason, the court will refuse his application,[86] however an administrator who is denied permission but insists on resigning and ceases to carry out his duties must naturally also be replaced.[87] A decision to ignore the court's refusal of permission should not be taken lightly, as the administrator may be liable to a fine.[88]

Where an administrator is to be replaced he will be subject to some ongoing duties. Firstly, he must, upon receiving notification of the court's decision, take steps to promptly transfer to his replacement any documentation and properties, together with the seal created for use in relation to the bankruptcy case and a report of progress to date.[89] The transfer process will be supervised by the court. If the administrator fails to carry out the transfer he may be liable to a fine.[90] In the event that the administrator is unable to effect the transfer the onus will be on his replacement to take control of the documents, properties etc. Secondly, the outgoing administrator must be ready at all times to answer the questions of the replacement administrator, the creditors' meetings and the court as to the performance of his duties.

In the event of replacement of the administrator the court will determine the level of remuneration due to both the outgoing and incoming administrators.[91]

### *Punishment*

As noted in the previous section, a fine may be imposed where an administrator ceases to carry out his duties and does not have permission to do so, or if he fails to transfer documents and properties to his successor as required. If a fine is imposed, an organization will be fined an amount between RMB 50,000 to RMB 200,000, while an individual may be fined an amount between RMB 10,000 and RMB 50,000. If the administrator refuses to accept the decision imposing a fine the court will refer the matter to a higher court for reconsideration.[92]

An administrator who resigns without permission, who fails to transfer the documents and so on to his replacement or who refuses an appointment as administrator without good reason may be suspended from the roster of those eligible for appointment for a period between one to three years or he may be removed from the roster permanently.[93]

---

85 Article 35, Appointment Regulations.

86 Article 35, Appointment Regulations.

87 Article 36, Appointment Regulations.

88 Article 39, Appointment Regulations; Article 130, EBL 2006.

89 Article 37, Appointment Regulations.

90 Article 39, Appointment Regulations; Article 130, EBL 2006.

91 Article 16, Remuneration Regulations. The total remuneration payable may not exceed the limits set out under Article 2 of these Regulations, discussed below.

92 Article 40, Appointment Regulations.

93 Article 39, second paragraph, Appointment Regulations.

## Administrator Remuneration

The establishment of an appropriate level of remuneration for administrators will be essential if appropriate firms and individuals are to be attracted to this new line of work, in light of its onerous responsibilities, attendant workload and the level of expertise required.[94] However, an excessive level of remuneration is likely to give rise to significant dissatisfaction among creditors, in view of the paucity of assets available in a typical bankruptcy case. Detailed provisions regarding the payment of remuneration are set out in the 'Regulations of the Supreme People's Court on the Determination of Remuneration for Administrators in the Hearing of Enterprise Bankruptcy Cases',[95] 'Remuneration Regulations', which were also passed by the SPC on 4 April 2007 and promulgated on 12 April 2007. Like the Appointment Regulations they came into force on 1 June 2007, on the same day as the EBL 2006. The stated aim of these Regulations is to ensure the just and effective hearing of bankruptcy cases and to normalize the work of the courts in determining the remuneration of administrators.

The Regulations set out the basis for the determination by the courts of the remuneration payable to administrators in carrying out the powers and duties that are set out in Article 25 of the EBL 2006. See further pp. 102-112 as to the extent of these powers and duties.[96]

### *Initial Identification of the Level of Remuneration*

The starting point in determining the level of remuneration payable will be the value of the debtor's estate, although, in cases where the administrator has been appointed by a competitive process, as discussed above, some adjustment may be made in light of the offer made by the administrator. The court is required to make an estimate of the value of the estate and the workload of the administrator and to make a preliminary scheme for the payment of the administrator (notified to the administrator in writing within three days and reported at the first creditors' meeting). This scheme may be adjusted where the creditors' meeting raises objections which are upheld, or where it proves necessary in the circumstances of the case. See further pp. 128-9 below. The remuneration which is ultimately agreed will be included in the plan for the distribution of the bankruptcy estate or, in reorganization proceedings, in the draft reorganization plan or draft settlement plan.[97]

The remuneration will be a ratio of the value of the estate, declining as the estate increases in value. The value of any collateral that is the subject of security

94 Shi (2007).

95 An English language translation of the Remuneration Regulations is available at Wang (2009b).

96 Article 1, Remuneration Regulations.

97 Article 10, Remuneration Regulations.

held by a secured creditor is not to be included in the calculation of the value of the estate. The ratios, set out Article 2 are as follows. If the value of the estate is:

- less than RMB 1 million, a ratio of 12 per cent or less will apply;
- RMB 1 million or more but less than RMB 5 million, a ratio of not more than 10 per cent will apply;
- RMB 5 million or more but less than RMB 10 million, a ratio of not more than 8 per cent will apply;
- RMB 10 million or more but less than RMB 50 million, a ratio of not more than 6 per cent will apply;
- RMB 50 million or more but less than RMB 100 million, a ratio of not more than 3 per cent will apply;
- RMB 100 million or more but less than RMB 500 million, a ratio of not more than 1 per cent will apply;
- RMB 500 million or more, a ratio of no more than 0.5 per cent will apply.

In recognition of likely differences in local economies it is possible for a higher court to make some adjustment to the ratios that are payable, taking account of local circumstances.[98] Where account is taken of an offer submitted by the administrator in a competitive appointment process, the remuneration cannot exceed these ratios.[99]

The calculation of the remuneration by reference to the size of the estate is perhaps surprising, since it may discourage an administrator from making full efforts to maximize the value obtained from the estate. It is also a rule that may operate harshly where the case is one of some complexity, since an administrator will inevitably have to spend more time on such a case than in a case involving an estate of equivalent value but straightforward issues. However, as discussed below, the Regulations also contain provision for an adjustment to be made to the amounts payable, in light of the circumstances of the case, which may mitigate any unfairness. The main alternative means of calculating the remuneration payable might have been a system based on the amount of time spent on a case. However such a system might have encouraged administrators to prolong proceedings in order to maximize the fees that they might claim,[100] so the motivation behind the Chinese use of ratios might have been to encourage efficiency.

98 Article 2, Remuneration Regulations.

99 Article 5, Remuneration Regulations.

100 See e.g. Finch (2009), p. 284, noting criticisms of lawyers' costs under the United States system.

*Adjustment of the Level of Remuneration*

The level of remuneration payable to the administrator may be adjusted by the court, either following an objection by creditors or, in light of the circumstances of the case.

*Objection by creditors* The level of remuneration payable to the administrator will come to the attention of creditors at the first creditors' meeting,[101] as a result of which it may be disputed. However creditors do not have the final say in the matter. In the event that the creditors' meeting objects to the remuneration payable to the administrator,[102] a request may be made to the court in writing, enclosing a resolution of the meeting. Upon receiving such an objection the court must, within three days, notify the administrator, who must, within a further three days, produce an explanation in writing. The court may hold a hearing to ascertain the views of the objecting creditors and the administrator before deciding whether to adjust the level of remuneration payable.

An adjustment may also be made in the event of objections by creditors to the administrator's remuneration being raised at a meeting between creditors and the administrator. In this event, the matter may be subject to negotiation.[103] If a consensus of opinion is reached, the court should be notified in writing, and a copy of the resolution made by the creditors' meeting should be provided. The court may then uphold the adjustment, provided that it does not contravene the terms of the law and that it does not harm the legitimate interests of others.

*Adjustment by the court in light of the circumstances* The level of remuneration initially determined by the court may prove to be inadequate. It may be adjusted by the court in light of the circumstance of the case and the performance by the administrator of his duties. In considering whether to make an adjustment, account will be taken of:

- the complexity of the case;
- the level of diligence with which the administrator has carried out his duties;
- the achievements of the administrator in reorganizing the company and settling claims;
- the risks and responsibilities borne by the administrator;
- the average disposable income and cost of living for residents of the place of residence of the debtor;
- any other circumstances that are relevant to the appropriate level of remuneration.

101 Article 6, Remuneration Regulations.
102 Article 17, Remuneration Regulations.
103 Article 7, Remuneration Regulations.

Such an adjustment may mitigate any harshness caused by the initial assessment of the level of remuneration in accordance with the ratios set out above.

*Payment of Remuneration*

The administrator's remuneration may be paid as a lump sum or in instalments, depending on what is appropriate in the circumstances.[104] The remuneration is payable from the debtor's estate in priority.[105]

In order to draw his remuneration, the administrator must submit a request in writing to the court, setting out an account of the debtor's estate from which remuneration may be drawn, the amount requested, when the administrator wishes for it to be paid and the duties that he has fulfilled.[106] Upon receipt of such a request the court shall, within ten days, determine the amount of remuneration to be paid.

In the event that the administrator chooses to hire another agency or professional to assist with the administration of the case, the remuneration that is due to this agent will be payable from the administrator's remuneration.[107] A similar rule applies in relation to the hiring of assistance by a liquidation group. In addition, the Regulations provide that working personnel sent by government departments to participate in the work of the liquidation group are not to receive compensation for doing so. In the case of other institutions or personnel, the level of remuneration payable will depend on the duties that they undertake.[108] The Regulations do not address the hiring of agents by individual administrators, presumably because the cases that they will be handling are regarded as sufficiently straightforward that agents will not need to be hired. It follows that, where an individual administrator chooses to engage an agent to assist with the case, he must fund this from his own remuneration.

If the administrator has been involved in the preservation, realization and delivery of collateral, they may claim compensation from the secured creditor.[109] In the event that no agreement can be reached between the secured creditor and the administrator regarding the level of remuneration, the court will determine the level of remuneration, taking account of the factors set out in Article 2 payable up to a maximum of 10 per cent more than the limits set out in that Article.

*Insufficiency of Assets*

In the event that the estate is of insufficient value for the payment of the administrator's remuneration the administrator must apply to the court for the

104 Article 3, Remuneration Regulations.
105 Article 12, Remuneration Regulations.
106 Article 11, Remuneration Regulations.
107 Article 14, Remuneration Regulations.
108 Article 15, Remuneration Regulations.
109 Article 13, Remuneration Regulations.

bankruptcy proceedings to be terminated. Such a termination could potentially enable a fraudulent case to be closed without consequence and without the recovery of assets which have been concealed.[110] However, the Regulations provide that the case may continue if an interested party, such as a creditor or a financier of the debtor is willing to pay the remuneration and expenses.[111] Where a third party advances funds for the remuneration of the administrator, these sums are payable as bankruptcy expenses.

## Conclusion

The Appointment Regulations may to a large extent be regarded as a transitional measure while the profession of administrator is still at an early stage of development. There will be a steep learning curve for many and it will be important for adequate training to be provided. Ultimately it may be anticipated that this profession will evolve to the extent that admission to the profession will require that a licence be obtained and that entry to the profession will be by means of a uniform examination.

## References

Blum, B.A. (2006), *Bankruptcy and Debtor/Creditor Examples and Explanations* 4th edn (New York: Aspen).

Booth, C.D. (2008), 'The 2006 PRC Enterprise Bankruptcy Law: the Wait is Finally Over' 20 *Singapore Academy Law Journal* 275.

Finch, V. (2009), *Corporate Insolvency Law Perspectives and Principles* 2nd edn (Cambridge: Cambridge University Press).

Li, S. (2001), 'Bankruptcy Law in China: Lessons of the Past Twelve Years' 5(1) *Winter Harvard Asia Quarterly* <http://www.asiaquarterly.com/content/view/95/40/>, last accessed 8 May 2009.

Paulus, C. (1998), 'The New German Insolvency Code' 33 *Texas International Law Journal* 141.

Shi, J. (2007), 'Twelve Years to Sharpen One Sword: the 2006 Enterprise Bankruptcy Law and China's Transition to a Market Economy' 16 *Norton Journal of Bankruptcy Law and Practice* 645.

Tang, A. and Au, P. (2007), 'China's Enterprise Bankruptcy Law: the Central Government's New Regulations on Bankruptcy Administrators' available at <http://www.hkicpa.org.hk/-APLUS/0711/p48_50.pdf>, last accessed 27 May 2009.

110 Shi (2007).

111 Article 12, Remuneration Regulations.

UNCITRAL (2005), 'Legislative Guide on Insolvency Law', <http://www.uncitral.org/-pdf/english/-texts/insolven/05-80722_Ebook.pdf>, last accessed 27 May 2009.

Wang, T. (2009a), 'Regulations of the Supreme People's Court on the Appointment of Administrators for Hearings in Cases of Enterprise Bankruptcy' 42 *Chinese Law and Government* 85.

Wang, T. (2009b), 'Regulations of the Supreme People's Court on the Determination of Compensation for Administrators in the Hearing of Enterprise Bankruptcy Cases' 42 *Chinese Law and Government* 94.

Wang, W. (2004), 'Administrator in New Bankruptcy Law of China', available from <http://www.iiiglobal.org/component/jdownloads/?task=viewcategory&catid=148>, last accessed 27 May 2009.

Zhang, H. (2009), 'A Notable Feature of China's New Bankruptcy Law: Administrator' 6 *International Corporate Rescue* 98.

# Chapter 7
# Bankruptcy Estate

Jianhua Xiao

The bankruptcy law system has as an aim the fair of distribution of the debtor's estate in liquidation.[1] The range of property that can be included in the estate and used for distribution in liquidation directly affects the entitlements of bankruptcy creditors. Hence, the question of how to correctly define the estate and determine the scope of the property of the insolvent enterprise is of very important significance for protecting the legitimate rights and interests of creditors.

## Overview of the Estate

### *Concept of the Estate*

The debtor's 'estate' is comprised of the property and the property rights enjoyed, operated or managed by the insolvent enterprise. The disposal of the estate by the bankruptcy administrator enables a distribution to be made in liquidation.

The concept of the estate may be considered from two aspects, according to its formal meaning and its substantive meaning.[2] In its formal meaning, the estate is the property of the bankrupt which is used for liquidation and the repayment of debts in bankruptcy proceedings. This meaning focuses on the estate as a concept within the distribution procedure and the direction of property. In its substantive meaning, the term 'estate' refers to the whole property of the bankrupt owned by the bankrupt, available for liquidation and repayment in bankruptcy at the declaration or application for bankruptcy and before the conclusion of bankruptcy proceedings. This meaning focuses on the scope and substance of the estate, its composition and the source of the property. Hence, generally speaking, the formal meaning is concerned with the concept of the estate while the estate in its substantive meaning is concerned with scope of the estate and its composition.

*Estate and bankruptcy estate* The notion of the 'estate' is mainly a concept derived from Anglo-American legal systems. For example, Section 541 of the Bankruptcy Code of the United States provides that the submission of the bankruptcy application will result in the automatic formation of the estate. In

1 Article 1, EBL 2006.
2 Wang (2004), pp. 178-9.

cases under Chapter VII of the US Bankruptcy Code, the estate is collected and sold by the trustee; and the proceeds from sale of the estate will be distributed to creditors consequently, according to their entitlements.[3] In continental law systems, the bankruptcy estate is further divided by scholars into the statutory estate, the existing estate and the distribution estate. The 'statutory estate' refers to the consortium of all the properties of bankruptcy properties, as specified in the bankruptcy law. The concept of the 'statutory estate' in theory underpins the duties of the bankruptcy administrator to occupy, control and manage the bankruptcy properties. In carrying out these duties, the bankruptcy administrator shall exercise rights including revocation rights and rights of claims *in rem*, and he will reclaim the properties of the statutory estate and attribute such properties to the bankruptcy estate. Similarly we may note Article 35 of German Bankruptcy Law,[4] which provides that: 'the assets involved in the bankruptcy properties consist of all the assets owned by the debtor at the commencement of bankruptcy proceedings and acquired during bankruptcy proceedings'. The 'existing estate' is comprised of the properties actually managed by the bankruptcy administrator, that is, the properties falling under the 'general occupation system' aimed at protecting the integrity and the security of the bankruptcy estate with the effect of preservation. The 'statutory estate' and 'existing estate' may not overlap entirely and the task of the bankruptcy administrator is to fill up the gap. For instance, disparities will arise if properties which should form part of the bankruptcy estate are transferred to a third party due to the fraud of the bankrupt; or if there are properties that should be attributed to a third party which are mixed with the bankruptcy estate. In the former case, the bankruptcy administrator shall exercise the right of veto to make the estate appreciate in value, because otherwise the existing estate is smaller than the statutory estate; and in the latter case, since the existing estate exceeds the statutory estate, such property shall be recovered by the real owner to reduce the bankruptcy estate. In addition, the exercise by a guaranteed party of exclusion rights or set off rights will also result in a change to the existing estate. The 'distribution estate' is the bankruptcy estate composed of the properties that are available for distribution to general creditors by the bankruptcy administrator after the settlement of debts holding priority. This is the last representation in procedure of the bankruptcy estate, and the distribution estate is certainly smaller than the statutory estate in scope.[5]

The new Chinese Enterprise Bankruptcy Law 2006, hereafter 'EBL 2006', adopts the concept of the 'estate'. Paragraph 2 of Article 107 of this law provides that the debtor is termed the 'bankrupt' upon a declaration of bankruptcy, and the bankrupt's property becomes the bankruptcy estate. Article 30 of the EBL 2006 provides that the debtor's property includes the entire property of the debtor at the acceptance of the application for bankruptcy together with the property acquired

3 Ji (2006), p. 193.

4 *Insolvenzordnung* of 1 January 1999.

5 Ding (2006), pp. 221-2.

by the debtor from the time of acceptance of the bankruptcy application to the conclusion of the bankruptcy proceedings.

*Nature of the Estate*

There are two theoretical doctrines regarding the nature of the estate. One is the doctrine of the 'object of rights', which holds that the estate is the object of rights, and its owner is the bankrupt. The other is the doctrine of 'subject of rights', which holds that in bankruptcy proceedings, the estate itself constitutes the subject of rights, having the nature of a judicial person and the qualifications of a civil subject. In the legal provisions noted above, the new Chinese bankruptcy law adopts the doctrine of object of rights.

*Legal Features of the Estate*

The issue of how to determine the property of the bankrupt at the declaration of bankruptcy is a core issue in the bankruptcy law. The accurate demarcation of the legal features of the estate is the premise and foundation for an accurate understanding of the scope of the estate. More specifically, the estate is comprised of the following four legal features:

1. The estate is comprised of the property and property rights enjoyed or managed by the insolvent enterprise. Firstly, the estate includes property in a broad sense, both tangible property and intangible property, as well as property rights. However, some personal rights, for example the right of name and the right of reputation, may not be separable from the debtor, and have no independent property content in themselves, so they do not belong to the estate. Secondly, since the estate is limited to the property owned or managed by the bankrupt, the property that is not owned or managed by the bankrupt shall not be treated as the estate but my be recalled by its right holder, such as the things prepared on a commissioned basis, things deposited, subjects of consignment sales, and borrowings of others.
2. The paramount purpose for establishment of the estate by law is to satisfy and protect the rights of distribution among bankruptcy creditors to the maximum extent. The special use of the estate is therefore for distribution in bankruptcy. It is notable that the estate does not treat as equal all the properties enjoyed or managed by the bankrupt. According to legal provisions, certain properties enjoyed or managed by the bankrupt may not be used for general bankruptcy distribution, such as collateral of the bankrupt. Hence, only the property available for bankruptcy distribution is included in the estate, while the property of the bankrupt that may not be used for bankruptcy distribution according to law falls outside the estate. In addition, the estate is the property that can be realized,

and property that cannot be realized may not be taken as the estate for liquidation distribution.

3. The estate shall be managed and disposed of by the bankruptcy administrator. The administrator is independent of the bankruptcy creditors and the bankrupt, and is responsible only to the court; and the administrator does not exercise the right of management and disposal for his or her own interest but for the interest of all the creditors of bankruptcy, in the interests of the justness of bankruptcy liquidation.
4. The estate is dynamic in time, since the estate is not limited to the property of the debtor at the declaration of bankruptcy, but rather may include the property disposed by the debtor according to law within a certain period before the declaration of bankruptcy[6] and the property acquired from the declaration of bankruptcy to the conclusion of bankruptcy proceedings, and even the property discovered and recalled during the additional distribution period after the conclusion of bankruptcy proceedings. In consequence, the value of the estate is not limited to the total amount of property at the declaration of bankruptcy, and during the bankruptcy proceedings its value may vary for reasons such as a change of amount resulting from the liquidation of the accounts receivable of the bankrupt. A further aspect of its dynamism is that the form of the estate is not static but will vary with the progress of the liquidation. For instance, if the equities held by the bankrupt are converted to currency, the estate may change from a property right to tangible property.

## Composition of the Estate

In this section the legislative model chosen in respect of the composition of the estate will firstly be considered before attention will turn to the details of the composition. Here consideration will be given as to the time when the estate comes into being, in addition to the assets which come within the scope of the estate and those which do not. Particular attention will be paid to recovery rights, exclusion rights, recall rights and set-off rights.

### *Legislative Models of the Scope of Composition of the Estate*

To determine the scope of composition of the estate, two legislative models can be identified as having been adopted by legislatures in their bankruptcy laws: firstly, a 'fixed legislation' model and secondly an 'expansion legislation' model.

The 'fixed legislation' model takes as the estate all the property of the debtor at the declaration of bankruptcy, including rights to claim property that may be exercised in the future. The term 'fixed' indicates that when bankruptcy is

6 See further Chapter 8.

declared, the scope of the estate is determined. Japan, Germany, the United States and some other countries adopt this legislative model. For example, paragraph 1 of Article 6 of Japanese Bankruptcy Law provides that all the property attributed to the bankrupt when bankruptcy is declared is the bankruptcy estate and paragraph 2 thereof provides that rights of claim of the bankrupt to be exercised in the future for reasons existing before the declaration of bankruptcy belong to the estate.[7]

The 'expansion legislation' model means that the estate contains not only the property of the debtor at the time of declaration of bankruptcy but also the property acquired before the conclusion of bankruptcy proceedings, and the scope of the estate still expands after the declaration of bankruptcy. The UK, France and Taiwan adopt this legislative model. For instance, Article 82 of the bankruptcy law of Taiwan provides that the following property shall be the estate: (1) all the property of the bankrupt when bankruptcy is declared, and rights of claim for property to be exercised in the future; (2) the property acquired by the bankrupt from the declaration of bankruptcy to the conclusion of the bankruptcy proceedings. The rights which are personal to the bankrupt and the property prohibited from detainment do not belong to the estate.[8]

The fixed legislation model is arguably more rational in theory: firstly, the scope of property may be clear when bankruptcy is declared, which is conducive to the rapid progress of bankruptcy proceedings and the quick payment of the creditors; secondly, new property which is acquired by the bankrupt after the declaration of bankruptcy can be disposed of freely, which is conducive to the resumption of business as soon as possible in reorganization proceedings and the reduction of social pressure; and thirdly, property acquired before the declaration of bankruptcy can be used to liquidate the credit rights existing before the declaration of bankruptcy while the newly acquired property may be used to liquidate new credit rights, which is relatively fair. However, the disadvantage of the fixed legislation model, in failing to provide appropriate protection for creditors, is also very obvious. On one hand, if the new activities carried out by the bankrupt before the conclusion of the bankruptcy proceedings fail, a secondary bankruptcy may follow, which will severely affect the normal payment to the creditors; and on the other hand, the debtor may make use of the time gap to evade debts and even deceive the creditors. Therefore, in the interests of sound governance in China, the new Chinese bankruptcy law adopts the expansion legislation model so as to prevent bankruptcy fraud and safeguard the legitimate rights and interest of creditors.

### *Time Span of the Existence of the Estate*

The time span of the existence of the estate, when the property owned by the bankrupt will belong to the estate, is directly related to the progress of the insolvency proceedings under the legislation.

7 Wang (2004), p. 181.
8 Wang (2004), p. 182.

In determining the commencement time, countries which take the declaration of bankruptcy as the commencement of bankruptcy proceedings provide that the property of the bankrupt at the declaration of bankruptcy is the estate. In contrast, countries which take the application for bankruptcy or the acceptance of the case as the commencement of bankruptcy proceedings generally provide that the property of the bankrupt at the time of submission of the application for bankruptcy (or the acceptance of the case) belongs to the estate. The new Chinese bankruptcy law has adopted the former mode whereby the computation of the estate starts from the declaration of bankruptcy.

By determining the time at which the computation of the estate is to end, in the 'fixed legislation' model the times of commencement and ending of the computation of the estate are identical. In contrast, under the 'expansion legislation' model, the commencement time and the ending time will differ. Under the EBL 2006, the determination of the estate must end before the conclusion of the bankruptcy proceedings.[9] After the conclusion of the bankruptcy proceedings, the bankrupt enterprise will be dissolved.

*Scope of Composition of the Estate*

The EBL 2006 does not expressly address the scope of composition of the bankruptcy estate. Generally speaking, according to the legislations of other countries and Chinese judicial practice, the estate of an insolvent enterprise shall cover the following contents:

1. All the property owned and managed by the insolvent enterprise at the time of the bankruptcy declaration. All the rights enjoyed by the insolvent enterprise, and including the property of a state-owned enterprise granted the right of operation and management,[10] as at the time of the bankruptcy declaration fall into the estate. The properties generally fall into the following four categories:
    a. tangible properties, including plant, machines and equipment, transport tools, raw materials, products and office articles;
    b. intangible properties, including land use rights, patent rights, rights of trade mark, copyright, know-how and franchises;
    c. currency and marketable securities; and
    d. interests in investments, such as equities in other corporations, enjoyed by the insolvent enterprise.
2. Property acquired by the insolvent enterprise between the time of the declaration of bankruptcy until the conclusion of the bankruptcy

9 Article 30, EBL 2006.

10 The assets which are possessed by the SOEs are not owned by the SOEs. They belong to the state. They are managed by the SOEs under the authority of the state. See Article 82, General Principles of Civil Law 1986.

proceedings. In accordance with Article 18 of the EBL 2006, the administrator may conduct necessary civil activities, and he has the right to decide on the continued performance of any contract not yet performed by the insolvent enterprise. The property acquired by the administrator as a result of the continued performance of a contract can be regarded as the result of a capital appreciation of the corporate person in itself, which constitutes an integral part of the property of the corporate enterprise. The kind of properties belonging to the estate and falling within this category, include the following:

a. the property acquired from the bankruptcy distribution of a debtor of the insolvent enterprise, and the property returned to the insolvent enterprise by a property holder who possesses the property for a legal reason;
b. the property acquired from the continued performance of a contract that has not yet been carried out. Since the contract is a bilateral contract, the estate has a corresponding obligation while receiving payment; and the corresponding obligation is generally in the nature of equivalent consideration. Therefore, the newly acquired property should not be regarded as an increase in the value of property but as an increase of property in physical form. In terms of the physical form, it can be regarded as a proceed of the estate arising after the declaration of bankruptcy;
c. the proceeds from investments enjoyed by the insolvent enterprise, such as annual distributions of bonuses as per corporate shares and distributed profits from joint ventures;
d. the interest from the estate, such as rent and bank interest;
e. the revenue from continued business carried out during the insolvency proceedings. It shall be noted that after the declaration of bankruptcy, the insolvent enterprise may carry out necessary business activities in the interests of the creditors of the insolvent enterprise, and the added income of the business thereof shall be incorporated into the estate; and
f. the property acquired on account of other legal reasons, such as compensation acquired due to another's infringement of the patent rights of the insolvent enterprise.

3. Other property rights that should be exercised by the insolvent enterprise. Included in this category are the following:
   a. property rights that should be exercised by the insolvent enterprise, including mining rights, rights of occupation, mortgage rights and liens, apart from the above-mentioned ownership, rights of management and use rights;
   b. contractual credit rights that should be exercised by the insolvent enterprise, such as rights to claim for the payment of the price of goods delayed by sales customers, and liquidated damages due to a related breach of contract;

c. the rights attached to bills held by the insolvent enterprise, such as the right to claim for payment and rights of recourse;
d. the rights of the company as a shareholder in respect of any shares that it holds. The rights of shareholders mainly include dividend rights and voting rights;
e. the intellectual property rights enjoyed by the insolvent enterprise;
f. sums due from promoters, which they are liable to pay where the registered capital of the promoters of the insolvent enterprise is insufficient. The promoters are required to make up for this deficiency, and the part that is made up shall belong to the estate;
g. property obtained through recovery by execution for the insolvent enterprise;
h. where the insolvent enterprise acquires subrogation right by law, the credit rights enjoyed accordingly shall be counted in the estate;
i. credit rights which have not yet fallen due prior to the start of bankruptcy shall be regarded as due when bankruptcy is declared, and shall be counted in the estate, with undue interest excluded; and
j. mortgaged property, property subject to a lien or pledged property with the priority right of repayment given up by the creditors; or any mortgaged property, property subject to a lien or pledged property which remains after the repayment of the secured credits in priority shall be included in the estate.

### Bankruptcy Recovery Rights

Upon the declaration of the bankruptcy of the debtor, the administrator will take over its internal affairs and the estate.[11] The debtor will lose the right to manage and dispose of the property and it will be difficult for the debtor to engage in any act that prejudices the interest of the creditors of the estate. However, within a certain time before the commencement of bankruptcy proceedings, as the time of the bankruptcy declaration approaches, the debtor may be tempted to carry out an act prejudicing the interests of the creditors, such as a transfer of property without compensation or a transaction at an obviously unreasonable price. If the bankruptcy law does not provide for the invalidity of those acts by force of law, it will prejudice the protection of the credit rights.[12] Thus, in order to preserve and augment the bankruptcy estate to the maximum extent possible, the administrator has powers to recover property. These powers are considered further in Chapter 8.

Once a bankruptcy application is accepted by the court, the administrator is entitled to recover property of the debtor which has been pledged or which is

11 Wang (2007), pp. 71-2.
12 Li (2005), pp. 17-18.

subject to a lien by making payment in respect of the debts which are secured by the property under the pledge or lien, or by providing another security which is acceptable to the creditor. If the value of the property for the pledge or lien is less than the value of the secured claim, the amount of the payment or substitute security should refer to the market value of the property after the bankruptcy case has been accepted.[13]

## Recall Rights

In bankruptcy cases, the estate will include diverse property interests. Recall rights arise in respect of property managed in the name of the insolvent debtor but owned by another. Diversity arises due to the complexity of the occupation and use by the debtor of others' property and its economic dealings with others. Hence, the creditors enjoy different rights in the property under management by the insolvent debtor, and one of them is the recall right.

### *The Concept of the Recall Right*

Article 38 of the EBL 2006 provides that an owner of the property occupied by the debtor may recall his property from the administrator after the court has accepted the application for bankruptcy, unless otherwise specified by the Law. Neither the property involved in this recall right, nor that in the exclusion right, belongs to the estate. The Regulation on Several Issues Concerning Hearing Enterprise Bankruptcy Cases, which was issued by the Supreme People's Court in July 2002 (hereinafter referred to as 'Regulation 2002'), provides in Article 71 that some properties do not belong to the bankruptcy estate, such as property which is possessed by the debtor under legal reasons such as a borrowing or a leasing agreement, and property which is used as collateral to secure debts, and specific property like land which is only owned by the state. The parties who enjoy recall rights are entitled to claim the property back, as stipulated in Article 71.[14]

Recall rights and exclusion rights are different. The subject matter of the recall right belongs to the owner, while the subject matter of the exclusion right belongs to the debtor for the purpose of guaranteeing certain credits as collateral. The recall right holder enjoys priority based on his ownership, which confers the attribute of exclusion. The exclusion right holder is normally a secured creditor who enjoys priority over unsecured creditors subject to the property as collateral.[15]

---

13 Article 37, EBL 2006, Wang (2007), pp. 201-2.

14 Article 72, Regulation 2002.

15 Wang (2007), p. 203.

### *Legal Features of the Recall Right*

The recall right has three features: firstly, the person entitled to exercise the recall right is the title owner of the property; secondly, the person subject to the obligation is the actual occupier of the property, i.e., the insolvent debtor; and thirdly, the exercise of the recall right is preferential and exclusive in nature, whereby in a bankruptcy case, the owner can directly recall the property occupied by the debtor without resort to the bankruptcy liquidation proceedings.

The exercise of the recall right is subject to time restrictions. The recall right should be exercised after the acceptance of the bankruptcy case and before the bankruptcy declaration. If the recall right is not exercised before the distribution of the estate, this shall be regarded as a waiver of the recall right. Accordingly, if the recall right is exercised after the distribution of the estate, it will be without any legal effect.

The exercise of the recall right takes place separately from the bankruptcy proceedings and there is no need for the claimant to go through a litigation procedure (absent any dispute). However, the recall of the property should be conducted via the administrator and no property may be taken away from the insolvent enterprise without the permission of the administrator.

If the owner of the property recalls property, such as things made on a commissioned basis and deposited things, to which there exist corresponding obligations of payment, the properties concerned may be recalled only after the payment of the processing fees and the safekeeping fees to the administrator.

The exercise of the recall right is limited to the recall of the original things. If the original things have been sold by the bankrupt before the acceptance of the case, the owner may not ask for the recall of the price. In this circumstance, the recall right holder becomes an unsecured creditor who can only obtain recovery from the distribution of bankruptcy property. The sale or loss of the original things leads to the loss of the recall right and changes to the debt structure of the bankrupt. However, if the original thing is sold by the administrator after the bankruptcy declaration, the owner of the recall right has the right to request the administrator to return the price received and it is unnecessary for the creditor to present a claim for these sums as an unsecured creditor in the liquidation.

### *Property Scope of the Recall Right*

The right extends to properties occupied and used by the debtor on the basis of such legal relations as warehouse storage, safekeeping, contractual processing, commissioned transaction, sales on agency, borrowing, deposit and leasing. However, the properties in relation to which recall rights may be exercised are not limited to those mentioned above, and also cover property in respect of which the debtor has received full payment, but which has not been transferred to the buyer under Clause (5) of Article 71 of the 'Regulation 2002'. The rights extend also to property the ownership of which has not been acquired in the transaction, with ownership retained by the counterparty of the debtor as specified in Clause (7). Property which is owned by the state is not transferrable under Clause (8), nor, according to Clause (9) is property which is owned by the labour union of the bankrupt enterprise. All the properties above-mentioned are not part of the bankruptcy estate, and their title owners can exercise corresponding rights thereof.

The debtor may intend to buy some goods and the goods may have been dispatched by a seller under delivery to the debtor. At the time when the court files the bankruptcy application, if the debtor has not received the goods and has not paid the price in full yet, the seller is entitled to exercise the recall right in respect of the goods under delivery. If the administrator thinks that the goods under delivery are very useful for the continued operation or reorganization of the insolvent debtor, the administrator is allowed to make full payment and request the seller to convey the goods.[16]

### *Damage To and Loss of the Subject Matter of the Recall Right*

Damage to the subject matter of the recall right may, in different degrees, reduce the value of the subject matter, depending on the level of damage sustained. Where the damage to the subject matter of the recall right occurs before the bankruptcy declaration, the right holder of the subject matter can participate in the bankruptcy proceedings as a creditor of bankrupt and may acquire compensation only based on the infringement or breach of contract by the debtor, reflecting the corresponding reduction of the value of the subject matter after exercise of the recall right. Where the damage to the subject matter of the recall right occurs after the bankruptcy declaration, the right holder shall acquire the full amount of compensation from the estate for the corresponding reduction of the subject matter upon payment of bankruptcy fees after the exercise of the recall right.

Where the subject matter of the recall right is lost, the right holder can not exercise the recall right but may instead claim compensation for the value of the subject matter. Where the loss of the subject matter occurs before the bankruptcy declaration, the right to claim compensation is exercised by the right holder who participates in bankruptcy proceedings as a creditor based on a tort claim or claim for breach of contract. Where the loss of the subject matter occurs after the bankruptcy declaration, the right holder shall acquire the full amount of compensation for the value of the subject matter from the estate after payment of bankruptcy fee.

Similar considerations to those applicable where the property is lost apply where the subject matter of the recall right has been destroyed.

16 Article 39, EBL 2006; Wang (2007), p. 205.

### *Subject Matter of the Recall Right Transferred by the Debtor or the Administrator*

Where the debtor has transferred the subject matter of the recall right to a transferee, and the transferee has not paid the consideration due to the debtor as transferor, the holder of the recall right, may ask the transferee to either pay the required consideration or to return the subject matter. Where the transferee has paid the consideration to the debtor or to the administrator, the right holder can only ask the administrator to return the amount of consideration for the subject matter. Where the amount of consideration paid no longer exists, if the transfer occurred before the bankruptcy declaration, the right holder shall participate in the distribution of the bankruptcy estate on the basis of a claim for the return of unjust enrichment and liquidated damages; and if the transfer occurs after the bankruptcy declaration, the right holder shall enjoy the right to claim for the full amount of liquidated damages after the payment of the bankruptcy fee as a debt of common interest.[17]

## Set Off Rights in Bankruptcy

Set off rights in bankruptcy arise where a bankruptcy creditor owes obligations to the bankrupt, where those obligations were incurred before the bankruptcy declaration, regardless of the categories of the debts and the time of expiration. Such rights are dealt with under Article 40 of the EBL 2006, which provides that a creditor who owes debts to the debtor, incurred before the acceptance of the filing of the bankruptcy petition, may request to the administrator that such debts are set off. Similar rights are common in other bankruptcy legislations around the world.[18]

### *Set Off Right of Bankruptcy and Set Off Right in Civil Law*

Compared with set off rights in civil law, the set off rights in bankruptcy have the following features:

1. The set off right in bankruptcy law may only be exercised by the bankruptcy creditor, while set off rights in civil law have no such restrictions, since both parties to the debts may make such claims. Such difference results from the features of the bankruptcy system itself.
2. The exercise of the set off right in bankruptcy is not restricted by the categories of debts and deadlines of performance thereof. In contrast, set off rights at civil law are conditioned on the subject matters of debts being

17 See p. 260 regarding debts of common interest.

18 See e.g. §553, US Code, Title 11; s. 553C Corporations Act 2001 (Australia); Insolvency Rules 1986, rr. 2.85 and 4.90. See generally Wood (2007).

of the same kind and both debts being due. Hence, debts of different kinds shall not set off against each other, and the debts that are not due shall not be set off. However, after the declaration of bankruptcy, all the debts shall be changed to monetary debts and treated as due.

3. Debts to which rights of set off are to apply in bankruptcy must be ones under which the bankruptcy creditor became liable to the bankrupt before the declaration of bankruptcy. Civil law does not impose equivalent restrictions on the time of formation of the debts that are eligible for set off.

*Exercise and Effect of Set off Rights*

The creditors of the bankrupt shall express to the administrator their intention to exercise set off rights.[19] Where the bankruptcy administrator acknowledges the claim of the creditor for set off, the effect of set off occurs. If the bankruptcy administrator holds an objection to the exercise of set off by the creditor, such objection shall be resolved by litigation. Whether the set off right shall be exercised or not is decided by the creditor; and if the creditor does not exercise the set off right, the bankruptcy administrator shall not automatically set off the debts and credits.

In terms of the period for the exercise of the set off right, paragraph 1 of Article 40 of the EBL 2006 provides that if the creditor owes debts to the debtor before the acceptance of the application for bankruptcy, the creditor may request to set off such debts through the administrator, Hence, the bankruptcy creditor may exercise the set off right from the time of the bankruptcy declaration until the conclusion of bankruptcy proceedings. Since the bankruptcy creditor can only present a claim for set off to the bankruptcy administrator, the exercise of the set off right can be made only after the appointment of the bankruptcy administrator.

*Circumstances Where No Set off Right in Bankruptcy Applies*[20]

The sole aim of the set off right in civil law is to avoid an increase of expense due to repeated performance, and there is no issue of unfairness to third parties, and thus no restrictions are imposed regarding the time of establishment of the credit rights. However, different considerations apply in relation to the set off rights in bankruptcy proceedings, since allowing set off means full recovery for the creditor and prohibiting set off means that the creditor will only receive proportionate payment, in accordance with the amounts payable under the bankruptcy proceedings. Accordingly the existence of a right to set off makes a big difference to the entitlements of the holder of the set off right in bankruptcy, as compared with other creditors. Furthermore, when the debtor is in financial

19 Wang (2007), p. 221.
20 Wang (2007), pp. 227-32.

difficulties in most cases, the creditors will fight against each other to set off their claims in respect of the debtor as early as possible, or the debtors of the debtor will try to acquire the debts of the creditors at lower prices for the purpose of set off. Therefore, restrictions are necessary to maintain the fairness among creditors and the EBL 2006 specifically provides for the following three situations where bankruptcy set off does not apply.[21]

1. Where, after the acceptance of the bankruptcy petition, a debtor of the debtor acquires the claim of a third party against the debtor.
2. Where a creditor gets into debt with the debtor while knowing either the fact that the debtor cannot pay off its due debts or the fact of application for bankruptcy; unless the debts undertaken by the creditor were incurred in accordance with legal provisions, or unless they occurred a year before the application for bankruptcy.
3. Where a debtor of the debtor who has known of the fact that the debtor cannot pay off the debts due, or the fact of application for bankruptcy, acquires a claim against the debtor; except where the claim was acquired by the debtor of the debtor in accordance with a legal provision or unless it was incurred for any cause which occurred a year before the application for bankruptcy.

## Conclusion

The provisions regarding the bankruptcy estate may be regarded as a great achievement in improving upon the old legislation. The new law stipulates the scope of the bankruptcy estate, bankruptcy recovery rights, recall rights and set off rights together with transaction avoidance provisions which will be fully discussed in the following Chapter 8. The new law has established an effective framework in relation to the bankruptcy estate which is important for the administrator, enabling him to collect, manage and dispose of the property, and is crucial for the maximization of the distributions to creditors. The EBL 1986 not only emphasizes the protection of creditors' interests as a whole, but also pays attention to fair recovery of individual creditor's claims and the rights of property owners.

## References

Booth, C. (2008), 'The 2006 PRC Enterprise Bankruptcy Law: The Wait Is Finally Over' 20 *Singapore Academy of Law Journal* 275.

Bufford, S. (2007), 'The New Chinese Bankruptcy Law: Text and Limited Comparative Analysis' 16 *Norton Journal of Bankruptcy Law and Practice* 697.

21 Article 40, EBL 2006.

Ding, J. (2006), 'On Nature of Bankruptcy Property' *Jiangxi Social Sciences* 221.

Epstein, D. et al. (2003), *Bankruptcy Law of the United States*, translated by Han Changyin et al. (Beijing: CUPSL Press).

Ji, Z. (2006), *Comments on Selected Cases of US Bankruptcy Law* (Beijing: University of International Business and Economics Press) (in Chinese).

Li, S. (2005), 'The Enactment of New Bankruptcy Law and the Chinese Credit Culture and System' *Jurists Review* 12 (in Chinese).

Li, S. and He, D. (2004), 'International Comparison on Several Major Issues Concerning Legislation of Bankruptcy Law' *Tribune of Political Science and Law* 59.

Shi, J. (2007), 'Twelve Years to Sharpen One Sword: The 2006 Enterprise Bankruptcy Law and China's Transition to a Market Economy' 16 *Norton Journal of Bankruptcy Law and Practice* 645.

Wang, X. (2004), *Bankruptcy Law Science* (Beijing: Renmin University of China) (in Chinese).

Wang, X. (2007), *Bankruptcy Law*, 2nd edn (Beijing: Renmin University Press) (in Chinese).

Wood, P. (2007), *Set-off and Netting, Derivatives, Clearing Systems* (London: Sweet & Maxwell).

Xie, J. (2005), *Chinese Bankruptcy Law System* (Beijing: People's Court Press) (in Chinese).

# Chapter 8
# Transaction Avoidance

Rebecca Parry

## Introduction

This chapter will consider the transaction avoidance laws contained in the Enterprise Bankruptcy Law 2006, 'EBL 2006'. Such laws are a key feature of any effective system of bankruptcy laws,[1] since they may be used to maintain and enforce the schemes set out under bankruptcy laws for the distribution of the estate of the insolvent company. The Chinese legislation indicates that the debtor's estate is regarded as being comprised of 'any property belonging to the debtor when the case is accepted and any property subsequently acquired'.[2] However there is significant potential for this estate to have been badly depleted prior to, or following, the opening of the case, so that the administrator is left with little, if anything, for distribution to creditors.[3] The transaction avoidance laws, if properly enforceable, may enable the administrator to restore the estate to a value approaching that which it would have had if the transaction had not taken place.

There are two main forms of behaviour that can undermine the scheme set out in the legislation and which are commonly targeted by transaction avoidance provisions around the world. Firstly, the scarcity of assets of a struggling company presents incentives for company managers to devise their own scheme of distribution prior to the company entering insolvency proceedings, paying some creditors ahead of others, or granting security over previously unsecured debts. Secondly, there are incentives for company managers to remove assets from the estate entirely, by gifting, or selling for minimal value, the assets to relatives or associates. The integrity of bankruptcy proceedings therefore depends in part on the availability of robust laws for the avoidance of such abusive transactions that deplete the bankruptcy estate or which otherwise interfere with the entitlements of creditors, collectively or individually, under the insolvency legislation. Without such laws and their effective enforcement, companies can be left as empty shells

1 For example, in the UNCITRAL Legislative Guide to Insolvency Law it is stated that 'an insolvency law should include provisions that apply retroactively to and are designed to overturn transactions, involving the debtor or assets of the estate, and that have the effect of either reducing the value of the estate or upsetting the principle of equitable treatment of creditors': recommendation 87.

2 Article 30, EBL 2006.

3 Seligson (1967), p. 292.

and carefully designed frameworks of entitlements set out under the insolvency legislation can be significantly undermined. This chapter will briefly sketch the transaction avoidance laws that were applicable under previous Chinese law before concentrating on the provisions of the EBL 2006. It will examine each type of voidable transaction in turn, with some brief comparisons to provisions to be found in insolvency systems in other countries where appropriate.

## Position under Previous Law

Mechanisms to support the fair distribution of the assets of insolvent companies were an area in which the Chinese law was hitherto largely ineffective. The previous Enterprise Bankruptcy Law (For Trial Implementation), enacted in 1986, hereafter 'EBL 1986', and judicial interpretations had stipulated relevant provisions similar to transaction avoidance rules applicable in mature systems of insolvency laws to be found elsewhere in the world. Firstly, Article 12 of the EBL 1986 provided that after the bankruptcy case was accepted by the court, any payment made to a particular creditor or creditors would be null and void, except where this was necessary for the normal production and operations of the debtor. The equivalent of this provision in the EBL 2006 is discussed further below. Secondly, Article 35 of the EBL 1986, a provision which bears similarity to provisions of some civil law bankruptcy systems, was the most extensive transaction avoidance provision. Article 35 provided that certain categories of transaction would be null and void if they were entered into during a period that would be deemed to have begun six months prior to the acceptance of the bankruptcy case by the court and which would end upon the date that bankruptcy was declared. The transactions that fell under this provision were: (1) the concealment, secret distribution or transfer of property without compensation; (2) the sale of property at an abnormally depressed price; (3) the securing with property of claims that were previously unsecured; (4) the early repayment of claims that were not yet due; and (5) the abandonment of a claim of the enterprise's own. The liquidation group, which bore responsibility for administering the bankruptcy proceedings, would have the right to apply to the court to recover any property involved in such a transaction and the recovered sums would be added to the bankruptcy estate. A similar provision appears in the EBL 2006, as discussed below.

Although this system of transaction of avoidance laws bears similarity to the systems that are applicable in some highly evolved systems of insolvency laws,[4] they were not effective to restrict fraudulent and abusive behaviour. Rather, under the EBL 1986 much use was made of the bankruptcy proceedings as a method

4 In many jurisdictions, transaction avoidance laws have been fully developed in insolvency laws. For a discussion of the position in England, see Parry (2001). For a detailed discussion of the Australian provisions see Keay (1997).

for companies to evade payment of their liabilities.[5] The valuable assets of state owned enterprises, 'SOEs' were commonly transferred or sold at unreasonably low prices prior to the commencement of the liquidation procedure, and the SOEs often gave an unfair preference to some creditors. The prevention of a recurrence of such behaviour will be a key task for administrators under the EBL 2006.

*Overview of the Provision under the EBL 2006*

The EBL 2006 contains a significantly revised scheme of several transaction avoidance provisions, of a range similar to those that would be encountered in other jurisdictions. As discussed below, the influences of German law, Australian law and Italian law may perhaps be most clearly identified in these laws. This avoidance system has the potential to effectively prevent the directors and managers of the company from engaging in abusive behaviour, and it could have a positive impact in assisting the administrator to maintain the asset pool of the insolvent company for distribution under the new liquidation proceedings in a manner envisaged under the law.[6] Under the new law the administrator is empowered to petition the court for the nullity of transactions falling within four main categories: firstly, dispositions of property following the acceptance of the bankruptcy case by the court; secondly, certain transactions that took place within a year before the application for bankruptcy was accepted by the court; thirdly, unfair preferences; and fourthly, dishonest transactions, in relation to which the administrator enjoys his widest powers.

Further powers, which enable the administrator to recover amounts due from capital contributories and to recover inappropriate income from company directors and other managers, will also be considered in this chapter, since they also augment the bankruptcy estate. These provisions are the only instances considered in this chapter where special provision is made for company insiders and in this respect the Chinese law differs from the laws in some other jurisdictions. For example, as discussed below, various time limits apply under the avoidance provisions but in no case is a separate time limit provided for a transaction with an 'insider'. Such special provision might have been made, as a company is more likely to grant favour to an insider, such as a company director. Not only may a director be able to identify at an earlier stage than other creditors the possibility of the company's financial difficulties but also, as an insider, he may be able to influence the company to advantage him or another insider. For this reason, special provision for insiders is found in insolvency provisions in other countries.[7] In these jurisdictions, longer time limits may be applicable to transactions with insiders, or the burden of proof in respect of certain matters may fall on the insider. Under the Chinese legislation,

5 Simmons and Jiang (2007), pp. 12 and 13.

6 Liu (2007), pp. 164-73.

7 For example, UK law refers to 'connected parties' under ss. 239(6) and 249; Australian law to 'related entities'; and the USA refers to 'insiders' under §547(b)(4).

the only separate provision made for insiders is to be found in Articles 35 and 36, discussed below.

### Void Dispositions: Article 16

The first provision of the EBL 2006 which must be considered, Article 16, is one that bolsters the managerial authority of the administrator. Upon the acceptance of the bankruptcy case by the court, an administrator will be appointed,[8] and he will assume the powers of management and disposal of the debtor's estate.[9] A system of entitlements of creditors will come into effect, requiring them to submit claims[10] and a distribution plan will then be drawn up,[11] reflecting a scheme of priorities set out under the EBL 2006.[12] See further pp. 259-263. Any payment of property to a creditor following the acceptance of the bankruptcy case by the court will interfere with this scheme unless it is made subject to tight controls. A strict approach is accordingly taken under Article 16, under which any payment made by a debtor to a creditor after the acceptance of the insolvency case by the court will be void.

It may be important in some circumstances for payment to be made to a creditor, in particular if the company's affairs are not to immediately cease, notably if the company is to be reorganized. For example, the payment of a supplier for continued supplies of goods or services may be necessary for continued trading. It is not, however, the case that no payment can be made but rather that the powers to make such a payment fall within the remit of the administrator, rather than the debtor. The administrator has powers under the EBL 2006 to manage and dispose of the company's property,[13] under which he may decide to continue the company's business, and he will be able to make payments under these powers. However, where such a disposition has a material effect on creditor interests this must be reported to the creditors' committee, or, if no such committee has been established, to the court.[14]

Provisions of a similar nature to Article 16 are common in insolvency systems around the world, however, differences of approach are notable. One limitation of the Chinese provision that may be noted is that it only covers the period after the case is accepted by the court. There does not appear to be any equivalent provision to cover the time between the bankruptcy application being made and the case being accepted by the court. This approach accords with the approach under Australian law. This jurisdiction had previously taken a stricter approach, providing

8 Article 13, EBL 2006.

9 Article 25, EBL 2006.

10 Article 48, EBL 2006.

11 Article 111, EBL 2006.

12 Article 113, EBL 2006.

13 Article 25, EBL 2006.

14 Article 69, EBL 2006.

that dispositions made following the presentation of a winding up petition were void and the impact of this provision was often significant.[15] However, legislative amendments[16] were made, as a result of which a disposition under Australian law will only be void if it took place after the winding up order was made and not if it took place during the interim period between an application for such an order being made and the order being made.[17] A similar amendment had earlier been made in New Zealand.

A stricter approach may be found in the equivalent provision in the UK under the Insolvency Act 1986, section 127, which applies from the time when a winding up petition is presented. A disposition made after this time may be termed a 'post-petition' disposition. Such a disposition is automatically void, unless the court gives permission for the disposition.[18] Similar provisions are applicable under United States law[19] and Irish law.[20] The approach of invalidating post-petition dispositions is that it enables the courts to exercise strong control over the estate of the debtor. This provision is, naturally, restrictive, however, and it might be contended that this is not justified, since the presentation of an application for bankruptcy proceedings does not guarantee that the court will accept the case, so that section 127 and its equivalents place an undue restriction on a company's affairs, effectively paralysing its business.[21] However the debtor's estate is arguably most vulnerable to depletion after the presentation of the application, which provides a justification for the stricter approach.[22] Presumably the Chinese legislature, in following the Australian and New Zealand legislation considered certainty in commercial dealings to be more important than the maximization of the pool of assets available for distribution to creditors.

Under the Chinese law, any dispositions that the debtor makes at the time between the bankruptcy application and the court's acceptance of the case must therefore be voidable on some other grounds, notably those set out under Articles 31, 32 and 33, discussed below, if they are to be challenged. The approach followed by the Chinese drafters places the onus on the administrator to challenge transactions falling within these provisions, an approach which is more beneficial to the parties, allowing business to be continued without express sanction.

---

15 Duns (2002), p. 181. See e.g. *Campbell v Michael Mount* (1995) 16 ACSR 296; *Bianco Hiring Services v Adelaide Truss and Frame* (1993) 11 ACLC 193.

16 S. 85, Corporate Law Reform Act 1985, inserting a new s. 513A into the Corporations Law, now s. 513A Corporations Act 2001. For critical discussion of the reforms see Keay (1997), pp. 177-81.

17 Ss. 468, Corporations Act 2001.

18 See *Re Gray's Inn Construction Co Ltd* [1980] 1 WLR 711.

19 § 549, Title 11, US Code. This provision is less restrictive than Insolvency Act 1986, s. 127 in that it exempts some transactions from its scope.

20 S. 218, Companies Act 1963.

21 Goode (2005), p. 493; Simmons and Smith (2000).

22 *Re Wiltshire Iron Company, ex p Pearson* (1868) LR 3 Ch App 443, pp. 446-7; *Coutts & Co. v Stock* [2000] 1 WLR 906, p. 909.

However, this convenience will potentially entail greater administrative expenses for the administrator in protecting the estate, since any transactions at this time which fall within these provisions are voidable, rather than void, as a result. One danger is that, due to this expense and the problems of proof, the administrator will not try to have post-petition dispositions set aside and so it may be a law which operates to the detriment of creditors. As it stands, Article 16 primarily emphasizes the displacement of the directors and managers of the debtor in managerial control of the debtor and underlines the control of the administrator over the estate.

## Transactions Within One Year Prior to the Acceptance of the Insolvency Proceedings: Article 31

Article 31 may be regarded as the key transaction avoidance provision of the EBL 2006, in light of its breadth and the range of transactions that it targets. It identifies the following as voidable transactions, where they took place within one year prior to the acceptance of the insolvency case:[23]

1. transfers of assets free of charge;
2. transactions in respect of which the company received an unreasonably low price;
3. the provision of property security in respect of an unsecured debt;
4. the repayment of a debt that has not fallen due;
5. the giving up of a claim as a creditor.

Each of these categories will be considered further below. Some of the types of voidable transaction listed in Article 31 are uncontroversial and are common in other jurisdictions, whereas others are less common worldwide.

### *Transfers of Assets Free of Charge*

The gratuitous transfer of an asset obviously depletes the bankruptcy estate. Since the company gains no benefit from such a transaction it is not an appropriate transaction for a time when the company is on the verge of insolvency and, in consequence, such a transaction is voidable.[24] No provision is made for categories of gratuitous transfer to be exempted from avoidance. In contrast, in Germany[25] and Scotland[26] exemptions apply in the cases of gratuitous transactions that are conventional gifts of minor value. Although no equivalent provision is made under

---

23 Article 31, EBL 2006.

24 See also e.g. Article 134, *Insolvenzordnung* (Germany); and s. 242 Insolvency Act 1986 (Scotland).

25 Article 134(2), *Insolvenzordnung*.

26 S. 242(4)(c), Insolvency Act 1986.

the Chinese provision, it is unlikely to be worth the while of the administrator to pursue a transfer of assets which is of low value.

*Transactions in Respect of which the Company Received an Unreasonably Low Price*

In contrast to the clear need for the avoidance of transactions for which no consideration is received, the impact of a transaction for which the company does not receive full price may be more marginal. The Chinese provision translates as targeting transactions where the debtor received an 'unreasonably low price'. In common with provisions in other jurisdictions,[27] no margins of unreasonableness are given in the Chinese provision, rather the matter of what is 'unreasonable' must be one of judgement. The valuation of assets is an inexact science in which differences of opinion are common. Moreover it is notable that, due to the newness of the Chinese legislation, there will be a shortage of trained and experienced valuers. As a result, it may be difficult to effectively assess whether the price is 'unreasonably low' and it is likely that transactions will only be challenged in instances where the consideration received by the company is greatly less than the consideration that it gave.

It is notable however that there may be good reasons why a struggling company may sell assets for a price below their full market value. For example a discount may be necessary in order to obtain a quick sale, so that the company may raise cash to meet urgent bills. At the time of such a sale it is not always obvious that the rescue effort is futile. In addition, the voidability of a sale at a low price would deter possible purchasers of assets from struggling companies. Arguably therefore not only the price but also the circumstances in which the transaction took place need to be taken into account in assessing whether the price that has been paid is unreasonably low. A more detailed provision of similar substance may be found in Australian legislation. Under that provision, in assessing whether a transaction is an 'uncommercial transaction', account must be taken of the benefit of the transaction for the company; any detriment arising from the transaction for the company; any benefits to third parties from the transaction; and any other relevant matters.[28] If a similar range of factors was taken into account by the courts in interpreting the Chinese provision it would arguably enable them to consider in all the circumstances whether the avoidance of the transaction was appropriate.

27 See e.g. s. 588FE (2A)(a)(i), Corporations Act 2001 (Australia), relating to 'uncommercial transactions'; s. 238, Insolvency Act 1986 (England and Wales), transactions at an undervalue, where the company must have received consideration 'significantly less' than it gave; s. 242 Insolvency Act 1986 (Scotland), applicable to 'gratuitous alienations', not made 'for adequate consideration'; § 548(a)(B) US Code, Title 11, transactions for which a company received 'less than a reasonably equivalent value'.

28 S. 588FB, Corporations Act 2001.

*The Provision of Property Security in Respect of an Unsecured Debt*

The provision of security in respect of a debt which was previously unsecured, which also falls under Article 31, alters the status of a creditor and earns him a place of priority in the scheme of asset distribution that he may be regarded as not having earned. The Chinese provision has equivalents in many other jurisdictions.[29] The conventional arguments in favour of the position of priority held by secured creditors rest on three main points: first, that the secured creditor bargains to obtain his security; secondly, that he provides value in return for the security, for example through a lower interest rate; and thirdly that his charge is registered.[30] None of these arguments applies in the case of an unsecured creditor, who has done nothing to earn priority gained at the last minute ahead of other unsecured creditors. In contrast, the provision of security in respect of fresh lending should arguably not fall within the administrator's powers of avoidance, an approach taken under similar English and Australian provisions, since unsecured creditors suffer no disadvantage.

*The Repayment of a Debt that has not Fallen Due*

The payment of a debt that has not fallen due may be regarded as an unfair preference of a creditor, since such a creditor would otherwise only be able to claim as an unsecured creditor in the bankruptcy. Special provision for the avoidance of a payment of a debt which has not fallen due appears in the legislation of some countries,[31] although in many other jurisdictions an early repayment is not subject to any special provision and so it will only be challengeable as a preference. In some jurisdictions which do contain provision for the avoidance of early repayments, a transaction of this type will only be invalid where the creditor knew of the debtor's insolvency, however there is no such restriction under Chinese law. The avoidance of an early repayment as a preference is also possible under Chinese law under Article 32, a provision which is discussed below.

*The Giving Up of a Claim as a Creditor*

If a company gives up a claim as a creditor, this will prejudice its own creditors, as the sums due to the debtor will no longer be available as part of the bankruptcy estate. This final category of voidable transaction enables the administrator to reassert the company's entitlement. Although express provisions to cover this type of transaction are relatively uncommon, there are some examples in

---

29 See e.g. s. 245 Insolvency Act 1986; Articles 130 and 131 *Insolvenzordnung*; s. 588FJ Corporations Act 2001 (Australia).

30 See Goode (1983-84).

31 See e.g. Article 65, *Legge Fallimentare*, Royal Decree 16 March 1942, no. 267 (Italy); L. 632-1, I(3), *Code de Commerce* (France).

other jurisdictions,[32] and in others a transaction of this nature will normally be challengeable on some other basis.

## Voidable Preferences: Article 32

Article 32 provides that if the debtor, at a time when the debtor was insolvent, repaid a debt to an individual creditor within a retrospective period of six months leading up to the court's acceptance of the insolvency case, the administrator is entitled to apply to the court for an order under which the repayment can be rescinded, unless the repayment was beneficial for the debtor's property.[33] The company must, at the time of the transaction, have met the conditions of insolvency established under the first paragraph of Article 2, that is, the company must either have been unable to pay its debts as they fell due and its assets must have been insufficient to meet its liabilities; or it must have obviously lacked liquidity. The other test, established in the second paragraph of Article 2, where the company is obviously likely to become insolvent, is expressed not to apply to Article 32.

In common with preference regimes worldwide, therefore, the provision does not concentrate merely on the fact that the transaction benefited the recipient. The defence that is available if the payment was beneficial for the debtor's property is a potentially broad defence that would enable account to be taken, for example, of a payment made to a creditor, without which the creditor would have refused to continue to supply the company with goods or services necessary to the company's survival. The approach of looking at the effect of the transaction but offering a defence is taken in some other jurisdictions[34] but it is not the only model of preference avoidance to be found worldwide. Other jurisdictions focus instead on the debtor's motivations in giving the preference;[35] and others on the state of knowledge of the creditor.[36] Arguably the model chosen by the Chinese drafters provides an appropriate balance between upholding the system of entitlements under the scheme of distribution in insolvency and enabling debtors to carry on business and it is a model that might be considered by other legislatures.

In another respect, however, Article 32 may be considered to be too narrow, since it appears to be confined to the payment of a creditor. Arguably a broader approach, enabling account to be taken of anything done to improve the position

32 See e.g. Article 67(2), *Legge Fallimentare*, Royal Decree 16 March 1942, no. 267 (Italy).

33 Article 32, EBL 2006.

34 See e.g. US Code, Title 11, §547, which provides several defences, most notably an 'ordinary course of business' defence in §547(c)(2). See also s. 243(2), Insolvency Act 1986 (Scotland).

35 See e.g. s. 239(5), Insolvency Act 1986 (England and Wales); Bankruptcy and Insolvency Act (R.S., 1985, c. B-3), §95 (Canada).

36 See e.g. s. 588FG(1)(b), Corporations Act 2001 (Australia).

of a creditor, not just payment, might have given the courts greater flexibility to neutralize an unfair advantage that has been gained by a creditor. For example, a creditor's position will be improved where the debtor has returned goods received from the creditor which it has not yet paid for, or where the debtor has granted security in favour of the creditor, although this latter type of transaction may be challenged under Article 31(3).

## Dishonest Transactions: Article 33

The following actions are invalid under Article 33 irrespective of the time at which they occur:

1. hiding or transferring property in order to evade the claims of creditors;
2. fabricating debts or admitting fabricated debts.[37]

Notably, in contrast to the other transaction avoidance provisions noted above, no time limit is specified within which these activities must have taken place.

The invalidity of dishonest transactions such as these, irrespective of the time at which they occurred, is common in insolvency systems.[38] Unlike many types of potentially voidable transaction there is little scope for argument that a dishonest transaction was somehow beneficial to the company. In practice the most difficult tasks for the administrator in challenging a transfer of property under this provision may be in tracking down the property that has been transferred and, assuming that this can be done, in proving that the hiding or transferring of property was done for the purpose of evading the claims of creditors.

## Sums Due from Capital Contributors: Article 35

Article 35 provides that if a capital contributor has failed to pay the full price of the shares that he has subscribed to, the administrator may require him to make up the balance, regardless of whether the limit of the capital contribution period has been

37 Article 33, EBL 2006.

38 Many of these provisions can be traced back to the *actio Pauliana* of Roman law, an action which has had a remarkable and enduring influence, since some jurisdictions employ this form of action today. The *actio Pauliana* also however, through its influence on the *Lex Mercatoria* had a bearing on the development of fraudulent conveyance provisions in England and Wales. Moreover, these fraudulent conveyance provisions in turn influenced the laws of the United States and Commonwealth countries. Therefore we find similar laws in both civil and common law jurisdictions. See for example s. 423 Insolvency Act 1986; sec. 588FE(5) Corporations Act 2001 (Australia); §133 *Insolvenzordnung* (Germany); Article 66, *Legge Fallimentare* (Italy).

reached. This provision would appear to only apply to share holders and not bond holders, since the term 'capital contributor' in this provision only refers to share holders. The new Chinese Company Law has allowed such capital contributors to make their contributions by instalments according to the incorporation contract; hence, they are liable to pay the remaining price within the prescribed period.[39] Article 35 was formulated upon the basis of a summary of the findings of a forum regarding the hearing of economic cases, which was issued by the Supreme People's Court in 1993.[40]

## Recovery of Inappropriate Income Paid to Company Officers: Article 36

Under Article 36 an administrator is able to recover any inappropriate income that has been acquired or misappropriated by a director, supervisor or managerial officer of the debtor through taking advantage of his position. Notably this provision does not require that the income should have been received by the officer within a particular period leading up to the acceptance of the insolvency case by the court, in contrast to Articles 31 and 32. Nor is it necessary for the company to have been insolvent at the time that the income was received by the company officer. It will therefore be easier for the administrator to pursue excess benefits under Article 36, even where the benefits would fall also under Article 31 or 32. Abuses by company officers have been common in the past and so the inclusion of this special measure is, perhaps, unsurprising.

The income received by the company officer would arguably extend, not only to salaries but also to bonuses and other benefits, such as the issuing of shares. If a broad view is taken, it may also extend to the giving of benefits to third parties.

The key question in assessing the benefits received by a company officer is likely to be whether or not this income is 'inappropriate'. This is a matter that would seem to require a consideration of a number of factors. A company officer with high levels of skills, experience or achievements is appropriately able to command a higher level of remuneration than one who is not so well qualified. Account may also be taken of the type of company and the nature of the tasks undertaken by the officer. However, rich benefits will tend to be inappropriate in cases where a company is short of cash flow.

The Chinese provision is relatively simple in nature but it has a similar aim to the more complex s. 588FDA of the Australian Corporations Act 2001, one of the newest Australian provisions.[41] The Australian provision requires a consideration of whether a reasonable person in the company's circumstances would have

39 Articles 26 and 81, Company Law 2005.

40 Wang (2007), p. 98.

41 This provision was introduced as a result of public outrage at the level of bonuses that were revealed to have been paid to directors of a company, One.Tel, which had become insolvent in 2001.

entered into the transaction, taking account of the benefits (if any) to the company of entering into the transaction; the detriment to the company of entering into the transaction; the respective benefits to other parties to the transaction of entering into it; and any other relevant matter.[42] These principles, and cases interpreting them, might be borne in mind by the Chinese courts in interpreting Article 36. However, at the time of writing, case law interpreting s. 588FDA has yet to emerge.

## Remedies

The provision of transaction avoidance laws is one thing; their effective enforcement is another and this is likely to be a key test of the effectiveness of the new system. Article 34 provides that the administrator is entitled to petition to the court for the recovery of property obtained as a result of a transaction that is voidable under Articles 31, 32 or 33.[43] However the law is vague as to the means of avoidance, since Article 34 merely states that the administrator 'shall recover the debtor's property'. No further details of the process of recovery are given. It is unclear, for instance, whether property that is no longer in the hands of the person who received it from the company can be obtained by the liquidator, or whether such a person can be made to compensate the insolvent estate. It is unclear whether, if the debtor's property has been sold, the administrator may instead seek recovery of the sale proceeds. Arguably a flexible approach is required to enable the interests of creditors to be most fully protected, although some protection may be required for those who have acquired property in good faith as a result of a voidable transaction, or where such a person has acquired property that was previously transferred under a voidable transaction.

## References

Duns, J. (2002), *Insolvency Law and Policy* (South Melbourne: Oxford University Press).

Goode, R. (1983-84), 'Is the Law Too Favourable to Secured Creditors?' 8 *Canadian Business Law Journal* 53.

Goode, R. (2005), *Principles of Corporate Insolvency Law* 3rd edn (London: Sweet and Maxwell).

Keay, A. (1997), *Avoidance Provisions in Insolvency Law* (North Ryde, NSW: LBC Information Services).

Liu, D. (2007), *An Analysis and Practice Guideline to the New Enterprise Bankruptcy Law* (Beijing: Law Press-China).

42 S. 588FDA(1)(c), Corporations Act 2001.

43 For a full interpretation of article 31, 32 and 33, see Wu (2006); Simmons and Jiang, (2007), p. 12.

Parry, R. (2001), *Transaction Avoidance in Insolvencies* (Oxford: Oxford University Press).
Seligson, C. (1967), 'The Code and the Bankruptcy Act: Three Views on Preferences and After-Acquired Property' 42 *New York University Law Review* 292.
Simmons, M. and Jiang, J. (2007), 'A New Insolvency Law in China' 4 *International Corporate Rescue* 10.
Simmons, M. and Smith, T. (2000), 'The Human Rights Act 1998: The Practical Impact on Insolvency' 16 *Insolvency Law and Practice* 167.
Wang, W. (2007), *The Interpretation and Substance of Bankruptcy Law* (Beijing: Law Press-China (in Chinese).
Wu, G. (2006), *Enterprise Bankruptcy Law of PRC: Interpretation and Application of Provisions* (Beijing: People's Court Press) (in Chinese).

# Chapter 9
# Filing of Claims

Bingkun Ye

## Introduction[1]

Frequently, the filing of the claims is regarded as a purely procedural issue. Rules on this issue mainly lie within guidelines established by the higher courts and by judicial experiences. However, as the conditions of filing can be regarded as the first gate by which a creditor enters the bankruptcy procedure, and the acceptability of the claims filed directly determines the extent to which a creditor can influence decisions in the procedure, and how much he can take back from the debtor's estate, the arrangements as to the processes of filing, checking, investigating, confirming and supervising greatly affect the efficiency and fairness of the whole bankruptcy procedure. The significance of these rules to the creditors' interests and the bankruptcy system can therefore be easily seen.

Before discussing the rules as to the filing of claims under the new law, it is necessary to give a brief introduction to the issue as it was dealt with in the People's Republic of China under the previous bankruptcy law system. In fact, there was no article that specially stipulated any rule as to the filing of claims under the previous Enterprises Bankruptcy Law (For Trial Implementation).[2] There was only limited reference made to the matter in this law: two sentences concerning the matters of the time-limit, the documentary requirements of the filing and the registration of claims could be found in the second part of Article 9 (headed 'Notification, filing and register of claims');[3] while another sentence, as to the power of checking and confirmation of claims filed, was included in the first part of Article 15 (headed 'Functions and powers of the creditors' meeting'). No guideline as to the practice

1 It should be pointed out that, as mentioned in the paper, that there are only a few statutes and guidelines as to the issues concerned with the filing of claims. Most arguments in this paper come from judicial practices and, some of them may differ between provinces and change from time to time.

2 Herein after the 'EBL 1986', or the 'old law'.

3 'Creditors who have been notified shall, within one month after receiving the notice, and creditors who have not been notified shall, within three months after the date of the public announcement, report their claims to the People's Court and specify the amount of the claims, as well as whether or not they are secured with property, and also deliver relevant materials of proof. Creditors who do not report their claims during these periods shall be deemed to have automatically abandoned their claims'.

was given in this law, which led to numerous confusions in judicial practice. Most criticism focused on the absence of supervision over the actions of the court,[4] since the court acted not only as the institute receiving and registering the filing,[5] but also was the one investigating and confirming the claims when there was debate concerning the conclusion drawn by the creditors' meeting[6] and the previous law provided no relief in respect of claims filed out of the limited period for filing.[7]

Under the title 'Filing of Creditors' Claims', Chapter 6 of the new Enterprise Bankruptcy Law of the PRC[8] is composed of fifteen provisions, from Article 44 to Article 58. Besides elaborate clauses on the treatments of particular kinds of claims, detailed rules are given as to the procedures of filing, registration, checking, investigation, confirmation of claims and the resolution of disputes regarding claims.

In comparison with the previous bankruptcy law system,[9] several improvements may be found in the new Law. Meanwhile, similar to reforms of other laws in the PRC, it should not be ignored that there are also shortcomings. The primary purpose of this chapter is not to analyse what the law should be, but rather it is to focus on introducing a brief procedural framework for the filing of creditors' claims in the new EBL 2006, though some comments may be given in discussion.

## Acceptability of Claims under the New Law

To some degree, the word 'claims' can be regarded as a central concept of the whole bankruptcy procedure. The scope of the concept in bankruptcy law determines whether the holder is permitted to file and thus participate in the procedure as a 'creditor' and enjoy rights and powers accorded by the law. The new law does not however give a definition of the concept, but rather its meaning is implicit in a listing of the treatments of particular kinds of claims in its provisions.

---

4 One of the most famous corruption cases, which happened in Shenzhen Intermediate People's Court in 2006, can be regarded as an illustration of the problems.

5 Article 9, EBL 1986.

6 Section 43, 'The Regulation on Several Issues Concerning Hearing Enterprise Bankruptcy Cases', issued by the People's Supreme Court on 18 July 2002.

7 The situation was changed in the 'The Regulation on Several Issues Concerning Hearing Enterprise Bankruptcy Cases', but only few claims could obtain relief while the conditions were rigorous. See Section 24 of the guideline.

8 Hereafter the 'EBL 2006', 'the law', or 'the new law'.

9 Before the new EBL 2006 came into force, there were different bankruptcy provisions for different enterprises. For instance, the previous EBL 1986 was applicable only to state owned enterprises while the bankruptcy provisions contained in the previous Civil Procedure Law were applicable to other types of enterprises.

*General Qualifications of the Claims*

Article 44 of the EBL 2006 prescribes that a creditor who holds a claim at the moment when the bankruptcy application is accepted by the court is permitted to file his claim pursuant to the law. Accordingly, one main condition for the claim to be filed is that it should exist at the time that the bankruptcy petition is accepted, except if the law expressly provides otherwise.[10] A claim which comes into being after this specified time point is precluded from being filed, however it may be regarded as a debt of common interest, described in Article 42 of the Law. If this is the case the claim will be payable in accordance with that provision in the event that it is necessary for the continued operation of the bankrupt's business or the progress of the bankruptcy proceedings. A claim may also be lodged in accordance with Article 42 if it stems from a tort arising after the beginning of the bankruptcy procedure.

Though it has not been clearly provided by the law, it is well accepted in judicial practices that there are also several conditions for the claims to be filed. Firstly, the claim should in nature be for a money-payment or be capable of being transferred to a claim for a money-payment. This approach comes from one of the traditional understandings as to the basic purpose of bankruptcy proceedings, which is to provide a special process to clear all the debts of the insolvent.

Secondly, it is widely accepted that claims that are unenforceable in law are prevented from being filed. Under Chinese law, several situations may lead a claim to become unenforceable in law. One possibility is that a claim may be regarded as revocable, null, illegal or out of a time-limit[11] in accordance with substantive laws such as the General Principles of Civil Law, the Contract Law and so on. Alternatively, a claim may also become unenforceable pursuant to Article 215 of the Civil Procedure Law for non enforcement, where an enforcement application has not been submitted during the two years since the obligation was ascertained by a judgment or arbitration decision.[12] It is said that these claims will lose legal protection and thus cannot be filed in the bankruptcy procedure.

*Dealing with Some Special Claims*

As mentioned above, the law has provided numerous detailed provisions as to the treatments of particular claims and these provisions will be considered in this section. They include: Article 46, which mainly concerns claims that are not yet due at the time when the bankruptcy petition is accepted and the interest accruing

10 See Articles 51, 54 and 55 of the EBL 2006.

11 Two years for normal claims, four years for claims relating to contracts for international sales of goods and contracts for technology imports and exports, and one year for some special claims, see Article 135 and Article 136 of the General Principles of Civil Law 1986 and Article 129 of the Contract Law 1999.

12 Two years since the judgment came into force.

upon all claims; Article 47, which sets out the treatment of claims which are subject to conditions or to a time limit and, claims which are still in litigation or in arbitration; Article 48, which prescribes a special procedure for the filing of employees' claims;[13] Article 50, which concerns the filing of joint claims; Article 51, which is specially for the claims of the guarantor or pledgor of the debts of the insolvent and those of any guarantor or any joint debtor; Article 53, which regulates the treatment of any claims to compensation arising from the frustration of contracts; Article 54, which deals with the position of an agent who acts in ignorance of the acceptance of the bankruptcy case; and Article 55, which mainly sets out how to deal with the claims of a payer of a negotiable instrument.

Meanwhile, there are also provisions in other laws, regulations and judicial interpretations by the Supreme People's Court which are concerned with this issue. Among them are several clauses in 'The Interpretation by the Supreme People's Court as to the Application of the Guarantee Law' which are related to the disposal of the claims of the guarantors and pledgors of the debtor.

*Claims which were not yet due at the time of acceptance of the proceedings* A basic principle contained in Article 46, which specifies the handling of claims which are not yet due when the bankruptcy petition is accepted, is that they should be regarded as having fallen due at the moment when the petition is accepted. Accordingly, these claims are permitted to enter the procedure. Furthermore, due to the divergency of the causes of claims not being due, the law contains several articles as to the handling of such prospective claims under different circumstances.[14]

Article 46 also provides that the interest accruing upon claims, if there are any, can only be calculated up until the day when the bankruptcy case is accepted. Interest after that day is precluded from being filed.[15] In respect of a claim which has not yet fallen due, although permission is granted for such claims to be filed, in practice, the interest in respect of such claims accruing before the day of acceptance, if there is any, should be omitted from the claim. The calculation to get the acceptable amount of the contingent claim could be set as below:

$$FC = PC \div (1 + R \times L/360)$$

Where FC = the amount of the claim that can be filed; PC = the total amount of the claim; R = yearly loan interest rate; and L= the length of the period (days).

*Compensation for the termination of contracts* Undoubtedly, the bankruptcy of a company directly influences the performance of contracts which the company has

13 See below.

14 See below.

15 See Article 61(3), Several Regulations in Handling Bankruptcy Cases by the Supreme People's Court. Although the regulations are for the application of the previous Bankruptcy Law, some judicial tendencies and opinions can be seen in it.

entered into. The bankrupt, as well as his contracting partners, immediately faces the problem of how to deal with the contract and, if the contract is terminated, the loss of the contracting partner caused by the termination. The administrator is permitted to decide whether or not to continue the performance or to terminate a contract that is still in performance at the moment when the court accepts the bankruptcy petition.[16] Meanwhile, the contracting partner is also able to suspend his performance, however the administrator can elect to continue the performance of the contract, in which event the insolvent should provide an acceptable guarantee in accordance with Article 69 of the Contract Law.[17]

If the administrator keeps silent for two months following the acceptance of the bankruptcy case; or he fails, after being urged to do so, to reply within 30 days; or, in the event that he chooses to go on with the performance but he cannot provide a guarantee from the assets of the insolvent or by a third party demanded by the counterparty, the contract is deemed to be terminated.[18]

If either the administrator expressly rescinds the contract or the contract is deemed to be terminated, the contracting partner has the right to file for compensation caused by the termination of the contract, besides his contractual claims. Additionally, differing from some other countries, it should be pointed out that, although pure economic loss is well protected under the Chinese contract law system,[19] it is not regarded as an insolvent credit and hence it is precluded from the filing.[20]

*Claims subject to conditions, time limits or legal proceedings* Frequently, claims, especially contractual claims, are subject to conditions or to a time period. The condition or time period set previously may not yet be fulfilled at the moment when the court accepts the bankruptcy application and thus the creditor's claim may not be due at that moment. Though the claims are eligible to participate in the procedure, pursuant to Article 47 of the law, there may be some differences between the treatments that they enjoy: claims that are subject to a time period may directly be deemed to be due according to Article 46; while for claims subject to conditions, due to the contingency of the conditions, it seems that, before the conditions are fulfilled, such claims can only be treated as 'uncertain claims' and the votes of their holders in the creditors' meeting will be prohibited until they can get temporary confirmations from the court.

For a claim which is still in procedure, either in litigation or in arbitration, when the bankruptcy petition is accepted, the opportunity to enter the procedure

16 Article 18, EBL 2006.

17 Article 68, Contract Law of the PRC 1999.

18 Ibid.

19 See Wang Jiafu (1991), p. 383. For discussion see Wang Liming and Cui Jianyuan (2003).There are arguments as to whether pure economic loss should be protected in bankruptcy.

20 S. 55, of the 'Regulations on Handling Bankruptcy Cases', issued by the Supreme People's Court.

is protected by the law also. However, as the facts concerned with the claim and its amount will be unascertained before a final judgment or arbitrational decision is given, such a claim will apparently be treated as an 'uncertain claim' although its filing is permitted.

*Joint credits and joint debts* In China's legal system, each creditor sharing a joint claim is empowered to ask for whole payment from the debtor. In order to avoid each of them filing the claim separately and thus confusing the administrator, creditors holding a joint claim are requested to file the claim as a whole or to delegate to one of them to file the claim.[21] In practice, to ensure the convenience of the filing and the claims of the other joint creditors, it is required that each of them should indicate the joint nature of the claim when filing.[22]

In contrast, as far as joint debts are concerned, each debtor has the obligation to pay off the whole of the debt and the joint debtor who has paid is permitted to ask for compensation from other joint debtors.[23] Thus, under the circumstance that one of the joint debtors becomes bankrupt, a joint debtor who has paid off the debt has the right to file for compensation in the bankruptcy procedure for his previous payment.[24] Where none of the other joint debtors has paid, the joint debtors, other than the insolvent, are permitted to file their prospective claims for compensation only when the creditor has not yet filed.[25] However, the law does not make clear whether the joint debtors should file their claims for compensation as a whole or separately. Theoretically, similar to joint creditors, they can only file as a whole. If this is the case, a problem similar to that in the case of the joint creditors may arise, namely how to determine the share which each joint debtor enjoys?

A joint debt may be proportional among the debtors in their internal relationship. But the proportion, except where it is concluded in a contract among them, can only be recognized by a court or arbitration institution in practice. Consequently, it seems that the accurate amount of the joint debtors' compensation or prospective compensation will remain in question until the proportion is concluded by a court or arbitrator, in the absence of such a contract concerned with the proportion, and such contracts rarely exist in reality.

Additionally, it may be the case that several of the joint debtors become insolvent. The creditor is permitted to file the whole of his claim in each bankruptcy procedure in this circumstance.[26] However confusion may arise too, as there is a risk that the creditor may get back an amount higher than the whole of his claim.

21 Article 50, EBL 2006.

22 See below.

23 Article 87, General Principles of Civil Law 1986.

24 Article 51, EBL 2006.

25 Article 51, EBL 2006.

26 Article 52, EBL 2006

For instance, if there are five insolvent companies jointly liable to a claim, then the creditor is permitted to file his claim five times according to the law. Supposing that the distribution rate of each bankruptcy is 25 per cent, 20 per cent, 30 per cent, 35 per cent and 40 per cent, the creditor will get back 150 per cent of his claim then. Thus, it seems the communication between, and harmonization of, bankruptcy procedures will become an issue in future practice in the absence of a regulation.

*Reimbursement of negotiable instruments* There is no question that the payer of a negotiable instrument, who made an acceptance or payment before the drawer became bankrupt, has the right to file for reimbursement in the bankruptcy procedure of the drawer if he has not obtained a full deposit from the insolvent in advance.

However, a question may arise in the event that the payer makes the acceptance or payment after the bankruptcy case has been accepted. There was legislative debate as to whether the payer has the right to file for reimbursement only when he is unaware of the bankruptcy, and if he should otherwise bear the loss caused by his negligence. However, the level of certainty, stability and predictability of the banks in making acceptance or payment of the negotiable instruments would undoubtedly be influenced by such a provision and would thus impact upon the utilization of the instruments, and the difficulty of proving the payer's unawareness is also notable.[27] Consequently, the legislator did not ultimately accept this option. It is contained in Article 55 that the payer, whether or not he was aware of the bankruptcy, is able to file for reimbursement under this situation.

*Claims of agents after the bankruptcy: Article 54* It may often be the case that an agent of the bankrupt, in unawareness of the bankruptcy, will continue to handle the affairs with which he has been entrusted and he will have to bear the risk that he will not be able to obtain reimbursement of payments made or the expenses incurred in dealing with the affairs of the insolvent principal. Article 54 of the EBL 2006 permits the agent to file his claims arising as a result of his actions in ignorance of the bankruptcy.

However, it may be frequently the case in practice that the immediate stoppage of commission leads to unreasonable loss to the principal and it will therefore be preferable for the agent, though being aware of the bankruptcy of the principal, to go on dealing with some affairs in the interests of the principal. Thus, though it is not contained in the provision, it could be suggested that when the agent acts

27 Japanese insolvency law regards the notice of the bankruptcy as evidence of the awareness of the payers, and the payments made after the notice are therefore deemed to be made in awareness of the bankruptcy. However such an approach would arguably be unfit for China, a country with a wide territory.

for the interests of the bankrupt, even if he is aware of the bankruptcy, his claims should also be protected.

*Claims of guarantors and pledgors of the insolvent* This section will consider two kinds of guarantees contained in China's legal system: ordinary guarantees and joint responsibility guarantees.[28] Where another company or person provides a joint responsibility guarantee for the insolvent, he is permitted to file the amount that he paid instead of the bankrupt, either partly or wholly, before the procedure is accepted. Where he did not, whether he is permitted to file in respect of the claim that he has guaranteed depends on whether the creditor has filed his claim. In the event that the creditor did, the guarantor is prevented from filing.[29]

So far as an ordinary guarantee is concerned, in normal situations, an ordinary guarantor has the right to refuse the creditor's demand for him to assume guarantee responsibilities before the principal contract undergoes judicial or arbitration procedures and until it is established that the debtor is incapable of paying the debt despite mandatory implementation against his properties.[30] However, when the principal debtor's bankruptcy case is accepted, the ordinary guarantor is deprived of the right and the creditor may ask him to take the responsibility directly.[31] Consequently, it may be seen that the creditor is empowered to choose between whether to file his claim in the principal debtor's bankruptcy procedure or to demand that the guarantor pays out the debt directly, regardless of which kind of guarantee has been provided.

Meanwhile, it is said that the guarantor should also be responsible for any part which the creditor has not been paid through the principal debtor's bankruptcy procedure if the creditor demands this within six months after the end of the procedure.[32] For instance, supposing that A has a claim of RMB 100 against B and that C provided a guarantee to B. When B becomes bankrupt and A chooses to file his claim in the bankruptcy procedure, providing that the distribution rate is 20 per cent, A will take away RMB 20 and ask C to pay the remaining RMB 80 within 6 months following the end of B's bankruptcy procedure. If A's choice is to directly ask C to take the guarantee responsibility, instead of filing in B's bankruptcy, he will get RMB 100 from C immediately and leave it for C to file in the bankruptcy for his compensation. This arrangement seems appropriate. But it should not be ignored that some extreme situations may happen during the bankruptcy procedure and the subsequent six months. For instance, if A chooses to file his claim in B's bankruptcy procedure, again receiving RMB 20, and the guarantor, C, becomes insolvent by the end of the six month period by which he was to pay the remaining

28 Article 16 of the China Guarantee Law 1995.

29 Article 51, EBL 2006.

30 Article 17 of the China Guarantee Law 1995.

31 Ibid.

32 Article 44, The Interpretations by the Supreme People's Court as to the Application of the Guarantee Law.

RMB 80, then, in the event that the distribution rate in C's bankruptcy procedure is 30 per cent, A stands to get RMB 24 from C's procedure. In total, he will get only RMB 44 back. In comparison with directly taking RMB 100 from C, A will suffer loss caused by the deterioration of C's financial situation. It should also not be ignored that a common phenomenon in Chinese financial practice is that many companies, whether relational (such as those which belong to the same group, or which have the same controller, or which hold shares in each other) or not, provide guarantees to each other and, the collapse of a company frequently brings about a domino effect. Thus, running faster than the toppling of another domino is crucial for the creditors. It may be unsurprising that they will prefer to claim against the guarantor, rather than filing their claims in the principal debtor's bankruptcy procedure, while their demands will undoubtedly quicken the collapse of the guarantor at the same time.

Additionally, it should be pointed out that, in accordance with the 'Interpretation by the Supreme People's Court as to the Application of the Guarantee Law',[33] when the creditor, in awareness of the bankruptcy, neither files his claim nor informs the guarantor of the bankruptcy of the principal debtor, the guarantor's responsibility as to the part which could otherwise have been paid in the bankruptcy procedure will be discharged.

Although it has not been addressed in the EBL 2006, a pledgor of the bankrupt who has provided security in respect of a debt of the bankrupt, should arguably also have the right to file his contingent claim as to the amount of his obligation. However, it is almost impossible to identify a clear amount as to his obligation, since the payment has not happened yet at the moment. Furthermore, as costs of the realization of security, such as the costs of evaluation and auction, and the interest on the debt,[34] should be paid firstly from the sum transferred from the secured assets,[35] it seems that the securer should also be permitted to include the possible costs and interests under the circumstance that the potential value of the bound asset is sufficient to pay all of the debt, the interests and the costs.

Attention should also be paid to the situation where there are several guarantors or pledgors, or a mix of both, to a claim. Although it has not been provided by the law, in a situation where several guarantors are concerned, it is arguable that, since a payment made by one of them leads to the discharge of all guarantors' obligations correspondingly, only the guarantor who has paid has the right to file for his compensation as to the part of his payment. So far as a mix of pledges and guarantees is concerned, as the guarantors are only responsible for the balance over the amount of the security,[36] guarantors are permitted to file for the balance only.

33 Article 45 of the Interpretation.

34 Article 74, Interpretations as to the Application of the Guarantee Law by the Supreme People's Court.

35 Ibid.

36 Article 28 of the Guarantee Law 1995. The Property Law changed the principle, with effect from 1 October 2007. In accordance with the new law, the creditor has the right

However a dispute as to the amount of the balance seems unavoidable without a valuation of the pledged assets.

*Claims Precluded*

Due to the absence of express provisions in the law, it is difficult to provide a clear list as to the scope of the claims that are precluded from filing. The list discussed below is only a rough summarization of judicial practices and, before an affirmation from the legislator or the Supreme People's Court, there may be divergences in different courts.[37]

*Criminal or administrative penalties and forfeits* Since the administrative punishments and criminal penalties applied against a company aim to punish the company's illegality, it is said that the liability should fall upon the company itself only. Where the company becomes bankrupt, its assets are regarded as a hotchpot for its creditors. It may be regarded as unfair for the innocent creditors to bear the charges caused by the company's illegality. Consequently, it has been provided in the 'The Regulation on Several Issues Concerning Hearing Enterprise Bankruptcy Cases' by the Supreme People's Court that penalties and forfeits, either administrative or criminal, can not be filed as claims in the bankruptcy procedure when they have not been enforced yet at the time when the bankruptcy case is accepted.[38] Meanwhile, since surcharges for overdue payment in judicial enforcements,[39] administrative charges, revenue and social insurance funds are punitive in nature, they are also precluded from filing.

*Costs of the creditors to file his claim and participate in the procedure* There will undoubtedly be some costs in creditors filing their claims and participating in the insolvency procedure. It is widely accepted that it is impermissible for these costs to be filed as claims in the bankruptcy procedure. The reasons are, firstly, that the

---

to select the realization of the security or to ask the guarantor take the full liability, see Article 176 of the Property Law 2007.

37 For instance, there are some differences in the guidelines in handling bankruptcy cases by the High Court of Beijing, Anhui Province, Fujian Province, Guangdong Province, Heilongjiang Province, Shangdong Province and Shanghai. Accordingly, what is listed in this section are those which are generally accepted, and they may be inapplicable in some provinces.

38 [2002] Fasi No. 23. Although it is a regulation regarding the application of the EBL 1986, some of its provisions, if they do not conflict with the EBL 2006, could be a point of reference in understanding the new law.

39 According to Article 232 of the Civil Procedure Law 2007, if the company fails to fulfil its obligations in respect of a payment of money within the time limit specified by the court in a judgment, order or any other legal document, it shall pay a multiplied rate of interest on the debt for the period of deferred fulfilment. For the deferred fulfilment of other obligations, it shall pay a surcharge also.

costs are spent for the interests of the creditors and secondly, that the costs will increase the burden on the debtor's estate and reduce the capacity of the debtor to pay off the claims, which will harm the creditors' interests as a whole.

*Shares in the company* It is generally accepted that the shares of the company, and all rights and claims incidental to the shares, are not regarded as bankruptcy claims and thus, they can not be filed by the shareholders in the bankruptcy procedure. The shareholders can ask for a distribution in respect of these claims only when there are assets left after all creditors' claims are fulfilled.

*Unenforceable claims and unprotected claims in law* As mentioned previously, there are numerous reasons in substantive law which can lead to a claim losing the protection provided by the law. One of the main reasons is if the contract has been adjudicated as illegal, null, void or revoked by a court or arbitration institution. For instance, a contract becomes null and void when the dissolving conditions are met or the termination time period agreed is reached; if it violates the compulsory provisions of the laws and administrative regulations; if it is concluded as a result of serious misunderstanding; or if it is obviously unfair and is petitioned by the party bearing the loss within one year following the conclusion of the contract; and so on.[40] Another reason is if the claim is out of the time-limit described in substantive or procedural laws.

*Costs and fees in criminal procedure* Similar to penalties and forfeits, when a company is the defendant in criminal proceedings at the time when the bankruptcy petition is accepted, or it is prosecuted subsequently, the costs and fees of the criminal procedure are prevented from being filed as claims in the bankruptcy procedure.

## Filing the Claims: Procedure and Effects of Filing

Different processes are established for employees' wages and entitlements, which need not be filed, and those of other creditors. The positions in relation to employee claims and non-employee claims must therefore be considered separately.

### *Filing of claims other than for employees' wages and entitlements*

The position in relation to claims other than by employees must firstly be considered.

*To file the claims: procedural and documentary requirements* According to the EBL 2006, an application filing the claims and all documents or evidences

40 See Chapter 3 of the Contract Law 1999.

attached should be submitted to the administrator.[41] Applications handed to any other institutes cannot be regarded as filings in law.

In practice, there are three requirements for the filing of a claim. Firstly, the applications should be written and they should include some basic information about the credit, including the amount and due time of the claim; how, when and where it came into being; whether there has been any payment; whether the claim is joint in nature; and whether it is guaranteed or secured. Secondly, evidences in support of the claim should be attached with the file. However no common guidelines have been provided by the legislator or the Supreme People's Court as to the level of evidence that will suffice. In practice, some preliminary evidence, such as a contract or documentary promise should normally be satisfactory. However, since the secured claims are preferential to unsecured ones, it is especially demanded that the secured creditor must submit detailed evidence concerned with the security. Thirdly, as the creditors of a joint claim are able to select whether to file their credits in whole or separately according to the EBL 2006, any one of them may ask the debtor to pay the claim in its entirety and the claim in whole will be destroyed when he has received the payment. In order to prevent the situation that only one, or some, creditors of a joint claim file their claims alone and hence harm the interests of other creditors who have not presented their claims, it is particularly required that a special explanatory term must be included in the application indicating the joint nature of the claim.[42]

Additionally, although it is not required in the clauses, additional information is necessary for the convenience for the administrator to register and check the filing, to edit the list of claims and to inform the creditor of any steps taken under the procedure. In particular some information regarding each creditor should be provided in the terms of the filing, such as his or her full name and contact information, the details of the bank and accounts to receive the distribution, the time of filing, and so on and so forth.

In practice, when the administrator is of the view that the documents and evidences presented by the creditor are not sufficient to enable the claim to be investigated, he may notify the creditor to provide further evidences or documents in due course.[43] Although no further direction has been given on how to deal with the claim when the creditor does not submit to his direction, as the right to investigate the claims is accorded to the creditors' meeting and the power to confirm the claims is left to the court only, it is clear that the administrator has no power to refuse the claim, but must leave the question to the first creditors' meeting and the court.

41 Article 49, EBL 2006.

42 Article 49, EBL 2006.

43 The Supreme People's Court, the 'Regulations on the application of laws in bankruptcy cases when the EBL comes into force' (in discussion).

*Changing or withdrawing the claim* Theoretically speaking, before the end of the procedure, a creditor is permitted to change or withdraw his filing at any time. However, several matters should be taken into consideration in practice. Notably, when the creditor reduces the amount of his claim, abandons a position of priority, or withdraws his claim, there is almost no negative impact on the interests of other creditors and the debtor. Thus, such a reduction, abandonment or withdrawal is acceptable and the creditor is allowed to reduce or re-file his claim in the prescribed filing period. However, where the creditor wishes to increase the amount of the claim or to ask for priority which has not been included in his previous filing, it is suggested that the part that is increased should be regarded as a new filing de facto. In addition, it is submitted that the request for a change should be by a normal written document and should also be accompanied by evidence where it is a request for the claim to be increased.

*Time-limit for the filing* In order to ensure the efficiency of the procedure, it is clearly stipulated that creditors should file their claims within the period specified by the People's Court. As far as the duration of this period is concerned, instead of listing a fixed length, as in the previous bankruptcy law,[44] the EBL 2006 states that it should not be shorter than 30 days and should not be longer than three months, from the time when the court issues acceptance of the bankruptcy case.[45] Under most circumstances, the court in practice will list the term for filing and give the contact details of the administrator in the notice. Although the length of this term seems to wholly depend on the discretion of the court and no direction has been given by the law itself or by the Supreme Court up until now, in practice particular factors which may be taken into account include: the scale of the debtor's business and estate, especially when the company has established branches and developed businesses in numerous regions or countries; the amount and the complexity of the potential claims; the locations of potential creditors and the degree of convenience for the claimants to make their filing.

If a creditor sends his filing petition or documents in the period, the claim should be regarded as filed during the period, even if the documents are not received during the period.

*Relief for filing out of the prescribed period* Previously, there was no opportunity for a creditor who did not file his claim within the prescribed term to participate in the procedure. In accordance with Article 9 of the EBL 1986, the claim would have been deemed as abandoned and would thus have been excluded, not only from the bankruptcy but also from any other procedures. The claim in fact would be destroyed in substance without any relief. Although the 'Several Regulations in Handling Bankruptcy Cases' issued by the Supreme People's Court subsequently

44 In the EBL 1986, the period for creditors receiving the notice from the court was one month and for those not receiving the notice it was three months from the date of notice.

45 Article 45, EBL 2006.

changed the situation,[46] the granting of permission for the creditor to file his claim out of the period was restricted to a narrow scope, namely where the creditor's failure to meet the deadline was due to force majeure or for another justified reasons.[47] Furthermore, the creditors' meeting was empowered to petition the court to reconsider the grant of permission if it disagreed with this decision.

Obviously, such a clause was too rigorous to the creditors to meet its terms and it arguably impaired the fairness of the procedure. Thus, the situation was changed under the EBL 2006. A creditor is now permitted to file his claim at any stage of the bankruptcy procedure.

Notwithstanding that the creditor is permitted to supplementarily file his claim up until the latest distribution of the debtor's assets,[48] or by the close of the bankruptcy procedure, he can only exercise his rights in such stages as are left and he may only participate in the distribution of the assets of the debtor which remain. Also, it is his responsibility to finance the checking, investigation and confirmation of his claim.

*Filing of the Employees' Claims to Wages and Entitlements*

Hitherto, no fund for the protection of employee wages in insolvency was established, either in law or in practice, except in a few cities such as Shenzhen, a Special Economic Zone. The only way for the employees of the bankrupt to get their wages and entitlements was for them to seek a payment from the assets of the insolvent company. Consequently, it is no surprise that, for the stabilization and harmonization of society, the protection of the employees' claims as to their wages and entitlements became an especially important theme in the legislative process which led to China's new bankruptcy law: see further pp. 297-301. In addition to the employee protection measures, consisting of the priority for their wages and entitlements (Arts 42, 48 and 113), the membership of the union delegation in the creditors' meeting (Art. 59) and the creditors' committee (Art. 67), and the votes of employee claimants upon a rescue plan (Art. 82), the law has provided a special procedure for the filing of the employees' claims.

It is unnecessary for the employees to file their claims for wages and entitlements in the procedure. This is because the administrator, after his appointment, is required to investigate the wages and entitlements and to make and publicize a special list of these claims (Art. 48). Furthermore, a special correcting procedure, different from that applicable in relation to other claims, is stipulated for these employees' claims. The employee is permitted to directly ask the administrator to correct the recording of his claims in the list and when refused, he is permitted to bring litigation to confirm his claims.[49]

46 Article 24, Regulations 2002.

47 See Article 76 of the Civil Procedure Law 2007.

48 Article 56, EBL 2006.

49 Article 48, second sentence, EBL 2006.

During the legislative process some arguments arose as to the scope of the employees' claims in the legislation. A phrase, which may be translated as 'labour claims', was used in the bills. It was argued that these words were ambiguous as to their scope and that they might be confused with other claims.[50] In order to avoid unnecessary confusion, it was suggested that a direct and clear description as to the scope of employees' claims would be better. The Law Committee considered that the employees' claims in the clause should be clearly and strictly limited, including: the wages, the costs of basic social security covering health insurance, and other entitlements set out in the laws and administrative regulations only.[51] Finally, in Article 48 of the EBL 2006, the scope became wider and clearer. It includes not only the wages, the basic pensions, health insurance premiums, and compensation prescribed in law and regulations, but it also includes the medical treatment subsidy and that for disability, and the compensation payable to a bereaved family. Accordingly, it seems that some claims of the employees, which are not listed in this provision, such as bonuses, are precluded from enjoying the special protection.

However, there is an absence of supervision of the operation of this special procedure in the legislation. As it is clearly stipulated that the employees' claims contained in the Article need not be filed and they are listed separately from the list of non-employee claims,[52] while it is said that a creditor is permitted to bring confirmation litigation in respect of the claims in the list of claims, it seems that the confirmation procedures which are applicable to other claims are inapplicable to employees' claims. If so, no opportunity to challenge these claims is given to either the debtor or the creditor. Thus, there is no supervision from the court to prevent the administrator from incorrectly increasing the amount of the employees' claims, either consciously or negligently.

### *Effects of Filing in Law*

The legal effects of filing the claims can be summarized in two main points, relating to the qualification for the creditor to participate in the bankruptcy procedure and the discontinuity of the time limits in other legislation. In respect of the first point, according to Article 59 of the EBL 2006, whether a creditor has the membership of the creditors' meetings depends wholly on a purely procedural condition, namely whether he has filed his claim in accordance with the law. As far as the second point is concerned, as the law permits the creditor to bring litigation against, or to seek arbitration with, the company after the end of insolvency procedure, in circumstances where the company has survived, the discontinuity of the time limit for the creditors' claim may be important for his interests in future.

---

50 See Law Committee of the NPC (2004).

51 Ibid.

52 Article 48, EBL 2006.

## Checking, Investigation and Confirmation of the Claims

### *Checking*

According to Article 57 of the EBL 2006, the administrator is liable to enrol all filings, to check the claims that have been filed and to make a list of claims. The list of claims, accompanied with all petitions and evidences attached, should be kept by the administrator and be available for all interested parties to refer to. Normally, secured claims should be listed separately from unsecured ones in the list.

Since the law does not indicate how the administrator can check the claims and what he can do when he has doubts about a claim, it may be argued that the process of checking by the administrator could entail a substantial investigation. However, as it is obviously impossible for the administrator to investigate all claims in such a short term, and the parties whose interests are affected ultimately are the creditors and the debtor, the right to investigate the claim is accorded to the first creditors' meeting under Article 58 of the EBL 2006.[53] Consequently, the checking by the administrator should be only preparatory and procedural in nature. That means that he should mainly ascertain the following:

- whether the filing satisfied the conditions set by the law;
- whether the claim should be precluded for illegality, whether it is out of the time-limit stipulated in other substantive laws or out of the legal period within which an application for enforcement must be made under the Civil Procedure Law;
- whether the documents and evidences provided by the creditors are sufficient (in practice, if he finds that they are not, the administrator can require the creditor to provide further evidence in due course) and whether the documents and evidences presented are genuine.

All defects that he finds in checking should be described in the list of claims and submitted to the first creditors' meeting with his comments.

### *Investigation*

The power to investigate the claims is given only to the first creditors' meeting under Article 58 of the law. The debtor, any creditors and the administrator are permitted to refer their doubts as to any claim listed. Meanwhile, the creditor to whom the doubts relate has the right to defend his claim and to show further evidences in the meeting.

Although it is not expressly addressed in the legislation, it can be concluded that claims filed later than the deadline specified by the court should also be investigated in the subsequent creditors' meeting.

53 See below.

It should be noted that, as the power to confirm the claims is given to the court, the creditors' meeting has no right to vote as to whether the claim is acceptable or not. In the event that no consensus can be reached at the meeting regarding a claim, the claim can only be submitted to and confirmed by the court.

### *Confirmation and Relief for the Disputes*

As mentioned, the law reserves to the court the power to confirm the claims. It is stipulated that the court will issue an order confirming the claims listed and approved unanimously by the debtor and all creditors in the creditors' meeting. Meanwhile, in accordance with Article 58, not only the debtor but also a creditor may bring a lawsuit before the court which has filed the bankruptcy case in respect of a listed claim which he disputes. Accordingly, firstly, the debtor may object to any claim listed, and secondly, any creditor is empowered to bring litigation against a record in the list as to the claims either of himself or of other creditors. Although the former situation may seldom happen in practice, it may be necessary when there are some mistakes or errors in the record by the administrator.

In addition, as the employees' wages and entitlements are filed by the administrator, rather than by the employees themselves, Article 48 of the EBL 2006 expressly states that the employees may directly ask the administrator to correct the record of their claim in the list in the circumstance where they disagree with the record and, they can petition the court when refused. Interestingly, though it may widely exist in practice, the law does not make a similar correcting arrangement for other creditors, yet litigation by creditors seems unavoidable even when the issue is merely a clerical mistake in the record. It is suggested, for the efficiency of the procedure, that a similar correcting arrangement for all creditors may be better than requiring litigation.

One may wonder why the law does not make it clear whether the disputed creditor is able to bring litigation to confirm his claim. Since the words employed by the law in describing the creditors who can trigger the litigation is those 'disapproving of a record in the list', it is apparent that the disputed creditor is disqualified, for he definitely will not disapprove of the record of his claim, except for mistakes in the record discussed above. It may be argued that, firstly, the right of the debtor and other creditors to challenge a claim through a lawsuit is well protected by the law. Either of them is well placed to go to court when he has doubts regarding a claim. Secondly, the influence of this omission upon the right of the doubted creditor to participate in the procedure and vote in the meetings is lessened by the introduction of temporary confirmation: according to Article 59 of the law, any creditor who has filed his claim according to the law can be a member of the creditors' meeting and, although his right to vote is strictly limited when his claim is 'uncertain', the court can make a temporary confirmation as to his claim for the purpose of his exercise of the right to vote. Accordingly, a creditor who has filed his claim in the appointed period can definitely be a member of the first creditors' meeting and, when his claim is disputed in the meeting or in a courtroom, he might arguably still have the opportunity to petition the court to issue a *temporary* confirmation and, if the court grants his petition, he will be enabled to vote in the meeting to the extent of the amount granted by the court in accordance with Article 59 of the Law, although there are several problems in the issuing of such a temporary confirmation that will be discussed further below.

However, several issues should also be taken into account: firstly, although the law has successfully improved the efficiency of the procedure by placing the burden of taking a lawsuit on the disputing parties, it keeps in question the matter of how to settle a claim which did not get unanimous approval in the creditors' meeting and where neither the debtor nor the opposing creditors submit the issue to the court subsequently. Under this circumstance, the claim cannot get an immediate order from the court since it has not been 'unanimously approved'. On the other hand, as there is no one who is empowered to bring confirmation litigation, it is impossible for the claim to be the subject of a confirmation judgment from the court too. A problem may arise as to how to deal with the claim. Thus, without the possibility for the disputed creditor to petition for confirmation, it seems that the claim can only remain 'uncertain' in the absence of a final judgment from the court. Undoubtedly, the situation will lead to confusion in further procedures.

Furthermore, leaving aside the argument as to whether claims disputed in the creditors' meeting could be included as 'uncertain claims', might it be supposed that the creditor could employ a temporary confirmation to vote? If the answer is 'yes', the law is uncertain as to several aspects of this possibility. Firstly, the law does not indicate the conditions that must be met if the court is to issue such a temporary confirmation. Secondly, the law does not design a practicable procedure for the issuing of such a confirmation. For instance, it does not indicate whether a hearing is necessary before the order is issued, whether an appeal against the order may be made, whether the order may be reconsidered and so on. Thirdly, the law does not make it clear whether the temporary confirmation remains in effect in the event that no dispute regarding the claim is presented to the court after it is issued. Fourthly, under the circumstance that a lawsuit against the claim is being handled by another court at the moment,[54] it keeps in question whether it is the court who handles the dispute or the court who accepted the bankruptcy petition which has the jurisdiction to accept the confirmation petition and issue the order.[55] Fifthly, in spite of a dispute as to whether the claim exists when the temporary confirmation is issued, or whether it comes into being subsequently, in the event that the dispute is finally resolved in a manner that conflicts with the temporary confirmation, the

54 See Article 20, EBL 2006.

55 Article 21, EBL 2006 indicates that all civil litigation concerning the bankrupt should be handled by the court which accepted the bankruptcy petition. But it does not indicate whether the court can issue a temporary confirmation when litigation is in process in another court. A conflict will undoubtedly be unavoidable between these two courts and their decisions.

law does not indicate how to deal with the vote and decision of the creditors' meeting prior to the final judgment.

Reference could be made to Japanese bankruptcy law, which may offer a preferable approach. Under the Japanese law, the burden of bringing litigation as to the claims which have previously been adjudged by the court is accorded to the objecting parties, while the doubted creditor may bring a lawsuit to confirm his claim when not.[56]

In so far as the administrator is concerned, it may be strange to find that the situation is different from that in other civil law countries, such as under the German and Japanese bankruptcy laws. In these countries, the administrator is permitted to begin litigation when he has doubts regarding the existence, or the amount, of a claim and the court must hear and issue an order as to his petition, while the EBL 2006 of the PRC keeps its silence as to this issue.[57] However, since the administrator is more professional than other participants under most circumstances, for the interests of the parties concerned and for the efficiency and fairness of the procedure, there is no reason to preclude him from petitioning the court. Furthermore, notwithstanding that the debtor and creditors are able to litigate, it is notable that in view of the time consuming and costly nature of the procedure, it is not impossible that none of them will prefer to take this step where they disagree with the claim in the creditors' meeting. Under this circumstance, it seems that the administrator is the proper person to break the impasse and seek relief when he is certain of the potential for material harm to be caused by the disputed claim to the interests of parties. Consequently, to some extent, this absence may be regarded as one of the shortcomings of the law.

Another aspect as to the confirmation litigation is that the law does not clearly stipulate the burden of the fees and costs arising in respect of the confirmation litigation. Since these fees are not included in the 'bankruptcy fees' prescribed in Article 41 of the law, it is obvious that they can not be paid from the debtor's assets. Accordingly, on one hand, it may be interesting to find that the law permits the debtor to file a lawsuit against a claim, while it does not clearly allow him to obtain the fees from the debtor's estate at the same time. Thus, it may lead to confusion. On the other hand, when it is a creditor who litigates against another creditor's claim, it seems that the only choice left for him is to pay all the costs arising in the confirmation procedure himself, while the benefits that he can get from such an action may be few, since he must share the profits of the litigation with all other creditors and the debtor. Obviously, the comparison between the cost and the benefit may lead to his reluctance to petition for confirmation. Yet, it may be true that these conditions are helpful in preventing creditors from taking unreasonable and unnecessary lawsuits and thus disturbing the progress of the bankruptcy procedure. But, when the creditor's objection is well founded, the interests of all concerned parties undoubtedly would be harmed by his reluctance. Thus, it can

56 Articles 244 to 248, Japanese Bankruptcy Law.

57 Though it may be argued that he can do so as the delegatee of the debtor.

be suggested that, for the purpose of making the relief more practicable and to encourage creditors to utilize it when essential, the fees and costs of confirmation litigation brought by the debtor, and those brought by creditors, which successfully wipe out the disputed claims, either partly or wholly, should be regarded as claims for the common interest of parties and thus be paid directly from the pool.

The procedure for confirmation litigation did not exist under the EBL 1986. In accordance with previous regulations, all claims concerning the interests of the bankrupt had to be decided directly by the court handling the bankruptcy case and such a decision was unappealable. It is said that the new mechanism provides more protections for the parties concerned, both substantially and procedurally.[58] Meanwhile, it should also be pointed out that the law is silent as to some procedural problems in the litigation. For instance, it does not indicate whether the debtor should be a party to the procedure when the action is petitioned by a creditor. More importantly, the law does not describe a special procedure for these litigations. Article 4 of the EBL 2006 provides that reference should be made to the procedure provisions contained in the Civil Procedure Law where no relevant rule appears in the insolvency legislation. Accordingly, it seems that the ordinary civil procedure rules provided in the Civil Procedure Law are applicable to the confirmation litigation. Undoubtedly, an ordinary procedure provides more procedural protection for the parties. For instance, the case may be handled by a different tribunal from the one dealing with the bankruptcy case; a hearing is necessary; the decision is appealable; and so on and so forth. But, due to the time[59] and cost-consuming[60] nature of proceedings, it can be argued that an ordinary civil procedure is unfit for confirmation litigation in bankruptcy, in which the efficiency of proceedings is crucial. For the efficiency of the bankruptcy procedure, it is suggested that a special procedure for confirmation litigation would be more desirable.

## Conclusion

In evaluating the filing procedures in bankruptcy, several factors should be taken into consideration. Among them, the certainty, rationality, practicability and efficiency of the procedure are most important factors for the protection of the interests of the parties concerned.

58 See the speech by the head of the 2nd Civil Division of the Supreme People's Court on the interpretations on the application of the EBL, 27 April 2007.

59 For instance, a period of not less than 30 days to provide evidences and a hearing are necessary in the procedure, the period of the first instance can be as long as six months and it is deferrable. The decision is appealable and the period for the appeal is three months and it is deferrable too.

60 All costs in normal civil procedure should be prepaid by the petitioner and, it seems the costs of professional services can not be avoided in most confirmation cases, due to their complication.

As mentioned previously, in comparison with the EBL 1986, the new law has taken a great step in restricting the involvement of the court. The role of court in the procedure of filing is restricted to an institute to confirm claims which have been unanimously approved in the creditors' meeting and to handle disputes as to contentious claims. Involvement from the court in the filing of claims is restricted to a limited range. Undoubtedly, the change in the law has transformed the court's role from that of a player to a superior. A tendency towards more certainty and rationality can be seen in these improvements. Yet, it may still be argued that the court retains too important a role in the procedure.[61] However, given the absence of experienced lawyers, auditors and even judges in liquidation issues, it was not feasible to leave all powers to administrators, given that this is a new office in China.

Another step which accords with the tendency of global developments in bankruptcy law is that the new law pays more attention to the protection of the parties concerned and the appropriate balance of their interests. In this regard, we may note the provision of relief for creditors seeking an out-of-period filing; the rights to dispute a claim in the courtroom; and the special filing and confirming procedures for employees' claims; and the change in the period for the filing from fixed to discretionary. These developments may be regarded as improvements in rationality.

Meanwhile, in comparison with the EBL 1986, advancement in the practicability and certainty of the procedure can also be clearly found in the new law. In order to prevent unnecessary uncertainty and impracticability, the law includes numerous articles that clearly direct the treatments of several claims, which would give rise to confusions in practices or in law without these guidelines.

The evaluation of the efficiency of a filing system should mostly focus on whether the creditors can enter the procedure as soon as possible; how efficiently any disputes concerning claims can be resolved; and how the impact of disputes as to the creditors' rights in the procedure may be reduced. To some extent, the new law has done much in this field. We may note here the removal of barriers to the creditors filing their claims; the nearly unconditional entitlement for the creditors to participate in the procedure; the introduction of the confirmation litigation procedure; and, more importantly, the process of temporary confirmation. However, as discussed previously, in reforming the filing procedure and creating some new mechanisms, the new law may potentially give rise to many procedural problems that may emerge in future. After all, China is undergoing an era of great change. However, it would be naïve to expect every aspect of a legal system in a society full of rapid changes to be perfect.

61 For a detailed discussion see Parry and Zhang (2008).

## References

Chen, Q. and Wang, G. (2004), 'The Establishment of Confirmation on Bankruptcy Claims' 6 *Enterprise Economy*.

Hao, H. and Wang, Z. (1999), 'The Creditors' Autonomy in Bankruptcy Procedure' *Forum on Civil and Commercial Law* 2 vols (Beijing: Law Press-China).

He, D. (2008), 'Examination and Admission of Deputed Insolvency Claims – And Perfection of China Enterprise Bankruptcy Law' 5 *Journal of Gansu Political Science and Law Institute*.

Law Committee of the NPC, 'The Report about the Amending of the Enterprise Bankruptcy Law of the PRC', 19 October 2004.

Li, G. (2006a), *Problems and Interpretations on the New Enterprise Bankruptcy Law* 1st ed. (Beijing: People's Court Press).

Li, G. (2006b), *The Understanding and Application on the New Enterprise Bankruptcy Law* (Beijing: People's Court Press).

Liu, M. (2006), 'Researches on Filing of Claims', 7 *Hubei Social Sciences*.

Liu, Z. (2009), 'Researches on Confirmation for Bankruptcy Claims', at <http://www.lawtime.cn/info/pochan/pczqqr/2008110743496.html>, last accessed 27 May 2009.

Parry R. and Zhang. H. (2008), 'China's New Corporate Rescue Laws: Perspectives and Principles' 8 *Journal of Corporate Law Studies* 113.

Shi, J., Jin, X. and Yuan, L. (2000), 'Confirmation of the Bankruptcy Creditors and Financial Control' 5 *Forest Engineering*.

Vanessa, F. (2009), *Corporate Insolvency Law: Perspective and Principles* 2nd edn (Cambridge: Cambridge University Press).

Wang, J. (1991), *Obligations in Civil Law* 1st ed. (Beijing: Law Press-China).

Wang, L. and Cui, J. (2003), *New Comments on the Contract Law: General Principles*, rev. ed. (Beijing: China University of Political Science and Law Press)

Wang, X. (2000), 'The Procedure of Confirmation on the Claim' 27th May, *People's Court Daily*.

Wang, X. (2002a), *Bankruptcy Law* 1st ed. (Beijing: China Renmin University Press).

Wang, X. (2002b), *Researches on Issues in Bankruptcy Law* 1st ed. (Beijing: Law Press-China).

Wang, Z. (2008), 'On the Objection Litigation for Claims Table in the New Bankruptcy Law: On Article 58 of the New Bankruptcy Law' 4 *Journal of Central South University*.

Wu, P. (2005), 'The Legal Consequence on Overdue Underclared Claims in Bankruptcy' 5 *Journal of Henan Finance and Taxation College*.

Wu, Y. (1994), 'The Bankruptcy of the Guarantee and the Obligation of Guarantee' Autumn vol. *Nanjing University Law Review*.

Xu, D. (1993), 'Bankruptcy and Guarantee' 1 *Legal Science and Practices*.

Zhu, C. (2006), 'Studying on Confirmation for Insolvent Credit and Act of Confirmation' 4(27) *Journal of Shaoguan Institute*.

# Chapter 10
# Creditors' Meeting and Creditors' Committee

Xin Ge

## Introduction

In the process of bankruptcy, it is evident that the interests of various creditors may give rise to conflict. Therefore the establishment of coordinating an effective means of involvement of creditors in the bankruptcy proceedings will be one of the main issues for the legislature to resolve.[1] Under the modern legislation of most jurisdictions in the world, the solution to this trouble is to establish during the bankruptcy proceedings autonomous creditors' regimes, such as creditors' meetings and/or creditors' committees, enabling creditors and their representatives (in the case of creditors' committees) to decide on critical issues and to monitor the process so as to ensure fairness and integrity.[2]

In conformity with this international model, the Enterprise Bankruptcy of the People's Republic of China, hereafter the 'EBL 2006' devotes an entire chapter, Chapter 7, to the creditors' meeting. The chapter consists of 11 Articles, and establishes the creditors' meeting as an authority for internally coordinating and formulating the joint ideas of all the creditors, and externally actualizing the creditors' rights by means of overseeing the proceedings. Due to the fact that the creditors' meeting is not a permanent organ, in cases where there are a large number of creditors the creation of a creditors' committee that will act on behalf of all the creditors provides for coherence and efficiency in the process, ancillary to the creditors' meeting, to conduct the supervision of the bankruptcy proceedings.

This chapter will provide a brief comparison in respect of provisions on the creditors' meeting that were contained in the 1986 Enterprise Bankruptcy Law of China (For Trial Implementation), hereafter the 'EBL 1986' and the new provisions of the EBL 2006 (superseding the EBL 1986), in order to highlight the improvements of the new law. The chapter will then sketch the outline of the regulations on the creditors' meeting and creditors' committee and will identify some matters that are not clearly set out regarding the creditors' meeting under the new law.

1 Zou (2005).

2 The World Bank (2001), p. 9.

## What are the Significant Changes from the Prior Bankruptcy Law?

The EBL 1986 contained only four articles in respect of the creditors' meeting, dealing with (i) the parties to attend the meeting; (ii) the calling and holding of the meeting; (iii) the powers of the meeting; and (iv) the meeting's resolution. Obviously, this limited approach was too simple to suit the trend of increasing complexity in enterprise insolvency proceedings.

The EBL 2006 'represents an amalgam of borrowing from international experiences and drawing on uniquely Chinese considerations'.[3] This legislative approach is reflected in the provisions on the creditors' meeting. An additional section dealing with creditors' committees has been added to Chapter 7, which deals with the creditors' meeting, in order to strengthen the supervision of the bankruptcy proceedings. The following changes are notable.

Detailed provisions have been enacted regarding the process of approval of resolutions by the creditors' meeting and objection and remedy mechanisms. See further pp. 198-9.

Specific provision is made regarding the voting entitlements of secured creditors who have not surrendered their priority right to be repaid. See further p. 188.

Powers for a creditor who considers that a resolution of the creditors' meeting has violated the law or damaged his interests to apply to the court for the resolution to be revoked.[4] See further 199-200.

Powers of the creditors' meeting to examine and confirm the amount of creditors' claims, which were prescribed in the EBL 1986, have been abolished. This previous provision presented a dilemma for the creditors' meeting as to whether a creditor who had presented a claim could attend the meeting and vote, and how much the claim would stand for. These matters would be settled only after the creditors' meeting had voted upon the claim of each creditor. On the other hand, any resolution to be passed by the meeting would be conditional upon the claim of each creditor participating in the meeting having been confirmed.[5] Under the EBL 2006, the creditors' meeting will only verify the claims that are submitted to it,[6] and the confirmation of the list of claims, where there is no disagreement regarding the claims that are listed, is a function of the judicial authority.[7] A creditor whose claim is unconfirmed may obtain temporary confirmation for the purpose of exercising his voting right.[8]

3 Shi (2007), p. 649.

4 See Article 64, EBL 2006.

5 Zou (1995), p. 147.

6 Article 58, EBL 2006.

7 Article 58, EBL 2006.

8 Article 59, EBL 2006.

Whereas the EBL 1986 emphasized in particular the court's control over the bankruptcy procedure,[9] the EBL 2006 relatively reduces the court's penetration and intervention, and gives more powers to the creditors' meeting and the administrator. The new law includes sufficient procedures to establish the relationship between the creditors' meeting and the administrator, with the creditors' meeting supervising the administrator, and the administrator having to compensate[10] the creditors for losses incurred due to the administrator's malpractice.[11]

## Provisions Regarding the Creditors' Meeting

### *Membership and Voting Rights in Creditors' Meetings*

Who is eligible to attend and vote at the creditors' meeting? Article 59 of the EBL 2006 provides that a creditor whose claim has been declared in accordance with law is entitled to attend the creditors' meeting with the right to vote. In general, the creditors who are entitled to attend the creditors' meeting will meet the following conditions:

1. their claim tallies with the related provisions of the bankruptcy law;[12]
2. as far as the first creditors' meeting is concerned, their claim has been legally presented within the legitimate term,[13] whether or not the claim and its amount are true; and
3. for the second and subsequent meetings that, upon examination, the court has confirmed his creditor's right.

The process of claim declaration requires creditors to present their claims for participation in the insolvency proceedings, those who fail to state their creditor status according to the EBL 2006 will lose the right to take part in the creditors' meeting and to vote. Nevertheless, under Article 56, 'claims which have not been declared within the time period established by the court may be supplementarily declared prior to the final distribution of insolvent property'. Creditors to whom this provision is applicable can still become members of the creditors' meeting.

Article 59 does not specifically classify creditors according to the character of the claims that they hold. However an analysis of the legislation reveals that the

9 Wang (2007), p. 93. In addition, the liquidation group's role is similar to that of the administrator under the EBL 2006.

10 See Article 130, EBL 2006.

11 Wang (2007), pp. 92-3.

12 See Chapter 6 of the EBL 2006, Filing of Creditors' Claims and Chapter 9 in this volume.

13 See Article 45, EBL 2006.

creditors who are present at the meeting can be divided into two types: those with voting rights and those without voting rights.

Those creditors with voting rights are members of the creditors' meeting, entitled to attend and express their opinions in the creditors' meeting, and further to vote on the issues to be resolved by the meeting. This class of creditors is composed of i) the holders of claims which have been directly allowed and are unsecured; ii) the holders of claims which have been legally allowed and are secured, with or without the priority right having been given up;[14] iii) the holders of claims that have been legally allowed and are secured but which have not been fully repaid, despite priority rights having been exercised; and iv) any guarantors, or co-debtors bearing joint and several liability with the debtor, who have made payment on account of the debtor's liability.[15] Upon a ruling of the creditor's right by the court, the creditor can be a member of the creditors' meeting and enjoy the right to vote.

Another group of creditors is comprised of those who can attend the creditors' meeting, and voice their opinions, but who cannot vote at the meeting, or whose voting entitlements are restricted. This group includes any creditor whose claim has not yet been confirmed and unless the court grants temporary confirmation of his claim, for the purpose of his exercising voting rights, such a creditor is prohibited from voting.[16] This group also includes any secured creditor who has not waived his right to priority of being repaid: such a creditor may not enjoy the right to vote in respect of any matter concerning the adoption of a composition agreement or the adoption of a distribution plan regarding the insolvent estate.[17]

*Creditors holding undecided claims* Can creditors holding undecided claimed vote at the meetings? In the process of the bankruptcy, there may be some claims that have not yet been determined, such as claims subject to conditions or to time limits; claims that are being heard by a court or arbitration panel; contingent claims; future rights to recourse against the debtor, and so on. Thus, the issues of whether the holders of such claims can vote at the creditors' meeting and, if so, what proportion of the vote their claims shall account for, will have to be decided by the court, under Article 59 of the EBL 2006. In the event that the court cannot determine the claim, this creditor will not be entitled to exercise voting rights at the meeting. It is noteworthy that the ruling by the court on this matter only relates to the procedural issues of whether or not the creditor is able to vote at the creditors' meeting and the proportion of the claim that his voting will

14 As mentioned in Part II(1), sometimes the voting right for a secured creditor who has not surrendered his position of priority of realizing the collateral will be restricted.

15 Li (2008), p. 348.

16 Article 59, second paragraph, EBL 2006.

17 Article 59, third paragraph, EBL 2006.

cover.[18] The ruling does not have the force of confirming substantive issues, such as the substantive validity of a claim against an insolvent debtor.[19] The dispute regarding the claim should be settled by bringing an action *in personam* based on the substantive laws.

*Creditors holding rights of exclusion* Can creditors with right to exclusion be members of the creditors' meeting? Generally, a creditor with right to exclusion is a secured creditor. The 'right to exclusion' refers to a claim against assets of the debtor, based on a mortgage, pledge, lien or similar. Such claims will be given priority repayment, ahead of the claims of the unsecured creditors. They will be repaid under general civil procedures without going through the bankruptcy procedures.[20]

The EBL 1986 stated that a creditor with the right of exclusion was a member of the creditors' meeting, and that such a creditor who did not abstain from the priority to be repaid would not have voting rights.[21] Such an approach may be regarded as having been unfair to this kind of creditor for two reasons. First, pursuant to the EBL 1986, the claim held by the creditor with the right to exclusion would have had to be examined and allowed at the creditors' meeting, like the unsecured creditor's claim, but, unlike unsecured creditors, the secured creditors would have had no access to voting. Second, on one hand the EBL 1986 did not vest the secured creditor with any voting rights on the motions of the creditors' meeting, but, on the other hand, it stipulated that all the resolutions of the creditors' meetings would become legally binding against the secured creditors. These disparities in rights were obviously detrimental to the legitimate rights of the secured creditor.[22]

Consequently, Article 59 of the EBL 2006 places ordinary creditors and secured creditors subject to the same creditors' meeting regime and they have the same voting rights on almost every issue except for the passing of a draft composition agreement or a proposal regarding the distribution of the bankruptcy estate.[23]

Also, it is a principle in China, as in other countries, that '[a] creditor is a lien creditor only to the extent of the value of its collateral'.[24] In the event that the amount of a claim held by a secured creditor is more than the value of the secured property, and the disparity in amount cannot be collateralized, the claim for the shortfall will be treated as an unsecured claim.[25] And moreover, in the event of a deficient amount, the creditor can gain voting rights on every issue at the creditors'

18 However, so far we have not seen a set of published criteria on the basis of which the court should decide upon the amount of claim.

19 Wang (2008).

20 Li (2000), pp. 307 and 318.

21 Article 13, EBL 1986.

22 Wang (2008).

23 Article 59, EBL 2006.

24 Epstein (2005), p. 3.

25 Article 110, EBL 2006.

meeting as a general unsecured creditor. Alternatively, where the secured creditor, for some purpose, abandons his repayment priority, he will have the same voting rights as the general unsecured creditors.[26] In practice, the consideration of whether it is in the interests of a creditor to waive this priority will depend on whether the voting right is more important and beneficial than the priority.[27]

Where the value of the collateral exceeds the value of the secured claim, the excessive amount after the redemption of the collateral will be part of the bankruptcy estate.[28]

*Entitlements of labour creditors* Compared to some other countries, China is facing a problem that some employees are owed wages and premiums in arrears. In consideration of protecting the employees' interests, Article 59 of the EBL 2006 states that the representatives of the employees of the debtor and of the trade union shall attend the creditors' meeting and may voice their opinions on matters of their concern.[29]

However, the Law is vague as to whether these representatives have voting rights and there exist three points of view on this question. Some argue that the labour creditors should neither be members of the creditors' meeting nor should they have voting rights, though they are also creditors of the insolvent debtor, inasmuch as the employment claim[30] stems from the labour relationship. It is contended that the labour relationship is, in essence, of a different nature from other types of business relationship which generate civil legal rights and obligations (including the creditor's rights), in light of the unequal relationship between employer and employee.[31] Further it is noted that, as under the bankruptcy laws of numerous

26 Article 110, EBL 2006.

27 Tang (2006), p. 207.

28 Li (2000), p. 320.

29 It is notable that there are some uncertainties relating to this provision which will have to be made clear in the future by either the legislature or the court. They include the following. Which issues does the term 'relevant issues' refer to? Through what procedure can the employee or trade union representatives be elected to participate in the creditors meeting? Is there any limitation to the number of representatives? And will the representatives attend the creditors meeting, where there is no employment claims against the insolvent debtor?

30 The relevant scope is expressly provided in Article 48: '[w]ages, medical fees, compensations for injury and disability, compensations due from the debtor to a bereaved family, basic pension and medical insurance premiums that the debtor was liable to pay into the employees' personal accounts, as well as other compensations that are payable by the debtor to the employees in accordance with laws and administrative rules and regulations, are exempt from being declared but shall be listed and announced by the Administrator after investigation'.

31 In the interests of employee protection the newly enacted (1 May 2008) Labour Dispute Mediation and Arbitration Law stipulates the labour administrative department shall provide guidance to labour dispute arbitration work within the administrative area

jurisdictions, the labour creditors are entitled to be paid in priority under China's bankruptcy law.[32] It is argued that the position of first priority held by labour claims in the distribution of the debtor's estate in liquidation means that the labour creditors' rights and interests will be sufficiently guaranteed, even if the labour creditors do not attend the creditors' meeting. A further point made to support this argument lies in the different process of identification of labour claims that is set out in the EBL 2006. The position that is applicable to non-employee creditors is set out in Article 59, which provides that only those creditors who have presented their claim against the insolvent debtor can be members of the creditors' meeting and enjoy the right to vote, and in Article 56, which provides that where a creditor fails to declare his creditor's right, he may not exercise relevant rights arising under the procedures prescribed in the EBL 2006.[33]

In contrast, in Article 48 it is provided that it is not necessary for labour claims to be declared to the administrator, since the administrator will create a list of labour claims upon investigation and that he will announce this list. In light of these differences in treatment, it is arguable that employment claim holders do not fall within the range of persons who can attend and vote in the creditors' meeting.[34]

A further observation, which may support this argument, is that the number of labour creditors is often relatively large, and it would not be feasible for all of them to attend the creditors' meeting. In addition, it may be noted that one of the voting rules requires a majority of those attending to consent to a resolution. A concern is that, in the case of a proposal with which the labour creditors disagree, the required majority in number could seldom be reached, which would effectively amount to a substantial power of veto in respect of resolutions at the creditors' meeting. Such a veto may affect the progress of the bankruptcy proceedings and may jeopardize other creditors' interests.[35]

A different opinion regarding the rights of the labour creditors' representative is that the representatives should enjoy some rights, including voting rights, to protect the employees' rights and interests, because the law's empowering of the representatives of labour creditors to join in the creditors' meeting, indicates that the status of those representatives is equivalent to that of a litigation representative for labour claimants.[36]

It is notable that, no matter what nature can be ascribed to labour claims, nobody can deny that the bankruptcy law should also safeguard the rights of labour creditors and that any activities that are needlessly harmful to the interests of labour creditors should be prohibited. In this case, if at the creditors' meeting, a proposal

---

and labour dispute arbitration commissions shall comprise the representative of the labour administrative department, labour union representative and enterprise representative.

32 See Article 113, EBL 2006.

33 Article 56, second paragraph, EBL 2006.

34 Li (2008), p. 353; Yin (2008), pp. 166-8.

35 Wang (2007), p. 287.

36 Tang (2006), p. 206.

may damage the labour creditors' rights and interests, they ought to have legally provided measures to challenge it, and it is obvious that only having undeclared labour creditors' rights and the first priority in liquidation are not enough, since this priority will take effect only at the stage of bankrupt liquidation. Except for stating their views at the creditors' meeting, the Law should offer some other remedies to the labour creditors, at least when composition[37] proceedings which may relate to the employees' crucial interests are concerned. From this angle, the EBL 2006 needs improvement in the future based on practice.

*Tax creditors* There is no special provision in EBL 2006 to indicate whether or not tax claims need to be declared to the administrator. This means that this kind of creditor will not have participation and voting rights in the creditors' meeting unless it puts forward its tax claim to the administrator in time like the other creditor (excluding the labour creditor for whom the Law has special provisions).[38]

As for participation in the creditors' meeting by the tax claim holder, in the event that the debtor has provided collateral in respect of its tax payment liability, pursuant to Article 38 of the Law on Administration of Tax Collection of China, the tax creditor has no voting rights at the meeting; whereas it will enjoy the voting rights if the debtor has not placed a collateral on its tax payment liability.[39]

*Attendance and voting by agents* Can the creditor authorize an agent to attend the meeting and vote? Pursuant to the EBL 2006, the creditor can either attend in person, or authorize his agent to attend the creditors' meeting. In this latter circumstance the creditor may exercise the right to vote by submitting a power of attorney to the court or the chairperson of the creditors' meeting.

A point that is worthy of emphasis is that, in conformity to Article 242 of the Civil Procedure Law of China, where a foreign creditor entrusts the agent to take part in the creditors' meeting, the power of attorney will not be valid unless it has been notarized by a notary in the country of domicile of the creditor, and then authenticated by the Chinese embassy or consulate accredited to that country; or alternatively it has gone through the verification formalities that are stipulated under any relevant bilateral treaty between China and that country.

In the event that a creditor domiciled in Hong Kong, Macau or Taiwan, intends to employ a mainland China lawyer to handle the bankruptcy issues on his behalf, the related power of attorney which is made:

37 However, under the reorganization procedure, the labour claim holders will vote on the reorganization plan as a group, as provided in Article 82 of the EBL 2006.

38 Another viewpoint holds that the tax claim cannot be subject to the civil law and bankruptcy law and that the claim holder is not a member of the creditors' meeting, for the tax claim originates from taxation, a kind of administrative legal relation between the State and the taxpayer, different from those claims that are rooted in civil and business activities. For details, see Xing (2007), p. 125.

39 Sun and Li (2008).

- by a Hong Kong resident, shall be first notarized by a Hong Kong lawyer (public notary) who has been duly appointed by the China Ministry of Justice, and then examined and delivered to the appropriate court on the mainland for the affixation of the seal by the Examination and Delivery Office, a department under the China Legal Service (H.K.) Ltd;
- by a Macau resident, shall be legalized by a Chinese public notary who is appointed and sent to Macau by the China Ministry of Justice, with the exclusive attesting seal affixed by China Legal Service (Macau) Ltd on it;
- by a Taiwan resident, shall be first legalized by a local Taiwan notary, and delivered to the mainland by the Taiwan Straits Exchange Foundation, by which the notarized documents will be remitted to a competent notary association in mainland China, and the latter will send it to the needed court.

*Non-voting Delegates*

Besides the above mentioned creditors, there are further parties who may attend the meeting as non-voting delegates:

As stated in Article 15 of the EBL 2006, such relevant personnel of the debtor as its legal representatives, financial managers and other operators, will be present at the creditors' meeting to answer the creditors' inquiries. Article 126 sets out relevant liabilities when they violate the above obligations, for instance, the imposition of a fine according to law;

> Due to the special function of the administrator, the EBL 2006 prescribes that the administrator shall be present at the creditors' meeting, and that he shall report upon the performance of its duties and functions and answer relevant inquiries from the creditors' meeting;[40]
> Representatives appointed by the capital contributors of the debtor may attend the creditors' meeting to discuss a draft reorganization plan;[41] and
> Representatives of employment creditors and the trade union shall be present at the meeting. The attendance of such representatives will be analyzed further below.

*Convening of the Creditors' Meeting*

Two types of creditors' meeting may be identified. One is the statutory meeting of creditors and the other is any discretionary meeting of the creditors.

---

40 Article 23, second paragraph, EBL 2006.

41 Article 85, first paragraph, EBL 2006. The second paragraph of this provision provides that where the draft reorganization plan involves the adjustment of investors' equities, such investors will vote. In this context, the meeting is not wholly a creditors' meeting.

*Statutory meeting of the creditors* The term 'statutory meeting' refers to the first meeting of creditors. This meeting is convened by the court and it cannot be cancelled unless 'the debtor's property is insufficient to cover the bankruptcy expenses and the bankruptcy procedure is concluded early'.[42]

It is provided in Article 62 of the EBL 2006 that the first creditors' meeting shall be convened by the court within 15 days of the expiration date of the term for claim declaration. The term for the claim declaration, within which creditors must present their claims, must fall within a range of no less than 30 days and no more than three months after the court's acceptance of an application for bankruptcy, therefore the first meeting of creditors may be held within 45 to 105 days after the date of the court's acceptance of the bankruptcy petition.

Since the statutory meeting is called by the court, what work will it prepare prior to the meeting? In conformity with the new bankruptcy law and the Supreme Court's judicial interpretation thereof, the following steps will be taken by the court:

- within 25 days from the day when it decides to accept the petition, it will notify the relevant creditors of the time and place where the first creditors' meeting is to be held;[43]
- it will draft the agenda of the first creditors' meeting;
- it will notify the debtor's legal representative or person in charge, the debtor's shareholders and the like, as well as its auditors and appraiser (if any) to attend the meeting.[44]

What is the business of the statutory meeting? As per Article 42 of the Regulations 2002, the meeting will:

- announce the functions and powers of the creditors' meeting;
- announce the results of the examination of the creditors' qualification;
- announce the chairperson of the creditors' meeting upon the court's designation;
- request the debtor's personnel to answer the creditors' queries;
- include the administrator's presentation of a report on the debtor's operation, property and debts; and
- examine the claims.

Where all the creditors' voting rights have been settled, the following additional resolutions may be considered at the statutory meeting, depending on the circumstances:

---

42 Article 40 of 'The Regulation on Several Issues Concerning Hearing Enterprise Bankruptcy Cases' promulgated by the Supreme People's Court on 30 July 2002 (hereinafter the 'Regulations 2002').

43 Article 14(6), EBL 2006.

44 Regulations 2002, Article 41.

- where, before the first meeting, the debtor puts forward a draft composition proposal the meeting will resolve on the draft composition proposal;[45] or
- where before the first meeting, the court has ruled and announced the debtor to be bankrupt, and the administrator has finished receiving and clearing up the property of the estate and has prepared the distribution proposal in respect of the estate, the meeting will also resolve on the distribution proposal.

*Discretionary meetings of the creditors* The term 'discretionary meeting' refers to any meeting which may be held after the statutory meeting. Such a meeting may be held where the court deems it necessary, or where the bankruptcy administrator, the creditors' committee, or any creditor representing one quarter or more of the total creditors' rights proposes to the chairperson of the creditors' meeting that such a meeting should be held.[46]

Who will convene the discretionary meetings? On this question, the provisions in the EBL 2006 seem varied and ambiguous: Article 62 provides that the court will 'convene' the first meeting; and that the subsequent discretionary meetings may be held when the court deems it necessary or where the administrator, the creditors' committee, or any creditors representing 1/4 or more of the total creditors' rights, propose to the chairperson of the creditors' meeting that a discretionary meeting should be held. In addition, Article 84 provides for the court to 'hold' a creditor's meeting to vote the draft reorganization proposal, while Article 96 authorizes the court to 'convene' a creditors' meeting to discuss the draft composition agreement. Obviously, 'holding' is different from 'convening' a meeting, however the Law lacks further instruction as to the different roles for the court.

The opinions from the judiciary and from scholars are also various: some hold that the discretionary meetings will be called by the chairperson of the meeting;[47] while others consider that the administrator can do this work, on the basis that it is a permanent office during the bankruptcy proceeding, and that the Law provides in Article 63 that the administrator shall notify the already-known creditors 15 days in advance in case of holding a creditors' meeting.[48] A third point of view is that the subsequent meetings can be convened either by the court or by the chairperson, in other words, both the court and the chairperson of the creditors' meeting have respective independent rights to call a creditors' meeting.[49]

Purely in consideration of the literal meaning, the third idea seems to be closest to the provisions listed above. It is expected that a clarifying supplement may be made by the Supreme Court in the future so that the role of each organ in the bankruptcy proceeding will be clarified and that these roles shall be effectively coordinated.

45 Li (2008), p. 354.

46 Article 62, second paragraph, EBL 2006.

47 Li (2008), p. 355; Wang (2008), p. 200.

48 Wang (2007), p. 96.

49 Tang (2006), p. 211.

*Powers and Functions of the Creditors' Meeting*

The powers and functions of the creditors' meeting are set out in Article 61 of the EBL 2006. This provision constitutes the legal authority for the meeting to undertake various tasks, and the yardstick for its legal activities. In particular, the provision gives authority for the following activities:

- verifying creditors' claims. At the meeting, the attending creditors will examine all the proofs for the declared claims, and are entitled to dispute the authenticity of each proof and question the declarer. Claims that are declared without objection by the creditors will be allowed on a preliminary basis by means of a resolution of the meeting and they will then allowed by a court ruling. Any dispute concerning the authenticity or amount of a claim that has been filed will be decided by the court;[50]
- petitioning the court to replace the administrator or to examine his expenses and remuneration, or for the administrator to be supervised. Where the court finds improper or unethical conduct on the part of the administration after investigation, it can rule to replace the administrator and appoint a replacement;
- electing and replacing members of the creditors' committee;
- deciding on the continuation or cessation of the business of the debtor. After the court accepts the petition for bankruptcy, and before the first creditors' meeting is held, it is the administrator that decides whether to continue or suspend the debtor's business.[51] Afterward, this decision will be made by the creditors' meeting;
- adopting reorganization proposals and composition agreements;[52] and
- adopting plans for the management of the property of the debtor, or the sale of the debtor's assets, or the distribution of property.

What responsibilities does the court possess at the first and subsequent meetings? In accordance with the provisions regarding the creditors' meeting under the EBL 2006, the functions and powers of the court are in particular the following:

- to convene and preside (before the appointment of the chairperson of the

50 Article 58, EBL 2006.

51 Article 25(5), EBL 2006.

52 It is noteworthy that the creditors' meeting's powers and functions in respect of composition and reorganization differ from each other when voting: the former meeting will act as one voting unit to calculate the total vote; and the latter will vote by groups, with the creditors classified into different groups as per the classes of claims that they hold (see Article 82, EBL 2006). Further, the debtor's investors (including shareholders) shall vote on the draft reorganization plan where the plan involves the adjustment of investors' equities (see EBL 2006. Article 85).

meeting) over the first meeting;[53]

- to designate the chairperson of the meeting from among the creditors with the right to vote;[54]
- to propose a discretionary meeting where it considers it appropriate;[55]
- to replace the administrator upon the application of the creditors' meeting;[56]
- to confirm the undecided claims and the amounts thereof;[57]
- to confirm the claims and the amounts thereof;[58]
- to revoke, where appropriate, a resolution and order the creditors' meeting to re-make a resolution according to the law, upon a creditor's application;[59]
- to convene the creditors' meetings in order for it to resolve on a reorganization proposal. In the event that the meeting adopts the proposal, the court will grant approval for the proposal by a ruling; alternatively, where a proposal fails to be adopted and fails to be approved, or where an adopted proposal fails to be approved, the court will rule to terminate the reorganization procedures and announce the debtor to be bankrupt;[60]
- to convene the creditors' meeting in order for it to resolve on a composition proposal: in the event that the meeting adopts the composition agreement, the court will confirm it by a ruling; alternatively, where the agreement fails to be adopted, or where an adopted proposal fails to be approved, the court will rule to terminate the composition procedure and announce the debtor to be bankrupt;[61]
- to decide on the management of the debtor's property, a plan of sale regarding the property of the estate, or a distribution plan, if needed;[62] and
- to reconsider, upon a creditors' petition, any previous rulings made by itself on the management of the debtor's property, a plan of sale of the property of the estate, or a distribution plan.[63]

*Chairperson*

What kind of creditor can be designated as chairperson of the creditors' meeting? At the first meeting, the chairperson of the creditors' meeting will be appointed. Article 60 provides that the chairperson will be designated by the court from

53 Article 62 first paragraph, EBL 2006.
54 Article 60, EBL 2006.
55 Article 62, second paragraph, EBL 2006.
56 Article 61(2), EBL 2006.
57 Article 58, EBL 2006.
58 Article 59, second paragraph, EBL 2006.
59 Article 64, second paragraph, EBL 2006.
60 Articles 84 and 88, EBL 2006.
61 Articles 96, 98 and 99, EBL 2006.
62 Article 65, EBL 2006.
63 Article 66, EBL 2006.

among the creditors with the right to vote.[64] As noted above, those creditors who have declared their claims will be entitled to participate in the creditors' meeting and vote. However, Article 60 is to some extent ambiguous in nature, since it does not expressly state whether a secured creditor can be the chairperson. As noted previously, a secured creditor holds no voting rights concerning the approval of a composition and distribution plan, given that he still holds the entitlement to be repaid in priority to other creditors. Therefore the secured creditor may be regarded as having partial voting rights. Arguably, it would be desirable for future related legislation to specify a secured creditor shall not be the chairperson.[65]

In addition, in the event that the creditor is selected as chairperson by the court is a legal person, the finally designated chairperson will be a natural person duly authorized by the body corporate.[66]

The EBL 2006 does not expressly state whether the chairperson of the creditors' meeting can resign and under what condition he can resign, therefore further supplementary provisions are needed. Moreover, this law is likewise silent on the right for the creditors to disagree with the candidate chairperson chosen by the court and on the right for the creditors' committee (or creditors) to supervise the chairperson, especially on the remedial measures in the event that that the chairperson has violated his duties.[67]

### *Resolutions at the Creditors' Meeting*

The EBL 2006 makes the following provision regarding resolutions adopted by the creditors' meeting in Article 64:

> A resolution made at a creditors' meeting may be deemed as being adopted provided that it is adopted by more than half of the creditors present at the meeting with voting rights and with claims that exceed half of the total value of unsecured claims, unless provided otherwise in this law.
>
> A creditor with the belief that a resolution made at a creditors' meeting violates the law and impairs his interests may, within 15 days of the adoption of the resolution, apply to the court to revoke the resolution and order the creditors' meeting to remake a resolution in accordance with the law.
>
> A resolution that is adopted at a creditors' meeting shall be binding on all creditors.

*Voting rules* The first paragraph of Article 64 deals with this issue. In the

64 Article 60, EBL 2006.
65 Wang (2007), p. 96; Han (2008).
66 Han (2008).
67 Tang (2006), p. 207.

insolvency legislation of some jurisdictions, such as England[68] and Canada,[69] a quorum requirement is applicable in respect of the meeting of creditors and the meeting shall not make a valid resolution in the event that the number of participants at the meeting is less than the quorum. The EBL 2006 lays no specific provisions on this issue, but in view of the rules of the meeting being based on the number of participants and the portion of the value of the claims of creditors represented by the participants, the quorum of the creditors' meeting should arguably be two or more entitled creditors, or otherwise the meeting should be postponed.[70]

As noted above, the criteria upon which the validity of a resolution is based contain a mixture of two approaches, based on both the number of participants at the meeting, and the portion that the value of the claims represented by the attending creditors bears to the value of the total creditors' rights, whether present at the meeting or not.

Based on the importance of the issues to be decided, the resolutions can be categorized into two kinds: special resolutions, which require the consent of a majority of the creditors present at the meeting, who hold claims of an amount which exceeds two-thirds of the total creditors' rights (in respect of a composition plan, the claims refer to those free from collateral);[71] and general resolutions of the type referred to in the first paragraph of Article 64.

Unlike the provision in Article 65 that the court will directly rule on matters relating to the adoption of a distribution plan in respect of the insolvent property where no resolution is made by the creditors' meeting on the matter after a second vote, the EBL 2006 lacks relevant provisions regulating the case where the amount of debts held by the participants at the meeting represents in value less than half of the total debts held by creditors, a state of affairs which gives the possibility of a standstill of the meeting or the invalidity of the resolutions.

### *Objection to a Resolution of the Meeting*

The second paragraph of Article 64 provides for the remedies where a creditor objects to the adopted resolution, based on a violation of the law and impairment of his interest. What must be kept in mind is:

- that the violation of law includes that of either substantive law or procedural law; and
- that the dissenting creditor may be among those who objected to the adopted resolution at the meeting, those who enjoyed the right to vote at the meeting but failed to attend the meeting, and those who did not have

---

68 R. 12.4A, Insolvency Rules 1986, (SI 1986/1925).

69 S. 106 of the Bankruptcy and Insolvency Act (R.S., 1985, c. B-3).

70 Zou (1995), p. 137.

71 For details, see Articles 84, 86 and 97, EBL 2006.

voting rights at the time when the resolution is passed but later acquired such rights;[72] and
- the ground for the dissenting creditor to petition the court to revoke the resolution is the resolution's violating the law and impairing his individual interests.[73]

In addition, as an experienced judge has noted,[74] this provision may be likely to trigger a long outstanding resolution or even a deadlock, for according to this Article, the court has no authority to directly rule on this disputed issue but may only charge the meeting with re-making a resolution. However, the task of actually organizing a creditors' meeting is costly and time consuming, and further, asking a creditor to cast a vote on the matter to which he objects is also extremely difficult. Accordingly, this judge has suggested the placing of a time limit for the meeting to re-make a resolution, or, authorizing the court to directly decide on this matter other than through having the resolution remade.

*Effect of the Resolutions*

The third paragraph of Article 64 provides that the resolutions of the creditors' meeting should be binding on all the creditors in the insolvency, whether or not they have attended the meeting, and whether or not they agree with the resolution. This approach may be criticized because the secured creditors have no voting right in respect of the distribution and composition plans, and will of course have no responsibility to be bound on such related resolutions from the angle that every right corresponds to an obligation. Further, the resolutions in relation to the composition agreement and the distribution plan are the common expression of intent of the ordinary creditors and they cannot alter the statutory priority of repayment of the secured claim and hence should have no effect on the secured creditors. Therefore, it is suggested that the resolutions of the meeting should be binding only on those creditors who have the voting rights in respect of the resolved issue.[75]

General resolutions will take effect upon adoption, whereas special resolutions shall not be effective unless the court approves them in a ruling.[76]

72 Wang (2007), p. 313.

73 It can be further provided in the future legislation that the cause of the petition shall include the violation of the common interest of all the creditors, like German Insolvency Statute Article 78 and Japanese Bankruptcy Law Article 184 (see Wang (2007), p. 313)

74 Chen (2006). But Wang Xinxin argues that in the event that the court considers that the property management plan or the distribution plan needs revising, it should only rule not to approve the plan, not change the plan, as formulation of these plans is the statutory authority of the administrator (see Wang (2007), p. 312).

75 Wang (2007), p. 311.

76 Articles 98, 86 and 116, EBL 2006.

## The Provisions Concerning the Creditors' Committee

In China, the first instance of the creation of a creditors' committee was in the Guangdong International Trust and Investment Corporation case, in which the claims of the top nine creditors by value were comprised, including the claims of six foreign creditors.[77] This practice was absorbed into the EBL 2006 and recently, the creditors' committee has facilitated a series of bankruptcy proceedings. For example, in the Hantang Securities Company bankruptcy case, the creditors' committee consisted of seven members, six of which were among the creditors with the highest value claims against the debtor and the other was an employee representative.[78]

Since Article 67 of the EBL 2006 provides that: '[t]he creditors' meeting may decide to establish a creditors' committee', it is clear that the committee is not a compulsory organ in bankruptcy proceedings and the decision as to whether or not it should be founded depends on the resolution of the creditors' meeting. Generally speaking, for bankruptcy proceedings involving only small amounts of claims or fewer creditors, the establishment of a committee may not be necessary.

### *What are the Relations between the Court, the Creditors' Meeting and the Creditors' Committee?*

For the reason that 'an insolvency proceeding is a judicial proceeding', and 'a party in interest cannot be denied an opportunity to appear before the court if it feels that its rights are not being adequately protected',[79] the court should play a crucial role in the bankruptcy process, and should be completely responsible for the smooth progress of the bankruptcy proceedings. Due to the fundamental role in the bankruptcy law of the creditors' meeting as a decision-making (resolution-adopting) authority comprised by all the creditors, enabling them to participate in the bankruptcy and exercise their collective authority, an important duty of the court in the insolvency proceeding is to facilitate the effective functioning of the creditors' meeting. The creditors' committee, as an ancillary organization can however represent the creditors' meeting and carry out the monitoring functions of the creditors' meeting[80] more easily and effectively than the meeting itself.

Further, although both the creditors' committee and creditors' meeting are to safeguard the interests of all the creditors, the former shall be bound by the resolutions of the creditors' meeting and the latter is superior to the former.[81]

77 Yang (2008), pp.181-2.
78 Yang (2008), pp. 179-80.
79 Legal Department of the International Monetary Fund (2008).
80 Li (2008), pp. 376-81.
81 Zou (2005).

### *How is the Creditors' Committee Comprised?*

As stated above, whether or not the creditors' committee should be established, depends on the resolution of the creditors' meeting. In practice, the key factors for consideration in setting up a committee are:[82]

1. the number of creditors;
2. the real value of the debtor's debts; and
3. the level of complexity that will be entailed in collecting, appraising and realizing the bankruptcy property.

A simple case will arguably not merit the establishment of the creditors' committee, so as to limit the costs that would otherwise be incurred.

Details of the required composition of the committee are provided in the first paragraph of Article 67 of the EBL 2006:

> The creditors' committee shall be comprised of creditor representatives, as selected at the creditors' meeting, as well as a representative of the debtor's employees or a representative of the trade union. The members of the creditors' committee shall be no more than nine persons.

The law is silent as to whether or not a representative of the creditors must be a creditor himself, and as to the minimum number of members of the committee. The appointment of the members of the creditors' committee is subject to the written approval of the court.[83] Nevertheless, there is no specified remedy in the event that the court does not ratify the member(s) of the committee.

The purpose of placing an employee or trade union representative on the committee is to safeguard the employees' interests in the debtor enterprise. However there is no further provision to guide how this representative is to be selected, beyond the requirement that the appointment should be ratified by the court in written form, like the appointment of the other members of the creditors' committee.[84]

In addition, the EBL 2006 does not specify the working mechanisms of the committee, such as quorum and voting rules. Therefore these details need to be made clear by the creditors' meeting resolution through which the committee is established.

### *What are the Monitoring Rights of the Creditors' Committee?*

The creditors' meeting has extensive powers to oversee the insolvency proceedings, however the legislation does not indicate that the creditors' committee can exercise

82 Li (2008), p. 383.

83 Article 67, EBL 2006.

84 Article 67, second paragraph, EBL 2006.

those powers, too. As per the law, there are two kinds of powers of the creditors' committee: general monitoring powers and special monitoring powers.

*General monitoring powers* It is provided in Article 68 that the creditors' committee shall perform such functions and duties as supervising the management, disposal and distribution of the debtor's estate, proposing that a creditors' meeting be held, and performing such other functions and duties as are authorized by the creditors' meeting. It is evident that the EBL 2006 takes a cautious approach in respect of the functions of the creditors' committee and it does not furnish the committee with more extensive authority.[85]

Notwithstanding the limited nature of the above functions, the EBL 2006 provides for two safeguarding roles for the creditors' committee. The first relates to the bankruptcy procedures: when performing its duties, the committee will have the power to require the administrator and the debtor to give an explanation as to any matter within the scope of its functions, or to provide the relevant documents. In the event that the administrator or the debtor should refuse to cooperate, the creditors' committee has the right to request the court to make a decision, and the latter shall make a decision thereon within five days.[86] The second enables the committee to propose that a meeting of the creditor's committee is convened.[87] It has been contended that this provision enables the committee to give substantive protection: where the committee is aware of activities on the part of the administrator or the debtor that are detrimental to the creditors' interests, it can propose that a creditors' meeting is held, and its supervisory function can be realized by presenting its opinions and asking the meeting to pass resolutions against the impairment.[88]

*Special monitoring powers* One of the key duties of the administrator is to manage and dispose of the debtor's estate and therefore one special function of the committee is to monitor the administrator's asset management and disposal activities on behalf of the creditors. The EBL 2006, in Article 69, requires the administrator to report upon the following significant activities affecting the interests of creditors:

- any transfer of the rights and interests in such realties as land and houses;
- a transfer of such property rights as the rights to mine exploitation, mining rights and intellectual property rights;
- a transfer of all the inventory or business operation;
- the granting of a loan;
- the provision of collateral on property;

85 Tang (2006), p. 232.

86 Article 68, EBL 2006.

87 Article 68(3), EBL 2006.

88 Tang (2006), p. 233.

- an assignment of rights as a creditors and a transfer of securities;
- the performance of any contract that has not been fully executed by the debtor and its counter party;
- a waiver of rights;
- a withdrawal of collateral; and
- any other property disposal that has a crucial impact on the creditor's interest.
- the second paragraph of this Article adds that in the event of no creditors' committee having been established, the administrator shall, when engaging in any of the significant activities noted above, report it to the court in a timely manner.

Nevertheless, it is doubtful whether the committee can effectively and fully perform the supervision functions set out in the EBL 2006, owing to the following unclear issues:

- Firstly, the Law does not vest the committee with more functions beyond those supervision powers mentioned above, which, however, seem very limited in nature. In practice therefore the committee may be unlikely to fulfil the function of representing the creditors' meeting and supervising the bankruptcy proceedings.[89] Further the EBL 2006 contains a lack of instructions regarding:
  - whether the administrator must report before carrying out the significant activities that he is supposed to report to the committee or whether this report need only be made after performing them;
  - what is the result for the administrator of reporting upon the significant activities; and
  - what consequences follow if a member of the committee causes damages or losses to the creditors' interests due to his intentional activity or negligence.
- Secondly, the EBL 2006 does not state how the representative of the employees or of the trade union on the committee is appointed, and the kind of powers that the representative has are also not clear.
- Thirdly, since the EBL 2006 is silent on the committee's working system, it may have been preferable for the Law to have provided that professionals shall be retained in the committee, in order for the committee to 'have access to impartial advice to ensure that the rights of creditors are being protected'[90] and to enable it exercise its duties smoothly and successfully.

89 Zou (2005).

90 The World Bank (2001).

## Conclusion

A number of improvements in relation to the creditors' meeting can be observed from the new bankruptcy legislation which emphasize the creditors' autonomy The creditors' meeting, as a standing body, plays a series of significant roles in bankruptcy proceedings, such as supervising the administrator, discussing and approving the reorganization proposal or composition agreement or the distribution plan of bankruptcy estate in the liquidation procedure. It is a crucial organization independent from the court and the administrator. The creditors' committee is a new creature of the EBL 2006 which is established under the selection of the creditors' meeting and written confirmation of the court. It has been conferred strong powers to supervise the debtor's property and administrator's conduct. Both the creditors' meeting and creditors' committee provide an effective framework for performing the function of supervising and protecting the interests of creditors.

## References


Chen, X. (2006), 'On Problems Involving the System of Creditors' Meeting in Bankruptcy Law' <http://www.foshancourt.org/program/article.jsp?ID=19909>, last accessed 10 March 2009.

Epstein, D. (2005), *Bankruptcy and Related Law in a Nutshell* 7th edn (St. Paul, MN: West Publishing Co.).

Han, C. (2007), 'Part 3 of Interpretation of the New Bankruptcy Law: Whether the Secured Creditor Can Be Designated Chairperson of the Creditors' Meeting' <http://www.hnqylawyer.com/pcqh/ShowArticle.asp?ArticleID=190>, from *People's Court Daily*, 30 January 2007, last accessed 25 September 2008.

Legal Department of the International Monetary Fund (1999), 'Orderly & Effective Insolvency Procedures Key Issues' <http://www.imf.org/external/pubs/ft/orderly/>, last accessed 25 September 2008.

Li, G. (2008), *Interpretation of the Clauses of the New Bankruptcy Law* (Beijing: the People's Court Press).

Li, Y. (2000), *The Bankruptcy Legal System* (Beijing: China Legal Publishing House).

Shi, J. (2007), 'Twelve Years to Sharpen One Sword: The 2006 Enterprise Bankruptcy Law and China's Transition to a Market Economy' 16 *Norton Journal of Bankruptcy Law and Practice* 649.

Sun, X. and Li, Y. (2007), 'On the Protection of Taxation Credit in the Settlement Procedure of Corporate Insolvency' <http://www1.cntl.cn/show.asp?a_id=6966&c_id=636>, accessed 25 September 2008.

Tang, W. (2006), *Interpretation and Application of the New Bankruptcy Law* (Beijing: China Legal Publishing House).

Wang, D. (2007), *Interpretation of the Difficult Points in the New Bankruptcy Law and Practical Implementation* (Beijing: Law Press China).

Wang, X. (2006), 'Consideration on Setting up the System of Creditors' Meeting in the New Bankruptcy Legislation' <http://www.lawtime.cn/info/pochan/pcqszqrhy/2006090127412.html>, accessed 10 March 2009.

Wang, X. (2007), *Bankruptcy Law* (Beijing: China Renmin University Press).

Wang, X. (2008), *Bankruptcy Law* (Beijing: China Renmin University Press).

World Bank, *Principles and Guidelines for Effective Insolvency and Creditor Rights Systems*, the World Bank, April 2001, p. 9, available at <http://siteresources.worldbank.org/-GILD/PrinciplesAndGuidelines/20162797/Principles%20and%20Guidelines%20for%20Effective%20Insolvency%20and%20Creditor%20Rights%20Systems.pdf>, last accessed 25 May 2009.

Xing, L. (2007), *The Latest Precise Explanation of Enterprise Bankruptcy Law* (Beijing: Law Press China).

Yang, J. (2008), *Precise Analysis on and Interpretation of the Latest Bankruptcy Law* (Beijing: China Legal Publishing House),

Yin, Z. (2008), 'Study on the Practice Regarding Insolvency Administrator', in Wang, X. and Yin, Z., *Bankruptcy Law Forum (1st Volume)* (Beijing: Law Press China).

Zou, H. (1995), *Comparative Study on the Bankruptcy Procedures and the Substantive System of the Bankruptcy Law* (Beijing: Law Press China).

Zou, H. (2005), 'Draft of New Enterprise Bankruptcy Law of China and Creditors Autonomy', <http://www.civillaw.com.cn/article/default.asp?=22963>, accessed 15 September 2009.

# Chapter 11
# Corporate Rescue

Haizheng Zhang

## Introduction

One of the most notable features of China's new bankruptcy law is the establishment of a revised corporate rescue regime. This regime was formed by reference to the corporate rescue laws including the US Chapter 11 and German insolvency law. It provides a debtor-friendly legal framework outside the liquidation proceedings for the purpose of reorganizing financially distressed but economically viable companies.[1] The ailing companies are able to gain respite from the debt enforcement efforts of individual creditors under the protection of an automatic stay. During this prescribed period, a reorganization proposal will be produced by an outside insolvency professional, or by the directors of the company under a debtor-in-possession (DIP) model. Once the proposal is approved by the meetings of creditors and sanctioned by the court, it will have binding effect on the debtor and all the creditors.

A number of beneficial effects of a successful corporate rescue effort may be noted, so that this outcome will often be preferable to an immediate liquidation. Firstly the rehabilitation of a company could avert a 'domino effect' caused by corporate failure, where the liquidation of the insolvent debtor brings about financial difficulties for closely related enterprises and for creditors. If the debtor can be rescued, these enterprises may avoid financial difficulties. In addition corporate rescue can maximize the economic value of the debtor,[2] bringing potential benefits for all stakeholders. As a result of the rescue effort, the debtor company may continue to run its business as a going concern as it did before and may keep its legal identity and market share. The preservation of the company and its business can enable a higher level of repayment to creditors than would be possible in liquidation. In some instances it can bring investment rewards for shareholders. Perhaps most importantly, a successful rescue effort can also maximize the level of job retention for employees. The preservation of jobs could undoubtedly not only allay the concerns of employees, who would, as a result, be in favour of increasing the possibility of rescue success, but it can also avoid potential social unrest. More broadly, from the perspective of the entire corporate sector of the state, an efficient and well-functioning rescue system could enhance the productivity and competitive

1 Shi (2007), p. 666.

2 Cork Report (1982), para. 204.

capacity of domestic industrial and commercial enterprises. Non-performing assets could be cleared away from the corporate and banking sector through formal or informal arrangements. In consequence, corporate rescue proceedings can definitely strengthen the vigour of enterprises and eradicate the potential risks of financial turbulence.

Although corporate rescue laws appeared in Chinese law as early as the EBL 1986, with the joint procedures of conciliation and reorganization, these provisions could not be taken to represent a Chinese corporate rescue culture on account of several reasons, such as the awkwardness of the proceedings and the high level of government interference. Therefore, the introduction of the reorganization procedure in the EBL 2006 may be regarded as the first arrival of a Chinese corporate rescue culture. The reorganization procedure is intended to provide enterprises with a second chance if insolvent liquidation can be avoided. This chapter focuses on this formal reorganization procedure, and also analyses informal rescue arrangements as well.

## The First Corporate Rescue Procedure in the EBL 1986

The old bankruptcy law established a corporate rescue regime, which was a dual procedure, comprising of conciliation and reorganization.[3] It only applied to debt-laden state-owned enterprises and was operated under the influence of government. The enactment of the EBL 1986, although a trial measure, was a great achievement which played a significant role in promoting the reforms of SOEs during the economic transition from the previous planned economy to a socialist market economy. The old bankruptcy law stipulated the joint procedure of conciliation and reorganization for the purpose of preventing the insolvent liquidation of SOEs and attached particular importance to the affected employees, especially as at that moment the protection of the social security system was far from adequate. However, from the perspective of judicial practice, this rescue regime was not suitable for the modern Chinese economy for a number of reasons. First of all, the joint conciliation and reorganization procedures could not be initiated directly by the debtor or creditors. A petition for liquidation had to be presented first by a creditor rather than the debtor. The applicant was required to attest that the debtor had incurred serious losses due to poor management and that it was unable to pay its due debts.[4] This condition

3 In this dual procedure, the insolvent SOE was required to produce a conciliation agreement which would stipulate a deadline for debt repayment. After the conciliation agreement was approved by the creditors' meeting and sanctioned by the court, it would have legal effect on the debtor and its creditors. At the same time, the superior department of the SOE controlled the process of reorganization, produced the reorganization proposal for the discussion by the workers' congress and then reported to the creditors' meeting. See Articles 18-20, EBL 1986. For further discussion see Wang (1998).

4 Article 3, EBL 1986.

placed insurmountable hurdles before petitioning creditors because they needed to prove that, not only was the debtor in insolvency, but also that the corporate failure was caused by the incompetence, irrationality, or poor decision-making of the management. It was therefore fundamentally difficult for creditors to get access to the joint proceedings of conciliation and reorganization. In addition, only the superior government department which was in charge of the debtor could apply to the court for the opening of the joint procedures. In the circumstance where there was no superior government department, the shareholders' meeting of the debtor would decide whether or not to apply.[5] If the superior department intended for the debtor to become subject to the rehabilitation procedures, an application needed to be presented within three months after the creditor's petition for bankruptcy was filed with the court.[6] Undoubtedly, the access to the joint proceedings of conciliation and reorganization was subject to strong influence by government authorities.

Once the rehabilitation application was accepted by the court, an automatic stay would be imposed on the debt enforcement activities of individual creditors. The debtor enterprise would be able to take a breath, to negotiate with creditors and to produce a conciliation agreement during the period of the automatic stay, which could not last more than two years. Normally, the conciliation agreement stipulated the reduction of unpaid debts and deferment of repayment.[7] Once the conciliation agreement was approved by the creditors' meeting and sanctioned by the court, it would bind the debtor and all the creditors. The court would declare the suspension of the bankruptcy proceedings, and accordingly, the debtor would be placed into the reorganization procedure. During the reorganization period, the superior government department was required to produce the reorganization proposal and the proposal would be sent to the worker's congress for discussion and negotiation. Creditors were not involved in the process of making the rescue proposal and did not have voting entitlements in respect of the proposal. The creditors' meeting only played the role of supervising the implementation of the reorganization proposal.[8]

It can be concluded that this joint conciliation and reorganization approach could not represent a true corporate rescue culture. Firstly, the debtor and its creditors could not easily and efficiently invoke the rescue proceedings because a series of awkward conditions established a threshold which was too high to reach in most instances. Secondly, the access to the reorganization process was controlled by government authorities, which to some degree had no incentive to bear such a 'costly, troublesome and sometimes risky mission'.[9] Thirdly, the joint procedure did not provide sufficient protection and entitlements to creditors. The creditors only had voting entitlements in respect of the conciliation agreement, and they could not have a voice in relation to the reorganization proposal. Fourthly, the undue interference of

5 Boyle (2006), p. 47; Ding (2003), p. 197.

6 Article 11, EBL 1986.

7 Article 18, EBL 1986.

8 Article 20, EBL 1986.

9 Wang (1998), p. 234.

government might cause unfair competition and break the market rules. Moreover, this interference tended to decrease the efficiency of reorganization because the officials were not bankruptcy law experts. Therefore, the cases which underwent this joint procedure were rare.[10]

### Informal Rescue Arrangements: the 'Changchun Approach'

The Changchun Approach, an informal rescue arrangement which was first created in 1996 in Changchun city (an industrial city and capital of Jilin Province), aimed to rescue the profitable assets of insolvent SOEs which could not avoid liquidation.[11] As long as the assets of these SOEs were still efficiently productive and their products had prospects of good sales, these assets could be deemed as profitable and be subjected to this approach which was described as a 'Purchasing-Sale Restructuring', 'PSR'. Under this PSR approach, the local government would inject legal registered capital and leased land to set up a new company, and then the profitable assets would be transferred from the old distressed enterprise to the new one. The process of transfer was according to the market-oriented method, and professional public agencies, including accounting firms and asset valuation firms were involved to ensure that this process was fair and transparent. It should be noted that this transaction could not proceed without the involvement and support of the major creditors, which were usually the 'big four' state-owned commercial banks and whose claims had to account for at least two-thirds of the total debts. The banks would make loans to the newly established company, which would be able to purchase the assets. When the old insolvent enterprise received the payment, it would be used to resolve labour claims and repay the debts of the major creditors, often the same banks.

It is clear that the state banks were the biggest beneficiaries of this debt-restructuring approach. They advanced healthy loans to the new company which offered a good prospect of repayment. In addition, there was a prospect that they might obtain some repayment from the old enterprise, which would enhance their recovery rate and get rid of some NPLs. It is therefore observed that the money under this approach went around in a circle and finally back into the banks.[12] However, in contrast to the financial creditors, other pre-existing creditors, such as small trade creditors and suppliers, would not benefit from this rescue arrangement, albeit that they would not get anything if this approach was not adopted. In other words, they were the forgotten classes in this PSR approach. It was indicated by these means that the government would prefer to enable someone to get something rather than for everyone to get nothing.

Three features of this Changchun PSR approach are worthy of particular note. First of all, the government was involved in the whole process. Although the

10 PricewaterhouseCoopers, Morgan Stanley and Asia Development Bank (2004).

11 For background knowledge, see Tang (2005).

12 Booth (2002), p. 23.

government did not play the leading role, without its mediation and facilitation the rescue attempt would be unlikely to succeed. Secondly, the power of labour was material. With the transfer of the profitable assets, the majority of workers would also transfer to the new company, with the production line and equipment, by new contracts of employment, however the redundant workers would lose their jobs. The old ailing enterprise had to satisfy their claims and rearrange their lives from the proceeds of the transaction, because of the inadequate social security system. Notably, if the worker's congress failed to pass the proposal in respect of the assets transaction, the restructuring would not be carried out. Thirdly, the small trade creditors and suppliers might be expected to be involved in the negotiation and to fight for their own interests, but, due to their weak bargaining position, their opinions might be overridden by the major financial creditors. According to the analysis of Professor Wang, the Changchun Approach was legal because all the interested parties had the opportunity to negotiate.[13] It is however arguable that, since all the creditors would vote in a single class and normally the value of the claims of ordinary unsecured creditors would be small, the creditors' meeting and the result of vote were at the mercy of financial creditors. It can be concluded that the small trade creditors and suppliers became the real victims in this approach.

## New Corporate Rescue Proceedings and Potential Weaknesses

### *Access to the Reorganization Procedure*

The new reorganization procedure has an enlarged scope of application, since it applies to all types of enterprises with legal person status, whether SOEs or non-SOEs. It also removes the involvement of government departments at the application stage, which had been required under the outdated joint proceedings of conciliation and reorganization in the EBL 1986. Since there is no 'out of court' appointment mechanism at the opening stage,[14] the procedure can only be initiated by the application of the debtor or creditors for a court order. In the circumstance where a creditor has applied for liquidation and the court has accepted the creditor's application, the debtor, or its shareholders who contribute to more than ten per cent of the debtor's registered capital, are entitled to petition for reorganization before the court makes a declaration of bankruptcy.[15]

The court shall accept the reorganization application if one of the following statutory conditions can be satisfied:[16]

13 Wang (2002).

14 In contrast to e.g. the United Kingdom Insolvency Act 1986, Sch. B1, paras 14 and 22.

15 Article 70, EBL 2006; Parry and Zhang (2008), p. 127.

16 Article 2, EBL 2006. Once the court thinks that the reorganization application meets the requirements stipulated in Articles 2 and 70, the court shall accept the application and

1. the debtor is unable to pay a debt which is due and the value of debtor's assets exceeds the value of its liabilities; or
2. the debtor is unable to pay a debt which is due and the debtor obviously lacks the capacity to repay its debts; or
3. the debtor is obviously likely to become unable to pay its debts.

See further Chapter 4 regarding the evaluation of these conditions.

The law is unclear about what the application materials should include. However, there is an article regulating the application materials for bankruptcy, rather than reorganization, under which it is stipulated that the applicant should submit an application form and relevant evidence.[17] The legislative lacuna in respect of reorganization applications may lead to at least two problems. Firstly, the applicant may wonder what materials and evidence could convince a judge to accept a reorganization application. If the applicant is a creditor, it could be easy for the creditor to prove that the debtor is unable to pay its due debts because the failure of the debtor to perform according to contract terms might be regarded as enough evidence. In contrast, it would be extremely difficult for a creditor to adduce evidence that the value of the debtor's liabilities exceeds the value of its assets, since the creditor has no access to the debtor's financial and accounting information. Therefore evidence of the debtor's failure to pay its due debts should arguably be sufficient to prove that the company is facing financial trouble and in need of immediate reorganization in order to avoid insolvent liquidation.[18] If the applicant is the debtor company, the applicant should arguably be required to submit relevant materials regarding the company's assets, financial and accounting information, unpaid wages and sums due in respect of the social insurance of employees. In addition, the debtor should provide an initial proposal for the reorganization, which may include details such as whether there is a potential investor who intends to inject fresh funding, and whether the company could obtain sufficient funds for continued trading during the reorganization period. This information should be sufficient to enable the judges to decide whether there is a reasonable prospect that the company can be rehabilitated and to determine that the applicant is not attempting to abuse the reorganization procedure to avoid debt enforcement. Secondly, the uncertainty of law in this aspect may provide a wide discretion to the court because there is no specific criterion according to which it should accept or refuse an application. For instance, pursuant to the current rescue law, theoretically any creditor is entitled to trigger the reorganization procedure. The law does not set out a requirement for the court to assess the value of this creditor's claim as a percentage of the value of the total debts, although it may be that in a particular case such an approach will be taken. A question that arises is

make a public announcement. The reorganization period starts from the court's acceptance of the application. See Article 71, EBL 2006; Wang (2007), p. 206.

17 Article 8, EBL 2006.

18 Parry and Zhang (2009).

whether the court should be satisfied with any claim of any creditor in deciding upon the debtor's inability to pay debts? Apparently, this is a legislative lacuna which may present difficulties for the judges. It may be argued that, if the value of the creditor's claim is very small, the court may dismiss the application and suggest that the creditor pursues his claim by other civil procedures. It should be noted that in this respect the English insolvency law has provided a good example, which addresses the tests of a company's inability to pay debts. The approach in English insolvency law has been elaborated at p. 79.

*Automatic Stay*

Once the court accepts the reorganization application, there will be an automatic stay on enforcement proceedings against the debtor. Under the protection provided by this moratorium, creditors cannot initiate legal actions against the debtor's property and secured creditors are not normally allowed to realize their collateral.[19] The legislation is not clear as to how long the moratorium will last. There is no automatic end to the moratorium in China's reorganization procedure, unlike under the English administration regime, where the effect of moratorium will be terminated at the end of one year when the appointment of administrator ceases to have effect.[20] It can be inferred that the period of the moratorium in China is identical to the period of reorganization, which starts from the court's acceptance of the application and persists until the termination of reorganization process under the court's declaration.[21] There are however two potential problems with the moratorium in reorganization. First, the moratorium is not watertight. Although normally the secured creditor is prohibited from exercising his right of enforcement, if the secured creditor is able to prove that the collateral is at the risk of being damaged, or that the value of the collateral might be reduced to an extent at which the interests of the secured creditor could be jeopardized, the secured creditor is entitled to apply to the court for a resumption of the right of enforcement during the reorganization period.[22] In addition, a property right holder, such as a lessor under a lease agreement or a landlord, is able under the reorganization process to repossess their property which is under the possession of a debtor where there are legitimate grounds for doing so.[23] Second, there is no interim moratorium to provide the debtor with protection during the period from the time at which the application for reorganization is filed with the court until the order of acceptance is made by the court. Individual creditors may therefore

19 Article 75, EBL 2006. See however the exceptional circumstances in which a creditor may realize collateral, discussed in the next paragraph.

20 IA 1986, Sch B1, para. 76. The period of administration, and with it the period of the moratorium, can however be extended.

21 Article 72, EBL 2006; Wang (2007), pp. 208-10.

22 Article 75, EBL 2006.

23 Article 76, EBL 2006.

initiate litigation against the property of the debtor during this period. As a result, the moratorium legislation is not wholly effective and sufficient. The inadequacy of the automatic stay may lead to a depletion of the debtor's property which will jeopardize the prospects of a successful rescue attempt.

### *Governance Structure of the Rescue Process*

The corporate reorganization procedure is intended to provide financially troubled but economically viable firms with a legal framework to enable them to continue their operation as a going concern, by negotiating with creditors and devising a feasible reorganization scheme. However, an important question is who should be in charge of the rescue process: the existing management of the debtor, or an independent insolvency professional? Under guidance produced by the World Bank, it is observed that:

> [T]here are three typical approaches in reorganization proceedings: (i) exclusive control of the proceeding is entrusted to an independent insolvency representative; or (ii) governance responsibilities remain invested in management; or (iii) supervision of management is undertaken by an impartial and independent insolvency representative or supervisor. Under the second and third approaches, complete administration power should be shifted to the insolvency representative if management proves incompetent, negligent or has engaged in fraud or other misbehavior.[24]

Under Chapter 11 of the US Bankruptcy Code, the incumbent management remains in control over the insolvent firm during the reorganization process and this arrangement is characterized as 'debtor-in-possession' (DIP).[25] One obvious advantage of the DIP model that it encourages voluntary filings for reorganization by the existing board of directors because they do not need to worry about the displacement of their managerial powers.[26] However, the US model might be criticized because the corporate failure may be caused by the poor management.[27] The capability and competence of the existing board of directors may be doubted by creditors who may be concerned about the potential abuse of the DIP process to the detriment of their interests. In contrast to the US DIP model, the British insolvency laws produce a 'practitioner-in-possession' model which gives control of the rescue proceedings to an outside insolvency expert.[28] An insolvency practitioner will be appointed to act as an administrator under the administration

24 The World Bank (2005).

25 Westbrook (2004), p. 795.

26 Hahn (2004), p. 117.

27 For evaluations of debtor in possession approaches see e.g. Moss (1998), p. 19; Qi (2008b); McCormack (2007); and Finch (2009), p. 287.

28 Finch (2005), p. 374.

regime, to take over a company from its incumbent management and to be in charge of rescue activities.

In China's new bankruptcy law, once a reorganization application is accepted, the court shall appoint an administrator to take over and manage the debtor's business and property.[29] The debtor is entitled to apply to the court for the proceedings to be converted into DIP proceedings under the supervision of the administrator during the reorganization period. Once the application for DIP proceedings is sanctioned by the court, the administrator shall relinquish control over the debtor's property and business affairs to the debtor.[30] It is however submitted that there are several problems which may impede the implementation and effectiveness of the Chinese modified DIP, which offers a hybrid of the US and British approaches, seemingly modelled on similar provisions of German law.

First, the new law provides the debtor with access to the DIP procedure by applying to the court for retention of control during the reorganization, but the law is not clear as to who is entitled to make such an application, whether it is the general meeting of shareholders or the board of directors. According to the Chinese company law, the management power of the board of directors is limited and normally the general meeting of shareholders makes the final decision regarding big business events, such as a merger with another company, or an increase in registered capital.[31] An application for the DIP, if granted, may have a crucial effect on the corporate administration of the distressed company in reorganization. Thus, on this logic, the board of directors should not be allowed to petition without the authority of the shareholders' meeting. This logic holds that if the board intends to apply for conversion to DIP proceedings, it must convene an interim meeting of shareholders for authority prior to filing the application in court. However it can be imagined that this process will cost time and money at a time when the company is short of both. Therefore, it is submitted that the board of directors should be authorized to make an application for DIP proceedings directly, in the interests of efficiency and cost-effectiveness, but arguably this approach might have been made explicit in the legislation.

Second, the factors that the court should take into account before granting a DIP application are unclear. This is a legislative lacuna which may provide the court with a wide discretion. It has been suggested that the court should fully investigate what caused the corporate distress: unpredictable market reasons or the incompetence of management? If the insolvency mainly resulted from poor management and decision-making, the court should unquestionably dismiss the

29 Article 73(1), EBL 2006. It should be noted that once the reorganization is accepted by the court, the managing power of the existing board will be suspended. The reorganization will be carried out under the charge of the administrator who is allowed to employ the managerial and business personnel of the debtor to manage the business affairs of the debtor. See Article 74, EBL 2006.

30 Article 73(2), EBL 2006; Wang (2007), p. 212.

31 Articles 47 and 109, PRC Company Law 2005.

DIP application. In addition, the judges need to assess whether or not the existing directors are able to manage the ailing company in continued trading during the reorganizing process. In other words, the court should evaluate the directors' experience and ability to deal with the balance of risk and return, to negotiate and produce a reasonable and practicable rescue proposal during the reorganization.[32] To this end, the debtor should submit the management records and board minutes along with the DIP application for the consideration of the court, to enable the court to evaluate the competence of directors. Moreover, the court should listen to the suggestions of the representatives of the labour union who are familiar with the management. The opinions of creditors are also very significant. After all, the creditors bear the risk and cost of a rescue attempt. They will lose more if the reorganization fails. Thus, it can be supposed that the court will not grant a DIP application if the creditors' meeting strongly opposes it.

The third problem is that is unclear how long the court shall be permitted to make the decision. In the interests of enabling the reorganization to proceed at an appropriate pace there should be a clear time limit under which the court must finish the investigation of a DIP application and decide whether or not to grant it, but the new law fails to provide this. In view of the above analysis, it can be assumed that it will take some time for the judges to complete their investigative work to reach a good decision.

It should be noted that, although all the matters discussed here have not been codified yet, it is expected that these shortcomings and ambiguities may be clarified by further legislation or judicial interpretations on the basis of practice.

### *Powers and Duties of the Administrator*

Once an application for reorganization is accepted by the court, the court will appoint an administrator who will take over the assets and business affairs of the enterprise. The administrator is entitled to exercise management powers in the reorganization period. The administrator must discharge his duties loyally and diligently, otherwise he may be punished with a fine upon a court order.[33] If the interests of the debtor, its creditors or a third party are damaged on account of a breach of this general duty, personal liability will be imposed upon the administrator.[34] Broadly speaking, the administrator has wide powers in bankruptcy and reorganization proceedings, but not as extensive as the powers of insolvency practitioners in some other jurisdictions. The administrator can decide whether to continue trading or not, before the creditors' meeting is convened.[35] In addition, the administrator is entitled to dispose of the company's assets. If the transfer involves real estate, such as land or houses, or rights, such as mining rights and intellectual

32 Wang (2007), pp. 211-16.

33 Shi (2007), p. 664.

34 Article 130, EBL 2006; Simmons and Jiang (2007), p. 12.

35 Article 25(5), EBL 2006.

property rights, the administrator is required to report to the creditors' committee, or the court in the circumstance where there is no creditors' committee.[36]

The primary duty of the administrator in reorganization is to produce a reorganization proposal within six months after the application for reorganization is accepted by the court and this period can be extended by three months by a court order. It is prescribed that the proposal of reorganization should address the following issues:

1. operational and business strategy;
2. categorization of creditors;
3. adjustment of claims;
4. proposal for satisfaction of debts;
5. implementation period of the proposed reorganization plan;
6. supervisory period for the implementation of the proposed reorganization plan;
7. other arrangements in favour of the reorganization of debtor.[37]

It should be noted that if the administrator fails to produce a reorganization proposal in the prescribed period, the court can terminate the reorganization procedure and declare the bankruptcy of the debtor, and accordingly the debtor will be automatically put into liquidation proceedings.[38] The administrator shall supervise the situation of the debtor during the reorganization period, and in any of the following circumstances the administrator shall apply to the court for termination of the reorganization procedure, a power of application in respect of which is also conferred on the interested parties:[39]

1. the business and financial situations of the debtor have run from bad to worse, and the debtor is unlikely to be rescued;
2. the debtor has acted with fraud, or for the purpose of decreasing the debtor's property in a wrongful manner, or the debtor has put the creditors into an obviously disadvantageous position;
3. the administrator is unable to perform his functions and duties because of the debtor's acts.

The court shall make a declaration to end the reorganization process and put the company into a liquidation procedure.

36 Article 69, EBL 2006.

37 Article 81, EBL 2006. It is important to note that the proposal of reorganization shall not reduce the amounts of unpaid social insurance which should be paid to the relevant government departments. This is why these government departments are not involved in the voting on the reorganization proposal. See Article 83, EBL 2006.

38 Article 79(3), EBL 2006.

39 Article 78, EBL 2006; Wang (2007), p. 231.

### *Voting Structure and Cramdown Rule*

The court is required to convene the meetings of creditors to consider and approve the reorganization proposal within 30 days after the proposal is submitted.[40] The proposal will become effective if it is approved by the meetings of creditors in different voting classes and sanctioned by the court. The approval of the proposal in each class needs the support of a majority in number of creditors present at the meeting and that the claims of creditors giving approval should represent at least two-thirds in value of the total amount of claims held by the class.[41] If the reorganization proposal involves the adjustment of the company's capital structure and the interests of shareholders, a separate voting class of shareholders should be convened.[42] In the voting structure, creditors will be categorized into different voting classes according to the nature and characteristics of their claims against the debtor.[43] Normally, they will be divided into four groups, respectively:

1. secured creditors;
2. employees with unpaid wages and social insurance;
3. creditors with tax claims;
4. ordinary unsecured creditors.

It should be noted that the court has the discretion in due course to organize a separate group of creditors from the group of ordinary unsecured creditors, comprised of those who hold relatively small claims in amount, in order to protect the interests of small creditors.[44]

Where the proposal is approved by all the voting classes, the administrator, or the debtor under DIP, shall within ten days present an application to the court for sanction of the approved proposal. If the proposal follows the rules of the reorganization procedure substantively and procedurally, the court shall within 30 days sanction the proposal and declare the termination of the reorganization procedure by a public notice.[45] Fundamentally, the voting structure is quite similar to the US Chapter 11 of Bankruptcy Code, the English Scheme of Arrangement under Part 26 of Companies Act 2006 and the German *Insolvenzplan* under Part 6 of the *Insolvenzordnung*.

Before the Chinese court decides whether or not to sanction the approved proposals, the judges will consider whether the interests of creditors and members of the company have been treated fairly and reasonably. It is unclear whether a dissenting creditor or member is entitled to petition to the court if he thinks that his

40 Article 84(1), EBL 2006.
41 Article 84(2), EBL 2006.
42 Article 85, EBL 2006.
43 Shi (2007), p. 668.
44 Article 82, EBL 2006.
45 Article 86, EBL 2006.

interests have been unfairly prejudiced in the reorganization process. Arguably the court should have a wide discretion to decline to sanction the proposal if a claim of unfair harm or material irregularity is justified.

It is important to note that there is a remedy in the circumstances where one or more classes of creditors fail to approve the proposal.[46] Firstly, the administrator may negotiate with the creditors of this class and make some modifications for further voting, but any such modification is not allowed to damage the interests of the creditors in the other classes and the shareholders of the company as well.[47] In the event that the creditors of this class refuse to vote or fail to give approval again at the further meeting, the administrator is still entitled to apply to the court for sanction and the court has discretion to override the objection of those creditors and make the order upon the satisfaction of three conditions, respectively according to the reorganization plan: that the claims of creditors in this class can be well satisfied; that all the creditors and shareholders in each voting class are treated fairly and reasonably; and that the reorganization strategy in the draft is feasible. This is the so-called 'cramdown' rule.[48] It is indicated by this provision that the judiciary holds the final say on the rescue scheme and that the power of the court is supreme to the authority of the creditors' meeting.[49]

If the reorganization proposal is not sanctioned by the court, the court shall terminate the reorganization procedure and declare the bankruptcy of the debtor.[50] Once the reorganization proposal is granted by the court, it will have a binding effect on the company and all the creditors.[51] The proposal should be implemented in compliance with the agreed terms under the supervision of the administrator.[52] If the debtor fails to perform its obligations under the reorganization proposal, the court shall terminate the implementation of the proposal and adjudicate bankruptcy upon the application of administrator or any interested party.[53]

### *Supervision of the Implementation of the Approved Reorganization Proposal*

Once the reorganization proposal is approved by the meetings of creditors and sanctioned by the court, the proposal will come into force and the company will be placed into the stage of implementation. The debtor is liable to perform the obligations in accordance with the terms of the reorganization proposal, and the administrator shall hand over the business and property to the debtor.[54] Every

---

46 Article 87, EBL 2006.
47 Qi (2008a), p. 21.
48 Qi (2008a), p. 21.
49 Shi (2007), p. 668.
50 Article 88, EBL 2006.
51 Article 92, EBL 2006.
52 Article 90, EBL 2006.
53 Article 93, EBL 2006.
54 Article 89, EBL 2006; Shi (2007), p. 665.

reorganization proposal should stipulate a supervision period within which the administrator should play a supervisory role. In this period, the debtor is required to report to the administrator regarding the progress of implementation of the reorganization proposal and upon the financial status of the company.[55] The administrator shall submit a supervision report to the court before the supervision period expires. The supervision period can be extended by a court order upon the application of the administrator. The appointment of administrator will cease to have effect after the administrator submits the supervision report.[56]

After the reorganization proposal is implemented, the debtor is no longer liable to pay the debts which have been reduced or discharged according to the terms of the reorganization proposal.[57] If the debtor company refuses to carry out, or is unable to implement the reorganization proposal, the court can terminate the implementation of the reorganization proposal and declare the bankruptcy of the debtor upon the application of the administrator or any interested party.[58]

## Notable Features of the Reorganization Procedure

### *New Financing*

The Chinese reorganization procedure borrows DIP financing, to some extent following the US DIP model. Such financing could enable the debtor to borrow money for continued trading by means of enabling a security on the debtor's property which has not been pledged as collateral to be granted in respect of a loan obtained for the purpose of continuing the debtor's business.[59] Although this provision is in line with common international standards, the problem is that when a company is in the slide into insolvency, there are normally no adequate assets available to provide collateral for a new security to guarantee a new loan.[60] In other words, this stipulation lacks operational specifics in Chinese reality.[61] In addition, a notable legislative lacuna of the Chinese reorganization regime is super-priority financing which is conducive to the generation of post-petition funds. It should be noted that such financing could encourage lenders to extend credit to the debtor for restructuring without concerns because post-petition lenders are able to jump ahead

55 Article 90, EBL 2006.

56 Article 91, EBL 2006.

57 Article 94, EBL 2006.

58 Article 93, EBL 2006; Qi (2008a), p. 23.

59 Article 75(2), EBL 2006; Qi (2008a), p. 22.

60 Under the US Code, Title 11, s. 364 the court can permit a 'priming lien' which is superior to an existing lien. The US provision is much more detailed than Article 75. See further Qi (2008c).

61 Shi (2007), p. 669.

of existing creditors including the secured creditors in the distributional queue.[62] In China's new bankruptcy law, there is one section which indirectly mentions the priority of new financing in the post-petition bankruptcy or reorganization in the context of the payment of labour compensation and social security expenses and other incidental debts.[63] It can be deduced from this section that the lenders could enjoy priority only in the circumstances where the money is borrowed for the specific purpose of payment of wages and social security expenses of the employees in the continued trading. Borrowing for the payment of labour wages and social insurance for the continued operation of debtor's business belongs to the category of debts of common interest, and debts of common interest have priority over existing unsecured debts.[64] However, the lenders cannot leapfrog over the existing secured creditors. Therefore, it can be said that this priority is limited, and different from the internationally recognized concept of super-priority. It can be concluded that the Chinese reorganization procedure fails to give the banks and potential lenders sufficient incentives to advance a loan in order to reconstruct a troubled firm. This explains why the Chinese banks are unwilling to lend to an enterprise which is in financial difficulty. In addition, although the Chinese banking sector has made great achievements in dealing with non-performing loans during the past decade, the current amount of non-performing loans of state banks is still RMB 1,251.78 billion which accounts for 6.17 per cent of the total commercial loans.[65] Thus, the banks are very prudent in lending, and the loan policy is very tight. One survey indicates that nearly 90 per cent of medium and small sized enterprises are encountering difficulties in raising funds from banks in China.[66] Apparently, at present the banks' attitudes and incentives are not conducive to reorganizing a company in financial distress.

### *Shareholders' Entitlements*

Corporate rescue laws may confer some powers and entitlements on the shareholders of a financially troubled company, although there is by no means a uniform approach to this issue internationally.[67] Broadly speaking, China's new

62 Gold, Morrison and Laughlin (2002).

63 Article 42(4), EBL 2006.

64 Article 43, EBL 2006. Debts of common interest are normally incurred in the post-petition of bankruptcy or reorganization for the benefit of all the stake-holders, and priority is given to such debts in the distribution: see pp. 260-1.

65 Zhang (2008), p. 162.

66 This survey was conducted by Standard Chartered and Chinese Academy of Social Science in 2007 under the support of Chinese National Development and Reform Commission, and with the involvement of more than 400 medium and small sized enterprises.

67 It should be noted that although this section discusses the shareholders' entitlements, the restrictions against shareholders during the reorganization period should not be ignored. Particularly, notable is Art 77 of the EBL 2006, which provides that the debtor's members

bankruptcy law is conducive to the protection of the rights and interests of the shareholders from three aspects.

First, the new reorganization procedure provides the shareholders with easy access to the rescue regime. It is stipulated that the financially distressed debtor, under the majority decision of the shareholders' meeting, is entitled to apply to the court for reorganization.[68] In order to prevent the majority shareholders from manipulating the shareholders' meeting, and to protect the interests of the medium and small shareholders, the new law allows shareholders who contribute to more than 10 per cent of the debtor's registered capital to trigger the rescue proceedings.[69]

Second, although the shareholders' controlling power is largely stripped in reorganization, they still have rights to be involved in the process of producing a restructuring proposal. In practice, it is unlikely that all the shareholders of a large publicly held company can be organized to discuss and vote on the reorganization proposal. Shareholders' rights of involvement can be more effectively realized through the establishment of a shareholders' committee, the members of which are either majority shareholders or elected, and are entitled to exercise such rights on behalf of all the shareholders.[70] It is noteworthy that China's rescue law also provides rights of involvement for shareholders in reorganization, through the appointment of representatives who are allowed to attend the creditors' meeting and to specially negotiate regarding the reorganization proposal.[71]

Third, since shareholders have a right to be involved, logically they should have the right to vote for the reorganization proposal. It is provided that a group of shareholders should be established to vote if the reorganization proposal involves the adjustment of the capital structure and existing shareholders' interests.[72] However, the veto of the shareholders' group cannot absolutely impede the approval of the rescue arrangement, because the court could cramdown the objection of the voting group of shareholders if the adjustment of the rights and interests of investors under the proposal is fair and equitable.[73] The importance of such a provision may be illustrated by reference to the reorganization of *Zhengzhou Baiwen*, where the majority of pre-bankruptcy shareholders were not happy with the arrangement for changing the capital structure and dissented against the transfer of their half of

who made capital contributions are not allowed to request the distribution of a dividend or other investment interests. In addition, if the debtor's directors, supervisors and senior management staff hold the company's shares, they are not permitted to transfer their shares to a third party during the reorganization period unless the transfer is sanctioned by the court. See Wang (2007), p. 228.

68 Article 70(1), EBL 2006.

69 Article 70(2), EBL 2006; Parry and Zhang (2008), p. 127.

70 Article 85(2), EBL 2006.

71 Article 85(1), EBL 2006.

72 Article 85(2), EBL 2006; see the reorganization case of *Canghua Chemical Industry Joint Stock Company* in 2007, see further Shanghai Securities News (2007).

73 Article 87(4), EBL 2006; Song (2006).

the share capital to the intended investor Sanlian Group.[74] Zhengzhou Municipal Intermediate Court established a principle that the pre-insolvency shareholders have no right to stop the approval and implementation of the rescue scheme during the course of reorganization.[75] The new law will enable the court to overcome similar hold outs.[76]

In short, China's reorganization procedure promotes the rights and interests of shareholders, and to some degree enables the generation of appropriate incentives for existing shareholders so that they may actively engage in a rescue attempt. These measures may be beneficial in that they may encourage shareholders to place their company into corporate rescue proceedings at an early stage. Such incentives are most important in private companies, where shareholders are commonly the governing directors. If they cannot get any benefit from the rescue procedure, they are likely to take over-risky activities to turn the business around and to delay filing. This could cause extra loss to creditors. Therefore, the entitlements for shareholders to be involved in the rescue process could incentivize shareholders to initiate rescue proceedings in a timely manner and provide support to the rescue attempt.[77]

*Protection of Labour Interests*

Traditionally, China's bankruptcy law has adopted an employee-friendly approach.[78] The new bankruptcy law continues to protect the interests of employees, mainly because of the, as yet, under-developed social security system. First, the employees have the rights to be informed and consulted, especially where the company is insolvent.[79] Second, where a creditors' committee is established, it is required that there should be one representative of the worker's congress on the committee.[80] This committee plays a significant role in supervising the administrator's conduct in relation to the management and disposal of the company's property. Third, in the process of approving the reorganization proposals, the meeting of employees should be convened to vote upon the proposals.[81] Fourth, the claims of employees

74 For the details, see Wei (2002), p. 100.

75 Zhang (2002).

76 Articles 85(2) and 87, EBL 2006.

77 Hart (1999).

78 See for example Article 4, EBL 1986 and Parry and Zhang (2008), pp. 117-19.

79 It is noteworthy that every enterprise has a labour union. A certain number of representatives of the labour union should be appointed to be directors or supervisors who are able to be involved in the decision-making process or the supervision of the management in the corporate governance structure, which enables the workers to exert their influence on significant commercial activities through their representatives in the board of directors and the supervisory board. For more information regarding corporate governance, see Miles and Zhang (2006) and Chapter 3 of this volume.

80 Article 67, EBL 2006.

81 Article 82(2), EBL 2006.

are conferred preferential status in the distribution order and so they should be paid in priority to the tax claims of the state and the claims of ordinary unsecured creditors.[82] Fifth, in the reorganization procedure, if the financially ailing company intends to dismiss more than 20 employees, or less than 20 but the number which is cut accounts for ten per cent of the total employees, this firm needs to notify the labour union or to provide an explanation for all the employees 30 days in advance. Meanwhile, this firm is required to report the plan of dismissal to the bureau of labour and social security in the local government for approval.[83]

All the above measures indicate that efforts have been made to provide protection for the affected employees of the insolvent company for the main purpose of achieving social stability.

### *High Level of Court Involvement*

Fundamentally, the Chinese reorganization procedure is a court-driven procedure within which the courts play a dominant role. It follows the tradition of civil law countries and the courts are involved in every major step of the reorganization procedure.[84] In some jurisdictions, by contrast, the court merely plays the role of removing uncertainty and resolving litigation. Notable examples are the English company voluntary arrangements and administration regimes which give wide powers to insolvency practitioners and have a reduced level of involvement of the court.

*Overview of the court's involvement* The court driven nature of the Chinese procedure can be seen from the following activities of the courts, occurring at all stages of the proceedings:

- The opening stage of the Chinese rescue process is under the control of the judiciary, and the procedure cannot be commenced without a court order.
- The court is liable to convene the meetings of creditors for the approval of the reorganization proposal.
- The proposal does not have a binding effect until it is sanctioned by the court.
- The legislation confers the power of cramdown on the court, which is entitled to override the objection of some voting class in certain conditions.
- Most importantly, as detailed further in subsequent paragraphs, the judiciary holds the final say on all the administrator-related issues including the administrator's qualification, appointment, replacement and remuneration.

82 Article 113, EBL 2006.

83 Article 41, PRC Employment Contract Law 2007.

84 Shi (2007), p. 665.

*The courts' role in respect of matters concerning administrators* Since China has no judicial experience of the newly established office of 'administrator', the Supreme People's Court is conferred the authority of stipulating relevant criteria to qualify and make a roster of the eligible law firms, accounting firms, bankruptcy and liquidation firms and individual practitioners for selection.[85] Under this authorization, the Supreme People's Court issued a judicial interpretation, which specifies the comprehensive rules of how to qualify and appoint an administrator in a bankruptcy or reorganization case.[86] See further Chapter 6. Under this interpretation, the judiciary takes complete control over the access to this market. It may be argued that the relevant administrative department (PRC Ministry of Justice) or an independent autonomous organization should discharge the function of qualifying the competent public agencies and insolvency professionals, rather than the judiciary. It may be contended that the judiciary is unsuited to take charge of the task of qualifying competent intermediary agencies and insolvency professionals because in this circumstance the judiciary is not only a rule-maker, but also a gatekeeper. It is also notable that the court holds the power to appoint an administrator in a bankruptcy or reorganization case and to determine the remuneration of the administrator.

All the significant powers relating to administrator issues have therefore been concentrated on the judiciary. In consequence, it might be very difficult to ensure that the judiciary is impartial, since it is not subject to checks and balances. The major concern is that, since the crucial powers, such as qualifying the eligible candidates, appointing an administrator and determining the remuneration of the administrator in a detailed case, are held by the courts, it may be difficult to ensure transparency and fairness, and to prevent the abuse of powers because of a lack of effective supervision.[87] Even though currently it is arguably immature to establish an autonomous body to qualify, manage and supervise the insolvency professionals, it is foreseeable that such a body might be established once this profession has evolved suitably.

The courts also have a monopoly over the power of designating administrators in bankruptcy and reorganization regimes.[88] It should be noted that there was a fierce debate about who should be entitled to appoint an administrator: the creditors' meeting or the court; and this debate to some extent delayed the final deliberation of the new bankruptcy law in the drafting process.[89] In addition, the court is involved in the decision of the administrator's remuneration. Although the

85 Article 22(3), EBL 2006.

86 'Regulations of the Supreme People's Court on the Appointment of Administrators for Hearings on Cases of Enterprise Bankruptcy', issued by the Supreme People's Court on 4 April 2007 and valid since 1 June 2007. For more information, see Chapter 6 of this volume and also Tang and Au (2007).

87 Parry and Zhang (2009).

88 Article 22, EBL 2006; Falke (2007), p. 69.

89 Booth (2008), p. 299; Shi (2007), p. 663.

creditors' meeting is entitled to petition to the court and oppose the remuneration scheme, the court will eventually determine it.[90]

*Challenges facing the judiciary* In terms of hearing bankruptcy or reorganization cases, there are two brief observations that may be made regarding big challenges for the Chinese judiciary. First, there are not enough competent judges with bankruptcy law expertise, particularly in geographical areas outside of the large coastal cities. Sufficient training programmes are required to develop the knowledge and skills of judges and it will be quite some time before judges acquire a good level of practical experience. Second, under the current political and legal structure, government intervention is always likely, especially regarding the reorganization of SOEs, listed companies or finance companies which may have a significant impact on the social stability of the local region.

## Conclusion

The establishment of the reorganization procedure is a remarkable achievement of the bankruptcy law reform, but the implementation of the rescue-oriented proceedings is not efficient and effective in judicial practice. Further clarifications and modifications are necessarily needed to remove the existing uncertainty and ambiguities. To this end, the Supreme People's Court has organized a review committee to identify the potential problems according to the experiences in bankruptcy and reorganization cases in judicial practice, and to produce a judicial interpretation which could resolve the weaknesses of the new law in the near future. In addition, future reforms may consider conferring more powers on the administrator and reducing the involvement of the court. The enforcement of the reorganization procedure also depends on some issues outside the legal rules of bankruptcy, such as an adequate social security system, an efficient and healthy banking community, competent judges, sufficient insolvency practitioners and judicial independence. Obviously, these background factors will take years to improve to an extent that a well functioning corporate reorganization legal framework can be effectively supported.

90 Article 28(2), EBL 2006. Under the authorization of the new law, the Supreme People's Court issued a judicial interpretation, 'Regulations of the Supreme People's Court on the Determination of Remuneration for Administrators in the Hearing of Enterprise Bankruptcy Cases' in April 2007 which specifically stipulates the rules regarding administrator's remuneration and the court's role. See Chapter 6 of this volume and Shi (2007), p. 665.

**References**

Booth, C. (2002), 'Corporate/Debt Restructuring: Japan, the Hong Kong SAR & the People's Republic of China: A Roundtable Discussion' 10 *American Bankruptcy Institute Law Review* 1.

Booth, C. (2008), 'The 2006 PRC Enterprise Bankruptcy Law: The Wait Is Finally Over' 20 *Singapore Academy of Law Journal* 275.

Boyle, C. (ed) (2006), *The Asia-Pacific Restructuring & Insolvency Guide 2006* <http://www.adb.org/Documents/Guidelines/restructuring-insolvency/restructuring-insolvency.pdf>, last accessed 6 March 2009.

Bufford, S. (2007), 'The New Chinese Bankruptcy Law: Text and Limited Comparative Analysis' 16 *Norton Journal of Bankruptcy Law and Practice* 697.

Ding, C. (2003), 'The New Development of Chinese Law on Corporate Rescue' *Insolvency Lawyer* 197.

Falke, M. (2007), 'China's New Law on Enterprise Bankruptcy: A Story with a Happy End' 16 *International Insolvency Review* 63.

Finch, V. (2005), 'Control and Co-ordination in Corporate Rescue' 25 *Legal Studies* 374.

Finch, V. (2009), *Corporate Insolvency Law, Perspectives and Principles* 2nd edition (Cambridge University Press).

Gold, H.J., Morrison, V.P. and Laughlin, A.M. (2002), 'Superpriority Financing: Last in Time First in Line' Wiley Rein LLP Press Release, published online 26 April 2001, available at <http://www.wileyrein.com/publication.cfm?publication_id=11386>, last accessed on 6 March 2009.

Goode, R. (2005), *Principles of Corporate Insolvency Law* 3rd edn (London: Sweet & Maxwell, London).

Hahn, D. (2004), 'Concentrated Ownership and Control of Corporate Reorganizations' 4 *Journal of Corporate Law Studies* 117.

Hart, O. (1999), 'Different approaches to bankruptcy', a paper presented at the Annual World Bank Conference on Development Economics, Paris, 21-23 June 1999.

McCormack, G. (2007), 'Control and Corporate Rescue: An Anglo-American Evaluation' 56 *International and Comparative Law Quarterly* 515.

Miles, L. and Zhang, Z. (2006), 'Improving Corporate Governance in State-Owned Corporations in China: Which Way Forward?' 6 *Journal of Corporate Law Studies* 213.

Moss, G. (1998), 'Chapter 11: An English Lawyer's Critique' 11 *Insolvency Intelligence* 17.

Parry, R. and Zhang, H. (2008), 'China's Corporate Rescue Laws: Perspectives and Principles' 8 *Journal of Corporate Law Studies* 113.

Parry, R. and Zhang, H. (2009), 'China's New Bankruptcy Law: Notable Features and Key Problems of Enforcement' (forthcoming, on file with author).

PricewaterhouseCoopers, Morgan Stanley and Asia Development Bank (2004), *The Asia-Pacific Restructuring and Insolvency Guide 2003/2004*, available at <http://www.asianrestructuring.com/>, last accessed 20 December 2008.

Qi, L. (2008a), 'The Corporate Reorganization Regime under China's New Enterprise Bankruptcy Law' 17 *International Insolvency Review* 13.

Qi, L. (2008b), 'Managerial Models During the Corporate Reorganisation Period and their Governance Effects: the UK and US Perspective' 29 *Company Lawyer* 131.

Qi, L. (2008c), 'Availability of Continued Financing in Corporate Reorganisations: the US and UK Perspective' 29 *Company Lawyer* 162.

Shanghai Securities News (2007), 'Reorganization or imitating ZhangBaiWen Model', <http://news2.eastmoney.com/071129,731487.html>, last accessed on 6 March 2009.

Shi, J. (2007), 'Twelve Years to Sharpen One Sword: The 2006 Enterprise Bankruptcy Law and China's Transition to a Market Economy' 16 *Norton Journal of Bankruptcy Law and Practice* 645.

Simmons, M. and Jiang, J. (2007), 'A New Insolvency Law in China' 4 *International Corporate Rescue* 10.

Song, X. (2006), 'The Court's Role in the Proceedings of Enterprise Bankruptcy and Restructuring and Problems that Needs to be Solved', a paper presented at the Forum on Asian Insolvency Reform, April 2006 in Beijing.

Tang, A. (2005), *Insolvency in China and Hong Kong: A Practitioner's Perspective* (Hong Kong: Sweet & Maxwell Asia).

Tang, A. and Au, P. (2007), 'China's Enterprise Bankruptcy Law: The Central Government's New Regulations on Bankruptcy Administrators', Hong Kong Institute of Certified Public Accountants, available at <http://www.hkicpa.org.hk/APLUS/0711/p48_50.pdf>, last accessed 20 December 2008.

Wang, W. (1998) 'Adopting Corporate Rescue Regimes in China: A Comparative Survey' 9 *Australian Journal of Corporate Law* 234.

Wang, W. (2002), 'The Bad Assets of Banks & Corporate Rescue in China' (Dec 2002), a paper presented at the Second Forum for Asian Insolvency Reform (FAIR) in Thailand.

Wang, W. (2007), *The Interpretation and Substance of Bankruptcy Law* (Beijing: Law Press-China) (in Chinese).

Wei, X. (2002), 'People's Republic of China: the Legal Features of Chinese Capital Markets in the Light of the Zhengzhou Baiwen Case' 23 *Company Lawyer* 100.

Westbrook, J. (2004), 'The Control of Wealth in Bankruptcy' 82 *Texas Law Review* 795.

World Bank, *Principles for Effective Insolvency and Creditor Rights Systems* (Revised Draft, 2005).

Xu, Y. (2006), *The Speech on Enterprise Bankruptcy Law* (Beijing: Law Press-China) (in Chinese).

Zhang, H. (2008), Making an efficient and well functioning corporate rescue system in Chinese bankruptcy laws: from the perspective of a comparative study between England and China (PhD thesis, University of Leicester).

Zhang, Y. (2002), 'The Urgency of Legalizing Corporate Reorganization – From the Perspective of Zheng Baiwen Case' *China Securities* 24 July.

# Chapter 12
# Composition

Xin Ge

## Introduction

In China, the composition procedure, as one of the bankruptcy preventive regimes, is referred to as a legal proceeding. An application for composition will be initiated by an insolvent debtor filing an application with the court. The aim of the composition by the debtor is to avoid insolvent liquidation. It entails a process of consultation and negotiation with the creditors' meeting, after which an agreement should be reached with a view to the resolution of the debtor's debt crisis by means of concessions by creditors. The composition will come into force upon the court's sanction.[1] The composition application can be made either at the time when the debtor files a bankruptcy petition, or after the court has accepted the petition but before it has declared the debtor to be bankrupt.[2]

Modern bankruptcy law places greater emphasis than hitherto on rescuing struggling but viable businesses. The Enterprise Bankruptcy Law of China (hereafter the '2006 EBL') follows this trend and it includes one chapter, Chapter 9, regulating the composition procedure.

This chapter will give a comprehensive analysis of the provisions of composition in the EBL 2006, including some case illustrations. The first part gives an overview of the composition regime in China. The second part examines the whole process of agreement of the composition: the initiation, adoption by the creditors' meeting and the court's sanction. The third part focuses on the effect, possible avoidance, and termination of the composition agreement; and the last part draws some conclusions.

---

1 For the definition of the term 'composition procedure' in the context of Chinese bankruptcy law, see also Li (2008), p. 458.

2 Article 95, first para., EBL 2006. Nevertheless, recently, a decision regarding the initiation of a composition procedure was made by a grassroots court in Guangdong Province in the spirit of new bankruptcy law and the superior court's opinion, after the debtor was declared to be bankrupt. For details see the website 'Coming Back to Life After Bankruptcy Announcement', (2008) and Wang (2008).

## Overview of the System of Composition in China

### *A Retrospective View of China's First Enterprise Bankruptcy Law of 1986 and Relevant Regulations*

The Enterprise Bankruptcy Law (for Trial Implementation), which was promulgated in 1986 and became effective in 1988, allocated six articles providing for composition linked with a reconstruction system which was only applicable to state-owned enterprises (SOEs). This law fused reconstruction with composition by indicating that the former is the premise of the latter and the latter is the only means of the former.[3] Later in 1991, the Civil Procedure Law was enacted, in which, under Chapter 19, there was only one article governing the composition of non-state-owned enterprises with the status of legal person.

The two separate laws each gave the right to petition for composition to different types of enterprises, and set out different procedures for each. However, these seemingly complicated provisions did not cover the bankruptcies of all kinds of enterprises that were emerging with the development of the market economy in China. Notably, neither applied to foreign investment companies and listed companies limited by shares. In addition, neither furnished details of all necessary substantive and procedural issues. In addition, compositions that involved SOEs were subject to severe government intervention, which obviously left little scope for the court to play a normal role in such composition proceedings.

In the new bankruptcy law, an improved composition procedure has been established to apply to all types of enterprises with separate corporate personality. The previous Chapter 19 has been abolished by the newly revised Civil Procedure Law with effect from 1 April 2008.

The EBL 2006 has made the following modifications to the composition regime:

- Treating different types of enterprises in a fair and equitable way and, to a large extent, eliminating government's involvement in the composition process.
- Creating separation between the composition and reorganization processes. Now the debtor can directly file for composition with the court or may file after the case has been accepted by the court but before the debtor has been declared bankrupt.
- Enhancing the operability of the composition regime by providing relatively detailed instructions as to the requisite conditions, procedures and rights and liabilities of each party involved.[4]

3 Li (2000), p. 386.

4 Wang (2008), pp. 249-50.

- Establishing an advanced system for composition rescission and composition invalidation, in order to tackle cases of dishonesty. Such provision can potentially safeguard the creditors' interests and help to maintain the order of the market economy.[5]

## Choosing between the Composition and Reorganization Procedures

Generally, in terms of character, both the composition and reorganization procedures may be regarded as parts of an insolvency preventive system, with the purpose of avoiding unnecessary insolvent liquidations. They often entail the consequence that creditors will suffer some reduction in the value of their rights against the debtor. Further, they both proceed subject to the will of the debtor's creditors; they are collective procedures; and the composition agreement or reorganization plan will only be effective subject to the condition of ratification by the court. Each of the procedures can easily be converted into a liquidation procedure in appropriate circumstances.

Differences in the composition and reorganization procedures are shown in Table 12.1. When attempting to rescue an insolvent company, debtors and creditors[6] will have to consider whether to commence a composition or a reorganization procedure with these factors in mind.

## Conversion between Composition, Liquidation and Reorganization Procedures

The reasons for initiation of composition and liquidation procedures may overlap, and so the interested parties will have the right to choose which approach to invoke. Generally, composition will be preferred to liquidation, and so in case of coexistence of both kinds of petitions, the court will order the company to enter into composition. In this respect, the EBL 2006 seems to have followed the United Nations' Legislative Guide on Insolvency Law by furnishing more flexible linkages between different proceedings, with a view to allowing conversion of one type of proceeding to the other in certain specific circumstances, and by including devices designed to prevent the abuse of insolvency proceedings to overcome delay, increased expense and inefficiency therein.[7]

---

5 Liu (2008).

6 Article 100 of the EBL 2006 defines the conciliated creditors as the unsecured creditors and accordingly their claims are conciliated claims. Unless otherwise specified, the creditors discussed in this chapter are the conciliated creditors.

7 United Nations (2005), p. 19.

**Table 12.1 Comparison between composition and reorganization**

| Composition (Chapter 9 EBL 2006) | Reorganization (Chapter 8 EBL 2006) |
|---|---|
| May be initiated only by the debtor (Art. 95). | May be initiated by the debtor, a creditor, or a shareholder whose contribution to the registered capital of the debtor enterprise accounts for over one tenth in value (Art. 70). |
| Dependent on the debtor being unable to pay its debts as they fall due, and on its assets being insufficient to meet its debts; or upon an obvious lack of liquidity (Arts 2 and 7). | Dependent on the debtor being unable to pay its debts as they fall due, and on its assets being insufficient to meet its debts; or upon an obvious lack of liquidity; or upon there being an obvious possibility of the debtor becoming insolvent (Arts 2 and 7). |
| The secured creditors can realize their collateral (Art. 96). | The realization of collateral on the debtor's specific properties is stayed (Art. 75). |
| Limited in scope. Implemented through a debt repayment scheme, which only concentrates on repayment of debts. | Actively enables the salvage and reconstruction of the insolvent debtor by means of adjustment of debts, re-arrangement of the business operation of the debtor and through the participation of various professionals. |
| Voted on by the creditors' meeting (Art 97). | Voted on by the creditors' meeting, and sometimes additionally by the shareholders' group attending creditors' meeting (Arts 82 and 85). |
| Simple, quick and less expensive. | Complicated, prolonged and expensive |
| Generally applicable to medium or small sized debtors requiring less complex rescue procedures. | Generally applicable to large scaled debtors requiring complex rescue process. |
| A ratified composition agreement is only binding on unsecured creditors who participate in the composition; and a secured creditor may realize its collateral upon a court's ratification (Art 100). | A ratified reorganization plan is binding on all the creditors, including secured creditors (Art 92). |
| No legal provisions regarding employment debts. | Stresses the protection of the employees' rights and interests in the debtor's enterprise by means of classifying the labour claim holders into a separate group when the creditors participate in the creditors' meeting to discuss the draft reorganization plan. (Arts 82(2) and 83). |
| No specification as to the supervision of the execution of a composition agreement. | Implementation is supervised by the administrator during the whole reorganization process. |

*Bankruptcy Liquidation Conversion into Composition*

In the event that that the debtor petitions for bankruptcy or the creditor applies for the debtor's bankruptcy, after the court's acceptance of the bankruptcy application but before a bankruptcy declaration,[8] the debtor is entitled to put forward a composition application and submit the composition agreement to the court. If the composition application satisfies requirements provided for in this law, as scrutinized by the court, the court shall rule to approve the composition.[9] This means that the liquidation procedure will automatically be turned into a composition procedure.

*Conversion into Liquidation*

There are four situations where the court shall rule to terminate the composition procedure, and declare the debtor to be bankrupt and to undergo the liquidation procedure: (a) if the draft composition agreement fails to gain the approval of the creditors meeting; (b) if the adopted composition agreement fails to be approved by the court;[10] (c) if the composition agreement was established by the debtor's fraud or other unlawful activities;[11] or (d) where the debtor is unable to implement the composition agreement or refuses to do so.

*Conversion between Composition and Reorganization*

Unlike the bankruptcy laws of many jurisdictions, there is no provision for the company to transfer between composition and reorganization and vice versa under the EBL 2006,[12] due to the differences between these procedures that were mentioned in the above chart. This omission may result in inefficiency and additional expenses.

Another unaddressed issue in the EBL 2006 concerns the application priority among reorganization, composition and liquidation proceedings where such applications are made by different eligible applicants simultaneously after the court's acceptance of the bankruptcy filing and before declaring the debtor to be bankrupt. Scholars have argued that the reorganization application should be accepted in priority to composition and that composition should have priority over a liquidation application,[13] due to the social effect and influence on the parties concerned that the three proceedings will induce.[14]

8 The time limit is not absolutely unchangeable (see supra n. 2).
9 Article 96, first paragraph, EBL 2006.
10 Article 99, EBL 2006.
11 Article 103, EBL 2006.
12 Li (2008), p. 18; Liu (2008).
13 Liu (2008).
14 Liu and Xie (2008).

### Course of Forming the Composition

While the EBL 2006 does not expressly address informal workouts or other alternative procedures such as debt write-offs, rescheduling, and debt-equity conversions, such approaches are made possible under composition provisions.[15] The first successful composition case[16] involving a listed company after the adoption of the new bankruptcy law, showing the whole stages of formation of the composition, is considered next.

China Liaoning International Cooperation Corporation (Group) Holdings Limited (hereinafter CLIC), was a listed company in China,[17] but its listing had been suspended as of 29 April 2004 due to great losses that it had incurred for three consecutive years. In February 2007 it filed an application in court for bankruptcy, in light of its inability to pay off due debts and the insufficiency of its assets to meet its debts.

The court consulted with the China Securities Regulatory Commission pursuant to the Securities Law and related regulations, and upon the Commission's permit, in October 2007 formally accepted the application for CLIC's liquidation.

Nearly one month later, CLIC applied to the court for composition and presented a composition proposal involving a reduction and restructuring of the debts and meanwhile, as an alternative, a liquidation plan. After examination and appraisal, the court sanctioned CLIC's composition proposal, as it held that the composition approach was more favourable to creditors than liquidation.

A creditors' meeting was then convened and 50 creditors attended representing claims amounting to 480 million RMB, which stood for 94.82 per cent of the unsecured claims. By open voting, a resolution for composition was adopted, with 42 voters[18] representing 419 million RMB, amounting to 82.7 per cent of the unsecured claims[19] approving the composition.[20]

Subsequently, the court ruled to ratify the composition agreement, terminate the composition proceeding and proclaimed its ruling.

The presiding judge in this case stated after the decision that there were four reasons why CLIC had chosen composition instead of reorganization: (a) the scale of this company was not large; (b) CLIC had been in serious financial difficulty and its assets were insufficient to pay the insolvency expenses; (c) its listing had been suspended for nearly four years and the termination of the listing would be completely ordered unless it was reconstructed and achieved a favourable financial balance by the end of 2007, and composition proceeding

15 Meng (2008).

16 Liu, Wang and Liu (2008); Li (2008).

17 In Shenzhen Stock Exchange, stock code 000638.

18 Over half of the attending creditors, as required by Article 97, EBL 2006.

19 Over two thirds of unsecured creditors' rights as required by Article 97, EBL 2006.

20 Yang (2008), p. 239.

would take less time than reorganization;[21] and (d) the strategic investor of CLIC was interested in and capable of successfully dealing with CLIC's debts, as surveyed by the court.[22]

From the above, it is clear that three stages must be undergone to form the composition from beginning to end: (a) submitting a composition petition to the court and drafting the composition agreement; (b) the holding of creditors' meetings discussing and adopting the resolution on composition; and (c) the court's sanction of the composition agreement. A successful composition must go through the above stages one by one. It results in (a) the possibility of the debtor's legal person status remaining intact and (b) that the debtor is no longer obligated to pay the debts reduced or discharged by virtue of the composition agreement after the implementation of the composition agreement.[23]

### *Composition Petition and Court's Scrutiny Thereon*

*What prerequisites are needed when petitioning for composition* As per Article 95, only a debtor satisfying the following substantive and formal prerequisites can be eligible to submit a petition with the court for composition.

The substantive prerequisites are as follows:

i. financial status: the composition procedure can be launched for the reason that the debtor is unable to pay off due debts, and its assets are insufficient to meet its debts or if it obviously lacks liquidity.[24]
ii. applicant: only the debtor can apply for composition,[25] as the most important factor for the composition is the debtor's sincerity – only if the debtor is sincere regarding the composition, can the creditor agree to make concession regarding debt repayment, which is the crucial component in the composition. Arguably, only the debtor is well placed to form a clear view as to whether the business in trouble deserves salvaging and as to the appropriate measures to do so.[26] If composition is put forward by the creditor, a dishonest debtor may be able to make use of this composition opportunity, to reach a composition with the creditors for the sake of

21 Article 56, Securities Law of the People's Republic of China (revised in 2005), provides that if a listed company has been operating at a loss for the latest three consecutive years and fails to gain profits in the year thereafter, the Stock Exchange shall decide to terminate the listing of its stocks.

22 Liu, Wang and Liu (2008).

23 Article 106, EBL 2006.

24 Article 2, EBL 2006.

25 Article 95, EBL 2006.

26 Chen (1991), p. 59.

ulterior ends, and thereby jeopardize the creditors' interests.[27] However, the restriction that only the debtor may apply does not mean that a creditor or the third party has no opportunity to do so. It is possible for a creditor or third party can gain control of debtor, for example, by means of a debt for equity swap or a purchase of shares sufficient for the ex-creditor or third party to control the passing of a resolution,[28] as there is no provision to forbid this kind of contribution under the Company Law (2005 revised).[29]

iii. timing of application: when the debtor meets the insolvency conditions as stated above, he can directly apply to the court; alternatively, he may apply after the insolvency petition has been accepted by the court but before the debtor has been declared to be bankrupt.[30] He may even file for composition after a declaration of bankruptcy.

iv. number of the creditors: Scholars in Taiwan hold that the existence of over two creditors is a prerequisite for the composition, as the composition regime in the bankruptcy law aims to achieve more than a person to person composition.[31] Although the EBL 2006 does not specify the number of the creditors against the debtor, it may be inferred from one of the voting rules for the passing of resolution on composition stipulating a requirement of a majority in number,[32] that the number of the creditors should be at least two or more, or otherwise no valid resolution can be made.

The formal prerequisites are as follows. When applying to the court, the debtor must submit an application for composition and an integrated draft composition agreement.[33] Where, after scrutinizing the application documents, the court finds that the documents are not in conformity with the law, the court will refuse to accept the application. In such circumstances the debtor can re-apply upon revision of the application documents.[34]

It is noteworthy that the situation stated in Article 19 of the EBL 2006 can also be applied in the composition procedure. This provision states that '[o]nce the court accepts the insolvency petition, all judiciary measures taken against the debtor's property for the purpose of preserving the property shall be removed and

27 Li (2000), pp. 373-4.

28 Li (2008), p. 464.

29 The Company Law 2005 sets out in Article 27: 'A shareholder may make capital contributions in currency, in kind or intellectual property right, land use right or other non-monetary properties that may be assessed on the basis of currency and may be transferred according to law, excluding the properties that shall not be treated as capital contributions according to any law or administrative regulation.' For detailed elucidation, see Wang and Xu (2008), pp. 86-9.

30 Article 95, EBL 2006.

31 See Qi (2004), pp. 373-4.

32 Article 97, EBL 2006.

33 Article 95, second paragraph, EBL 2006.

34 Tang (2006), p. 302.

execution proceedings shall be stayed'. It is necessary to address here the order of events during the composition:[35]

- The debtor submits application for composition with the court.
- The court scrutinizes the application documents, rules its ratification for composition procedure, if appropriate, and announces the beginning of the composition. From now on, the secured creditor can realize his collateral.[36]
- The creditors' meeting is convened to discuss and vote upon the draft composition agreement.[37]
- If the voting requirements are satisfied, the composition agreement is reached by the debtor and creditors' meeting. In the event that there is collateral to guarantee the performance of the agreement, the collateral provider will also sign the composition agreement.
- The signed agreement will be presented to the court for sanction. Upon sanction, the administrator will transfer the property and business affairs to the debtor and submit to the court the working report concerning his performance of his duties and functions. The composition procedure is then terminated.[38]
- After the court's sanction of the composition agreement, the debtor should carry out its obligations in a timely manner, and repay its debts as per the agreement.[39]
- The last step is the execution of the composition agreement. Since, upon the termination of composition proceedings, the creditors' meeting and its committee are dissolved and the administrator stops his work, the means of monitoring the debtor should be included in the composition agreement, in order to protect the creditors' rights and interests, as the law is silent about supervision at this time.[40]

*What will be scrutinized by the court in reviewing the application documents?* Article 96 of EBL 2006 lays down that 'After ascertaining that the composition application satisfies the requirements provided for in this law, the People's Court shall rule to approve the composition, and announce it to the public'. Due to the fact that the composition in nature is a contractual activity for handling the relations of rights and obligations between the debtor and the creditors through consultation, the scrutiny of the application documents for composition should consider the form of the documents; even if involving substantial contents, and the court's scrutiny mainly focuses on the debtor's sincerity in relation to

35 Xing (2007), pp. 176-7.
36 Article 96, EBL 2006.
37 Article 97, EBL 2006.
38 Article 98, EBL 2006.
39 Article 102, EBL 2006.
40 Wang (2008), p. 256.

the composition, as well as on the lawfulness of the fundamental issues in regard to composition.[41] The substantial conditions should be examined by the creditors' meeting.[42]

As for the aspects of the application documents to be examined, the Law does not give detailed provisions.[43] However, generally, in practice, the court will inspect:

- whether the applying debtor meets the insolvency conditions in Article 2 of the EBL 2006, since a non-debtor applicant, or a debtor not meeting the insolvency conditions, cannot apply;
- whether the application, composition agreement and the related necessary evidence have been submitted all together;
- whether the scrutinizing court has jurisdiction[44] over the application.[45]

*Out-of-court workouts* Additional to the kind of composition mentioned above, the EBL 2006 provides another approach, an out-of-court workout, which is a unanimous agreement made between the debtor and all his creditors (including the secured creditors) as to the disposal of debts and claims after the insolvent application has been accepted by the court. Where such an agreement has been reached, the debtor and creditors may request that the court rules to approve the composition agreement and to terminate the insolvency procedure,[46] no matter how the accepted insolvency case is going under the guidance of the court.

There are no specific procedural requirements set out in the EBL 2006 in this regard; the debtor and all the creditors can freely negotiate for composition, as long as they are willing to do so. Further, in case of reaching an out-of-court workout, an application for out-of-court workout need not be submitted to the court in advance, as the successful out of court composition depends only on whether the debtor and all the creditors can enter into a composition agreement, and on the court's subsequent ruling or sanction.[47]

As put by one scholar,[48] the out-of-court workout agreement, in light of the legal fact that the debtor and all of the creditors rearrange or readjust the debts and claims, will result in the change of the civil substantive rights and obligations between the debtor and the creditors. That is, the debtor will not be liable for

---

41 Li (2008), pp. 467-8.

42 Wang (2008), p. 251.

43 Some scholars like Wang Xinxin has suggested the Supreme People's Court to supplement the detailed provisions thereon in the judicial interpretations for the EBL 2006, see Wang (2007), p. 325.

44 For provisions regarding jurisdiction, please refer to the previous interpretation of Article 3 in the EBL 2006.

45 Xing (2007), p. 176.

46 Article 105, EBL 2006.

47 Xing (2007), p. 187.

48 Zou (2008), p. 76.

the debts to the full extent incurred prior to the establishment of the out-of-court workout agreement, instead he will only be required to repay the debts as stipulated in the out-of-court workout agreement. Moreover, where the debtor does not or is unable to carry out this agreement, the creditors can petition to the court for the debtor to be declared bankrupt; but in this situation, a new bankruptcy proceeding will be initiated and the commitment made by the creditors under the agreement to reduce the claims is still valid and therefore only the claims not yet repaid under the terms of the out-of-court workout agreement can be legally laid and included in the distribution of the debtor's bankruptcy estate.

It is notable the out of court composition differs from the kind of composition mentioned in the following part in this chapter.

*Composition Agreement*

A composition agreement is an agreement made between the debtor and two or more creditors under which the creditors agree to accept in full satisfaction of their claims only a specified partial payment.[49] Under Articles 103 and 104 of the EBL 2006, although this agreement will take effect upon sanction by the court, the creditors cannot directly enforce this payment obligation through the court in the event that the debtor fails to pay the debt which he has committed to pay in the composition agreement. Rather, a creditor in this position will have to ask the court to terminate the implementation of composition agreement and to order the debtor to go through the liquidation procedure.

An example relates to Jinan Qingqi Motorcycle Co., Ltd (hereinafter Qingqi), a listed company in respect of which a creditor had presented a petition for liquidation in September 2003 and which subsequently requested composition. In December 2003, it reached a composition agreement at the creditors' meeting and was salvaged from bankruptcy. As per the composition agreement, Qingqi would clear off 40 per cent of the principal amount of the declared indebtedness within three months upon the date when the agreement came into effect, and the other 60 per cent would be paid up by an associated company of Qingqi; as consideration, the creditors discharged Qingqi and its associated company from any other debts except the principal amount outstanding.[50]

*Establishment of the composition agreement* There are two prerequisites for the establishment of the composition agreement:

- The debtor submitting a draft composition agreement to the court, which is actually an offer to be made to the unsecured creditors regarding the settlement of the debt disputes through composition. This is the premise for the establishment of a composition.

---

49 Epstein (2005), p. 113.

50 See JRJ.com (2003).

- The creditors' meeting passing the draft composition agreement, which means the composition is ultimately established. The creditors' meeting will put the draft composition to a vote. Under Article 97, the composition agreement is deemed as being adopted in the event of an affirmative vote of a majority in number and two thirds in value.[51] Moreover, the composition agreement is not required to set forth a statutory proportion of the repayment by the debtor to the creditor.[52]

*Effect of the approved composition agreement* The composition agreement is concluded by the presentation of the debtor's offer to the creditors' meeting and the meeting's subsequent discussion and acceptance of the offer through voting. But, owing to the provision that only upon the court's approval can the agreement take legal effect, the agreement is created by the debtor, the creditors and the court together.

The procedural effect of the composition agreement is the termination of the composition procedure and suspension of the bankruptcy procedure. The administrator shall transfer the property and business affairs to the debtor and submit a working report concerning his performance of his duties and functions to the court.[53]

The composition has the following effects upon the debtor:

a. Restrictive measures imposed upon the debtor in relation to matters such as assets disposal and the discharge of debts, will be released, and the debtor will be bound by the composition agreement.[54]
b. The debtor will be required to clear the debts as per the time limit and amounts provided in the composition agreement, or otherwise the composition will be annulled, and bankruptcy declared.[55]
c. During the period of performance of the composition, the debtor may not violate the provided terms and conditions in the composition to render extra benefits to specific creditor(s) and therefore to damage other creditors' interests.
d. After the full implementation of the composition agreement, the debtor is freed from paying the debts reduced or discharged as per the composition agreement.[56]

---

51 However, it is submitted that despite no provision setting a limit on number of the participants in the creditors' meeting appearing in the EBL 2006, in practice, the court and the chairman of the creditors' meeting should take careful account of the number of the creditors' meeting participants, so as to avoid the creditors' meeting being controlled by creditor(s) holding two thirds claims in value of all the claims against the debtor. See Xing (2007), p. 178.

52 Wang (2008), p. 254.

53 Article 98, EBL2006.

54 Wang (2008), p. 256.

55 Articles 102 and 104, EBL 2006.

56 Tang (2006), p. 310.

The composition has the following effects on the creditors:

a. All the conciliated creditors are bound by the sanctioned composition agreement, whether or not they have attended the creditors' meeting, as long as they have declared their claims, whether or not they agreed to the composition agreement. They will request the debtor to pay back their debts as per the scheme provided in the composition agreement and the part of their claims which is excessive of the scheme will not be discharged by the debtor.
b. Those who fail to declare their claims are prohibited from realizing these claims during the implementation of composition agreement but may realize their claims under the repayment terms provided in the composition agreement after the composition agreement is implemented.[57]
c. As stated above, the secured creditors are not bound by the composition agreement and they may realize their collateral. This kind of realization will probably lead the debtor to lose the material ground for composition and may therefore result in the composition agreement not being executable. Thus, to avoid the occurrence of the above situation, it is better for the debtor to consult completely with the secured creditors in respect of the secured claims before petitioning with the court for composition.[58]
d. The composition agreement will have no effect on new claims incurred after the beginning of the composition procedure, as these new claims can be ascribed to the common interests and shall be paid off instantly from the debtor's property.[59]

The effect of the agreement on a guarantor or a joint debtor of the debtor is as follows. It is stated in Article 101 of the EBL 2006 that a creditor's claim against the guarantor and other joint debtors of the debtor are not affected by the composition agreement, which means that the composition agreement does not have the legal effect of changing the debt obligation which should be undertaken by the guarantor, joint debtors and collateral provider of the debtor. In other words, the concession on debt reduction or extension made by the creditors to the debtor does not act on these guarantors, or joint debtors as well as collateral providers who, on the contrary, should assume the liability on guarantee or joint and several liability. If, for example, the composition agreement provides that the debtor will repay the previous debts in the proportion of 70 per cent, and be exempt from the remaining debts, the guarantor, joint debtors and collateral provider of the debtor will still have to be accountable for 100 per cent repayment liability for the previous debts. That is to say, after being repaid by the debtor as per the composition agreement, the creditors still have the right to request

57 Article 100, third paragraph, EBL 2006.

58 Xing (2007), p. 181.

59 Articles 42(4) and 43, EBL 2006.

the guarantor, joint debtor or the collateral provider to repay the debts reduced under the composition agreement: in the example given, 30 per cent of the debts.[60]

In addition, at the expiry of the term as stated in the previous contract, the guarantor or joint debtor will have to bear relevant liability for the debtor, and may not enjoy the interests of debt extension resulting from the composition agreement. Although the guarantor and the joint debtor can obtain subrogation after paying off the debt for the debtor, the claim to be exercised by the guarantor, joint debtor or the collateral provider is restricted by the debt reduction and extension as set out in the composition agreement.[61]

### *Enforceability of the Composition Agreement*

On this issue, there are two sharp viewpoints among scholars: one holds that the composition agreement cannot be compulsorily enforced, as it only gains its meaning and significance in procedure law, rather than in substantive law, and so its effectiveness is based on the court's sanction.[62] The opposite argument is that the composition agreement can be enforced through litigation or by other methods, in the event that the debtor fails to implement it.[63]

The EBL 2006 clearly provides that the composition agreement has no compulsory enforcement effect, and in the event that the debtor is unable to, or refuses to, implement the composition agreement, the court shall rule to terminate the implementation of the composition agreement, upon a request by the creditors, and will then declare the debtor to be bankrupt.[64]

### *Null and Void Composition Agreement*

Article 103 provides that the composition agreement established by the debtor's fraud or other unlawful acts shall be ruled by the court to be null and void and the debtor shall be declared to be insolvent. After scrutiny, the invalidation will be ruled by the court, either resulting from its own ascertainment of the debtor's illegal activity, based on its authority, or upon the creditor's application when the creditor finds the debtor to have violated the composition agreement.

As interpreted by scholars, the term 'fraud' means that the debtor intentionally conceals the truth or fabricates the falsity, so as to mislead the creditors' meeting into passing the resolution on the composition agreement. The term 'other unlawful activities' refers to the acts conducted by the debtor as provided in Article 52 of the Contract Law of the People's Republic of China, such as malicious collusion to

60 Wang (2008), pp. 257-8.
61 Ibid.
62 Tang (2001), p. 359.
63 Xie (1987), p. 214; Li (2000), p. 381.
64 Article 104, first paragraph, EBL 2006.

damage the interests of the State, with a collective or a third party; an act with an illegitimate purpose concealed under the guise of a legitimate act; an act damaging the public interests; or an act violating the compulsory provisions of laws and administrative regulations.[65]

From the above Article 103, it is easily found that the composition agreement is very much like a civil contract and the concept of 'Fraud' in this Article is also based on the Contract Law. But, as far as the effect of a composition agreement formed by the debtor's fraud or other unlawful activities is concerned, in the view of a scholar in Taiwan, through composition, the creditors can neither obtain the right to compulsory enforcement of the composition agreement, nor can they pursue payment of the unpaid debt under the civil procedure law. Thus, the legislator should in particular provide for legal remedies in the bankruptcy law when the composition agreement is informally terminated.[66] It is regrettable that the EBL 2006 is silent on such an issue as whether, where the debtor breaches the composition only against one or two creditors, and not all the creditors, a composition concession made between the above creditor(s) and the debtor can be abandoned, and as to the subsequent remedy measures.[67] Thus, in order to protect such individual creditors, a regime of 'rescission of the composition concession' may be borrowed in the future by the legislature. This term means that, where the debtor fails to perform according to the conditions of the composition agreement, an individual creditor may rescind his expression of intent in the composition agreement separate from the creditors who have agreed under the agreement. This is a remedial measure for the individual creditor in case of the debtor's breach of the composition agreement.[68]

The legal consequence of a null and void composition agreement is also different from the consequences under general civil contract law. The second paragraph of Article 103 states, '[w]here the circumstances prescribed in the preceding paragraph occur, the repayment obtained by conciliated creditors based on the performance of the composition agreement need not be returned at the same proportion of payment as other creditors obtain'.

### *Termination of Composition*

There are two kinds of termination of the composition: one is based on the court's ruling, also called rescission of the composition, and the other results from the implementation of the composition agreement coming to an end.

65 Tang (2006), pp. 313-14; Xing (2007), p. 183.
66 Chen (1991), p. 97, cited in Li (2008).
67 Li Guoguang (ed.) (2008), p 484.
68 Li Yongjun (2000), p. 384.

*Rescission of Composition Proceedings*

As mentioned above, the first paragraph of Article 104 gives two conditions for the court to rule to terminate the composition agreement (i) that the debtor is unable to, or refuses to, implement the composition agreement; and (ii) that the creditors request the court to make such a ruling.

As per the law, the legal consequences of the rescission of composition are as follows:

- the court adjudges the debtor bankrupt and the debtor enters into the liquidation procedure;
- the claim concessions agreed by creditors in the composition agreement lose their effect,[69] which indicates that the creditors still have the right to have their claims confirmed and repaid as per the proportion that their original claims account for in the whole claims against the debtor.

The termination of the composition agreement has no retrospective effect on the amount of claims repaid to the creditors. Payment obtained by creditors owing to the implementation of the composition agreement remains effective with the unpaid portion of the claim deemed as a bankrupt claim.[70] However, it is added in the law that the aforesaid creditors may continue to receive a distribution only if the other non-conciliated creditors are paid at same proportion as was received by those who have been paid.[71]

The new claims incurred during the composition procedure will be repaid on a basis preferential to other claims.[72]

Security provided for the implementation of the composition agreement, including the collaterals provided by the debtor over his specific property and any collateral and any guarantee provided by any third party, will not be affected and remain as effective within the secured scope.

When a debtor is declared bankrupt after going through the composition procedure, any creditors who did not lay their claims before the court within the time limit confirmed by the court may have their claims supplementarily declared, however this may only be done prior to the final distribution of insolvent property as per Article 56.

Rescission of the composition concession is distinguished from rescission of the composition proceeding, though they both result in the termination of the implementation of the composition agreement in the following aspects:

a. a creditor must apply to the court for the rescission of the composition

69 Article 104, second paragraph, EBL 2006 .

70 Ibid.

71 Article 104, third paragraph, EBL 2006.

72 Articles 42(4) and 43, EBL 2006.

proceeding and rescission must be ruled by the court, whereas the rescission of composition concession will be expressed directly by the individual creditor to the debtor;

b. rescission of the composition proceeding may occur for the reasons legally provided, while rescission of the composition concession is only limited to the occasion where the debtor fails to pay money when it is due;
c. the rescission of the composition proceeding has effect on all the creditors, but the rescission of composition concession only affects a creditor who individually terminates his composition agreement; and
d. rescission of the composition proceeding will result in the composition procedure turning into a liquidation procedure, whereas the rescission of composition concession will merely make void the unimplemented amount of claim owed by the debtor under the composition agreement and the composition procedure will still proceed.[73] This creditor's rights will revert to their original amount prior to reaching the composition agreement, however, in order that the composition agreement is not undermined, a claim cannot be made by this creditor against the debtor until the debtor totally fulfils its obligations under the composition agreement to other creditors. Only at that time, in the event that the debtor fails to carry out his repayment obligation, can this creditor initiate a civil proceeding against the debtor for the outstanding debt.[74]

It should be noted that when the debtor breaches the composition agreement to any degree, as per the EBL 2006, one or more creditors may request that the court terminates the agreement. This provision seems to require only a low level of cessation of implementation of the agreement, because pursuant to the literal meaning of Article 104 first paragraph, as long as the debtor is unable to, or fails to, implement its obligations under a composition agreement for whatever reason and now matter by how much it fails, the court shall, upon request of the creditor in the composition, rule to terminate the composition, and adjudge the debtor bankrupt. There is the potential for the strict scope of this provision to easily destroy the previous endeavours made by the debtor and the creditors in agreeing the composition. It has been suggested[75] that only upon an application by a majority of creditors whose claims account for a great number of creditors' total claims, for example, over two thirds or three fourths of the total claims, ought the court to be able to rescind the composition agreement.

Further, proposals[76] are made regarding the unclear parts of the EBL 2006:

1. that the Law may specify that creditors only have the right to initiate

73 Wang (2008), p. 334.
74 Li (2008), p. 484.
75 Li (2008), p. 485.
76 Idid.

such an application within a very short period, such as ten days, after the court sanctions the composition, and that the creditors applying for the termination of the composition agreement, should have dissented against the resolution of the composition or that they should have been not present at the creditors' meeting evidencing the adopted resolution's impartial relief; and

2. that creditors can appeal against the court's ruling within a limited period as per the civil procedure law as a legal remedy in the event that the court rejects the creditors' application for termination of the composition agreement.

*Termination of Composition Due to Finished Implementation or Expiry*

At the end of the implementation, or at the expiry of the composition agreement where the creditors have been repaid under the conditions as set out in the composition agreement, the agreement will automatically terminate with two legal effects: (i) the bankruptcy proceeding is closed; and (ii) the debtor is no longer obligated to pay the debts which have been reduced or discharged in the light of the composition agreement, namely, the debtor is only required to pay such proportion of the debts as agreed in the composition and all the debts that are part of a composition agreement are extinguished once a composition has been terminated or ends.[77]

The consequence of full implementation of the composition agreement may again be illustrated by reference to the Qingji composition, which was mentioned above. After Qingqi finished repayment to 421 creditors as per the composition agreement, but nine creditors failed to draw the repaid amount on schedule, Qingqi applied to the court for putting the payment not collected by the nine creditors in the public notary office for escrow, and the court permitted it. On 26 April 2004, the court, upon scrutiny, decided to terminate Qingqi's bankruptcy proceeding.[78] After over four years endeavour, at the beginning of 2008, the company was estimated to be profitable.[79]

## Conclusion

Generally speaking, the composition proceeding employed in the EBL 2006 provides the debtor with a diversified option for corporate rehabilitation, with a relatively simple procedure and low opportunity cost entailed in coming through composition.[80] The cases concerning Qingqi and CLIC have evidenced that

77 Article 106, EBL 2006.
78 Yang (2008), pp. 246-7.
79 Zheng (2008).
80 Zou (2008), pp. 66-7.

composition is a useful tool to salvage companies on the brink of liquidation. More importantly, recently, with the global economy in an economic downturn, caused in part by the global credit crunch, 'predictability regarding what will happen if a business gets into financial difficulties is of wider economic importance',[81] especially to emerging markets like China, in terms of social and economic stability. In the meantime, however, it is undeniable that there exist some functional defects in the composition proceeding: (a) it is very hard to directly rescue the financially troubled company; (b) it has no binding effect on secured creditors, and the latter's realization of collateral may make it impossible for the whole business to keep its operations going; (c) it lacks legitimate means to safeguard the performance of the composition agreement.[82]

## References


Chen, R. (1991), *Bankruptcy Law* (Taiwan: San Min Book Co. Ltd).

Epstein, D. (2005), *Bankruptcy and Related Law in a Nutshell* 7th edn (St. Paul, MN: West Publishing Co.).

JRJ.com (2003), 'Jinan Qingqi Will Escape from Bankruptcy because of Composition' (published online 30 December 2003) <http://news1.jrj.com.cn/news/2003-12-30/000000721753.html>, last accessed 27 September 2008.

Li, G. (2008), *Interpretation of the Clauses of the New Bankruptcy Law* (Beijing: People's Court Press).

Li, H. (2007), 'A Sudden Turn for the Better regarding S*ST CLIC Bankruptcy and Restructuring Restarting for Wan Fang Yuan's Intervention' (published online 22 November 2007) <http://www.chinanews.com.cn/cj/ssgs/news/2007/11-22/1084898.shtml>, last accessed 26 September 2008.

Li, S. (2007), 'Composition Regime' available at <http://www.legaldaily.com.cn/misc/2007-02/11/content_539512.htm>, last accessed 22 May 2008.

Li, Y. (2000), *The Bankruptcy Legal System* (Beijing: China Legal Publishing House).

Li, Y. (2008), 'On the Procedures Structure in Bankruptcy Law', in Wang, X. and Yin, Z. (eds), *Bankruptcy Law Forum* (1st Volume) (Beijing: Law Press-China, Beijing).

Liu, X. and Xie, X. (2008), 'Reorganization Has the Failing Listed Company Revitalize', *People's Court Daily* (published online 14 May 2008) <http://rmfyb.chinacourt.org/public/detail.php?id=119231>, last accessed 25 September 2008.

Liu, X., Wang, G. and Liu, B. (2008), 'Composition: Another Regenerating Approach, People's Court Daily' (published online 18 July 2008) <http://


81 Parry (2004), p. 3.

82 Wang (2008), p. 248.

rmfyb.chinacourt.org/public/detail.php?id=120847>, last accessed 26 September 2008.

Liu, Z. (2006), 'Problems of connecting the Old and New Bankruptcy Laws and the Current Main Tasks of the Judiciary' (published online 2 November 2006) <http://www.fszjfy.gov.cn/program/article.jsp?CID=563050727&ID=13554, last accessed 25 September 2008.

Meng, L. (2007), 'China's New Bankruptcy Law: A Long-Awaited Compromise', (published online January 2007) <http://www.dlapiper.com/china's_new_bankruptcy/>, last accessed 30 September 2008.

National People's Congress Financial and Economic Committee (2004), 'Elucidation on the Enterprise Bankruptcy Law of the People's Republic of China (Draft) – The Motion on submission for deliberation of the Enterprise Bankruptcy Law of the People's Republic of China (Draft)' (published online 28 June 2004) <http://www.chinacourt.org/html/article/200406/28/121112.shtml>), last accessed 13 February 2009.

Parry, R. (2004), 'Introduction', in Gromek Broc, K. and Parry, R. (eds), *Corporate Rescue: A Overview of Recent Developments* (The Hague: Kluwer Law International).

Qi, S. (2004), *Research on Insolvency Law* (Xiamen: Xiamen University Press).

Tang, W. (2001), *Study on Insolvency Procedure and Legislation* (Beijing: People's Court Press).

Tang, W. (2006), *Interpretation and Application of the New Bankruptcy Law* (Beijing: China Legal Publishing House).

United Nations (2005), *Legislative Guide on Insolvency Law*, available at <http://www.uncitral.org/pdf/english/texts/insolven/05-80722_Ebook.pdf>, accessed 25 September 2008.

Wang, H. (2008), 'Shanhui Court for the First Time Successfully Applying Composition Procedure After an Enterprise Was Declared to Be Bankrupt and Obtaining Good Results' <http://www.gdcourts.gov.cn/xwcz/fyxw/t20080807_18139.htm>, last accessed 26 September, 2008.

Wang, H. (2008), 'Coming Back to Life after Bankruptcy Announcement', (published online 7 August 2008) <http://www.sanshui.gov.cn/main/dwzw/xwdt/sssc/2008080756253.shtml>, last accessed 26 September 2008.

Wang, X. (2007), *Bankruptcy Law* (Beijing: China Renmin University Press).

Wang, X. (2008), *Bankruptcy Law* (Beijing: China Renmin University Press).

Wang, X. and Xu, Y. (2008), 'On the Reorganization Legal System of Listed Companies' in Wang, X. and Yin, Z. (eds), *Bankruptcy Law Forum* (1st Volume), (Beijing: Law Press-China).

Xie, B. (1987), *General Theory on Insolvency Law* (Wuhan: Hunan University Press).

Xing, L. (2007), *The Latest Precise Explanation of Enterprise Bankruptcy Law* (Beijing: Law Press-China).

Yang, J. (2008), *Precise Analysis on and Interpretation of the Latest Bankruptcy Law* (Beijing: China Legal Publishing House).

Zheng, Y. (2008), 'Jinan Qingqi Will Make up the Deficits and Get Surpluses', Shanghai Securities Daily, (published online 9 January 2008) <http://www.cnstock.com/paper_new/html/2008-01/09/content_60516111.htm>, last accessed 27 September 2008.

Zou, H. (2008), 'Analysis on and Application of Enterprise Regeneration Procedures in Our Country' in Wang, X. and Yin, Z. (eds), *Bankruptcy Law Forum* (1st Volume), (Beijing: Law Press-China).

# Chapter 13
# Winding Up Proceedings

Weiwei Zheng

## Introduction

The design of appropriate bankruptcy liquidation procedures is a problematic issue, which has been the subject of much significant research in recent years. Following a protracted reform process, China's new Enterprise Bankruptcy Law, hereafter the 'EBL 2006', contains detailed stipulations regarding bankruptcy liquidation procedures. Under the procedures set out in the EBL 2006, the court will make a bankruptcy declaration in respect of a debtor who satisfies the insolvency conditions set out in Article 2. After the debtor is declared to be bankrupt, the debtor will become termed as the 'bankrupt', its property will form the bankruptcy estate, which should be liquidated and the proceeds distributed to all the creditors under the scheme of priorities set out in the EBL 2006.

Liquidation is a means of clearing the debts of the bankrupt, with the fundamental purpose of 'realization of the fair distribution of bankruptcy property between all the creditors'.[1] This chapter will examine liquidation-related issues, drawing upon judicial practice. Following this, it will proceed to a discussion of the conversion of bankruptcy property, the distribution of this property among all the creditors and the termination of bankruptcy procedures. Finally, it will take a case study approach to analyse some key issues in the operation of liquidation proceedings.

## The Bankruptcy Declaration and Its Legal Effect

A declaration of bankruptcy against the debtor by the court, means that the court is satisfied that the debtor has serious financial difficulties. Such a declaration will have a series of legal consequences, as set out in the EBL 2006.

### *Bankruptcy Petition*

A bankruptcy petition[2] may be filed with the court where the debtor satisfies the tests of insolvency set out in Article 2.[3] These tests are satisfied where either the

---

1 Li (2008), p. 12.

2 See further Chapter 4 regarding the presentation of the petition.

3 Article 7, EBL 2006.

debtor is unable to pay off its debts as they fall due and its assets are insufficient to pay off its liabilities; or if it obviously lacks liquidity.[4] The means by which these states of affairs must be proved are unclear. See further Chapter 4 where these tests are discussed in further detail.

The bankruptcy petition may be presented by the debtor or, if the debtor is unable to pay its debts as they fall due, by a creditor.[5]

### *The Specific Effects of the Bankruptcy Declaration*

A bankruptcy declaration enables the collective handling of claims and debts between an insolvent debtor and its creditors through the bankruptcy procedures. However, the EBL 2006 provides that a bankruptcy declaration may only be made in respect of an enterprise with legal person status, therefore such a declaration cannot be made in respect of an individual.[6]

As for the notification of the ruling of the bankruptcy declaration, Article 107(1) of the EBL 2006 provides that, where the court declares the debtor to be bankrupt, 'it shall, within five days of its ruling, serve the ruling to the debtor and the administrator and, within ten days of its ruling, it shall notify the debtor's known creditors and make an announcement'.[7]

The administrator, where a declaration of bankruptcy is made in respect of a company, shall apply to the incorporation registry authority for the cancellation of its legal personality after the termination of bankruptcy procedure.[8]

It is notable that the bankruptcy declaration depends on a state of continued insolvency. For example, the debtor himself or a third party may liquidate the debtor's due debts, and as a result the debtor will no longer have to conform to the substantive essentials of insolvency, as they are set out in Article 2. According to Article 108 of the EBL 2006, the court shall rule to terminate the bankruptcy procedure and make an announcement to this effect if one of the following events occurs prior to the declaration of bankruptcy: (1) A third party either provides security or pays off the debtor's due debts; or (2) The debtor pays off in full all of its due debts.

### *The Legal Effects of the Bankruptcy Declaration*

The bankruptcy declaration, as one kind of judicial act, will produce a series of legal effects. In particular, the following effects may be noted.[9] Firstly, there are

4 Article 2, EBL 2006. For criticism of these insolvency requirements see Bufford (2007).

5 Article 7, EBL 2006.

6 See further pp. 76-77 regarding this restriction.

7 Article 107(1), EBL 2006.

8 Article 2, EBL 2006.

9 Wang (2007a), p. 307.

remarkable differences in status that the debtor will undergo upon being adjudged bankrupt. After the adjudication of bankruptcy, the debtor becomes the bankrupt, and the debtor's legal personality and civil rights will be restricted by the bankruptcy procedures. The bankrupt's estate will fall under the management of the administrator and the bankrupt will lose his rights to manage his property. In the bankruptcy liquidation procedures, the bankrupt can only passively accept the actions of the administrator in selling off the debtor's property, in distributing property to creditors and in eliminating the legal personality of the debtor company. In contrast, during a reorganization period, the debtor may, upon the debtor's request and upon the approval of the court, manage its property and handle its business affairs under the administrator's supervision.[10]

Secondly, the debtor's property after the bankruptcy declaration will comprise the bankruptcy estate. The scope of the estate is considered further in Chapter 7.

Thirdly, the bankruptcy declaration gives rise for a need for the debtor's creditors to obtain special permission to exercise their rights. Before the bankruptcy declaration is made, all creditor's enforcement efforts will be subject to a stay.[11] After the bankruptcy declaration, a creditor is not entitled to obtain, in respect of debts incurred prior to the bankruptcy declaration, payment in priority but may only obtain payment according to the distribution plan of the bankruptcy property. Furthermore, a creditor can only obtain realization according to the scheme of entitlements and the distributional order applicable in liquidation in accordance with the legal rules. Nevertheless, this rule has an exception, under Article 109 of the EBL 2006: when the debtor is declared to be bankrupt a secured creditor is entitled to obtain payment in priority, by means of the assets to which his security relates. It is of note that this entitlement is not limited by the distribution plan of the bankrupt property; and this approach is called the 'exclusion right system' in the continental law systems.[12] In the bankruptcy procedures, the exertion of the exclusion right arises during the process of reporting claims and confirmation. However a creditor who has not filed his claims on time is not permitted to enjoy and exercise the exclusion right.[13] Moreover, a creditor who has not filed his claims on time is not allowed to enforce his security over the collateral outside of the bankruptcy procedures. The exertion of the exclusion right may enable a secured creditor to be paid off completely. If the value of the asset subject to a security is more than the amount of the debt, the remaining part of the collateral will belong to bankruptcy property and will be used for distribution to unsecured creditors.[14] Article 110 further provides that where a creditor does not exercise the rights referred to in Article 109 his claim shall be treated as a general one; and that a secured creditor

10 Article 73, EBL 2006.
11 Wang (2007a), p. 310.
12 Xiu (2008), p. 72. See further p. 141 and 189.
13 Article 56(2), EBL 2006; Wang (2007a), p. 316.
14 Wang (2007a), p. 317.

whose priority is waived shall be treated as an ordinary unsecured creditor.[15] When the company is declared bankrupt, a secured creditor who has given up security over collateral will be treated as an unsecured creditor and will receive payment at the same level as other unsecured creditors in accordance with the statutory order for the distribution of the bankruptcy estate. The bankruptcy legislations of common law countries have not developed the concept of the exclusion right, but have developed different systems regarding the priority of security interests.

## The Disposition and Distribution of the Bankruptcy Property

In the bankruptcy liquidation, the claims of creditors in relation to the bankruptcy property will mainly be settled in cash. The administrator will undertake a process of selling non-cash assets before implementing the final bankruptcy distribution, and may offer a discount to facilitate a quick sale. However, in light of the insolvent status of the enterprise, the enterprise's property will be insufficient to satisfy the claims of all the creditors. Therefore, the EBL 2006 provides rules for the creditors' fair reimbursement in the bankruptcy liquidation process, through stipulations relating to the order of distribution of the estate and the priority of claims to the bankruptcy property.

### *The Disposition of the Bankruptcy Property*

Under the process of disposition of the bankruptcy property, following the bankruptcy declaration, the administrator will sell the non-cash bankruptcy property in the conventional way, transforming the bankruptcy estate into cash assets, to facilitate the liquidation distribution.

Generally speaking, where the debtor is to be liquidated, rather than reorganized, there is no possibility that the debtor can be saved, and the administrator will formulate a plan of disposition of the bankruptcy property without undue delay and submit it to the creditors' meeting for discussion.[16] The administrator shall dispose of the bankruptcy estate in a timely manner in accordance with the disposition plan which has been approved by the creditors' meeting or sanctioned by the court if the plan is not approved by the creditors' meeting.[17] A prompt approach could save time and prevent the procedure from being protracted. However, it will not necessarily enable the bankruptcy estate to be realized to the maximum extent.

With regard to the disposition of the bankruptcy estate, Article 112(1) of the EBL 2006 provides that bankruptcy property shall be sold off by auction

15 Article 110, EBL 2006.

16 Article 111(1), EBL 2006.

17 Article 111(2), EBL 2006.

unless otherwise provided in resolutions made by the creditors' meeting.[18] Auction is a method entailing the sale of the bankruptcy property by public tendering. Adopting the auction method may raise the property's price by means of competition between willing buyers, and so it can provide an advantageous means of protecting the creditor's overall benefits. However, it is notable that some properties are not suitable for sale by the method of auction because of legal barriers or other reasons. For example, this method would not be appropriate if special procedures are applicable to the property. For example, a transfer of securities must be carried out through the stock exchange,[19] while private company shares may be subject to restrictions on transfer and to pre-emption rights.[20] In recognition that some properties might not be easily disposed of through the auction, Article 112(3) further provides that property which is not capable of being auctioned, or whose transfer is restricted, as required by state law, shall be disposed of in accordance with the means prescribed under state law.[21] The bankruptcy property could be sold as a whole or in parts. For example, intangible assets and other assets could be disposed of separately.[22] Whichever means the bankruptcy property is sold by, a going concern sale is likely to bring more proceeds than a piecemeal sale.

*The Distribution of the Bankruptcy Estate*

In distributing the bankruptcy property the administrator shall apply the bankruptcy estate to pay off the bankruptcy creditors as far as possible with fair regard to legal order and legal procedure. Under the EBL 2006 it is provided that the distribution of the bankruptcy property shall be made in cash unless the creditors' meeting resolves otherwise.[23] The creditors' meeting might decide to adopt other means of distribution after consultation. For example: (1) the distribution of non-cash assets, might be appropriate where the costs of realizing the cash value of the goods would be high or where some creditors have special demands for particular assets and they are prepared to give a reasonable price for them, and to accept a reasonable valuation etc; (2) the distribution of property rights, including creditor's rights, stockholder's rights, intellectual property rights may be appropriate where they cannot be realized as cash, or where they can only be realized as cash at high cost.[24]

The administrator is required to formulate the plan of distribution of the bankruptcy property without undue delay and to submit it to the creditors' meeting

18 Article 112(1), EBL 2006.
19 Article 39, Chinese Securities Law 2005.
20 Articles 72 and 73, Chinese Company Law 2005.
21 Article 112(3), EBL 2006.
22 Article 112(2), EBL 2006; Wang (2007a), p. 329.
23 Article 114, EBL 2006.
24 Wang (2007a), p. 338.

for discussion.[25] The following details should be included in the distribution plan: (1) the name and address of creditors participating in the distribution; (2) the total amount of the claims validly submitted for participation in the distribution; (3) the total amount of distributable bankruptcy property; (4) the order, proportion and amount of the bankruptcy property available for distribution; (5) the intended means of distribution of the bankruptcy property.[26]

The plan of distribution in respect of the bankruptcy estate formulated by the administrator can take legal effect in two ways: through approval by the creditors' meeting and then the court, or through the approval of the court in circumstances where the creditors' meeting has rejected the plan.

Firstly, the plan is voted upon and may be passed by the creditors' meeting. After formulating a disposition plan in relation to the bankruptcy property, the administrator shall propose that the chairman of the creditors' meeting holds the creditors' meeting promptly according to Article 62(2) of the EBL 2006.[27] Where the distribution plan is adopted by the creditors' meeting, the administrator must then submit the plan to the court for approval.[28] The court will examine the authenticity, the accuracy and the validity of the distribution plan, and will approve the plan if it satisfies legal conditions.

If however the distribution plan fails to meet the approval of the creditors' meeting after two votes, it will be ruled upon directly by the court.[29] The court is able to approve a distribution plan in relation to which the creditors' meeting has failed to pass a resolution.[30] It is not difficult to see that this stipulation is aimed at preventing the creditors' meeting from voting on these matters many times without any resolution, a state of affairs which would cause an increase in the costs of the procedure and cause damage to the level of benefits for creditors.

The administrator will implement the distribution plan as approved by the court.[31] The distribution of the bankruptcy property might be implemented by means of a single distribution or a distribution in instalments. If the distribution of bankruptcy property is implemented through a single distribution, the administrator shall announce the bankruptcy liquidation as a distribution. Where a distribution in instalments is to be implemented by the administrator in accordance with the distribution plan the administrator shall announce each amount of distributed property and the claims in relation to which the distribution is made. In terms of a final distribution in the form of a lump sum, the administrator shall make a public announcement including a number of matters relating to the entitlements of

25 Article 115, EBL 2006.
26 Article 115(1), EBL 2006.
27 Article 62(2), EBL 2006.
28 Article 115(2), EBL 2006.
29 Article 65(1), EBL 2006.
30 Article 65, EBL 2006.
31 Article 116(1), EBL 2006.

conditional creditors, as specified in paragraph 2 of Article 117,[32] namely whether relevant conditions for the payment of conditional creditors have been met at the date of announcement or whether any sums that have been set aside for conditional creditors can be distributed to other creditors. These issues will be considered in more detail below.

*The Unclaimed Distribution of the Bankruptcy Property*

Sums must be set aside by the administrator in three main situations. These situations are discussed below and the manner of treatment of unclaimed distributions is also considered.

Firstly, the administrator may have set aside sums for possible distributions to conditional creditors. The conditions for the payment of these sums will have been specified, together with any conditions in which the arrangement will terminate.[33] These deposited sums shall be distributed to other creditors provided that the conditions for initiation have not been met or that the termination conditions have been met. An announcement will be made regarding the distribution of the deposited sums upon the public announcement of the final distribution. In the event that the initiation condition has been met and the termination conditions have not been met at the time of the public announcement of the final distribution, the sums deposited by the administrator for conditional creditors shall be delivered to them.[34]

Secondly, the administrator is required to retain any distribution shares which have been unclaimed by creditors. Sums which have been retained in this manner and which have not been claimed by creditors within two months after the public announcement of the final distribution shall be regarded as disclaimed distributions and they will be available for distribution to other creditors by the administrator or the court.[35]

Thirdly, the administrator is required to retain a share of distribution monies for the settlement of claims which are pending under litigation or arbitration. Sums which have been deposited for this purpose and which have not been claimed by creditors within two years after the termination of the bankruptcy procedure shall become available for distribution to other creditors.[36]

*The Distributional Order of Priority*

The matter of greatest concern in the distribution of the bankruptcy estate shall be the order of payment for the creditors and the priority of their claims to the

32 Article 116(2), EBL 2006.
33 Article 117(1), EBL 2006.
34 Article 117(2), EBL 2006.
35 Article 118, EBL 2006.
36 Article 119, EBL 2006.

bankruptcy property. Creditors' claims will be ranked at different levels, according to their nature and attributes, and the distribution at each level shall follow the *pari passu* principle. The distribution order gives an indication of the government's attitudes and value orientations. The most striking example of the balance to be achieved in legislative values in China relates to the relative claims of employees and secured creditors. Under the old bankruptcy legal framework, secured claims were realized from the proceeds of the sale of collateral outside of the bankruptcy estate. This meant that secured debts enjoyed priority over the unsecured debts, including tax claims and employees' claims.[37] During the economic transition in the mid-1990s, the state adopted the 'planned bankruptcy' programme which emphasized the protection of labour interests in the bankrupcies of SOEs, an approach which was necessitated because of the inadequate social security system, and conferred super-priority on the claims of the redundant workers, who were ranked ahead of secured creditors.[38] The issue of the appropriate distribution order between secured claims and employees' claims was long debated throughout the legislative process of the new bankruptcy law.[39] The draft of June 2004 conferred priority on secured creditors, in accordance with the old law.[40] However, this arrangement was reversed by the draft of October 2004.[41] As discussed further below, the EBL 2006, as enacted, favours the interests of secured creditors. To some extent, this fierce debate protracted the legislative process. The EBL 2006 makes arrangement for the order of payment and reflects the legislative value orientation of the new bankruptcy law.

First of all, insolvency costs and debts of common interest enjoy priority entitlements in the scheme of distribution of the bankruptcy property. The term 'insolvency costs' refers to the essential costs and the expenses of maintaining bankruptcy procedures, such as case fees, the administrator's remuneration, and fees for the management, disposition and distribution of the debtor's property. The term 'debts of common interest' refers to miscellaneous debts arising in contract and tort in the course of the administration of the bankruptcy estate, for example, debts arising from a request by the administrator or the debtor to ask a contractual counterparty to perform the unfinished contract of both parties; claims in respect of unjust enrichment; claims in tort arising from damage caused by the administrator or relevant personnel in the course of their performance of their duties; or claims in tort arising from damage caused by the debtor's property.[42] Insolvency costs and debts of common interest occur after the commencement of the bankruptcy procedures, and may be regarded as the reasonable expense of maintaining the bankruptcy procedures. If these two expenses were not

37 Article 32, EBL 1986.

38 For more details regarding 'planned bankruptcy', see Chapter 15.

39 Shi (2007), p. 672.

40 Article 121, June 2004 draft.

41 Article 127, October 2004 draft.

42 Article 42, EBL 2006.

safeguarded, the bankruptcy procedure could not be continued. It is of note that insolvency costs should be treated as having priority as between insolvency costs and debts of common interest.[43]

If insufficient sums are available to meet all of the insolvency costs or debts of common interest, any payments should be made *pro rata*.[44] Where the insolvency state is insufficiently valuable to meet the insolvency costs the administrator must apply to the court for the bankruptcy procedures to be terminated.[45] The court will rule to terminate the proceedings within 15 days of receiving such a request and will make an announcement accordingly.[46]

Secured creditors are next in the sequence of priorities, ahead of the other creditors' claims. Article 109 of the EBL 2006 provides that a secured creditor is entitled to obtain payment in priority by means of the specific assets which are subject to the security that he holds.[47] Stipulation of the exclusion right in respect of these assets, as discussed above, enables the secured creditor to obtain satisfaction of his claim in priority to other creditors. The right to enjoy priority in respect of specific property of the debtor is a common feature which appears in most countries' bankruptcy law. Nevertheless, an exception may arise in relation to the rights of specific creditors which are stipulated by other laws and regulations, such as maritime law, air law, etc, as enjoying priority rights. Where such a position of priority is granted, the insolvency legislation may make provision for conflicts between such specific creditors' rights and the secured creditor's rights in the bankruptcy law, and may provide that the specific creditors' rights have liquidation priority over the secured creditor's rights in most situations.[48] The EBL 2006 places the payment of taxes after the secured creditor's rights and at present it is not clear whether other specific creditors' rights are payable prior to the secured creditor's right, other than under a transitional provision regarding the payment of employee claims occurring prior to the EBL 2006 coming into effect.[49] With the development of a market economy in China, other laws and regulations may also stipulate new types of creditors' rights as having priority, in order to adjust each kind of social relationship.

Additionally, the EBL 2006 gives priority to the employees' wages and welfare claims in the distribution of bankruptcy property. This approach is consistent with the protection generally afforded to employees in other jurisdictions and the relevant international convention.[50] Historically, a fundamental principle of

---

43 Article 43, second sentence EBL 2006.

44 Article 43, third sentence EBL 2006.

45 Article 43, fourth sentence EBL 2006.

46 Article 43, fourth sentence EBL 2006.

47 Article 109, EBL 2006.

48 Wang (2007), p. 237.

49 Article 132, EBL 2006.

50 For example, the 'Convention on the Protection of Worker's Claims in the Event of the Insolvency of their Employer' requires that the workers' claims should be paid prior

bankruptcy law is the fair and equal treatment of creditors, and, as such, it may be contended that the number of priorities should be kept to a minimum.[51] The priority in bankruptcy distribution in China has been complicated by strong arguments that the employees of the bankruptcy enterprise should be strongly protected.[52]

In nature, the justifications for the priority of employees' claims relate to the citizen's basic right to subsistence, which may include the right to suitable living conditions and the health and welfare of family members.[53] The impact of the bankruptcy case on social relationships is relatively complex; and the handling of the insolvency event should pay attention to the potential economic impact on the creditor, particularly aiding social minority groups. Protection of the personal interests of the employees of the bankrupt enterprise may mobilize the individual enthusiasm of the employees; it may also better promote prosperity and the development of the social economy. Meanwhile, the protection of the interests of employees of the bankrupt enterprise is a social policy reflected in the EBL 2006; it is an important feature, to maintain social stability and guarantee fair treatment under the bankruptcy procedure.[54] In the long run, special arrangements may be made by the legislature in relation to other social minority groups. Bankruptcy legislation is just one piece of legislation in an overall package of market reforms in the area of labour and employment affecting employees' interests.[55] A well developed and thorough approach to employee protection requires a synergy between bankruptcy law and other laws, in particular Labour Law and social security systems.[56]

Finally, where the bankrupt is in arrears with social insurance premiums and taxes, such sums will also receive priority of payment. Article 113 of the EBL 2006 stipulates that after the payment of insolvency costs and debts of common interest from the bankruptcy estate, the remaining debts shall be made in the following categories and in the following order: (1) wages, medical fees, compensations for injury and disability, compensations for a bereaved family owed by the debtor to

---

to the claims of non-privileged creditors, the privileged claims of the State and the social security system and most other privileged claims. The EBL 2006 gives priority to employees' claims over ordinary claims and tax claims, which satisfies the level of protection required by the Convention. The UNCITRAL Legislative Guide on Insolvency Law also points out that in a majority of countries, workers' claims constitute a class of priority claims, which, in a number of cases, rank above tax and social security claims but not secured claims: UNCITRAL (2005), para. 72.

51 Harmer (2000), p. 49.

52 Shi (2007), p. 670.

53 Liu (2007), p. 346.

54 Wang (2005), p. 38.

55 Shi (2007), p. 674.

56 A recent development is that China adopted the Employment Contract Law on 29 June 2007 (effective as of 1 January 2008), which greatly increases the employees' protection in many aspects. It can be expected that the implementation of the Employment Contract Law will have a positive effect on the implementation of the EBL 2006.

the employees, basic pension and medical insurance premiums defaulted by the debtor and due to be paid into the employees' private accounts, other compensations payable by the debtor to the employees in accordance with law and administrative rules and regulations; (2) social insurance premiums, other than those stated in the previous paragraph, defaulted by the bankrupt and tax payable by the bankrupt; (3) general bankruptcy claims.[57] Where the bankruptcy property is insufficient to pay off all of the debts within a particular category, distribution shall be made on a *pro-rata* basis.[58] The wages of directors, supervisors and senior managerial personnel of the bankruptcy enterprise shall be calculated in light of the average wage of the general employees of the enterprise.[59]

From what has been outlined above, it may be seen that arrears in respect of social insurance premiums are to be paid ahead of general bankruptcy claims in order to maintain the social benefits of workers and the social security system. Similarly, tax claims might also involve the national public interest; and such claims are also to be paid in priority.

## The Termination of the Bankruptcy Procedure

Where there are no funds remaining for distribution, either because all available sums have been distributed, or because there were no funds to distribute in the first place, steps will be taken to terminate the proceedings:

- Following the final distribution of the bankruptcy property, the administrator must without undue delay submit a distribution report to the court and request the court to terminate the bankruptcy procedure.[60]
- Where there are no funds available for distribution Article 120 of the EBL 2006 states that the administrator shall request the court to terminate the bankruptcy procedure.[61]

Where a request for the termination of the proceedings has been made, the court shall make its decision as to whether or not the proceedings shall be terminated within 15 days of the administrator's application. In addition, the court shall make a public announcement of the termination ruling.[62]

After the termination of the bankruptcy procedure, the legal person status of the enterprise will be eliminated. To this end, the administrator shall apply to the incorporation registration authority for the cancellation of registration within ten

57 Article 113(1), EBL 2006.
58 Article 113(2), EBL 2006.
59 Article 113(3), EBL 2006.
60 Article 120(2), EBL 2006.
61 Article 120(1), EBL 2006.
62 Article 120(3), EBL 2006.

days of the ruling of termination entered into by the court.[63] During the course of the winding up of the affairs of the enterprise, the administrator assigned by the court is engaged in the receipt, storage, disposition and distribution of the bankruptcy estate. When the ruling of termination is made by the court, the administrator shall terminate his duties and functions on the day following his application for the cancellation of the company's registration, unless there remains pending litigation or arbitration.[64]

Provision is made for additional repayment of bankruptcy property within two years of the termination of the bankruptcy proceedings. Specifically speaking, if, after the bankruptcy property is distributed finally or the bankruptcy procedure terminates, it is discovered that the bankrupt has new distributable property, the creditors are entitled to petition the court to permit the implementation of an additional repayment in conformity with the distribution plan.[65]

The EBL 2006 stipulates that the additional repayment may arise in the following two circumstances: (1) where property which is recovered in accordance with Article 31,[66] Article 32,[67] Article 33[68] and Article 36[69] of this law is discovered; or (2) if other distributable property of the bankrupt is discovered.[70] Therefore additional distributions will mainly relate to sums recovered in the context of transaction avoidance litigation, as well as property received within two years of the termination date of the bankruptcy procedure. The regulations for the implementation of the additional repayment are somewhat restrictive, since only property recovered within two years after the termination of the bankruptcy

---

63 Article 121, EBL 2006.

64 Article 122, EBL 2006.

65 Article 123, EBL 2006.

66 Under Article 31, EBL 2006, the administrator may request that the court revokes transactions of various types that have occurred within one year prior to the acceptance of the insolvency case. These activities are: (1) a transfer of property without consideration; (2) a transaction at an obviously unreasonable price; (3) the provision of security in respect of unsecured debt; (4) the payment of an undue debt; (5) the waiver of a claim. See further pp. 154-7.

67 Under the EBL 2006, Article 32 the administrator may request that the court rescind payment made to a specific creditor within the period of six months prior to the acceptance of the insolvency case and at a time when the debtor was insolvent within the terms of Article 2(1), unless this specific payment is beneficial to the debtor's property. See further pp. 157-8.

68 Under the EBL 2006, Article 33 it is provided that the following activities involving the debtor's property are void: (1) hiding, transferring property for the purpose of evading debts; (2) fabricating debts or recognizing fabricated debts.

69 Under Article 36 of the EBL 2006 the administrator shall recover any inappropriate income acquired and property misappropriated by a director, supervisor or other managerial officer of the debtor by taking advantages of their position.

70 Article 123(1), EBL 2006.

procedure, can be the subject of the additional repayment.[71] The petition for additional repayment should be presented within the two year limitation period. Property that is discovered after this limitation period is not capable of giving rise to an additional repayment. In addition, the guarantor and other joint debtors of the bankrupt are not discharged from paying remaining unpaid debts in accordance with liquidation procedure after the termination of the bankruptcy procedure.[72] This is because the guarantor or the joint debtors assume joint and several liabilities in respect of the debtor's unpaid debts. The creditors are entitled to enforce claims against the guarantor or the joint debtors, and an additional payment has to be made if they are capable of making the payment. In the circumstance where an additional payment made by the debtor could enable the creditors to be paid in full, the guarantor or the joint debtors will not be liable.

## Approaches of the Chinese Courts in Bankruptcy Liquidation Cases under the EBL 2006

This section will consider two case studies which illustrate the operation of the liquidation provisions under the EBL 2006.

### *Case 1 – Beijing Bowan Clothing Equipment Sales Outlet*

The distribution plan in a bankruptcy liquidation shall be implemented in accordance with the rules prescribed under the EBL 2006 for the protection of the creditors' legitimate rights and interests.[73] This case study, which concerns the bankruptcy case of Beijing Bowan Clothing Equipment Sales Outlet in 2007, will illustrate the basic course that such proceedings will take. The company, hereafter 'Bowan Sales Outlet' was a state-owned enterprise, established on 21 August 1984 with registered capital of RMB 500,000. Due to the unpredictability of the market, and poor management and operation, the enterprise began to experience financial difficulties in 1998. Over the following years the company's cash flow was insufficient and its losses increased. Consequently, it was unable to pay its debts and to carry on its business without being propped up by the state. An audit of the company's affairs, up to 8 June 2007, revealed that Bowan Sales Outlet had gross assets of RMB 5,718,368.23, and total liabilities of RMB 10,071,013.20. The ratio of assets and liabilities was 176.12 per cent. When the court accepted the bankruptcy application in this case, the claims filed by creditors came to a total amount of RMB 9,186,323.89.

Beijing Chaoyang District Court found that Bowan Sales Outlets was unable to pay its due debts, and that its property was insufficient to meet all of its debts. The

71 Article 123(1), EBL 2006.

72 Article 124, EBL 2006.

73 China Beijing Court Website. Available at <http://bjgy.chinacourt.org/>.

application for the bankrupt liquidation of Bowan Sales Outlets had to conform to the insolvency conditions set out under the EBL 2006. In light of the facts outlined above, the court found these conditions to be met and legally declared Bowan Sales Outlet to be bankrupt in accordance with the EBL 2006. After the announcement of the bankruptcy, the administrators appointed by the court performed the duties of dealing with the bankruptcy estate of Bowan Sales Outlet, and produced a distribution plan in respect of the bankruptcy property. Later, the court convened the creditors' meeting, at which the administrators submitted the distribution plan for approval by the creditors' meeting. The distribution plan would not become effective until it was sanctioned by the court. Finally, the bankruptcy estate was distributed. The winding up of the company protected the creditors' legitimate rights and interests effectively.

*Case 2 – Shanghai T & E Limited Company*

As noted above, the employees of a bankrupt enterprise are entitled to obtain payment in priority under the EBL 2006, for the protection of the employees' legitimate rights and interests.[74] In the bankruptcy case of Shanghai T & E Limited Company in 2008, the Shanghai Jinshan District Court adopted the stipulations in the EBL 2006 relating to the payment of arrears in respect of wages, compensations and the support fees, etc. It was apparent that the employees' legitimate rights and interests were protected in accordance with legal requirements, maintaining social harmony and stability.

The case concerned three related companies, whose brief details are as follows:

- Shanghai T & E Limited Company, hereafter 'Shanghai T & E' was a limited liability company owned by foreign investors and established in March 2004. The company's registered residence was located at Shenzhuang Town in the Minhang District of Shanghai. The company's actual business place was located in the Xingta Industrial Zone of the Jinshan District of Shanghai and its registered capital was 20,000,000 US dollars.
- The Shanghai T & E General Power Equipment Limited Company, hereafter 'General Power', was a limited liability company under the ownership of foreign investors, established in July, 2002. The residence of this company was located in the Xingta Industrial Zone in the Jinshan District of Shanghai, and its registered capital was 15,500,000 US dollars.
- The Shanghai Meihao Electric Appliance Limited Company, hereafter 'Meihao Electric' was a limited liability company owned by foreign investors and established in April 1998. This company's registered residence was located in Meilong Town of the Minhang District of Shanghai, and its actual

74 China Shanghai Court Website. Available at <http://www.hshfy.sh.cn/fyitw/gweb/>.

business place was located in the Xingta Industrial District of the Jinshan District of Shanghai. Its registered capital was 1,200,000 US Dollars.

Therefore, all three companies were foreign-owned enterprises.

In February 2008, the actual controller of the three companies, Mr Pan, went missing and the companies' suppliers sued in abundance. The assets and the bank accounts of the three companies were frozen by the court, and the companies' production operation could not be carried on. On 14 April 2008, the Shanghai Jinshan District Court received a bankruptcy application in respect of Shanghai T & E from Suzhou Jinhai Machinery and Electronics Science and Technology Company, and Shanghai Brilliant Trading and Development Limited Company; a bankruptcy application in respect of General Power from the Shanghai Grow Development Limited Company; and a bankruptcy application in respect of Meihao Electric from the Shanghai Yisitai Plastic and Rubber Product Limited Company.

The Jinshan District Court heard the bankruptcy application and made a report and request to Shanghai No. 1 Intermediate Court for guidance. The application was eventually accepted by the Jinshan District Court in accordance with this guidance.[75] The administrator appointed by the court appropriately dealt with the labour-related issues, took over the assets of the company and carried on the audit and valuation in accordance with the original plan. At the same time, in order to guarantee the security of the companies' assets, the administrator signed an agreement with a security company, and invited specialized security personnel to safeguard the companies' assets.

The bankruptcy case of Shanghai T & E was the first case under the EBL 2006 to come before the Shanghai Jinshan District Court. The case not only involved numerous creditors, but it was also of a complex context. In order to guarantee that the bankruptcy liquidation was implemented in an overt, fair and justified manner, protecting the creditors' legitimate rights and interests, the administrators of Shanghai T & E, General Power and Meihao held a partial creditor's symposium under the Jinshan District Court's instruction on 4 August 2008.

On 10 September 2008, the Shanghai Jinshan District Court held the first creditors' meeting according to the stipulations of the EBL 2006. On 30 October 2008, an auction company conducted two auctions of land parcels and the corresponding engineering foundation located in Shenzhuang Town in the Minhang District of Shanghai which belonged to Shanghai T & E. The sale price was agreed at RMB 55,000,000. The competitive buyer paid the full auction cost of RMB 55,000,000 on 20 November 2008.

Shanghai Jinshan District Court found that the three enterprises were in arrears, owing wages and labour-related compensation payments to 372 employees at a total amount of RMB 3,000,000. Before the acceptance of the bankruptcy case,

75 A common practice of the Chinese judiciary, when a court encounters difficulty in a trial, is for this court to ask for technical help or guidance from its upper-level court.

the unpaid wages and compensation payments had been made under the court's hearing, and the court's adjudication had become effective.

Under the stipulations of the EBL 2006, the scheme of distribution of the bankruptcy property should be voted upon and passed by the creditors' meeting, and by a ruling of the court, after which it will be carried into effect. The hearing process of insolvency cases entails a period of time for the convening of the creditors' meeting; therefore, it was impossible to promptly compensate the employees of the three companies for any arrears in respect of wages and labour-related compensation payments. A proposal from the Shanghai Jinshan District Court was discussed and passed by the creditors' committee, and then Jinshan District Court decided that the employees should be compensated in arrears in the amount of RMB 3,000,000 for sums due in respect of wages and compensation payments. These payments were made in advance and distributed to more than 370 employees of the bankruptcy enterprise. No provision for such a payment to be made is included in the EBL 2006, however, this payment enabled the payment of labour-related claims to be expedited. Such intervention may be necessary in future cases to prevent potential social unrest. From this example it is apparent that the protection of the legitimate rights and interests of employees remains the biggest issue of concern for the employees in a bankruptcy case under the EBL 2006.

## Conclusion

The liquidation procedure is a key process which enables insolvent enterprises to be wound up. It regulates the disposal of the remaining assets of the debtor and emphasizes a process of orderly distribution to creditors from the proceeds of sales of assets falling within the bankruptcy estate, whether by going concern sale or piecemeal sale. The new bankruptcy law has resolved what was a fierce debate in relation to the relative priorities in the order of distribution between secured debts subject to collateral and labour claims, with the former having prevailed. The new winding up procedure largely improves upon the old one and arguably provides an effective exit route for the insolvent enterprises which fail to effectively compete in the market.

## References

Bufford, S. (2007), 'The New Chinese Bankruptcy Law: Text and Limited Comparative Analysis' 16 *Norton Journal of Bankruptcy Law and Practice* 697.

China Beijing Court Website, available at: <http://bjgy.chinacourt.org/>.

China Shanghai Court website, available at: <http://www.hshfy.sh.cn/fyitw/gweb/>.

Harmer, R. (2000), *Insolvency Law Reform in the Asian and Pacific Region*, Vol. 1 Law and Policy (Manila: Asian Development Bank).

Li, J. (2008), 'Discussion on Procedure and Structure of the Bankruptcy Law', published in the first edition of *Bankruptcy Law Forum* (Beijing: Law Press-China) (May) 2008, at 12 (in Chinese).

Liu, D. (2007), *Understanding and Operation Instructions of the New Bankruptcy Law* (Beijing: Law Press-China).

Shi, J. (2007), 'Twelve Years to Sharpen One Sword: The 2006 Enterprise Bankruptcy Law and China's Transition to a Market Economy' 16 *Norton Journal of Bankruptcy Law and Practice* 645.

UNCITRAL (2005), 'Legislative Guide on Insolvency Law', <http://www.uncitral.org/pdf/english/texts/insolven/05-80722_Ebook.pdf>, last accessed 27 May 2009.

Wang, W. (2007a), *The Sum and Substance of Bankruptcy Law* (Beijing: Law Press-China) (in Chinese).

Wang, D. (2007b), *Difficult Explanation and Practice Operation of the New Bankruptcy Law* (Beijing: Law Press-China).

Wang, X. (2005), 'Discussion on the New Insolvency Law Legislation in Length and Breadth' 4 *Journal of Capital Normal University* 38.

Xiu, X. (2008), 'Discussion on Exercise to Eliminate Right of the Bankruptcy Law' 4 *Contemporary Law* 72.

Chapter 14

# Improper Trading in Bankruptcy and Director Liabilities

Bin Wang

## Introduction

The function of bankruptcy law is to regulate the order and equity of distribution of resources, to protect the legal rights of creditors as well as debtors, and to maintain the order of the market economy. As the last resort for market entities to quit the market, bankruptcy law must protect creditors' rights and reconstruct the market credit system. Therefore, bankruptcy laws in different countries set up legal liability systems in order to punish improper trading in bankruptcy and compensate creditors. As with any other branch of law, bankruptcy law without an integrated legal liability system will not be effective. At present, bankruptcy fraud and avoiding paying debts are serious, as a result of the lack of an effective legal liability system in bankruptcy law. This is one of the focuses of new bankruptcy legislation in China under the Enterprise Bankruptcy Law, hereafter 'EBL 2006'.

It is in the interests of an ordinary enterprise, as a debtor in the market, for emphasis to be put on the potential liabilities of directors, supervisors or senior managers in the event of its bankruptcy; otherwise it will lose its ability to attract credit. The lack of a bankruptcy liability system for senior managers has caused huge debts to be left unmet and has given rise to serious unemployment, while senior managers have escaped liability. The EBL 2006 puts more emphasis than hitherto on bankruptcy liability, and, together with the Company Law, Securities Law and Amendment Six to the Criminal Law, sets up a whole bankruptcy liability system, including civil, administrative and criminal responsibilities for improper trading before and during bankruptcy.

Legal liability premises that legal obligations do exist, and legal liability is the guarantee of legal obligation. Legal liabilities in bankruptcy law arise in respect of various forms of malpractices, including bribery, corruption, embezzlement and negligence, a range which is almost the same as those of like kinds of malpractice that are punishable outside of bankruptcy. This chapter will only focus on the analysis of special legal liabilities in the EBL 2006 and will compare the EBL 2006 regime with that applicable under the Insolvency Act 1986 in the UK. Compared with the EBL 2006 in China, the present bankruptcy law in the UK may be regarded as a perfect legal liability system. This chapter will, on the basis of comparing the EBL 2006 and the Insolvency Act in the UK, introduce the new system of improper trading and personal liability in bankruptcy law in China.

The new bankruptcy law prescribes two legal liabilities: bankruptcy liability and legal liability for bankruptcy.

## Bankruptcy Liability

Bankruptcy liability is referred to as the responsibility of a director, supervisor or senior manager if he violates his obligations of being honest and diligent and this leads to enterprise bankruptcy. Bankruptcy liability and legal liability for bankruptcy are different. The biggest difference is that bankruptcy liability deals with the illegal activity in enterprise management before, not during, the bankruptcy, mainly comprises neglect of duty of the manager, and protects the order of enterprise management and the rights of enterprise owners.

Individual responsibility of the directors in bankruptcy law is the direct result of the trend of strengthening the protection of creditors' rights. 'Traditional company law almost exclusively puts all emphasis on the relationship between the company and its members and between directors and shareholders, instead of the rights of the employees, the creditors and the consumers of the company's products',[1] accordingly, traditional company law was confronted with challenges from the theory of economics and company law.[2] The enforcement of liquidation rules has become an important method of protecting the creditors.[3] Since an investigation can be carried out during liquidation to ascertain whether the manager of a company has followed the rule of protecting the rights of the creditors and the company, accordingly, the liability of the manager for not following the rule may also be assessed.[4] It is for this reason that bankruptcy liability exists in bankruptcy laws in different countries.

Enterprise bankruptcy, which marks the end of an enterprise, has a significant impact on the rights of the shareholders, the creditors and the employees in the enterprise. If a director, supervisor or senior manager violates his obligations of being honest and diligent and this leads to enterprise bankruptcy, he will be held liable. There are similar clauses in the bankruptcy laws in different countries, such as under the Insolvency Act 1986.

Before the EBL 2006 was enacted, bankruptcy often gave rise to a problem of huge undischarged debts and serious unemployment, yet no senior managers were held to be liable for bankruptcy. Accordingly, article 6 of the EBL 2006 prescribes that 'In the hearing of a bankruptcy case, the court shall guarantee the legitimate rights and interests of the employees of the insolvent enterprise and subject its

1 Zhang (2000), p. 232.
2 See e.g. Parkinson (1995); Dine (2000), Ch. 1.
3 Zhang (2000), p. 232.
4 Han (2003), p. 30.

managers to legal liabilities'. Article 125 of the EBL 2006 provides that 'Where a director, supervisor or senior manager violates his obligations of being honest and diligent and this leads to enterprise bankruptcy, he shall be subject to the relevant civil liabilities according to law'. As discussed below, the consequences for a director can include a period of disqualification.

These articles in the EBL 2006 provide responsibility for a director, supervisor or senior manager if he violates his obligations of being honest and diligent and this leads to enterprise bankruptcy, marking a big step forward in bankruptcy legislation. This responsibility includes civil, criminal responsibility and disqualification.

*Disqualification*

Article 125, paragraph 2 of the EBL 2006 prescribes that 'no person under any circumstance as prescribed in the preceding paragraph may, within three years as of the day when the procedures for bankruptcy are concluded, assume the post of director, supervisor or senior manager of any enterprise'. This article, in content, is consistent with Article 147 of the Company Law.

*Civil Responsibility in Bankruptcy Liability.*

There is no specific provision in the new bankruptcy regarding civil responsibility for senior managers. However, Article 150 of the Company Law provides that 'if a director, supervisor or the senior officer causes detriment to the company while performing his duties in violation of laws, administrative regulations or the articles of association, he shall be liable for the loss so caused'. Since a director, supervisor or the senior officer owes a fiduciary duty to the company and its shareholders, he shall bear liability to compensate for the losses that he makes. Before the bankruptcy, the company may start legal proceeding for damages, and a shareholder may start a derivative suit as well.[5] However, it is the administrator who can start legal proceedings against senior managers of the company during the procedure for bankruptcy.

*Criminal Responsibility in Bankruptcy Liability*

Article 131 of the EBL 2006 provides that 'Any entity that violates the provisions of the present Law in a way which constitutes a crime shall be subject to criminal liabilities according to law'. The EBL 2006 applies to all corporations, including state-owned and non-state owned corporations. The senior manager will assume corresponding responsibility for his conduct where he violates his fiduciary duty, such as by misappropriation or bribery. The problem is whether a director, supervisor or senior manager who violates his obligations of being honest and diligent, leading to enterprise bankruptcy, shall be subject to criminal

5 Zhang (2003).

responsibility. Article 168 of the Criminal Law provides that only a person-in-charge directly responsible of 'a state-owned company or enterprise, who practices favoritism or irregularity and causes bankruptcy or serious loss to the company or enterprise' shall assume criminal responsibility. Therefore, we hold the view that under the current criminal law, a director, supervisor or senior manager of a non-state-owned company violating Article 125 of the EBL 2006 does not commit a crime.

What is worth mentioning is that the legal liability prescribed in the old Bankruptcy Law 1986, hereafter EBL 1986, was bankruptcy liability.[6] It can be seen that the bankruptcy liability prescribed in the EBL 2006 is quite different from that under the EBL 1986. First, bankruptcy liability applies to both state-owned enterprises and non-state-owned enterprises. Second, the comparatively wider scope of the liable party mentioned in the EBL 1986, including legal representative and the leading official of the department in charge, reflects that this law was enacted in the days of the planned economy, while the scope of the EBL 2006 only covers directors, supervisors and senior officers. Finally, the bankruptcy liability mentioned in the EBL 1986 is mainly administrative responsibility supplemented by criminal responsibility, instead of civil responsibility. In contrast, the EBL 2006, mainly gives rise to civil responsibility and to criminal responsibility when committing a crime. Although it is not clear in the EBL 2006 to whom the wrongdoer shall be liable, and what kind of civil responsibility the wrongdoer shall assume, the author holds the view that the responsibility here is not only to the bankrupt enterprise, but also to creditors. This change makes the indirect relationship between directors and creditors direct in special circumstances, breaking the tradition of company law.

It must be clarified that bankruptcy law, which deals with the legal relationship during the procedure of bankruptcy, is not the main legal basis for the bankruptcy liability of the director, supervisor or the senior officer before the procedure of bankruptcy. It is company law that may tell whether a director, supervisor or the senior officer fulfils his obligations of being honest and diligent. Articles 21, 149, 150, 152 and 153 of the Company Law provide the obligations of a director, supervisor or the senior officer to be honest and diligent, as well as the legal

6 Article 42 provided that after an enterprise was declared bankrupt, the government supervisory departments and audit departments would be responsible for pinpointing the responsibility for the bankruptcy of the enterprise. Where the legal representative of the bankrupt enterprise bore the major responsibility for the bankruptcy of the enterprise, administrative sanctions would be applied. Where the superior departments in charge of the bankrupt enterprise bore the major responsibility for the bankruptcy of the enterprise, administrative sanctions would be applied to the leaders of such superior departments in charge. With respect to the legal representative of the bankrupt enterprise and the leaders of superior departments in charge of bankrupt enterprise who, due to neglect of duty, caused the bankruptcy of the enterprise, resulting in a major loss of state property, criminal responsibility would be investigated in accordance with Article 187 of the PRC Criminal Law.

responsibility he should assume if he fails to do so. Nevertheless, Article 125 of the EBL 2006 is arguably too general. According to this article, a director, supervisor or the senior officer shall be held liable where his violation of the obligations of being honest and diligent leads to enterprise bankruptcy. It may be difficult even for the court to conclusively identify the real cause of bankruptcy so as to hold a director, supervisor or the senior officer accountable, since a company does not go bankrupt overnight and its downfall may be attributed to a variety of reasons. In view of these ambiguities, the UK 'wrongful trading' provision in section 214 of Insolvency Act 1986 is worth considering.

'Wrongful trading' in section 214 of Insolvency Act 1986 is a significant system for personal liability of a director in British bankruptcy law. This section is much more specific than Article 125 of the EBL 2006 of China, although it has a wide range of application. Liability may arise under section 214, if, at some time before the commencement of the winding up, the director knew or ought to have concluded that there was no reasonable prospect that the company would avoid going into insolvent liquidation. In such circumstances a director is expected to place the company into liquidation. If the director fails to do so and decides to carry on trading and this leads to insolvency, he may be ordered by the court to contribute personally to the assets in the liquidation upon the liquidator's application. Accordingly, wrongful trading is referred to as the conduct of continued trading when the company has gone into insolvency or bankruptcy. Conditions of 'wrongful trading' include: (1) the company must have gone into insolvent liquidation; (2) the director must have known, or he ought to have concluded, that there was no reasonable prospect that the company would avoid going into insolvent liquidation; (3) the defendant must have been a director or shadow director[7] at the time of trading; and (4) no statutory defence is applicable, that is, there is no evidence that the director has taken every step to avoid the creditors' losses. In determining the matters dealt with under (2) above, section 214 provides a dual objective and subjective standard, that is:[8]

> the facts which a director of a company ought to know or ascertain, the conclusions which he ought to reach and the steps which he ought to take are those which would be known or ascertained or reached or taken, by a reasonably diligent person having both: (a) the general knowledge, skill and experience that may reasonably be expected for a person carrying out the same functions as are carried out by that director in relation to the company and (b) the general knowledge, skill and experience that the director has.

7 Shadow Director refers to a person in accordance with whose directions or instructions the directors are accustomed to act: Insolvency Act 1986, s. 251. See further *Re Euro Express Ltd, Secretary of State for Trade and Industry v Deverell* [2001] Ch. 340.

8 S. 214(4), Insolvency Act 1986. See Han (2003).

Therefore a defendant will be judged by the standards that would be expected of a 'reasonably diligent' person carrying out the functions that were entrusted to the defendant[9] and it will be no defence if the defendant did not have adequate knowledge, skills or experience for the role. However if the defendant's knowledge, skills and experience are high, he will be judged by those standards, even if they are greater than would have been needed for the functions that he was carrying out.

Consequently, section 214 applies to the occasion where the company does not take proper measures to protect the creditors' rights where the company is facing inevitable insolvent liquidation, rather than to the improper management which leads to bankruptcy. Therefore, a director's performance or omission will constitute improper trading if it does not take all steps to reduce the creditors' losses within reasonable limits. If a director shuts the book too early when realizing that insolvency is inevitable this will potentially constitute wrongful trading. Positive or passive conducts out of the scope of management, such as omission in exercising the company's creditor rights, failure to maintain the company's assets, overpayment to directors, trading at an unreasonably low price after a shutout, are matters that may lead to the personal liability of a director.

A further UK provision which is worthy of note is section 213, applicable where a company is being wound up and giving rise to liability for 'fraudulent trading'. Fraudulent trading is referred to as a person may be held liable where they were knowingly party to the carrying on of business with intent to defraud the company's creditors, or creditors of any other person, or where the company's business was carried on for any fraudulent purpose. A person held to be liable for fraudulent trading will be liable to make contributions to the company's assets as the court thinks proper, a provision which is compensatory in nature, rather than punitive.[10]

According to the UK Insolvency Act 1986, a director will assume the following two responsibilities where he is found liable for 'fraudulent trading' or 'wrongful trading':

1. *Making contributions to the company's assets*. When 'fraudulent trading' or 'wrongful trading' occurs, the liquidator can apply to the court for an order that a director is to be liable to make such contributions to the company's assets as the court thinks proper. It needs to be pointed out that, firstly, the amount of the contributions is within the court's discretion; and secondly, the contributions belong to the bankrupt company, for the benefit

9 Taking account of the type of company of which he was a director: *Re Produce Marketing Consortium Ltd* (1989) 5 BCC 569.

10 Insolvency Act 1986, s. 213(2); *Morphitis v Bernasconi* [2002] EWCA Civ. 289; [2003] Ch. 552. Separate criminal liability for fraudulent trading may be imposed under Companies Act 2006, s. 993.

of creditors generally, rather than to one creditor or a group of creditors.[11]

2. *Director disqualification.* The court may make a disqualification order against the director for fraudulent trading or wrongful trading, disqualifying him from being a director within a certain period of time (15 years at most).[12] The disqualification order stops the disqualified director, within the specified period of time, from: (a) being a director of a company, or acting as receiver of a company's property or in any way, whether directly or indirectly, being concerned or taking part in the promotion, formation or management of a company without first obtaining the permission of the court, and (b) being an insolvency practitioner. No permission to be an insolvency practitioner may be obtained.

## Legal Liability in the Procedures of Bankruptcy

The other liability provided in the EBL 2006 is legal liability for default in the procedures of bankruptcy. This liability may arise where the debtor or other obligors have violated his or their legal obligations in the procedures of bankruptcy which have been initiated according to the Bankruptcy Law by the court. The sections with respect to the legal liability in the procedures of bankruptcy protect the fair order of discharge and the interests of all the creditors. The responsible entities of the legal liability in the procedures of bankruptcy include the bankrupt company, its legal representative, responsible individuals, bankruptcy administrators, and even third parties.

Articles 126 to 131 of the Bankruptcy Law stipulate legal liability in the procedures of bankruptcy for violating the following obligations:

### *Liability for Non Compliance with the Obligation of Illustration*

Article 126 stipulates that:

> Where any staff member of a debtor is obligated to attend the creditors' meeting yet, without any justifiable reason, fails to do so upon summon of the court, the court may summon him by force and impose upon him a fine according to law. Where any staff member of a debtor violates the provisions of the present Law by refusing to comply with the obligation of illustration or to answer enquiries

11 Previously the court had powers to order a defendant found liable under the fraudulent trading provisions to reimburse particular creditors: *Re Cyona Distributors Ltd* [1967] Ch. 889 and *Re Gerald Cooper Chemicals Ltd* [1978] Ch. 262. See Farrar (1994), p. 494.

12 S. 10, Company Directors Disqualification Act 1986. A disqualification application is more likely to be dealt with under s. 6 of the same Act.

> or where he produces any false statement or answer, the court may impose upon him a fine according to law.

The obligation of illustration is a significant obligation which shall be fulfilled by the debtor. In fulfilling the obligation of illustration the obliged person must meet two requirements: first, the obliged person must answer the enquiries upon summons in a specified place without absence or delay unless for justifiable reasons; and second, the obliged person must illustrate faithfully without holding back and must not make any false or one-sided statements. Violation of the 'obligation of illustration' arises where the person who is obligated to illustrate does not fulfil his obligation intentionally and thus interferes with the procedures of bankruptcy.

The bankrupt company who is under an obligation of illustration is the debtor, who is obligated, through relevant personnel, to attend the meeting of the creditors,[13] and this obligation of illustration may also fall on financial and accounting personnel, as well as managerial personnel. These persons, with relevant documents of the company in hand, are familiar with the management, assets, finance and employee resettlement of the bankrupt company. It is necessary that these insiders should illustrate the situation of the bankrupt company to the meeting of creditors and the administrator and should provide assistance to the meeting of creditors and the administrator in receiving the debtor's assets and dealing with the debtor's business. Article 126 which stipulates the obligation of the insiders to comply with the obligation of illustration and the legal responsibility for violating this obligation, is designed to enable the meeting of creditors and the administrator to acquire accurate information regarding the debtor's assets and to deal with the assets.[14]

The legal representative of the company, or other obliged persons, shall be held liable for a refusal to answer the inquiries, or for the making of a false statement. The legal responsibilities stipulated in Article 126 of the EBL 2006 are as follows:

1. summoning by force, which applies in the situation where any staff member of a debtor who is obligated to attend the creditor's meeting fails to do so without any justifiable reason upon summon of the court;
2. a fine, which applies to all the situation where any staff member of a debtor violates the obligation of illustration.

A summoning by force and a fine are both coercive measures in civil suits as well as in bankruptcy law. No specific procedures regarding these two coercive measures are stipulated in bankruptcy law, however Article 4 of the EBL 2006 provides that 'the procedures for hearing a bankruptcy case shall, in the absence

13 Article 15, EBL 2006.

14 Wang (2007), p. 369.

of relevant provisions in the present Law, be governed by the relevant provisions of the Civil Litigation Law'.

Different coercive measures apply to different conducts in violation of the obligation of illustration. To be specific, (1) the court may summon by force the obligor who refuses to attend the creditor's meeting, and may also impose upon him such fine as the court thinks proper at the same time; (2) the court may impose such fine as it thinks proper upon the legal representative or other persons under the obligation of illustration who refuse to fulfil their obligation; (3) the court may impose a fine as it thinks proper upon the legal representative or other person subject to the obligation of illustration who produces a false statement.[15]

There are similar provisions in the UK Insolvency Act 1986. According to sections 210 and 211 of Insolvency Act 1986, when a company is being wound up, whether by the court or voluntarily, any person, being a past or present officer of the company, shall not make any false representations or make any material omission in any statement relating to the company's affairs. Compared with China's EBL 2006, the obligation of illustration stipulated in the UK Insolvency Act 1986 applies to the occasion where a company is being wound up either by the court or voluntarily, and the obliged persons include any person being a past or present officer (including a shadow director) of the company. Accordingly, the UK Insolvency Act 1986 is worth an examination for its wider scope of the obligation of illustration. Moreover, the major difference between the two laws is that the obligation of illustration in China's bankruptcy law emphasizes that the obligor must illustrate in certain occasions, while the UK equivalent puts more emphasis on the completeness and authenticity of the illustration. The differences between the legislation in China and the UK represent differences in legal values, that is, different attitudes to the relative priorities of the positive interference of public authority and the rule of autonomy of the will.[16]

### *Legal Liability for Violation of the Obligations of Submission and Transference*

Article 127 applies where a debtor violates the provisions of the EBL 2006 by refusing to submit any required material to the court; or by submitting thereto any fraudulent statement on the debtor's financial status, its checklist of debts, its checklist of the creditor's rights, its financial statement or payment statement of its employees' wages or social insurance premiums. In the event of such a violation, the court may impose a fine upon the directly liable person according to law.

Liability arises under the second paragraph of Article 127 where any debtor violates the provisions of the EBL 2006 by refusing to transfer its assets, seals or materials, such as accounting records and documents, to the administrator; or where he fabricates or destroys the relevant materials of financial evidence, thereby

15 Li and Song (2006).

16 Li (2008).

making the debtor's financial status unclear.[17] In the event of such a violation, the court may impose a fine upon the directly liable person according to law.

*Violation of the obligation of submission* The 'obligation of submission' is the basic obligation of the debtor, who shall submit related documents to the court, whether the bankruptcy procedures are instituted by a creditor or the debtor. Article 8, paragraph 2 of the EBL 2006 prescribes that where a debtor files a bankruptcy application with the court, the debtor shall submit a statement on financial status, checklists of its debts and claims, relevant financial statements, a resettlement scheme intended to be adopted for employees, as well as the payment documents of employee wages and social insurance premiums. Article 11, paragraph 2 of the EBL 2006 prescribes that 'where a creditor files a bankruptcy application, the court shall serve it on the relevant debtor within five days from the day when a decision is made. The relevant debtor shall, within 15 days from the day when the decision is served, submit to the court its statements on financial status, a checklist of debts and claims, relevant financial and accounting statements, as well as the payment documents of employee wages and social insurance premiums'. In these explicit terms, the EBL 2006 gives clear provision regarding the obligation of submission and the range of the documents to be submitted.

A person subject to the obligation of submission will generally be the legal representative of a company and, by decision of the court, the financial manager or the key person-in-charge, and such a person will be liable where they refuse to submit the necessary legal documents or where they submit fraudulent documents in order to conceal the company's properties and avoid paying debts. It is worthwhile noting that damaging consequences of the interference with bankruptcy procedures are not a precondition of violation of the obligation of submission. However, the harmful consequences of the violation shall be taken into consideration by the court in considering the appropriate sentence for violation.

A person subject to the obligation of submission who fails to fulfil this obligation shall commit a criminal offence and be subject to a fine. A fine is a common punishment, and a crime will be constituted if the obligor violates the obligation of submission seriously. What crime does a person who fails to fulfil his obligation of submission commit? The present Criminal Law has no related provisions, except the crime of concealing or deliberately destroying financial vouchers, financial account books or financial statements, as prescribed in the Amendment to the Criminal Law 1999. Acts that will constitute a violation of the obligation of submission include: (a) refusing to submit legal documents; and (b) submitting fraudulent documents. Obviously, these conducts are different in substance from what is prescribed in the Amendment to the Criminal Law 1999. Where the violator of the obligation of submission also conceals or deliberately destroys financial vouchers, financial account books or financial statements, he

17 Wang (2007), p. 371.

will be held criminally responsible. Otherwise, violation of the obligation of submission alone does not constitute the foregoing crime.[18]

Article 1 of the Amendment to the Criminal Law 1999 prescribes that 'Whoever conceals or deliberately destroys financial vouchers, financial account books or financial statements, if the circumstances are serious, shall be sentenced to fixed-term imprisonment of less than five years or criminal detention, and/or be imposed a fine not less than RMB 20,000 but not more than RMB 200,000. Where a unit commits the crime as mentioned in the preceding paragraph, it shall be imposed a fine, and the persons who are directly in charge or persons who are directly responsible for the offence shall be punished according to the preceding paragraph'. Therefore, the debtor, as well as the persons who are directly in charge or persons who are directly responsible for the offence, will be held criminally liable if they violate the obligation of submission and such violation constitutes the crime of concealing or deliberately destroying financial vouchers, financial account books or financial statements at the same time.

*Violation of the obligation of transference* Violation of the 'obligation of transference' arises where a person who is obliged to transfer the company's assets, seals, or materials, such as books of accounts and documents, refuses to do so, or fabricates or destroys the relevant materials of financial evidences.

Bankruptcy procedures will be officially launched once the court accepts the bankruptcy application.[19] After that, the debtor's assets, as well as other related materials, shall be transferred to the administrator, so that the administrator may get a full understanding of the property status of the company. The obligor shall be held liable where he violates the obligation of transference and the leads to the confusion of assets.

Two kinds of legal responsibility are applicable to the violation of the obligation of transference:

a. a fine, which applies to the persons who are directly responsible for the violation, will be imposed as the court thinks proper; and
b. a criminal penalty, which applies to the persons who violate the obligation of transference and this violation constitutes a crime.

Conduct which amounts to a violation of the obligation of transference may also amount to a crime according to the present Criminal Law and its amendments, mainly the crimes prescribed in Chapter V 'Crime of Encroaching on Property'[20]

18 Chen (2008).

19 On the effects of acceptance see *inter alia* Articles 13-21, EBL 2006.

20 The Crimes of Encroaching on Property result from the violation of the obligation of transference, see articles 270, 271 and 272 of the Criminal Law.

and in Chapter III section III 'Crime of Disrupting the Order of Administering Companies and Enterprises'.[21]

Compared with the elaborate provisions regarding the obligation of submission and transference in China's EBL 2006, section 209 of the UK Insolvency Act 1986 prescribes that 'When a company is being wound up, an officer or contributory of the company commits an offence if he destroys, mutilates, alters or falsifies any books, papers or securities, or makes or is privy to the making of any false or fraudulent entry in any register, book of account or document belonging to the company with intent to defraud or deceive any person'. A person guilty of an offence under this section is liable to imprisonment or a fine, or both.[22] Section 208 (1)(e) also provides that 'When a company is being wound up, whether by the court or voluntarily, any person, being a past or present officer of the company, commits an offence if he ... after the commencement of the winding up, prevents the production of any book or paper affecting or relating to the company's property or affairs'. These sections represent the legal values of the principle of good faith.

### *Legal Responsibility for Bankruptcy Fraud*

Bankruptcy fraud, as the most common type of improper trading, is the main target of attack by the bankruptcy laws in all countries. In China, fraud in bankruptcy cases in order to avoid paying debts is particularly serious. Some debtors make use of the bankruptcy procedures to avoid paying debts by fraud in connivance with local governments. These conducts prejudice the interests of the creditors and the employees, disturbing the economic order. A prime example is the Sichuan Zhongjiang Silk Corporation (SZSC) bankruptcy case. SZSC, established in 1982, was a state-owned trading company with a raw silk and pod franchise, whose main business was pod purchase and distribution. From 1995 to 1999, SZSC had good record of annual profit and paid extra income tax and special agriculture tax up to RMB 13,344 million. From 1998 to 1999, SZSC was classified as a super and first class enterprise by its main creditor, Bank of Agriculture Sichuan Branch, and AA class enterprise by Bank of China Sichuan Branch. Before SZSC was announced bankrupt by the court, the book value of its assets was RMB 119.64 million, debts were RMB 86.7657 million, the net worth of the company was RMB 38.8758 million, and the asset-liability ratio was 72.52 per cent; with almost no overdue loans or unpaid bank interest. The only due debt was RMB 1 million from the Finance Bureau of Zhongjiang County. At that time, SZSC's business and assets were both in good order with RMB 0.792 million in bank deposits and RMB 12.155 million worth of stock in trade, mainly dry pod which were easy to sell.

21 Crimes which result from violating the obligation of transference of Disrupting the Order of Administering Companies and Enterprises refer to the destruction, mutilation, alteration or falsification of any books, papers or securities.

22 S. 209(2), Insolvency Act 1986.

However, under the political control of the Party committee and the government of Zhongjiang County, the Finance Bureau of Zhongjiang County, as SZSC's creditor, applied to the court for the bankrupt liquidation of SZSC on 14 December 2000, although during the last 11 months in 2000 SZSC had RMB 1.067 million of profit. On the same day, the court of Zhongjiang County accepted the application and made an announcement of SZSC's bankruptcy and the company was transferred to the control of the bankruptcy liquidation group. Thereafter, the government of Zhongjiang County and Sichuan Tianyou Company, a private enterprise, established New Century Silk Company (NCSC), which purchased SZSC by auction under the arrangement of the local government. In this bankruptcy case, a loan of RMB 40 million from the Bank of Agriculture Zhongjiang Branch became a bad debt.

In order to launch bankruptcy procedures, the Party committee and the government of Zhongjiang County arranged for ten affiliated companies of SZSC to go bankrupt and, as a result, SZSC lost its creditor's rights against these companies. Besides, SZSC was ordered to pay back most of the loan from the Finance Bureau of Zhongjiang County (RMB 16 million) with RMB one million remaining unpaid. The Finance Bureau of Zhongjiang County, as SZSC's creditor, applied to the court for the bankrupt liquidation of SZSC on 14 December 2000. The Party committee and the government of Zhongjiang County also ordered SZSC to withdraw money and make a false account so as to give the false impression of insolvency due to serious losses. As planned beforehand, the government of Zhongjiang County appointed an official as the head of the bankrupt liquidation group before bankruptcy, and ordered SZSC, the court and other related authorities to cooperate in the bankruptcy procedures.

On 31 July 2001, the television programme of 'Topics in Focus' of CCTV brought the SZSC case to light. From 12-17 June, a united investigation group consisting of related departments of the State Council, the main creditor banks and the Supreme Court carried out an investigation in depth. Accordingly, the key persons in charge in the Party committee, the government and the court of Zhongjiang County were punished according to the law.[23]

The SZSC bankruptcy case is a typical example of a fraudulent bankruptcy under the control of the local government. In this case, the Party Committee and the government and the court of Zhongjiang County controlled the bankruptcy procedures by exercising influence on the related departments and the court, making the bankruptcy law and the relative procedures an empty process. The court of Zhongjiang County, controlled by the local government without judicial independence, made a decision to accept the application for bankruptcy on the same day that the creditor filed the application, without either legal examination or reasonable notification of the declaration of the creditor's right. Through this typical fraudulent bankruptcy and manipulative 'insolvency', the wrongful traders caused a huge loss of state assets and infringed the interest of the creditors, as

23 See China Daily (2008).

well as the investors, seriously undermining the legal and social credit system. It shows that in the shift from the planned economy to a market economy, the local governments have on occasions had their own vested interests in mind and they, driven by these interests, have kept bargaining with the central government. This phenomenon is common in China. A similar situation happened in the 'Holland Village' bankruptcy case,[24] in which the author took part. Accordingly, it is arguably necessary to enact a uniform bankruptcy law against fraudulent bankruptcies.

Generally speaking, a company applying for bankruptcy without due causes will not be punished by bankruptcy law. According to United States bankruptcy law and judicial practice, the debtor does not need to prove its situation of assets and liabilities when applying for bankruptcy, that is to say, a company may apply for bankruptcy and liquidation although it is far from being insolvent. Since the bankruptcy procedure is, compared with certain civil enforcement procedures, a discharge procedure, the debtor may choose to undergo a bankruptcy procedure instead of an enforcement procedure for strategic reasons, in order to discharge its debts without due cause.[25] In addition, in a bankruptcy procedure, the causes of bankruptcy may vanish as a result of market changes or asset appreciation; nevertheless, the bankruptcy procedure will keep going. However, a debtor applying for bankruptcy without due cause will not necessarily be punished by law.

In theory, a company transferring or disposing of its properties by means of concealing its properties, or fabricating debts or by any other means going through a false bankruptcy, so that the interests of the creditors or any other person are severely injured, is considered to be a bankruptcy fraud and constitutes a crime.[26] In addition, Articles 31, 32 and 33 of the EBL 2006 prescribe the voidable transactions, discussed further in Chapter 8. The acts stipulated in Articles 31 and 32 are revocable acts, and the acts in Article 33 are invalid acts. The administrator is entitled to claim the property back if the debtor's transactions are established under the above articles. The transactions under Articles 31, 32 and 33 do not necessarily amount to crimes. Article 32, which provides that the debtor confers preferential status on a particular creditor, would not, without more, constitute the crime of bankruptcy fraud. Article 31(1) and (2) respectively stipulate the transferral of property without consideration and the transferral of property at a seriously unreasonable price. Article 33 prescribes the void acts which include the concealment or transfer of property by the debtor for the purpose of avoiding debts; and the fabrication of debts or recognition of fabricated debts. Article 31(1), (2) and 33 will not constitute the crime of bankruptcy fraud unless these acts cause serious damage to the interests of creditors.[27] Therefore, the author holds the view

24 No more details about this case were available at the time of writing because it was just under the bankruptcy procedure.

25 See further Delaney (1992), highlighting potential abuses of the United States bankruptcy system.

26 Article 6, Criminal Law Amendment 6, 2006.

27 Zeng (2006), p. 171.

that the provision regarding bankruptcy crimes in Amendment 6 to the Criminal Law still leaves much to be desired.

Seemingly, the EBL 1986 prescribed liability for bankruptcy fraud, stipulating that the legal representative of the debtor, or any other directly liable person, would be subject to civil liabilities for compensation[28] or, when constituting a crime, criminal punishment.[29] Nevertheless, the effective way to protect the victim's interest in civil activities is to provide civil compensation, for which no provision was made in the old EBL 1986. Administrative punishment upon the leaders of a company is of little practical significance. Since administrative punishment is based on a subordination relationship, it cannot be applied to most enterprises except for state-owned enterprises. Furthermore, administrative punishment has no punitive function in a market economy.

The EBL 1986 prescribed criminal liability for bankruptcy fraud. However, after the new Criminal Law came into effect in 1997, an analogous system was replaced by the principle of a legally prescribed punishment for a specified crime. Since there is no provision concerning the crime of bankruptcy fraud in the new Criminal Law, the lack of provision for civil liability, administrative liability and criminal liability in the liability system under the EBL 1986, has resulted in a situation where the wrongdoer will not be held liable for his wrongful trading. Accordingly, the cost of complying with the law is equal to the cost of breaking the law while the income from the latter is much higher than the former. This absence of deterrence is why bankruptcy fraud is rampant in practice.

Besides, the EBL 2006 removes administrative liability and enacts provisions of criminal liability, which, together with the Amendment to the Criminal Law, strengthen the liability system for bankruptcy fraud. A person suspected of bankruptcy fraud may violate the General Rules of Civil Law, Company Law, Accounting Law, Criminal Law and other laws at the same time, and will be under criminal sanction pursuant to these laws. Article 131 of the EBL 2006 prescribes that 'Any entity that violates the provisions of the present Law in a manner which constitutes a crime shall be subject to criminal liabilities according to law'. Compared to the crime of bankruptcy fraud prescribed in the Bankruptcy Law of Japan, the EBL 2006 of China, together with Amendment 6 to the Criminal Law, has set up a framework of the crime of bankruptcy fraud with Chinese characteristics.

Article 6 of Amendment Six to the Criminal Law inserts a new Article 162(II), as follows:

> Where any company or enterprise transfers or disposes of its properties by means of concealing its properties or undertaking fabricated debts or by any other means or goes through false bankruptcy so that the interests of the creditors or any other person are severely injured, the persons-in-charge who are held to be

---

28 Article 128, EBL 2006.

29 Article 6, Criminal Law Amendment 6, 2006.

> directly responsible and other directly liable persons shall be sentenced to fixed-term imprisonment of not more than five years or detention, and/or shall be fined RMB 20,000 up to RMB 200,000.

This is referred to as the crime of false bankruptcy. This provision marks a quantum leap forward, because bankruptcy fraud was not deemed as a crime according to the Criminal Law of China previously. This newly added crime is designed to work with the EBL 2006 so as to improve the liability system of bankruptcy law.

However, a potential problem with this article must also be pointed out. False bankruptcy arises where the debtor applies for bankruptcy without due causes of insolvency in fact. The debtor who defrauds the creditor in false bankruptcy shall be punished according to the Criminal Law. In China, it is notable that more frauds happen in real bankruptcy cases instead of false bankruptcy cases. In real bankruptcy cases, many debtors have due cause for their insolvency application but go on to commit fraud in these validly opened bankruptcy procedures. Literately speaking, fraud in a real bankruptcy case cannot be punished in the name of the crime of false bankruptcy according to Amendment Six to the Criminal Law. Some scholars hold the view that where a debtor either 'transfers or disposes of its properties by means of concealing its properties or undertaking fabricated debts or by any other means' or where it 'goes through false bankruptcy', the crime of false bankruptcy will be constituted, and the presence of both of the foregoing conditions at the same time is not necessary. This approach may make up for the apparent deficiency.

### *Domicile Restriction*

Article 129 of the EBL 2006 provides that 'Where any staff member of a debtor, in violation of the provisions of the present Law, unlawfully leaves his domicile, the court may admonish or detain him, and may additionally impose a fine upon him according to the law'. This article prescribes the liability for failing to follow the domicile restriction provision, which restricts freedom of action during the bankruptcy procedures. Under the principle of domicile restriction, set out in Article 15(4), it is provided that 'from the date when the court decides to accept an application for bankruptcy until the date when the bankruptcy procedures are concluded, the relevant personnel of the debtor shall not leave the debtor's place of domicile in the absence of permission from the court'.

In bankruptcy procedures, the legal representative, the financial manager and the key person-in-charge are obligated to cooperate with the court or the administrator.[30] Therefore, their freedom to leave the debtor's domicile will be restricted in order that the court or the administrator can find them. Similar provisions can be found in foreign bankruptcy laws. For example, violation of the domicile restriction constitutes a crime under Article 377 of the Bankruptcy Law

30 Article 15, EBL 2006.

of Japan, which provides that '1. The person under custody escapes or meets or communicates by mail with others will be sentenced to imprisonment for not more than 1 year or a fine of not more than 50,000 yen. 2. the bankrupt who leaves his domicile in the absence of permission of the court will be punished according to section 1 of this article'.[31]

The EBL 2006 prescribes compulsory measures instead of criminal liability regarding the violation of domicile restriction. Pursuant to Article 129 of the EBL 2006, the court can admonish or detain a transgressor of the domicile restriction, and may also impose a fine upon him. Admonition, mainly by verbal criticism, should arguably apply to those who cause less serious harm to the bankruptcy procedures, while detention should apply to those who cause comparatively serious harm. The amount of the fine imposed by the court should be as it thinks proper.

## Legal Liability for an Administrator for Violation of his Fiduciary Duty

Although the main focus of this chapter is on the liability of company directors, mention should also be made of potential liabilities of the bankruptcy administrator. Article 130 of the EBL 2006 provides that:

> Where a bankruptcy administrator fails to perform his functions and duties in a diligent and faithful manner according to the provisions of the present law, the court may impose a fine upon him according to the law. Where any loss is incurred by a creditor, a debtor or a third party, the bankruptcy administrator shall be required to compensate for such losses according to the law.

The principle of fiduciary duty, sometimes called the duty of honesty or duty of good faith, comes from the theory of trust law in Anglo-American law countries and applies to relationships in the context of company law, partnership law and bank law. It is accepted by most scholars that fiduciary duty is the legal duty of the fiduciary, in acting on behalf of the beneficiary, based on the fiduciary relationship. Since the bankruptcy administrator is the legal trustee of the bankruptcy property, he will be subject to corresponding fiduciary duties, including the duty of honesty and trustworthiness. The administrator will violate his fiduciary duty where he fails to perform his functions and duties in a diligent and faithful manner.[32]

The bankruptcy administrator plays a key role in the liquidation procedure and owes fiduciary duties as a faithful administrator. Accordingly, Article 27 of the EBL 2006 provides that 'the bankruptcy administrator shall perform his functions and duties in a diligent and dutiful manner, and shall faithfully perform his duties as well'. Upon his appointment as the bankruptcy administrator by the court, the administrator shall pay close attention to bankruptcy property and affairs

31 Shen (1993), p. 207.

32 Feng and Ai (2002).

and shall act diligently in relation to the bankruptcy property. If the bankruptcy administrator fails to do so and accordingly causes loss to the bankruptcy estate, or if he infringes the legal interest of the bankrupt company, the creditor or other interested parties, he will be held liable. If the interest of the bankruptcy estate conflicts with the administrator's own interest, he shall, pursuant to his duty of honesty, put the former over the latter, and he cannot seek an illegal interest for himself or others. The administrator will bear a corresponding responsibility if his illegal act infringes the interest of the debtor, the creditor and others.[33]

Matters that will amount to a violation of the administrator's fiduciary duties include neglect of duty, malpractice, and abuse of his power of office and so on. Among these matters, malpractice is relatively common.

The administrator will be liable in damages for neglect of his duty and infringement of the interest of the debtor, the creditor and others. At present, both the civil law system and the common law system take fault liability as the principle of imputation.[34] Based on the trust that the court and the creditors place in the administrator, the administrator must meet three requirements, necessary skills, reasonable care and diligence, fairness and honesty.[35] The measure of damages will reflect the real loss suffered. Complete damage compensation by the bankruptcy administrator is theoretically feasible. However, with the increase of the size of the bankruptcy enterprises, the bankruptcy administrator, such as an accounting firm or law firm or other trustee organization, may not be able to pay the full amount of compensation.

Generally speaking, the bankruptcy administrator's resources may be far less than the bankruptcy estate. Therefore, it will undermine the balance between risk and profit to order the bankruptcy administrator to compensate for all the potential losses, at least where he has not acted in a dishonest fashion. Where the potential scope of liability is too large, the incentive for professionals to act as bankruptcy administrators will be hindered. Accordingly, it is necessary to set up the system of a maximum compensation limit so as to control the practice risk of the bankruptcy administrator to a reasonable range. At present, there is no provision concerning a maximum compensation limit in the bankruptcy laws in different countries.

Where any loss is incurred by a creditor, a debtor or a third party as a result of the bankruptcy administrator's dereliction of his duty, the bankruptcy administrator shall potentially be subject to criminal liabilities according to the law. It is noteworthy that we cannot make a simple equation between the bankruptcy administrator's violation of his obligations of being honest and the crime of dereliction of duty as prescribed in Chapter IX of the Criminal Law. The crime of dereliction of duty is referred to as that of a public servant of a state organ who abuses his power of office or neglects his duty and thus causes a heavy loss to public property or the interests of the state or the people. The subject of this crime is limited to the public

33 Article 130, EBL 2006; Wang (2007), p. 376.

34 Zhang (2002), p. 228.

35 Yang (2007).

servant of a state organ. The bankruptcy administrator is not a public servant of a state organ, although he is appointed by the court. Therefore, the bankruptcy administrator is not a due subject of the crime of dereliction of duty.

What crime is committed if the administrator violates his fiduciary duty and thus causes loss to a creditor, a debtor or a third party? Theoretically, there are two possible types of crime that are relevant, that is, a crime that can be committed by a common subject and a crime that can only be committed by the administrator. The latter will be focused on. Since the EBL 2006 does not clearly stipulate the crime of the administrator, the matters of whether the administrator commits a crime and what crime is committed shall be decided according to the Criminal Law. One important point that should be noted is that the criminal liabilities of the person in charge in a state-owned enterprise and in a non-state-owned enterprise are different, and so are the liabilities for infringing on the property of a state-owned enterprise and a non-state-owned enterprise. The Criminal Law of China emphasizes the protection of state-owned property. Accordingly, the legal offence relating to the property of a state-owned enterprise results in criminal liability more frequently.

Therefore, in analysing a case, it is necessary to distinguish between administrators in bankruptcy procedures concerning state-owned enterprises and those concerning non-state-owned enterprises, because there are significant differences in the constitution of crimes and the names of crimes between the malpractices of either administrator. Some conduct will constitute a crime if practised by the administrator in a state-owned enterprise, but will not if practised by the administrator in a non-state-owned enterprise. In bankruptcy, the interested parties of the bankrupt enterprise have changed. The creditors, instead of the shareholders, become the main controllers of the enterprise, and the managers elected by the shareholders are replaced by the administrators appointed by the creditors or the court. That is to say, the bankruptcy administrator is actually the person in charge in the liquidation of a state-owned enterprise during a bankruptcy.

Accordingly, the bankruptcy administrator of a state-owned enterprise may be considered to commit one of a number of crimes that may be committed by the person in charge of a state-owned enterprise. These crimes are mainly prescribed in Section III, 'Crime of Disrupting the Order of Administering Companies and Enterprises', and Chapter III 'Crime of Disrupting the Order of Socialist Market Economy', Part II of the Criminal Law of China. These provisions deal with matters such as selling the state-owned assets at a low price, being defrauded in the course of entering or performing a contract due to a serious neglect of duty, the taking of advantage of a post to make a profit for a relative or friend, and so on. The crimes that may be committed by the bankruptcy administrator include but are not limited to the aforementioned crimes.

## Bankruptcy Crimes, Evaluation

It can be seen that bankruptcy crimes, which are very harmful, are easily found in bankruptcy procedures. As a German scholar has said, a common bankruptcy crime is more harmful than one hundred thefts.[36] Therefore, bankruptcy crime is prescribed in bankruptcy laws in different countries. As noted previously, Article 131 of the EBL 2006 provides that 'Any entity that violates the provisions of the present Law in a manner which constitutes a crime shall be subject to criminal liabilities according to law'.

Simply speaking, a bankruptcy crime is an illegal act which violates the Bankruptcy Law and the Criminal Law at the same time. Concrete analysis is necessary to tell which acts constitute crimes and which crimes they constitute.

Taking together Article 131 of the EBL 2006, the Criminal Law and Amendment one and six to the Criminal Law, crimes that may be committed during bankruptcy proceedings may include but are not limited to: the crime of disturbing liquidation in order,[37] the crime of negligence of the person-in-charge directly responsible for a state-owned company, enterprise or institution and the crime of a public servant's abuse of his power of office, the crime of false bankruptcy, the crime of offering and accepting bribes.

Due to the particularity of bankruptcy, bankruptcy crimes infringe upon the rights of not only the creditors and the bankrupt enterprise, but also the employees in the bankrupt enterprise and the whole society, and they endanger the public order. Therefore, the bankruptcy laws in different countries pay attention to bankruptcy crimes. There is a separate chapter in the EBL 2006 concerning legal liability; however, compared with the bankruptcy legal systems in other countries, China still has a long way to go in establishing a sound framework for its bankruptcy system.

In English law, an extensive list of bankruptcy crimes appears in Part IV, Chapter X of the Insolvency Act 1986. This chapter prescribes bankruptcy offences, in respect of matters including non-disclosure; concealment of property; concealment, destruction, mutilation or falsification of books and papers; the making of false entries in the debtor's books or papers; and the fraudulent disposal of property. Compared with the Insolvency Act 1986, the crimes prescribed in the EBL 2006 of China are too simple and ineffective to combat crimes.

In order to improve the bankruptcy crime system of the EBL 2006 and to keep the bankruptcy procedures proceeding smoothly, China shall, by learning from foreign countries' advanced experience in legislation, prescribe more precisely the crime of dereliction of duty in bankruptcy; the crime of bankruptcy fraud against third parties; the crime of violating domicile restriction; the crime of violating the obligation to make statements; the crime of bribery in bankruptcy, and so on. Traditionally, no criminal liability provisions are prescribed in the commercial

---

36 Lin (1981), p. 31.

37 Article 162, Criminal Law 1997.

laws of China, therefore, the new bankruptcy crimes shall be prescribed in the new amendments to the Criminal Law.

## Conclusion

Improper trading in bankruptcy and liability for such trading are special systems in bankruptcy, whose most important function is correction, so as to protect the creditors' interests. Such provisions are the last resort in upholding the integrity of a bankruptcy system and are emphasized in the bankruptcy laws of every country. Chapter 11 in the EBL 2006 of China, which contains such provisions, marks a big step forward in the establishment of a legal liability system in bankruptcy. This chapter provides an article-by-article analysis of the concept of improper trading in bankruptcy and both civil and criminal liability as prescribed in the EBL 2006 of China, and compares the EBL 2006 of China with equivalent provisions of the UK Insolvency Act 1986. In introducing and analysing the EBL 2006 the author has attempted to provide an impersonal and neutral viewpoint and to elaborate upon the provisions of the EBL 2006.

## References

Chen, Z. (2008), 'The Study of Legislation on Bankruptcy Crimes', available at <http://www.law-lib.com/Lw/lw_view.asp?no=962>, last accessed 31 March 2009.

China Daily (2008), 'Why a Company That Make Profits Went Bankrupt All of a Sudden? – The Study of Silk Corporation (SZSC) Bankruptcy Case' *China Daily*, 23 October 2008.

Delaney, K.J. (1992), *Strategic Bankruptcy* (Berkeley: University of California Press)

Dine, J. (2000), *The Governance of Corporate Groups* (Cambridge: Cambridge University Press).

Farrar, J. (1994), 'The Responsibility of Directors and Shareholders for a Company's Debts under New Zealand Law', in Ziegel, J. (ed), *Current Developments in International and Comparative Corporate Insolvency Law* (Oxford: Clarendon Press).

Feng, G. and Ai, C. (2002), 'The Study of Obligation of Honesty and Credibility and Civil Responsibility of Controlling Shareholder', in Wang, B. (ed), *Financial Law Journal* 6th edn (Beijing: Law Press-China).

Han, C. (2003), 'Personal Bankruptcy Liability of a Director to Enterprise Bankruptcy' 21 *Law Review* 1.

Li, S. (2008), 'Bankruptcy Announcement', available at <http://news.sina.com.cn/o/2008-02-03/092813377027s.shtml>, last accessed 27 May 2009.

Li, S. and Song, X. (2006), *The System Design and Operation Guide of Enterprise Bankruptcy Law of the People's Republic of China* (Beijing: People's Court Press) (in Chinese).

Lin, S. (1981), *Economic Crime and Criminal Law in Economy* (Taiwan: Sanmin Press).

Parkinson, J.E. (1995), *Corporate Power and Responsibility* (Oxford: Clarendon Press).

Shen, D. (1993), *The Study of Bankruptcy Law in a Comparative Way* (Beijing: Foreign Trade and Education Press) (in Chinese).

Wang, W. (2007), *The Sum and Substance of Bankruptcy Law* (Beijing: Law Press-China).

Yang, B. (2007), 'The Civil Responsibility of Bankruptcy Administrator', <http://www.lunwentianxia.com/product.free.5930490.1/>, last accessed 31 March 2009.

Zeng, J. (2006), *Criminal Law Amendments: Background, Explanation and Application* (Beijing: China Legal Press).

Zhang, M. (2000), 'The Protection of Creditors in Enterprise', in Wang, B. (ed.), *Business Law Review* (Beijing: Law Press-China).

Zhang, M. (2002), *The Study of Theory of Fault Liability in Tort* (Beijing: China University of Political Science Press) (in Chinese).

Zhang, M. (2003), *Interest Balance in Company Law* (Beijing: Beijing University Press).

# PART III
# State-owned Enterprises and Financial Institutions

# Chapter 15
# Bankruptcy of State-owned Enterprises and Planned Bankruptcy

Haizheng Zhang

## Introduction

Under the planned economy and the process of economic transition, the bankruptcy of a state-owned enterprise (SOE) was not only an economic and legal issue, but also a complicated political issue, with which the government was usually concerned. Even at the present, it remains an awkward matter for the state to deal with. The main reason is the inadequate social security system which is unable to provide sufficient protection to redundant workers. The SOEs are the major providers of social welfare. Once the SOEs are liquidated, the laid-off workers will have nowhere to claim unpaid wages and social benefits except the local government. This is why the Chinese government has always been active in dealing with the liquidation and reorganization of SOEs. The planned bankruptcy programme, an expedient administrative measure, was launched in the mid-1990s under this background with the intention to provide special care to the claims of employees, even at the expense of financial creditors. This chapter will explore planned bankruptcy related issues and the state's roles in the financing of ailing SOEs and the disposal of non-performing loans (NPLs). It will start with a discussion of the characteristics and reform of SOEs.

## Features, Problems and Reform of State-owned Enterprises

A Chinese enterprise, formulated upon state-owned assets, is like a cell which 'performs a specific function in order to contribute to the efficient functioning of the whole organism'.[1] Particularly in the era of the planned economy, the production and sales of SOEs were arranged by the government authority under public ownership and one SOE could not trade with other enterprises freely. In addition, the banks provided finance to enterprises at the behest of government agencies, rather than basing such lending on market rules on a commercial base.

1 Clarke (1992), p. 306.

In short, political connections between the state and the enterprises outweighed market considerations.[2]

It should be noted that in general there are four remarkable features of the SOEs. Firstly, a SOE is not merely a legal-economic entity, but also a political entity which involves the political power of the Chinese Communist Party (CCP). In this context, 'the enterprise's motivation was not only confined to the pursuit of profits and innovation; political motivation was also added'.[3] It is impossible for the state to seek the maximization of profits at the expense of political interest. The CCP tends to pay more attention to special concerns over laid-off workers, social security and stability, which may slow down the speed of the economic reform, and the bankruptcy or debt-restructuring of distressed enterprises.[4]

Secondly, although the state has decentralized some autonomy of management to enterprises and loosened its control over propaganda and press with the development of the market-oriented reform, it has never relaxed the power over the nomination and dismissal of personnel of the SOEs.[5] The board of directors is appointed by the CCP, which also elects the managers of every department, directly or indirectly. The state owns the enterprise and the relevant government agencies act as the shareholders. Because of the triple roles of the state, as the real owner of the enterprise, the regulator of business affairs and the appointer of directors and senior management staff, political intervention is easily exerted by the state over the business life of the enterprise. Undoubtedly, the enterprise may not have the right incentives to pursue profits. As the shareholders, the government agencies may also be reluctant to force the enterprise to take risky activities, because the officials of such agencies are concerned with political risk more than commercial risk. In addition, 'managers and boards of directors tend not to resist arbitrary government intrusion into all areas of business operations'.[6] They do not expect to have any debate or conflict with their appointer, since this could jeopardize their job and leadership of the enterprise. Therefore, this is also a big challenge to the corporate governance structure of the SOEs, which may reduce the competitiveness of SOEs against private enterprises.

Thirdly, it is noteworthy that every enterprise has a labour union. A certain number of representatives of the labour union must be appointed to be directors or supervisors, who are able to be involved in the decision-making process or the supervision of the management in the corporate governance structure. Therefore the workers are able to exert their influence on significant commercial activities through their representatives in the two boards.[7] This arrangement reflects a unique

2 Ewing (2005), p. 322.

3 Yang (2006), p. 44.

4 Guo (2003), p. 572.

5 Yang (2006), p. 52; Tan and Wang (2007), p. 155.

6 Tenev and Zhang (2002), p. 99.

7 The corporate governance of Chinese enterprises, whether SOEs or private enterprises, adopts a two-tier board system similar to the German structure. Directors are

Chinese characteristic, that the workers are the real masters of the enterprise. In addition, in the old corporate rescue regime of the outdated Enterprise Bankruptcy Law (for Trial Implementation) 1986, the worker's congress in the enterprise was entitled to discuss the reorganization plan issued by the superior department of the debtor enterprise and supervise the implementation of the plan.[8] It is also notable that the new Enterprise Bankruptcy Law 2006, hereafter 'EBL 2006', also stipulates that there should be one representative of the labour union in the creditors' committee which is authorized to perform a series of important functions in the bankruptcy and corporate rescue proceedings.[9]

Fourthly, under the state-planned economy, the SOEs were responsible for the provision of social welfare to the workers. This social security system was very different from that under, for example, the UK system, in which the government provides welfare benefits, such as health care, state pensions and redundancy benefits, to the employees. In China, each SOE was a self-sufficient 'welfare society' which offered medical care, life-long employment and housing.[10] The Chinese government adopted the social policy of 'high employment, low wage, high subsidy and high welfare' which meant that the SOEs had to raise huge amounts of social security funds from their annual profits.[11] The government provided a limited amount of subsidy only in the circumstances where the SOEs failed to raise sufficient social welfare funds.[12] In addition, the SOEs were also liable to take care of the livelihood of the workforce by means of providing basic facilities such as hospitals, nurseries, schools, and canteens which catered for the need of workers and their family members.[13] This was why the people who worked in the SOEs were regarded as holding an 'iron rice bowl'. It was undeniable, however, that this enterprise-financed social security system caused many negative effects. Firstly, it created a heavy financial burden on the SOEs, which constrained the enlargement of production scale and enhancement of productivity. In addition, the employees might not have the right incentives to innovate and improve efficiency under the coverage of the 'iron rice bowl' which could lead to laziness and equalitarianism.[14] Furthermore, there was a troublesome issue about whether facilities such as

---

the members of the management board which is in charge of managing the company's property and business affairs. Supervisors are the members of the supervisory board which primarily undertakes the statutory functions of monitoring the financial situation and business operation of the company and directors' conduct. For more details, see Chapter 3 of this volume and Miles and Zhang (2006), p. 213.

8 Article 20, EBL 1986. The 'superior department' means a specific government agency which is in charge of SOEs.

9 Articles 67 and 68, EBL 2006. See further Chapter 10 of this volume.

10 Leung (2003), p. 77.

11 Wang (2001), p. 64.

12 Lin and Kangas (2006), pp. 63-5.

13 Tang (2005), para. 3.22.

14 The concept of 'equalitarianism' is explained at Chapter 1 of this volume above. See also Wong (2004), p. 156.

hospitals and schools should be categorized as part of the bankruptcy estate when the SOE was placed into bankruptcy proceedings. Although these facilities belonged to the debtor enterprise, they were closely related to the daily lives of the workers. The law was silent as to this sensitive issue, which was usually resolved by administrative measures.[15] Finally, the over-tight connection between SOEs and employees inevitably had a great impact on the implementation of the EBL 1986 and the drafting process of the new EBL 2006. The bankruptcy of a SOE meant the termination of the high welfare provision, which had the potential to invoke social unrest under the old system, given the inadequacies of the social security system.

*Comparison with UK State Provision*

Striking contrasts can be made with the situation in the UK, as an example of a state with a well developed system of welfare provision, containing measures that enable employees to look to the state for financial provision in the event of the insolvency of their employer. When a British company is insolvent, the employees are able to claim for their back wages and benefits through a series of routes. The insolvency legislation has conferred preferential status upon labour claims ahead of unsecured creditors in the distribution of the bankruptcy estate.[16] The employees used to share the distributional priority with the Inland Revenue and HM Customs and Excise, but now have become the principal preferential creditors since the preference of Crown debts was abolished by the Enterprise Act 2002 reforms.[17] It is noteworthy that the employees' claim for remuneration with preferential status is limited to £800 and that the amounts beyond this limit are dealt with as an ordinary unsecured debt.[18] In addition, the sums available under this preferential claim may be influenced and reduced by a prior ranking claim with security like the fixed charge. However, this disadvantage may not bother the employees too much, since they are entitled to claim their unpaid wages and pensions and the like from the social security system, which is then subrogated to the rights of the employee. The employees are likely to obtain their entitlements more quickly through these means and they will not have to worry that there are insufficient sums to pay them. The labour-related laws enable employees of an insolvent company to claim for a wide range of entitlements against the state National Insurance Fund (NIF).[19] This is a more secure and productive way for employees to benefit, and it is therefore commented that 'the advantages of the

15 Chen (2000), pp. 58-9. Normally, such assets were not treated as bankruptcy property and would be taken over by the local government. Wang (2007), p. 390.

16 Insolvency Act 1986, s. 175.

17 Davies (2003), p. 30.

18 Insolvency Act 1986, Sch. 6, paras 9 and 12; Insolvency Proceedings (Monetary Limits) Order 1986 (SI 1986/1996), Article 4.

19 Employment Rights Act 1996, ss 166-70 and ss 182-90. Frisby (2000), p. 249; Eldridge (2001), p. 21.

[NIF] route are that [NIF] entitlements are guaranteed as opposed to preferred'.[20] In addition, the English employment laws are very conducive to the continuation of employment contracts when a transfer of business takes place, according to the Transfer of Undertakings (Protection of Employment) Regulations 2006 which are intended to protect employees from unfair dismissal.[21] The purchaser under the sale of an insolvent business is liable to inherit contractual obligations to the affected employees. In other words, when the business of a company is sold, the affected employees will be transferred to the transferee who shall accept the existing terms of the employment contracts. Any dismissal because of the transfer or a reason connected with it, is regarded as unfair dismissal and the employee is accordingly entitled to compensation, unless the dismissal is for, or principally for, an economic, technical or organizational reason.[22]

It is noteworthy that SOE reform is the most crucial component of China's market reforms.[23] Under the passive impact of the old economic system, which provided a lack of operational autonomy and appropriate incentives, SOEs failed to compete with private and foreign-invested enterprises in competitive industries. With the further decentralization of management and decision-making power,[24] SOEs could self-arrange production and sale according to the supply-and-demand rule on a commercial basis. The 'big pot', a legacy of the former planned economy, was abandoned by the reform which purported to get rid of equalitarianism and restore the incentives and creativity of workers and the vigour of enterprises.[25] The eventual aims of the SOE reform are to build an efficient corporate governance structure[26] and to formulate a modern enterprise system by means of clear corporate property rights and ownership structures, manifest autonomy of operation and relevant responsibility, separation between SOEs and government agencies, and scientific management.[27]

## State Involvement in SOE Bankruptcies

State involvement in the affairs of struggling SOEs has tended to be very significant and a number of initiatives will be described in this section. This activity is likely

20 Finch (2009), p. 757.

21 For more discussion about the new Transfer of Undertakings (Protection of Employment) Regulations 2006, SI 2006/246, 'TUPE 2006', see Upex and Ryley (2006); McMullen (2006), p. 113.

22 Directive 2001/23/EC, Article 4 (1); TUPE 2006, Reg. 7 (1)(2).

23 For an overview of SOE reform, see Garnaut, Song, Tenev and Yao (2005), pp. 2-11; Holz (2003).

24 See Lardy (1998), pp. 22-4 and Naughton (1995).

25 Deng (1993), p. 155.

26 See further Chapter 3 of this volume.

27 Tenev and Zhang (2002), p. 36; Ewing (2005), p. 317.

to diminish in the near future, although it is unlikely that state involvement will disappear completely.

*Planned Bankruptcy*

As noted previously, the two main obstacles to the implementation of bankruptcy proceedings in relation to SOEs have been the large amounts of non-performing loans in the state-owned banks and labour-related issues. Rather than ensuring the effectiveness and efficiency of the implementation of bankruptcy laws, the government has been more concerned with the potential social unrest which would inevitably be caused by the possible collapse of a financial institution and the protest of laid-off workers as a result of the bankruptcy of SOEs. Huge efforts have been made by the State to secure social stability which has been the main priority of the Chinese Communist Party at all times.

In 1994, the central government launched a Capital Structure Optimization Programme (CSOP)[28] in 18 pilot cities including Shanghai, which aimed to support financially ailing but still viable enterprises, to close down completely failed enterprises by administrative directives, rather than bankruptcy laws and market rules, and to cope with the arrangement of the unemployed workers appropriately.[29] This programme restricted bankruptcy and encouraged mergers of loss-making SOEs with profitable SOEs.[30] It was treated as an important remedy to deal with the liquidation of SOEs which could not be rescued, and to facilitate debt-restructuring under administrative measures.[31]

The bankruptcies of SOEs in the 18 test-point cities was followed by a series of administrative decrees out of the proceedings of existing bankruptcy laws under the CSOP. Under this approach, referred to as 'planned bankruptcy' or 'administrative closure', special policies were adopted in relation to employees, who enjoyed the main priority in the distribution of assets.[32] In other words, all the proceeds of the bankruptcy estates were employed to realize the claims of employees, whether or not the assets were subject to a security. The proceeds from the sale of an SOE's land use rights were used for the resettlement of the laid-off workers in priority. Obviously, this rule contradicted the distributional principle which had been

28 An official document, entitled 'Notice relating to carry out the bankruptcy of SOEs in some pilot cities', was issued by the State Council in October 1994 (the so-called 'Notice No. 59').

29 Tang (2005), para. 5.79.

30 Harmer (1996), p. 2571.

31 Booth (2008), p. 280.

32 Article 1 of the 1994 Pronouncement clearly stipulates that 'in any implementation of SOE bankruptcies, it is the responsibility of the relevant local government to ensure that all steps and all measures are to be taken, practically at all costs, to firstly settle properly workers of the bankrupt enterprise, and to preserve social stability.' See Tang (2005), para. 5.80.

established by the 1986 law, and partially pursued social stability at the expense of the interests of banks and secured financiers. In essence, planned bankruptcies of debt-laden SOEs were carried out under administrative arrangement rather than legal process. The numbers of and processes of planned bankruptcies were tightly under the control of government, which set aside financial resource to resolve the labour-related issues and bad loans of state banks.[33]

It was noteworthy that the applicable scope of the policy bankruptcy programme was enlarged to 56 cities in 1996 and 111 in 1997, and eventually to the national level under a directive issued by the National Bankruptcy Liaison Group (NBLG), which stipulated that, as long as the SOEs were listed in the programme sanctioned by the State Council, the bankruptcy or merger of such SOEs should comply with the special policies, rather than the existing bankruptcy laws.[34]

There were several notable features of planned bankruptcy. First, special policies originally applied only to industrial SOEs, and the scope gradually was enlarged to all types of SOEs. Second, the process of planned bankruptcy was under the charge of central or local government. The superior department of an insolvent SOE would produce the proposal of bankruptcy. Once the proposal was approved by the local government, it would be sent to the local court which would follow the special policies and terms of the proposal when hearing the bankruptcy case. Third, special policies encouraged mergers. If a profitable enterprise merged with an insolvent SOE, such enterprise could benefit from special tax policies. Fourth, super-priority was given to the labour claims of affected employees, who were arranged at the top of the queue for payment. Fifth, bank creditors were allowed to be involved in the process of making a proposal of bankruptcy. Representatives of financial creditors could be nominated as members of the liquidation group that would administer the case.[35]

In the process of economic transition, the programme of planned bankruptcies did play a significant role in the adjustment of capital structures, the large-scale closure of debt-laden SOEs and the arrangement of laid-off workers, with the aim of optimization of resources and the avoidance of social unrest. The policy bankruptcy process had been applied to over 4,000 economically distressed SOEs by the end of 2006, with a further 2,000 SOEs intended to be subject to the process by the end of 2008.[36] Under the special policies the central government properly resolved the arrangement of over 8 million unemployed workers. During the planned bankruptcies the non-performing loans of state banks and the losses of Assets Management Companies (AMCs) were written off to a total amount of RMB 223.8 billion yuan (US$28 billion).[37] In addition, central government provided financial support by subsidizing to an amount of RMB 49.3 billion yuan.

33 Shi (2007), p. 656.
34 Sun (2003), pp. 19-21 (in Chinese).
35 Wang (2007), p. 387.
36 Zhonglicheng Accounting Firm (2007).
37 Xu (2006), pp. 397-412.

By the end of 1997, the economic losses of state-owned and state-controlled large and medium sized enterprises reached RMB 66.6 billion yuan, however, by 2003, the financial position changed and the state-owned and state-controlled large and medium sized enterprises made a profit of RMB 378.4 billion yuan.[38] Needless to say, the programme of policy-oriented bankruptcies obtained some positive results in the process of SOEs reform.

However, upon closer inspection it may be seen that the programme of planned bankruptcies under special policies caused a number of severe problems which may be considered to have undermined the achievements of the economic reform. First of all, the implementation of planned bankruptcies blocked the application of the bankruptcy law proceedings and led to unfair competition between the SOEs and non-SOEs. In addition, under the framework of planned bankruptcy, judges had to follow the terms of the bankruptcy proposals which were approved by the local government. The government domination might be regarded as undue administrative intervention, especially under the current political structure in which the judiciary is not completely independent. The bankruptcy expertise of judges could not be developed because the use of special policies was favoured over the use of the EBL 1986. Most importantly, the banking community was hostile to the planned bankruptcy programme because the secured claims of state banks were ranked behind the employees' claims in the distribution order, which explicitly violated the principle established by the EBL 1986.[39] The special policies conducive to the arrangement of the workforce resulted in a huge increase in the NPLs of state banks, which gave rise to the potential risks of financial collapse.[40]

### *Disposal of Non-performing Loans*

The planned bankruptcy programme caused serious problems for the financial community, one of which was the huge accumulation of NPLs. The state banks had previously been subject to the government-dictated lending, which meant that the banks had to advance loans to the SOEs directly under administrative order, rather than according to commercial principles on the basis of market forces, in order to keep the loss-making SOEs away from the brink of insolvency and maintain existing employment for the avoidance of social unrest.[41] Although the government clearly understood that it was just an expedient, the government still directed its solely owned banks to lend for the short-term value of social stability at the price of the rise in NPLs. In addition, the enforcement of debts owed to state banks was very weak and vulnerable. Since both the SOEs and banks were owned

38 Wang (2007), p. 389.

39 Article 28, EBL 1986.

40 It should be noted that some SOEs wrongfully made use of these special policies to evade their debts owed to banks, which was called 'false bankruptcy, real escape'. See Tang (2005), para. 5.81.

41 Lardy (1998), p. 83.

and operated by the state, metaphorically the debt-enforcement of banks seemed like taking money out from the left pocket and putting it into the right one. This was why the state banks normally did not have any incentive to claim.[42] Moreover, in order to ensure social stability, the government's attitude was rather to sacrifice the interests of state banks for the priority of the social security obligations to the employees in the planned bankruptcy programme. These obligations included unpaid wages, social insurance benefits like pensions and medical care, and compensation payments according to relevant laws and obligations.[43]

Because of the weakness left by the old economic structure, the state-owned banks suffered from serious issues, notably the high level of NPLs, surplus and untrained staff, and an inefficient corporate governance structure. Due to the lack of effective internal control and adequate supervision, the amount of NPLs in the 'big four' commercial banks had already reached RMB 1 trillion (equivalent to £66 billion) by 1997.[44] Although China was not significantly affected by the Asian Financial Crisis, the NPLs ratio of the 'big four' was still as high as 40 per cent in 1998.[45] Obviously, there existed potential risks of financial collapse in the state banks, which had drawn the attention of the central government. In order to eliminate the financial risks and enhance the competitiveness of the 'big four', the State Council set up four asset management companies in 1999, which were mainly used to acquire and transfer the NPLs from the 'big four' by reference to the experience of the US and some Asian countries. This approach was intended to mitigate financial risks, reduce the NPLs of banks and enable the balance sheets of the state banks to be improved. In addition, it was conducive to the realization of debt-equity swaps and restructurings of the capital and debts of the financially distressed SOEs. The establishment of AMCs enabled the 'big four' commercial banks to improve their positions strategically by eliminating their bad and doubtful loans in order to improve their financial state and to strengthen their ability to compete with foreign banks. In addition, AMCs, as specialized financial institutions, had advantages over banks of capabilities in collection, management and sales of assets. Professional skills are required to realize a high rate of recovery and cash return in the methods that were adopted, of the sale of the portfolio or repackaging of non-performing assets for sale to domestic or international investors, methods which will now be discussed in more detail.

When dealing with the non-performing loans, the AMCs will assess their potential value from two aspects. One is an immediate disposal for a quick cash return. Normally, this 'sale' method includes the re-packaging of non-performing loans in order to cater to the special needs or preferences of the external purchasers. The other is to invest extra funds in the non-performing loans, if there are some reasonable prospects that the value of them is likely to go up, in order to realize

42 Parry and Zhang (2008), p. 113.
43 Wang (2007), p. 139.
44 Tang (2005), para. 3.66.
45 Thomas and Ji (2006), p. 21.

a higher rate of recovery. Undoubtedly, this approach will entail more risks.[46] In addition, another main function of AMCs is to help the debtor company to restructure through its financial difficulty in order to avoid eventual failure, especially in the case of a state-owned enterprise. One strategy of debt restructuring is a debt-equity swap. According to s. 43 of the PRC Commercial Bank Law 2003, commercial banks are not allowed to invest in enterprises and to be shareholders of enterprises. Therefore, the conversion of debt to equity in respect of non-performing loans could not be carried out by the banking community. It is submitted that this is another reason why it was necessary to set up AMCs, where the debt-equity swap and debt restructuring could be implemented by AMCs in order to avoid violating the rules of the Commercial Bank Law. It should be noted that by the end of March 2004, the four AMCs had already dealt with bad loans of RMB 528.68 billion and realized RMB 105.47 billion in cash recoveries, which accounted for 19.95 per cent of NPLs.[47]

### *Banking Reform*

The successful reduction of the NPLs provided a good preparation for the transformation and listing of the 'big four' state banks. In 2004, the State Council had injected US$45 billion from the state's foreign exchange reserve into two state-owned banks, respectively Bank of China (BOC) and China Construction Bank (CCB), each of which was allocated US$22.5 billion. Undoubtedly, the injection of capital further improved the position of state banks and paved the way for the eventual reform of commercialization.[48] By the end of 2006, it was praiseworthy that the NPLs ratio of the 'big four' had decreased into one digit (9.5 per cent) and the banks' capital adequacy had met the international standard.[49] Such developments indicate that the state banks have reached a healthy and stable status, in contrast to the position several years ago when the state banks were technically insolvent under the high NPLs ratio. In addition, three of the 'big four' (Bank of China, China Construction Bank and Industrial and Commercial Bank of China) have successfully transformed into joint stock companies and listed in China and overseas, and the fourth one, Agricultural Bank of China, has also finished its transformation and is attempting to be listed in the near future.

### *State Financing of SOEs*

In the previous centralized planned economy and at the beginning of the economic reform, the Chinese central government used to set aside a large amount of

46 Tang (2005), para. 3.63.

47 Statistics are available at the official websites of China Securities Regulatory Commission and AMCs. See also Tang (2005), para. 3.65.

48 Tang (2006), para. 3.66.

49 *People's Daily*, 22 August 2006.

funds from the annual budget to assist distressed state-owned enterprises and rearrange the laid-off workers. This situation is changing very fast, along with the establishment of the emerging socialist market economy and entry into the WTO. In recent years, only 10 per cent of state-owned enterprises' total funding has been derived from the state budget.[50] This trend is in line with the principles of competition law, which strongly restrict the government from stepping in, in order to maintain fair competition among economic entities in the free market.[51]

Although the situation that the state tended to habitually bail out distressed state-owned enterprises has changed so far, the state may still be likely to provide financial aids to salvage some ailing SOEs, in particular large and influential enterprises, the life or death of which will have a significant impact on the stability of the local region.[52] In addition, the state can act as a coordinator in bankruptcy and reorganization cases regarding SOEs. When the rescue process or negotiation falls into difficulty or deadlock, the local government and relevant agencies may assist in providing solutions to the disagreements, offering special policies to the troubled firms and mitigating the dissatisfaction and concerns of the affected employees. The administrator and court will to some extent rely on the local government in relation to labour-related issues, in light of the still underdeveloped social security system. In the near future, continued state involvement of this nature in the bankruptcy and corporate rescue cases of SOEs is likely to persist.

## Conclusion

It should be noted that the programme of policy bankruptcies was the outcome of a specific historic stage and was an expedient in the process of economic transition. The state-owned Assets Supervision and Administration Commission officially declared that the planned bankruptcy programme would end its mission at the end of 2008 and the newly enacted bankruptcy law would apply to all types of enterprises.[53] At the time of writing it was not clear whether this target had been met, since no information was available on official websites.[54] If achieved,

50 Allen, Qian and Qian (2005), p. 80.

51 For the relevant provisions of state aid in the EU, see Articles 87-92 EC Treaty; Hancher et al. (2006).

52 Parry and Zhang (2008), p. 140.

53 Article 133 of the EBL 2006 merely reserves the process of planned bankruptcy for SOEs to the regulations issued by the State Council before this new law came into force. There will be about 2,000 out of 100,000 SOEs which are allowed to continue to benefit from the special policies during the period from 2005 to 2008.

54 On previous occasions there had been some slippage in the targets set for the closure of the planned bankruptcy programme. See Booth (2008), p. 287, predicting that administrative closures may persist 'for many more years to come'.

the termination of the planned bankruptcy system will symbolize the gradual establishment of the market economy status of China.[55]

## References

Allen, F., Qian, J. and Qian, M. (2005), 'Law, Finance, and Economic Growth in China' 77 *Journal of Financial Economics* 57.

Booth, C. (2008), 'The 2006 PRC Enterprise Bankruptcy Law: The Wait Is Finally Over' 20 *Singapore Academy of Law Journal* 275.

Chen, F. (2000), 'Chinese Bankruptcy Law: Milestones and Challenges' 31 *St. Mary's Law Journal* 49, 58-9.

Clarke, D.C. (1992), 'Regulation and its Discontents: Understanding Economic Law in China' 28 *Stanford Journal of International Law* 283.

Davies, S. (ed) (2003), *Insolvency and the Enterprise Act 2002* (Bristol: Jordans).

Deng, X. (1993), *Selected Works of Deng Xiaoping 1982-1992*, Vol. 3 (Beijing: Renmin Press).

Eldridge, R. (2001), 'TUPE Operates to Damage Rescue Culture' (September) *Recovery* 21.

Ewing, R.D. (2005), 'Chinese Corporate Governance and Prospects for Reform' 14 *Journal of Contemporary China* 317.

Finch, V. (2009), *Corporate Insolvency Law: Perspectives and Principles* 2nd edn (Cambridge: Cambridge University Press).

Frisby, S. (2000), 'TUPE or not TUPE? Employee Protection, Corporate Rescue and "One Unholy Mess"' 3 *Company Financial and Insolvency Law Review* 249.

Garnaut, R., Song, L., Tenev, S. and Yao, Y. (2005), *China's Ownership Transformation: Process, Outcomes, Prospects* (Washington, D.C.: World Bank and the International Finance Corporation).

Guo, S. (2003), 'The Ownership Reform in China: What Direction and How Far?' 12 *Journal of Contemporary China* 553.

Hancher, L. et al. (2006), *EC State Aids* 3rd edn (London: Sweet & Maxwell).

Harmer, R.W. (1996), 'Insolvency Law and Reform in the People's Republic of China' 64 *Fordham Law Review* 2563.

Holz, C.A. (2003), *China's Industrial State-owned Enterprises: Between Profitability and Bankruptcy* (Singapore: World Scientific).

Lardy, N.R. (1998), *China's Unfinished Economic Revolution* (Washington D.C.: Brookings Institution Press).

Leung, J. (2003), 'Social Security Reforms in China: Issues and Prospects' *International Journal of Social Welfare* 73.

55 This view is expressed by Professor Dr Li Shuguang who is the chief drafter of the new Enterprise Bankruptcy Law 2006. See: <http://www.gog.com.cn/gzrb/g0403/ca632689.htm>.

Lin, K. and Kangas, O. (2006), 'Social Policymaking and its Institutional Basis: Transition of the Chinese Social Security System' 59 *International Social Security Review* 61.

McMullen, J. (2006), 'An Analysis of the Transfer of Undertakings (Protection of Employment) Regulations 2006' 35 *Industrial Law Journal* 113.

Miles, L. and Zhang, Z. (2006), 'Improving Corporate Governance in State-owned Corporations in China: Which Way Forward?' 6 *Journal of Corporate Law Studies* 213.

Naughton, B. (1995), *Growing Out of the Plan: Chinese Economic Reform 1978-1993* (Cambridge: Cambridge University Press).

Parry, R. and Zhang, H. (2008), 'China's Corporate Rescue Laws: Perspectives and Principles' 8 *Journal of Corporate Law Studies* 113.

Shi, J. (2007), 'Twelve Years to Sharpen One Sword: The 2006 Enterprise Bankruptcy Law and China's Transition to a Market Economy' 16 *Norton Journal of Bankruptcy Law and Practice* 645.

Simmons, M. and Jiang, J. (2007), 'A New Insolvency Law in China' 4 *International Corporate Rescue* 10.

Sun, Y. (2003), *Bankruptcy Law: Legal Theory and Practical Analysis* (Beijing: People's Court Press) (in Chinese).

Tan, L. and Wang, J. (2007), 'Modelling an Effective Corporate Governance System for China's Listed State-owned Enterprises: Issues and Challenges in a Transitional Economy' 7 *Journal of Corporate Law Studies* 143, 155.

Tang, A. (2005), *Insolvency in China and Hong Kong: A Practitioner's Perspective* (Hong Kong: Sweet & Maxwell Asia).

Tenev, S. and Zhang, C. (2002), *Corporate Governance and Enterprise Reform in China: Building the Institutions of Modern Markets* (Washington, D.C.: World Bank and the International Finance Corporation).

Thomas, S. and Ji, C. (2006), 'Banking on Reform' 33 *China Business Review* 20.

Upex, R. and Ryley, M. (2006), *TUPE: Law and Practice* (Bristol: Jordans).

Wang, M. (ed) (2001), *Restructuring China's Social Security System* (Beijing: China Development Press).

Wang, W. (2007), *The Interpretation and Substance of Bankruptcy Law* (Beijing: Law Press-China) (in Chinese).

Wong, L. (2004), 'Market Reform, Globalization and Social Justice in China' 13 *Journal of Contemporary China* 151.

Xu, Y. (2006), *The Speech on Enterprise Bankruptcy Law* (Beijing: Law Press-China) (in Chinese).

Yang, G. (2006), 'An Institutional Analysis of China's State Power Structure and its Operation' 15 *Journal of Contemporary China* 43.

Zhonglicheng Accounting Firm (2007), 'Approach to the end of 2008 – The Deadline for Planned Bankruptcy', available at <http://www.falvfagui.com/taxnews/shushiuyawe/200712/5189817.html>, last accessed on 31 March 2009.

# Chapter 16
# Bankruptcies of Financial Institutions

Yongqian Xu and Weiwei Zheng

## Introduction

The appropriate approach to insolvent financial institutions has been a matter of concern for governments across the world in recent months. This matter is addressed under the new Chinese bankruptcy law, and as a result, China has embarked on a process of establishing a framework to enable problematic financial institutions to obtain an exit route where they have suffered from poor management and operations. The new law may accordingly play an important role in eliminating financial risks and achieving financial security. However further regulations which will flesh out the details in relation to insolvencies of financial institutions were, all the time of writing, still awaited.

The appropriate approach to the bankruptcies of financial institutions has become more and more of a concern for the public with the establishment of the emerging Chinese socialist market economy and the deepening of financial reforms because it involves massive claims by creditors, complicated business transactions and potential effects on the stability of the financial market.[1] Under competitive mechanisms in the environment of a market economy, especially with the door gradually opening to foreign financial organizations, some Chinese financial institutions are on the slide into difficulty in operation, and are facing difficulties in paying off their due debts. Under such circumstances, those financial institutions which can be rescued may find a way out of their difficulties by restructuring or reconciliation. The only suitable approach for those which offer no prospect of salvage may be to put them into bankruptcy proceedings, ending up with liquidation.

By reference to the Chinese regulatory framework, it is notable that the old bankruptcy regime was silent regarding the bankruptcies of financial institutions, and the legislative lacuna caused many problems in practice. Those finance companies, which were poorly managed and debt-laden, could not be put into bankruptcy proceedings because there was no legislation and no regulations handling the liquidation-related issues of financial institutions. Therefore, those financially ailing finance companies might cause further loss to their customers and creditors, and the state had to provide economic aid to bail out those companies in order to maintain the financial stability of the market. In the drafting process of the

1 Shi (2007), p. 659.

new Enterprise Bankruptcy Law, hereafter 'EBL 2006', the reformers reached the consensus that relevant legislation or regulation should be enacted to deal with the bankruptcy-related issues of financial institutions. However, the issue of whether to integrate the bankruptcy provisions in respect of financial institutions into the bankruptcy law or to make separate legislation in this regard caused much debate throughout the drafting process.[2] Eventually only one article was included in the EBL 2006, which formulates a foundation for the treatment of the bankruptcies or reorganizations of financial institutions, which include commercial banks, securities companies and insurance companies.[3] In accordance with this article the State Council will provide implementation measures, although such measures have not as yet been enacted.[4]

This chapter will comprehensively describe the historical development of the legislation in relation to the bankruptcy of financial institutions, explore the roles of the article which provides a legal ground for the exit or restructuring of financial institutions and examine the detailed procedures.

## History of China's Bankruptcy Law Legislation for Financial Institutions

According to the traditional Chinese ideology, financial institutions cannot fall into insolvent liquidation. Nearly all the financial institutions are owned by the state and these institutions have significant influence on people's daily life and social stability. Because of this, mechanisms to deal with the bankruptcies of financial institutions have not previously been enacted, and people have been unable to accept the fact of eventual failure of a financial institution.

### *Reasons for Drafting the Provisions Handling Bankruptcies of Financial Institutions*

In China, the socialist market economy has been established gradually, and the financial market system, as an essential part of the market economy, is undergoing a great transformation. The rule of market economy emphasizes competition, under which those enterprises which fail to compete will fall by the wayside and those which succeed will survive. There is no exception for companies in the financial market. During the process of economic transition, many Chinese financial institutions, especially commercial banks, were in financial difficulty, and the government took great efforts to eliminate the financial risks of troubled banks by setting up asset management companies (AMCs) and transferring bad loans from banks to AMCs for the purpose of improving the balance sheet of those

2 Booth (2008), p. 288.

3 Article 134, EBL 2006.

4 Wang (2007a), p. 33.

problematic banks.[5] Since the legal framework for dealing with the bankruptcies of financial institutions was non-existent, some finance companies could not be wound up by bankruptcy proceedings and some administrative measures had to be adopted. For instance, Hainan Development Bank (HDB), set up as a stock bank in 1995, in 1998 became the first bank in China to close down in 50 years. This commercial bank was closed by the People's Bank of China (the central bank of China) by administrative means due to a serious systematic repayment crisis.[6] China Agriculture Trust Investment Corporation, a trust and investment company, was another example of an administrative closure. The 1999 insolvency of Guangdong International Trust Investment Corporation (GITIC) is both the only bankruptcy case, as opposed to administrative closure, so far concerning a financial institution in Chinese history, and also the largest bankruptcy case since China was founded in 1949.

Eventually, the legislative lacuna could not persist and this promoted the stipulation of provisions concerning the bankruptcy of financial institutions. In addition, bankruptcy legislation could provide an effective exit route for those insolvent financial institutions which could not be rescued. Such provision is vital for the efficient redeployment of resources in the field of financial market. Moreover, as state-owned enterprises (SOEs) in commerce and industry, financial institutions are wholly-owned by the state, or under the complete control of state. They are operated under the instructions of relevant government departments, and administrative interference is unavoidable. During the economic transition, some commercial banks fell into financial trouble because of policy loans and triangular debts, where a lender is unable to repay its debts because its borrowers are unable to repay their debts. The banks may not have had the incentives to enforce the SOEs to make repayments, and the state was reluctant to urge the banks to initiate legal action against the SOEs. Because both the enterprises and banks were state-owned, enforcing the claims could be described as taking the money out from the left pocket and putting it into the right one. The state would never ignore the bad debts incurred from the policy loans, and would provide financial aids to improve the financial situation of banks. It can be observed that the risks of debt-laden SOEs were shifted to financial institutions, and were eventually shifted from financial institutions to all the taxpayers. The administrative closure, which was usually adopted by the state, was however inadequate to handle the bankruptcy of financial institutions.

Although provisions regarding the bankruptcies of financial institutions subsequently appeared in some laws of China, the regulations on the substantive rights and proceedings were very simple and inadequate. For example, Article 71 of the Commercial Bank Law 1995 provided that a commercial bank, which was unable to pay its debts, could be declared bankrupt by the court, with the consent of the People's Bank of China. In 2003, the China Banking Regulatory

5 See further pp. 303-4.

6 Tang (2006), p. 4. See further Chi (1998).

Commission (CBRC) was established, and since then a bankruptcy declaration by a commercial bank has required the consent of the CBRC, under the amended Commercial Bank Law. A similar provision for insurance companies can be found in Article 86 of the Insurance Law, requiring the consent of the China Insurance Regulatory Commission (CIRC).[7] Meanwhile, both of these provisions provided for the appointment of a liquidation group, the members of which were nominated by the local governments. Article 71 of the Commercial Bank Law of the People's Republic of China also set out a paragraph stipulating that the 'repayment of the principal of savings deposits of individuals and interest thereon shall be given a priority after the liquidation expenses, the wages owed to the employees and labour insurance premiums have been paid'.[8] A similar priority for the indemnification or payment of insurance money is provided by the Insurance Law 1995.[9] In addition, the transfer of the debtor company's life insurance contracts and reserve funds to other insurance companies is also stipulated.[10]

These legislations represented an improvement upon the previous non-existence of bankruptcy regulations in relation to financial institutions, but their effectiveness was limited. The most critical issue was whether these provisions offered sufficient protection for depositors, creditors and taxpayers. To be honest, China does not have adequate experience in coping with the bankruptcies of financial institutions, especially in the circumstance where most of the banks and other financial institutions are owned by the state, and the history of non-state-owned financial institutions is relatively short in China.[11] As to the cases of the bankruptcies of financial institutions, judges could not find a juridical basis and rule by which to handle such cases because of the lack of legislation in this area and lack of experience of such cases. Hearing a bankruptcy case in respect of a financial institution relied on the limited skill and expertise of judges in courts at all levels, while the bankruptcy proceedings were going on. If the judges encountered some tricky issues which they were unable to resolve, they tended to ask the Supreme People's Court (SPC) for help and instruction. A judicial interpretation might be issued by the SPC, based on the limited experience of trials, for the guidance of similar cases in the future. The judges were usually placed in an uncomfortable position when they were facing the bankruptcy-related issues of finance companies, because of the legislative lacuna, which demonstrated the need for the creation of a legal regime to deal with the bankruptcies of financial institutions. Therefore, bankruptcy legislation regarding financial institutions became an urgent issue to eliminate the failed financial institutions from the competitive market, replacing the process of administrative closure under government policy and guidance.

7 Insurance Law was promulgated on 30 June 1995, and amended on 27 October 2000.

8 Article 71, Commercial Bank Law 1995.

9 Article 88, Insurance Law 1995.

10 Article 87, Insurance Law 1995.

11 Shi (2007), p. 660.

In the *China Financial Stability Report 2007* it was stressed that the stability of state finance is not in pursuit of zero closedown of financial institutions, but rather, the mechanism is established to let the poorly-run financial institutions be eliminated.[12]

*Drafting Process of Bankruptcy Legislation Regarding Financial Institutions*

There was a heated debate throughout the whole drafting process as to whether the EBL 2006 should apply to financial institutions or whether the bankruptcy of financial institutions should be subject to separate legislation. There is no international consensus on this issue. The UNCITRAL Legislative Guide acknowledges that it may be necessary for special provision to be made for enterprises of a specialized nature, including banking institutions.[13] In the US, the Bankruptcy Code generally excludes financial institutions,[14] and in the UK, provision regarding financial entities can be found in financial markets legislation.[15] Not only the insolvency procedures that are applicable to ordinary companies are available but also some specialist provision has been made for failing banks.[16]

There is one view that, since the bankruptcies of financial institutions involve a large number of clients and creditors in banks, insurance companies, and other financial institutions, the bankruptcies of such institutions should only be carried out when the relevant insurance system is established,[17] otherwise it will lead to social instability. In the draft of 2002, commercial banks were to be explicitly excluded from the scope of application of the bankruptcy law. It was argued that the new bankruptcy law should apply to commercial banks and insurance companies, but that securities companies and trust companies should be excluded because they would seek special treatment.[18] As for the bankruptcy of commercial banks and insurance companies, the Commercial Bank Law 1995 and Insurance Law 1995 have relevant provisions, so these two kinds of financial institutions were to be excluded, while the other financial institutions were to be included in the new bankruptcy law. The new bankruptcy law did not adopt the above points, and set out one article on the basis of the June and October 2004 drafts, providing that the bankruptcy of banks, insurance companies and other financial institutions should be handled by the implementation regulations, based on the new law and related laws to be issued by the State Council.[19] At the time of writing no such laws

---

12 People's Bank of China (2007).
13 See the UNCITRAL (2005), pp. 40-41.
14 Shi (2007), p. 659, citing 11 U.S.C.A. § 109(b)(2), (b)(3) and (d) (2005).
15 S. 359, Financial Services and Markets Act 2000.
16 Banking Act 2009, Part 2.
17 Miao (2008), p. 201.
18 Booth (2008), p. 288.
19 Article 149, October 2004 draft; Article 134, EBL 2006; Booth (2008), p. 288.

had yet been issued, although they were put on the legislative agenda as far back as February 2008.

## The Roles of Article 134 on the Bankruptcy of Financial Institutions

For the first time, the bankruptcy of financial institutions is addressed in the EBL 2006, which in effect proclaims that China's market economy has accepted the possibility of the bankruptcy of financial institutions. The EBL 2006 authorizes the financial supervisory and administrative agencies to handle matters in respect of the problematic banks and other financial institutions. This is consistent with the existing rules in relation to the bankruptcy-related issues of financial institutions in the existing Chinese laws which can be found in the Commercial Bank Law, Securities Law and Insurance Law. In the meantime, the new bankruptcy law empowers the State Council to draft relevant detailed regulations in relation to bankruptcy-related matters in respect of financial institutions. The application of these regulations in the near future will open a new era for the development of the legal framework towards the bankruptcy of financial institutions.

### *The Scope of Financial Institutions and the Supervisory and Regulatory Institutions*

Basically, the new bankruptcy law provides a very extensive definition of the term 'financial institution'. Article 134, applies to 'financial institutions', which are those financial entities which are under the supervision of three agencies under the State Council, respectively, the Banking Supervisory and Regulatory Commission (BSRC), the Securities Supervisory and Regulatory Commission (SSRC) and the Insurance Supervisory and Regulatory Commission (ISRC), mainly including commercial banks, securities companies and insurance companies, but these are not all of them.[20] In addition, as for specific categories of financial institutions, they include: (1) institutions under the supervision of the People's Bank of China and the State Bureau of Foreign Exchange Control, such as the Huijin Corporation, supervised by the Bureau of Foreign Exchange Control; (2) financial institutions dealing with futures and financial derivatives; (3) financial institutions under the supervision of financial departments, such as the financial group of companies, such as Zhongxin, Everbright, etc and the four financial assets management companies, respectively Xinda, Huarong, Great Wall and Dongfang; and (4) the financial institutions under the supervision of the Ministry of Agriculture and other departments, such as the rural credit cooperatives, involved in the business of depositing money from the public and advancing loans. Therefore, the financial supervisory agencies are not only the BSRC, SSRC and ISRC, but also the People's

20 Article 134(1), EBL 2006.

Bank of China, the State Bureau of Foreign Exchange Control, the Ministry of Finance and the Ministry of Agriculture.[21]

*The Application for the Bankruptcy of Financial Institutions*

Although financial institutions are enterprises, their business and assets are different from those of enterprises in the industrial and commercial sector. Consequently, their bankruptcies cannot be treated in the same way as those of ordinary enterprises. In the bankruptcy of an ordinary enterprise, only the debtor and its creditors can initiate the application for bankruptcy.[22] If an enterprise has been placed in the process of dissolution and the remaining assets of the enterprise are not sufficient to satisfy the debts of all the creditors, the staff who are in charge of the liquidation of the company may also present a petition for bankruptcy.[23] However, in the practice of the bankruptcy of a financial institution, the clients and creditors of the financial institution are unlikely to initiate bankruptcy proceedings because thousands of clients and creditors are involved in businesses with the financial institution. One claimant may be unable to prove that this financial institution is insolvent, and is less likely to convince judges of this fact. However, if an insolvent financial entity cannot be placed into bankruptcy proceedings, further debts will be accumulated and losses to clients and creditors will be increased. Here arises a question as to who will be the appropriate applicants? Article 134 of the EBL 2006 empowers the financial supervisory and regulatory agencies under the State Council to petition to the court for bankruptcy or reorganization.[24] There does not as yet appear to be general consensus as to the effect of this provision on the ability of debtors or creditors to file petitions.[25] However, the BSRC, the SSRC and the ISRC are the main petitioners to initiate the bankruptcy of commercial banks, securities companies and insurance companies. This arrangement demonstrates that the financial supervisory agencies have greater control in coping with the financial difficulties of financial institutions. The financial supervisory agencies are in an advantageous position in this regard, since they have a more precise estimate of the risks of financial institutions under their supervision. Therefore, the power to petition for bankruptcy, which is conferred on the supervisory agencies, is appropriate and necessary for the prevention and disposal of the business risks, and to protect the interests of clients and creditors.

21 Wang (2007b), p. 391.
22 Article 7, EBL 2006.
23 Article 7(3), EBL 2006.
24 Article 134(1), EBL 2006.
25 Booth (2008), p. 289.

### *Takeover and Custody by Financial Supervisory Agencies*

The EBL 2006 adopts the measures of takeover and custody in respect of the financial institutions subject to financial risks by the financial supervisory agencies, in light of the relevant laws and administrative regulations. Once a financial entity falls into financial difficulty, the relevant financial supervisory agency may attempt to deal with the financial risks in respect of the problematic entity through takeover, custody or reorganization.[26] If the financial entity still cannot be turned around, the normal approach is for it to be put into administrative closure or bankruptcy proceedings. In order to prevent individual creditors from initiating civil actions or executions against the property of the troubled financial entity, the financial supervisory agency is entitled to apply to the court for a stay, under which any civil action or execution procedure against the entity cannot be initiated.[27] After the takeover or custody of a financial institution, the court could consider a petition of a creditor against the financial entity, and may support the petition and restore the suspended proceedings according to relevant laws.[28]

### *Empowering the State Council to Formulate Regulations on the Bankruptcy of Financial Institutions*

Article 134 empowers the State Council to produce detailed provisions according to the EBL 2006 and the Commercial Bank Law, Insurance Law and Securities Law[29] to deal with the particular issues in the bankruptcies of financial institutions, in order to ensure that the bankruptcy regime for financial institutions can be used effectively in practice.[30] The special issues that are expected to be resolved by means of this regulation are: (1) the provision of a specific definition of 'financial institution' with the intention to include financial institutions that are funded by foreign investors; (2) the conditions under which an applicant may petition for the bankruptcy of a financial institution; (3) provision as to whether, in addition to the financial supervisory agencies that are entitled under Article 134 to present a bankruptcy petition, the debtor and creditors may also apply for the bankruptcy of a financial institution; (4) the sequence of distribution in the bankruptcy of a financial institution, under the recommendation that priority be conferred to personal savings; (5) special requirements for the supervisors of the bankruptcy cases involving financial institutions and supervisory measures; (6) special regulations regarding applications by creditors and rights to attend the creditors' committee; (7) powers of special management and disposal of the assets in the

---

26 Article 134(1), EBL 2006; Wang (2007b), p. 393.

27 Article 134(1), EBL 2006.

28 Article 108, Civil Procedure Law 1991; Article 20, EBL 2006.

29 Securities Law was promulgated on 29 December 1998 and amended on 10 October 2005, effective as of 1 January 2006.

30 Article 134(2), EBL 2006.

bankruptcy of financial institutions; and (8) the establishment of an investors' fund, insurance of savings, a fund for the protection of securities investors, policy holders and futures investors.[31] Currently, the State Council is drafting bankruptcy regulations regarding financial institutions. The drafting group has not reached consensus as to whether the State Council shall produce a uniform regulation for handling the bankruptcies of all the financial institutions, or whether it shall make separate regulations to which commercial banks, securities companies and insurance companies are subject.[32]

### *Establishment of a System of Bankruptcy for Financial Institutions with the Combination of Administrative Power and Judicial Power*

Prior to the establishment of a uniform bankruptcy regime in relation to financial institutions, one matter of concern is the placing of authoritative power and judicial power in the right place in the process of bankruptcy of financial institutions. The advantages of administrative power are flexibility, promptness, and high efficiency; while its disadvantages are high cost, low transparency, and the possibility of a violation of the principle of fairness and justice. Compared with administrative power, judicial power has high authority and enforceability; while its disadvantage is that it is time-consuming.[33] There is no doubt that China's bankruptcy legal framework in respect of financial institutions should adopt a combination of administrative power and judicial power, and for administrative power to act as a necessary complement for judicial power.

Administrative measures combined with judicial approaches can be summed up as follows. Financial institutions are subject to the financial supervisory agencies, and the financial supervisory agencies will decide whether to implement legal measures, such as liquidation and restructuring, or authoritative means such as administrative takeover and custody.[34] However, the matters of the distribution of assets in the bankruptcy of a financial institution, disputes in the process of bankruptcy, the initiation of the bankruptcy proceedings and the adjudication of bankruptcy are all in the charge of the Chinese judiciary. In this way, an effective combination of administrative power and judicial power can be achieved.

## Conclusion

Although there is only one provision in the new law concerning the bankruptcy of financial institutions, this provision may be regarded as a great achievement.

31 Li (2008), p. 27.

32 Information is available at <http://business.sohu.com/20080331/n255998063.shtml>.

33 Zhang (2008), p. 232.

34 Ibid. at 233.

It is clear that it is not possible in only one provision to cover all the issues regarding the bankruptcy or reorganization of financial institutions. Accordingly the EBL 1986 in Article 134 also authorizes the State Council to produce detailed regulations. At present, the State Council is planning to enact the implementation measures in relation to the bankruptcy of financial institutions, including commercial banks, securities companies, insurance companies and other financial institutions. It appears that the legal issues relating to the insolvency of financial institutions may be clarified in the near future. A pragmatic consideration will be carried out to minimize the impact and aftermath of the bankruptcies of banks and financial institutions, and simultaneously to provide the maximum protection to the interests of depositors, creditors and taxpayers.[35] There is still however much progress to be made in the formulation of an adequate and effective framework to handle the bankruptcy and reorganization related issues of financial institutions.

## References

Booth, C. (2004), 'Drafting Bankruptcy Laws in Socialist Market Economies: Recent Developments in China and Vietnam' 18 *Columbia Journal of Asian Law* 93.

Booth, C. (2008), 'The 2006 PRC Enterprise Bankruptcy Law: The Wait Is Finally Over' 20 *Singapore Academy of Law Journal* 275.

Chi, F. (1998), 'Rise and Fall of the Hainan Development Bank', <http://www.worldbank.org/html/prddr/trans/oct98/cfulin.htm>, last accessed 27 May 2009.

China Daily (2008), 'China Legislates on Bankruptcy of Banks' (published online 9 February 2008), <http://www.Chinadaily.com.cn/China/content_6446300.htm>, last accessed 27 May 2009.

Li, S. (2008), 'On the New Bankruptcy Law and the Device of System of Bankruptcy of Financial Institutions', in *Bankruptcy Law Forum* (Beijing: Law Press-China) (in Chinese).

Miao, Y. (2008), 'On Establishment of Bankruptcy System of China's Financial Institutions', in *Bankruptcy Law Forum* (Beijing: Law Press-China) (in Chinese).

People's Bank of China (2007), *China Financial Stability Report 2007, a Report by the Financial Stability Analysis Group of the PBA* (China Financial Publishing House), published online at <http://www.pbc.gov.cn/english//detail.asp?col=7000&ID=3>, last accessed 27 May 2009.

Shi, J. (2007), 'Twelve Years to Sharpen One Sword: The 2006 Enterprise Bankruptcy Law and China's Transition to a Market Economy' 16 *Norton Journal of Bankruptcy Law and Practice* 645.

35 *China Daily* (2008).

Tang, W. (2006), *A Comparative Analysis Between the New and Old Enterprise Bankruptcy Law and Case Materials* (Beijing: China Legal Publishing House) (in Chinese).

UNCITRAL (2005), *Legislative Guide on Insolvency Law* (New York: United Nations).

Wang, W. (2007b), *The Interpretation and Substance of Bankruptcy Law* (Beijing: Law Press-China) (in Chinese).

Wang, X. (2007a), *Bankruptcy Law* 2nd edn (Beijing: Renmin University Press) (in Chinese).

Zhang, S. (2008), 'Study on Legal System of Financial Institutions Quitting Market-Survey Starting from the Article 134 of the New Bankruptcy Law', in *Bankruptcy Law Forum* (Beijing: Law Press-China) (in Chinese).

# PART IV
# Cross-border Insolvencies

# Chapter 17
# Cross-border Insolvency[1]

Jingxia Shi

Recent decades have witnessed a worldwide explosive growth of cross-border bankruptcies, as a result of the increasing integration of the global economy. Generally, universality and territoriality are the starting points for discussions of cross-border bankruptcy issues.[2] Given the diversity in domestic legislations attributable to different political goals and cultural expectations,[3] the realm of cross-border bankruptcy has long been chaotic. International efforts in this field, notably the 1997 UNCITRAL Model Law on Cross-Border Insolvency and the 2000 European Union Regulation on Insolvency Proceedings,[4] have sought to create a degree of convergence across the globe, featuring facilitated cooperation in dealing with cross-border cases.[5]

Likewise, in addition to accelerated growth in foreign investment and trade, globalized production and distribution of goods and services renders it unavoidable that China will encounter more and more cross-border insolvency cases. There is only one article dealing with this important subject in the 2006 Enterprise Bankruptcy Law of the PRC, hereafter the 'EBL 2006'.[6] In addition to the lack of specifics in this article, the absence of reported cross-border cases since the EBL 2006 came into force on 1 June 2007, makes it helpful to review, in this chapter, several cases which took place prior to the enactment of the EBL 2006, in order to acquire a basic sense as to how Chinese courts dealt with those cases. This chapter proceeds as follows. After a description of the previous legal

1 The research and writing of this chapter is supported by the EYPT (the Excellent Young Teachers' Programme of MOE, P.R. of China).

2 See e.g., Fletcher (1999) p. 369; see also Blom-Cooper (1954), pp. 11-12, 14-17; Honsberger (1980) pp. 633-5; Powers and Mears (1985), pp. 305-7; Unger (1985), pp. 1154-5; Westbrook (1991), pp. 512-19; Westbrook and Gaillard (1994), p. 573.

3 See e.g. Boshkoff, D. (1994), p. 936.

4 Council Regulation (EC) No 1346/2000 of 29 May 2000 on insolvency proceedings (OJ 2000 L 160, p. 1).

5 The outcomes of these efforts most significantly include the UNCITRAL Model Law on Cross-Border Insolvency adopted in 1997, and the EU Regulation on Insolvency Proceedings, enacted in 2000. In addition, there are various recommendations or cooperation models developed in judicial practice, such as the NAFTA Cross-Border Protocol in Bankruptcy Matters, Guidelines Applicable to Court-to-Court Communications in Cross-Border Cases adopted and promulgated by The American Law Institute in 2000, etc.

6 Article 5, EBL 2006.

vacuum and inconsistent judicial practice, the chapter then examines two important cases specifically involving the effect of foreign bankruptcy judgments and the extraterritorial effect of Chinese bankruptcy proceedings. Thereafter, Article 5 of the EBL 2006 will be analysed and some critiques are offered on its insufficiency. The potential prospect for legal development in this field is to be addressed as well.

## The Legal Lacuna Prior to the EBL 2006

China launched its economic reform and open door policy in 1978. With more and more foreign-related investment enterprises in China, cross-border failures of enterprises also came to China. But China was devoid of explicit legislation on cross-border bankruptcies at a national level prior to the EBL 2006.[7] The 1986 Enterprise Bankruptcy Law (for Trial Implementation), hereafter 'the 1986 EBL', only applied to State-Owned Enterprises (SOEs) and excluded all vehicles for foreign investment.[8] The bankruptcy sections in the 1991 Civil Procedure Law (CPL) were too simple to touch upon any specifics on cross-border bankruptcy though this law was applicable to foreign-related legal persons.[9] Other laws and regulations concerning foreign investment enterprises at that time were also silent on this issue.[10] The 'Foreign-related Enterprises Liquidation Regulations'[11]

7 Some bi-lateral trade treaties which have been concluded with key trading partners have enabled foreign proceedings to be recognized: Wouters and Tang Liangyuan (2008). However these treaties do not expressly deal with cross-border insolvencies.

8 The 1986 EBL was promulgated at the 18th Session of the Standing Committee of the 6th National People's Congress on 2 December 1986, effective as of 1 November 1988. For the English version of EBL, see Boshkoff and Song (1987); see also Zheng (1987). The matter of whether the 1986 EBL should include foreign investment enterprises was debated at length. See Zheng (1987), p. 685 and Cho (1996), p. 746.

9 The Civil Procedure Law of the PRC was adopted and came into effect on 9 April 1991. Its bankruptcy provisions are very short and basically replicate main elements of the EBL despite some substantive differences. See Chang (1999), pp. 22-3. The 1991 Civil Procedure Law was amended on 28 October 2007, effective as of 1 April 2008. The amended 2007 version of CPL deleted Chapter XIX on bankruptcy provisions, given the fact that the EBL 2006 was adopted and came into force and thus it becomes unnecessary for the CPL to include bankruptcy provisions.

10 The Chinese legislation on foreign-related enterprises includes: 'The Law on Sino-Foreign Equity Joint Ventures of P. R. of China' (July 1979, as amended in 2001), 'The Law on Wholly-Owned Foreign Enterprises of P. R. of China' (April 1986, as amended in 2000), 'The Law on Sino-Foreign Contractual Joint Ventures of P. R. of China' (April 1988, as amended in 2000) and accompanying Implementation Rules. These Laws and Rules are, without exception, silent on bankruptcy issues although they mention the termination and non-bankrupt liquidation of these enterprises.

11 'Foreign-Related Enterprises Liquidation Regulations' were promulgated by the Ministry of Foreign Trade and Economic Co-operation (MOFTEC) and effective as of 9 July 1996.

provided the procedures for voluntary liquidation but remained silent on the bankrupt liquidation of foreign-related enterprises.

Article 73 of the Judicial Interpretation promulgated by the Supreme People's Court, 'SPC'[12] in 2003 stated that the bankrupt enterprise's properties situated outside the territory of China should be pursued by the liquidation team. It seems safe to infer that the bankrupt enterprise's properties should include those assets located outside the territory of China. But this Judicial Interpretation did not set out measures to facilitate the pursuit of those properties by the liquidation team.

Interestingly, bankruptcy provisions for foreign-related enterprises had, however, already been developed at a local level in Guangdong Province[13] and Shenzhen Special Economic Zone, 'SEZ'.[14] The Shenzhen Regulations stated that a bankruptcy declaration made in accordance with the bankruptcy law of a foreign jurisdiction would be of no effect against the property of the debtor situated in the Shenzhen SEZ.[15] However the bankruptcy estate in the proceedings opened by Chinese courts could include all assets of the debtor.[16] The rationale behind these provisions was to protect the interests of Chinese citizens and corporations. This approach might be understandable from a viewpoint of pure protectionism. Nonetheless, such an approach was hard to justify when it came to creditors' equality, given that it assumed a double standard and induced unfair results for creditors. In the meantime, these provisions laid much emphasis on the territoriality factor, an unappealing practice with a view to cross-border

12 'The Regulation on Several Issues Concerning Hearing Enterprise Bankruptcy Cases' (Interpretation No. 23 [2002] of the SPC) was adopted at the 1232nd meeting of the Judicial Committee of the Supreme People's Court on 18 July 2002, and came into effect as of 1 September 2002.

13 'Guangdong Special Economic Zone Foreign-Related Companies Bankruptcy Regulations' (hereafter the 'Guangdong Regulations') were promulgated by the Standing Committee of the Guangdong People's Congress on 20 October 1986, effective as of 1 January 1987. These Regulations were repealed by the 1993 Guangdong Province Company Bankruptcy Regulation. The new Regulation contains no provisions on cross-border insolvency.

14 In 1979, the Chinese government created in Southern China four Special Economic Zones (SEZ) where foreign investment enjoys preferential treatment. The four SEZ include Shenzhen, Zhuhai, Xiamen and Shantou. Shenzhen has the largest number of foreign investors in China. The proximity to Hong Kong gives Shenzhen great access to one of the largest consumer markets in the world. The 'Regulations on Foreign-Related Companies Bankruptcy in the Shenzhen Special Economic Zone' (hereafter 'Shenzhen Regulations') were promulgated on 7 December 1986 and became effective as of 1 July 1987. The Rules were repealed by the 1993 Shenzhen Special Economic Zone Enterprises Bankruptcy Regulations. Likewise, this new Regulation does not contain provisions regarding cross-border bankruptcy.

15 Shenzhen Regulations, Article 5.

16 Shenzhen Regulations, Article 31. This article stated that the bankrupt estate includes the debtor's assets when it was declared bankrupt. It is arguably inferred from this article that the debtor's assets shall include its overseas assets.

cooperation. Under this approach, when Chinese courts refused to recognize the effect of foreign bankruptcy proceedings upon the debtor's assets in China, a foreign liquidator might have to file *de novo* a bankruptcy case against the debtor in order to reach these assets. The added cost entailed in the duplication of proceedings would inevitably decrease the amount of payment for creditors involved.

When the proceedings, at the request of a foreign liquidator or creditors, entailed a takeover of the debtor's assets situated in China, a share transfer was a preferred approach compared to the direct turnover of the assets. According to the Guangdong Regulations, a foreign liquidator was entitled to advise as to how to dispose of a foreign debtor's assets.[17] The debtor's assets, however, could be disposed of, in general, by the way of a share transfer. There were different requirements as to share transfers, subject to the form that a foreign-related enterprise took. The procedure for share transfer involving wholly-owned foreign enterprises was simpler than that in relation to Sino-foreign joint ventures.[18] The latter had to obtain the approval of the Chinese partner whereas the former did not impose this requirement. The rationale behind this distinction was to protect the Chinese partner from unexpected loss due to the foreign partner's bankruptcy.[19] In addition, a share transfer had to receive necessary sanction from local government. The proceeds from share transfer could not be transferred out of the SEZ until the liquidation expenses, taxation and other local liabilities had been repaid.[20]

These provisions had two notable aspects. On the one hand, the bankruptcy in a foreign jurisdiction would not deprive the debtor of the ability to dispose of its own assets located in China. On the other hand, permitting a foreign debtor to pursue his assets in China by way of share transfer would not affect the business operation of a foreign-related enterprise, thereby protecting the Chinese partner's interests. However in practice, it is difficult to free foreign-related enterprises from adverse affect once foreign investors fail in other jurisdictions. Furthermore, these provisions invite criticism due to the administrative intervention involved in the process of assets disposal.

---

17 Guangdong Regulations, Article 40.

18 'The Law on Sino-Foreign Contractual Joint Venture of People's Republic of China' (2000), Article 10; The Implementation Rules for the Law of Sino-Foreign Contractual Joint Venture of People's Republic of China (2000), Article 23; 'The Law on Sino-Foreign Equity Joint Venture of People's Republic of China' (2001), Article 4; The Implementation Rules for the Law on Sino-Foreign Equity Joint Venture of People's Republic of China (2001), Articles 23, 24; 'The Law on Wholly Foreign-Owned Enterprises of People's Republic of China' (2000), Article 5; 'The Implementation Rules for the Law on Wholly Foreign-Owned Enterprises of People's Republic of China' (2000), Articles 23, 24.

19 Guangdong Regulations, Article 44. This article provided that the disposal of the assets, which was to take the form of share transfers or the assignment of rights and interests, was not to be made if the transfer would have had any adverse effect on the normal production and operation activities of the company.

20 Guangdong Regulations, Article 45.

## Judicial Practice: the Effect of Foreign Bankruptcy Proceedings in China

The business operation of foreign-related enterprises in China can be affected by the foreign investor's bankruptcy in other jurisdictions. In particular, the matter of how to deal with the debtor's assets situated in China inevitably has been a tough issue. The legal void prior to the EBL 2006 gave rise to many difficulties in judicial practice. Notably, aside from certain bi-lateral agreements,[21] there was no legislative foundation for Chinese courts to recognize foreign bankruptcy proceedings.[22] The following were several cases indicating that Chinese courts dealt with the problem in an inconsistent way.

### *The LMK Nam Sang Dyeing Case*

The first failure of a foreign-related enterprise took place in Shenzhen when LMK Nam Sang Dyeing Factory, hereafter 'LMK', collapsed.[23] LMK, operated by a Hong Kong company, was a wholly-owned foreign enterprise. In 1983, LMK became insolvent when its controlling parent company was being wound up by a Hong Kong court. The Peat Marwick Accounting Firm, as the receiver appointed in the Hong Kong proceeding, approached the local Chinese authorities to claim the control of LMK's assets in Shenzhen. Without legislative guidelines at that time regarding the recognition of such an insolvency proceeding, this case was not dealt with as a formal bankruptcy proceeding.[24] The Chinese court simply allowed Peat Marwick to negotiate with the local government. Peat Marwick succeeded in gaining control of LMK's assets and then distributed them in the Hong Kong proceeding.[25] The LMK case displayed an urgent need for China to deal with the bankruptcy of foreign-related enterprises, and led to the appearance of the Shenzhen Rules that were noted above.[26]

---

21 See Wouters and Tang Liangyan (2008).

22 For more information and discussion on these cases, see Lewis and Booth (1990) (providing a case digest). Despite this, some liquidators from Hong Kong in many unreported cases could have had their appointment and status recognized in the mainland courts. See also Shi (2001), pp. 36-40; Zhang and Booth (2002), pp. 34-5. Generally, courts in coastal cities, like Guangdong, tend to adopt a more sophisticated approach, recognizing that the debtor is undergoing bankruptcy in a foreign country and enabling its administrator to represent it in lawsuits in China. If the court is unwilling to grant the request, it may also question the status of the debtor's administrator as the representative of the debtor.

23 See Toronto (1990), pp. 290-91.

24 See Seebach (1995), p. 353.

25 See Toronto (1990), pp. 280-81.

26 It is not clear whether there were Chinese creditors and how their claims were dealt with in this case. But given the fact that the LMK case happened at an early stage of the Chinese 'open door policy' and at a time of pressing need for China to attract foreign capital to accelerate its economic development, it was very likely that foreign creditors were in fact given priority in this case.

*Liwan District Construction Company Case*

In the case of *Liwan District Construction Company v. Euro-America China Property Limited*, the defendant, a company registered in Hong Kong, concluded several contracts with the plaintiff. The plaintiff lodged a complaint in Guangzhou Intermediate People's Court based on the defendant's breach of contract. The case became more complicated when the defendant was wound up by a Hong Kong court.[27] In this case, the mainland court made its decision mainly under contract law principles, with little regard to bankruptcy issues.[28] When it came to cross-border issues, the court seemed to apply a territoriality approach without recognizing the appointment of a Hong Kong representative by the Hong Kong court, further holding that he lacked the authority to represent the defendant in Chinese litigation. Accordingly, the Hong Kong representative was unable to exercise the power given to the liquidation committee under the 1986 EBL.[29] The court's primary intention appeared to protect the Chinese party's interests.

*BCCI (Shenzhen Branch) Case*

BCCI was a banking group with headquarters in Luxembourg and with many subsidiaries and branches across the globe. BCCI also set up a branch in Shenzhen and operated its business in China. In the early 1990s, BCCI was declared bankrupt in more than 70 jurisdictions.[30] The Shenzhen Branch of the Bank of China, the biggest creditors of the BCCI Shenzhen Branch, applied to Shenzhen Intermediate Court, hereafter 'SIC' to declare the BCCI Shenzhen Branch bankrupt. SIC accepted and heard the case in 1992. In response to the applications filed by Chinese creditors, SIC promptly issued an order to freeze the assets of the BCCI Shenzhen Branch that were located in China. Pursuant to Article 5 of the Shenzhen Rules and Articles 241 of the 1991 CPL (as amended in 2007), SIC appointed a liquidation committee to take charge of the liquidation of the BCCI Shenzhen Branch. Accordingly, the Chinese creditors only participated in the proceeding opened by SIC (termed a 'small-pond plan'), without being involved in the global liquidation of BCCI (termed a 'big-pond plan'). The report of the liquidation committee indicated that the total assets of BCCI in China amounted to US$20 million, but with nearly US$80 million liabilities. These assets were distributed among domestic creditors under the Chinese bankruptcy procedure.[31] In this case, the Chinese bankruptcy proceeding opened by SIC made it possible for Chinese creditors to get quick repayment, but it seemed to have reduced the amount of

---

27 With respect to the details of this case, see Lewis and Booth (1990).

28 See Booth (1995).

29 See further Lewis and Booth (1990), pp. 33-4.

30 With regard to an overview of BCCI insolvency proceeding at a global level, see Grierson (1994), pp. 220-25; and Grierson (1996).

31 See Shi (1999), p. 70; and Xu (1997), pp. 59-60.

repayment should they participate in the global liquidation.[32] This case indicated that the Chinese courts might stick to a territoriality approach in dealing with cross-border bankruptcy cases.

*B & T Case: The Recognition of Foreign Bankruptcy Judgments by a Chinese Court*

As the only previous case in which a Chinese court recognized a foreign bankruptcy judgment in China, the *B & T* Case deserves a detailed examination. This case arose out of an application for recognition of bankruptcy judgments made by Italian courts. Notably a Treaty on Judicial Assistance in Civil Matters between the People's Republic of China and the Republic of Italy, hereafter 'The Sino-Italy Treaty', had been concluded and it was of assistance in this case.[33] An illegal transfer of corporate shares complicated the issue, although the Chinese court granted the application.

*The petitions of the applicant* In this case, B & T Ceramic Group s.r.l., 'B & T', domiciled at *Via Calzavecchio n.23, Casalecchio d/R* (Bologna), Italy, filed a petition on 18 December 2000, applying for recognition and enforcement of the following judgments and related matters:

- First, recognition of the No. 62673 Bankruptcy Judgment which had declared the E.N.Group s.p.a. (E.N.) bankrupt and which was made by a Milan Court (Italy) on 24 October 1997;
- Second, recognition of an adjudication Order on the Transfer of Confiscated Assets made by a Civil and Penal Court in Milan 30 September 1999;[34]
- Third, a request that the whole assets of the bankrupt E.N., including its 98 per cent shares in Nanhai Nassetti Pioneer Ceramic Machine Co. Ltd. (Nanhai Nassetti), should be fully delivered to B & T with the consequence that B & T should enjoy full rights of control over these assets;
- Fourth, confirmation that B & T holds 98 per cent shares of Nanhai Nassetti, and a resumption of the legitimate status of B & T in this corporation.[35]

---

32 In the global liquidation of BCCI which lasted for several years, the creditors finally recovered about 40 per cent of their claims as a result of effective cooperation among the liquidators and courts in different jurisdictions. See Burton (1999).

33 This treaty was concluded on 20 May 1991 between China and Italy, approved by the Standing Committee of the National People's Congress on 1 July 1992.

34 The main contents of this adjudication order is about the purchase of the bankrupt E.N. Group s.p.a. by B & T Ceramic Group s.r.l. As a result, the bankruptcy administrator should turn the whole bankruptcy assets of EN Group s.p.a. over to the purchaser – B & T Ceramic Group s.r.l.

35 No. 633 *Fozhongfajing chu zi* (2000) Civil Decisions made by Foshan Intermediate People's Court, Guangdong, at 1-2.

The reasons for the above petitions mainly lay in an illegal transfer of corporate shares of Nanhai Nassetti, which had been done by bankrupt E.N. On 2 May, 1999 E.N. entered into a share transfer agreement with Broao Win International Limited (a Hong Kong-based corporation, hereafter 'Broao Win'), transferring 98 per cent of the shares of Nanhai Nassetti to Broao Win at the cost of US$5.39 million. This share transfer was approved by Nanhai Foreign Economic and Trade Bureau (FETB) on 21 July 1999. However, given the fact that E.N. had been declared bankrupt when this transfer was made, it undoubtedly infringed upon the applicant's rights as the only legitimate holder of shares in the overseas corporations of E.N., including its 98 per cent shareholding in Nanhai Nassetti.[36]

*Background* Nanhai Pioneer Mould Co. Ltd. was incorporated, with the approval of Nanhai FETB in Nanhai City, Guangdong Province, China, as a Sino-foreign equity joint venture on 4 March 1993. In this joint venture, the Chinese partner was Nanhai Jili Ceramic Industry Co. Ltd. and the foreign partner was Nassetti Ettore s.p.a., an Italian company. On 26 December 1995, the total value of investment of Nanhai Pioneer Mould Co. Ltd. was changed into US$6.1 million, among which the registered capital amounted to US$5.5 million. Ninety-eight per cent of the shares of the joint venture were held by the Italian partner. At the same time, the name of Nanhai Pioneer Mould Co. Ltd. was changed into Nanhai Nassetti Pioneer Mould Co. Ltd.[37]

On 9 May 1997, the name of Nassetti Ettore s.p.a. was changed again into E.N. Group and a voluntary winding-up of its predecessor was commenced at the same time. E.N. was shortly declared bankrupt, according to judgment No. 62673 made by the Milan Court on 24 October 1997.[38] However E.N. still operated its business in China, despite its being declared bankrupt. On 19 November 1997, the name of Nanhai Nassetti Pioneer Mould Co. Ltd. was changed into Nanhai Nassetti Pioneer Ceramic Machine Co. Ltd., 'Nanhai Nassetti'. Moreover, after the disputed share transfer took place, the joint venture obtained *de novo* a Certificate of Joint Venture from Nanhai FETB, which recorded Nanhai Jili Ceramic Industry Co. Ltd. as the Chinese partner and Broao Win as the foreign partner.[39]

On 14 April 1999, Bankruptcy Division of Milan Court made an 'Order on the Sales of Subsidiaries and Branches of E.N. by Way of Wholesale Instead of Auction'. Pursuant to this Order, the bankrupt E.N., and two overseas corporations in which E.N. held shares, equipments and machines, trademarks, patents and business networks, were sold to B & T as a whole package without exception.

36 Written Application for Recognizing and Enforcing Judgments Made by Foreign Courts, filed by B & T Ceramic Group s.r.l. on 18 December 2000, at 2.

37 Supra note 35, at 2.

38 Bankruptcy Declaration made by Bankruptcy Division of the Milan Court (Italy) on 24 October 1997.

39 Annexure 2 to Written Application for Recognizing and Enforcing Judgments Made by Foreign Courts, filed by B & T Ceramic Group s.r.l. on 18 December 2000, at 2.

On 30 September 1999, the Civil and Penal Court in Milan Court made an Adjudication Order on the Transfer of Confiscated Assets, ordering the bankruptcy administrator to turn all assets of the aforesaid corporations over to the purchaser, B & T for its free control.[40]

*The opinions and decisions of the court* The Guangdong Foshan Intermediate People's Court, hereafter the 'Foshan Court', heard this case. The Foshan Court took the view that the Milanese No. 62673 Bankruptcy Judgment of 24 October 1997 and the Adjudication Order of 30 September 1999, conformed to the conditions for recognition of judgments and decisions made by foreign courts that were specified in the Sino-Italy Treaty and other relevant Chinese laws and regulations. As a result, the validity of the Bankruptcy Judgment and Adjudication Order would be honoured in China.

However, the court could not resolve the request by the applicant for the 98 per cent shareholding to be turned over to him, or confirm the 98 per cent shareholding by directly issuing a writ of execution, given that the said 98 per cent shareholding had been transferred to the third party, Borao Win. Therefore, this petition was not dealt with in this decision. The applicant would be able to continue to pursue its rights by filing another application with this decision as its legal basis.[41]

With these opinions in mind, further pursuant to Article 267[42] and Article 268[43] of the Civil Procedure Law, 'CPL' of the PRC and paragraph 1 of Article 20, Article 21, and Article 26 of the Sino-Italy Treaty,[44] the Foshan Court made a final decision to:

1. Recognize the validity of the No. 62673 Bankruptcy Judgment made by Milan Court on 24 October 1997; and to

40 Ibid., at 2-3.

41 Supra note 35, at 3.

42 Article 265 of the CPL (as amended in 2007) provides that if a legally effective judgment or written order made by a foreign court requires recognition and enforcement by a People's Court of the PRC, the party concerned may directly apply for recognition and enforcement to the intermediate court of the PRC which has jurisdiction.

43 Article 266 of the CPL (as amended in 2007) provides that in the case of an application or request for recognition and enforcement of a legally effective judgment or written order of a foreign court, the court shall, after examining it in accordance with international treaties concluded or acceded to by the PRC or with the principle of reciprocity and arriving at the conclusion that it does not contradict the basic principles of the law of the PRC nor violate State sovereignty, security and social and public interests of the country recognize the validity of the judgment or written order, and, if required, issue a writ of execution to enforce it in accordance with the relevant provisions of this Law.

44 The most significant articles of the Treaty between China and Italy include Article 20, Article 21 and Article 26. Article 20 deals with the scope of application. Article 21 involves the circumstances under which decisions may be denied recognition and enforcement, and Article 26 concerns the effects arising from the recognition and enforcement.

2. Recognize the validity of the Adjudication Order on the Transfer of Confiscated Assets made by the Civil and Penal Court in Milan on 30 September 1999.[45]

*Comments and Remarks on the Interpretation of the EBL 2006 in Light of the B & T Case*

The *B & T* case is, to this author's knowledge, the first case in which a Chinese court formally and explicitly recognized the validity of a bankruptcy judgment made by a foreign court. In this sense, it was a landmark decision, although China does not, for various reasons, have a precedent system. This case to some degree could serve as an indicator of the elements that might be taken into account by a Chinese court when it is requested to recognize a foreign bankruptcy judgment.

The second sentence of Article 5 of the EBL 2006, in its current form, grants the court great discretion when it comes to the recognition and enforcement of a foreign bankruptcy judgment:

> Where a judgment or ruling of a foreign court concerning a debtor's property located within the People's Republic of China requires the recognition of and execution by a Chinese court, the Chinese court shall, based upon relevant petitions or requests, review the foreign judgment and rule to recognize and execute the judgment in accordance with international agreements to which China is a party, or based on a principle of mutual reciprocity after ascertaining that there is no violation of basic principles of Chinese law, no detriment to state sovereignty or security, security and social public interests and no harm to the legitimate rights of interests of Chinese creditors.

It should also be pointed out that the 1991 CPL (as amended in 2007) and international treaties concluded or acceded to by China are very relevant as well. More specifically, Articles 265 and 266 of the 1991 CPL (as amended in 2007) on the recognition and enforcement of foreign courts' judgments and decisions can be invoked, where necessary, to determine the suitability of a foreign bankruptcy judgment for recognition and enforcement.[46] In the *B & T* case, the Sino-Italy Treaty laid a foundation to recognize the Italian bankruptcy judgments. As a matter of fact, the purpose of this Treaty is to provide mutual judicial assistance in civil and commercial matters and it is not a special vehicle to deal with bankruptcy

45 Supra note 35, at 3-4.

46 In fact, among the very few international agreements on cooperation in civil and commercial matters, the Rome Convention of 14 July 1970 on the Mutual Recognition and Enforcement of Judgments in Civil and Business Matters, and the Brussels Convention of 27 September 1968 on Jurisdiction and the Enforcement of Judgments in Civil and Commercial Matters, exclude insolvency-related matters from the scope of application.

cases. However, like the 1991 CPL (as amended in 2007), it can be employed to resolve such cases, since the Treaty does not exclude bankruptcy matters.

Now, even after the enactment of the EBL 2006, a treaty or a relationship between China and the relevant foreign jurisdictions will still be significant, due to the lack of specifics of Article 5, where an application for recognition and enforcement of a foreign bankruptcy judgment is filed before a Chinese court. The principle of reciprocity is another element to be considered, though the basis upon which the existence of reciprocity is to be determined remains an open question.[47] Therefore, it is still difficult to determine how, and the extent to which, a foreign bankruptcy judgment is likely to be recognized by Chinese courts before a more detailed judicial interpretation is issued in the future.

*The eligible applicant and Chinese court's jurisdiction* Pursuant to Article 265 of the 1991 CPL (as amended in 2007), the applicant in the *B & T* case could either have been B & T or the Milan Court. But the Sino-Italy Treaty limits the eligible applicant only to the party concerned. Therefore in this case, only B & T could serve as an applicant. Not every treaty that China concludes or accedes to imposes the same restrictions.[48]

The EBL 2006 grants the jurisdiction in respect of a bankruptcy case to the court where the debtor is domiciled. Given that the recognition and enforcement of foreign bankruptcy judgments involves foreign elements, the jurisdiction of such cases may fall into the scope of an intermediate court.[49] This jurisdiction requirement is intended to ensure the better hearing of foreign-related civil and commercial cases. In the *B & T* case, Nanhai Nassetti was registered in Nanhai city, and so was subject to the geographic jurisdiction of Foshan Intermediate People's Court.

*Judicial review of the foreign bankruptcy judgement* For the purpose of recognition and enforcement, the requested Chinese courts will review or examine the relevant foreign bankruptcy judgment or decision.[50] A practical question arises as to how wide the scope of this review is. For example, in the *B & T* case, should the Foshan Court have reviewed the procedural matters or substantive matters on which the Italian Courts made the judgments? Generally, a substantive review

---

47 Article 265, 266 of the CPL (as amended in 2007). The requirement of reciprocity goes against international trends in this regard. For instance, The 1997 UNCITRAL Model Law on Cross-Border Insolvency only provides a public policy exception for not recognizing a foreign bankruptcy judgment: Article 6, UNCITRAL Model Law.

48 For example, 'The Treaty on Judicial Assistance between China and Turkey' states that all applications shall be lodged by the court which makes the judgment or decision.

49 Article 3, 'Judicial Interpretation on Several Issues concerning Jurisdiction on Civil and Commercial Cases Involving Foreign Elements', *Fa shi* [2002] No. 5, adopted by the Supreme Court on 25 December 2001 and effective as of 1 March 2002.

50 Article 266, 1991 CPL (as amended in 2007) of the PRC.

emphasizes local laws and somewhat disregards the differences between domestic laws and foreign laws. The outcome might challenge the authority of foreign judicial practice.[51] In contrast, a procedural review of foreign judgments is more acceptable, especially in the context of international co-operation in bankruptcy cases. The Sino-Italy Treaty expressly states that the judicial review conducted by the court deciding the matters of recognition, shall be limited to the conditions specified by this Treaty. The Foshan Court in the *B & T* case reviewed and examined the documents submitted by the applicant and relevant procedural matters, without touching upon substantive matters. This approach conforms to general practice and the provisions contained in the Sino-Italy Treaty. However it remains to be seen whether the same approach would be taken in a case where there is no Treaty or equivalent to assist the court.

*The legal effects following the recognition* Perhaps this is most controversial aspect of this case was the existence of an illegal transfer of corporate shares. As commonly recognized, a bankruptcy adjudication stops the debtor from disposing of its assets when an administrator is appointed. But in this case, E.N. still transferred its shares in Nanhai Nassetti in 1999 despite its having been declared bankrupt in 1997. This undoubtedly constituted an illegal transaction. The background for this transfer was uncharted, but the transfer itself did make this case more complex since the substantive rights of B & T were not realized with its application being granted by Foshan Court.

Moreover, according to the 1991 CPL (as amended in 2007) and other relevant Chinese laws, the recognition and enforcement of foreign judgments and decisions are separate things. The realization of substantive rights largely relies on enforcement, while recognition is a prerequisite. The decision made by Foshan Court recognized the validity of the Italian bankruptcy judgments and adjudication orders, but left the enforcement matters to other proceeding which the applicant might initiate.

Interestingly enough, the applicant, B & T, finally realized its substantive rights through diplomatic approaches, instead of by pursuing further judicial proceedings. Nanhai FETB had to approve the change from Borao Win to B & T as the holder of the 98 per cent shareholding in Nanhai Nassetti. This approval ignored the rights and interests of Borao Win, since there was no consideration made for this change. If there was no conspiracy between Borao Win and E.N. with respect to the share transfer, Nanhai FEBT could have faced an administrative proceeding brought by Borao Win as a *bona fide* transferee, although this did not happen.

Suppose that B & T had brought another proceeding in order to realize its rights based on the decisions granted by the Foshan Court. A series of issues would have arisen before the court, such as the jurisdiction, the nature and effects of the share transfer between E.N. and Borao Win, the ownership of 98 per cent shares in Nanhai Nassetti, special issues as to enforcement of corporate shares,

51 See Xu (1995), pp. 333-4.

the protection of the Chinese partner and creditors, the maintenance of normal business operation of the joint venture, etc. It was not clear why B & T failed to pursue its rights via diplomatic means, rather than judicial proceedings. In consequence, the failure regretfully painted an incomplete picture of cross-border bankruptcy practice by a Chinese court.

It is difficult to provide a full account of Chinese cross-border bankruptcy practice from these few cases of *Liwan*, *LMK*, *BCCI* and *B & T*. The protection of local creditors is a priority for Chinese courts.[52] At the same time, while the notion of international cooperation is still a relatively new idea to Chinese courts, the Foshan Court in the B & T case displayed a change in this regard.

## Judicial Practice: The Extraterritorial Effect of Chinese Bankruptcy Proceedings – the *GITIC* Case

There has likewise been no reported case thus far concerning the effect of China's outbound proceedings since the EBL 2006 came into effect. In respect of outbound proceedings, the first sentence of Article 5 provides that:

> Insolvency proceedings commenced in accordance with this law shall have binding effect on the debtor's property that is located outside the territory of the People's Republic of China.

In considering this provision reference may be made to the bankruptcy of Guangdong International Trust Investment Corporation (hereafter 'GITIC') in early 1999,[53] which made a major contribution to the debates on Chinese cross-border bankruptcy.[54] The GITIC case is the largest bankruptcy case since the PRC was founded in 1949. Notably, the Hong Kong High Court, for the first time, recognized the effect of the GITIC bankruptcy proceedings, which had been opened by the Guangdong People's High Court, 'GPHC', on GITIC's assets located in

52 As a matter of fact, the concern for the protection of local creditors is blameless since it is a standard that is fairly and widely accepted as a legitimate criterion on which national courts in an international context may base any use of their discretionary powers. See, e.g. the former US Bankruptcy Code, s. 304 (c)(2) (now repealed).

53 GITIC, as one of a select group of 'champions of economic reform', was established in March 1984 and later became the second largest foreign debenture issuer in China and a fund-raising arm for the Guangdong provincial government as well. In August 1988 it was registered in Hong Kong as an overseas company. GITIC had the most spectacular rise and fall in the business history of China. See e.g., Chinaonline (1999).

54 As the first case concerning the bankruptcy of a leading state-owned financial institution in China, the GITIC case involved the largest-ever amount of assets and foreign debts, drawing international attention in a short period of time. See e.g. Chang, (1999), p. 43; see also *AsiaPulse News* (2000); Shi (2001), pp. 40-42.

Hong Kong and further refused to make absolute a temporary garnishing order applied by a local creditor.[55]

The *GITIC* case was the first case, and the only case to date, in which a Chinese bankruptcy proceeding has been recognized in another jurisdiction. The case took place between CCIC Finance Limited (CCIC, the plaintiff) and GITIC (the defendant) and GITIC Hong Kong (Holdings) Limited (GITIC HK, the Garnishee) and was tried by the Hong Kong High Court in 2001.[56] This case unveils the elements which are considered crucial for the recognition of a bankruptcy proceeding by a Hong Kong court. Moreover, the case itself might generate some positive implications for China's ongoing judicial practice regarding cross-border bankruptcies. In particular, it may enlighten us that when a Chinese court hears a cross-border bankruptcy case, the honoring of the principle of creditors' equality is likely to be of paramount significance.

### *Factual Background*

Before the *GITIC* case took place, CCIC,[57] the plaintiff and judgment creditor, obtained in the Hong Kong High Court a default judgment against the defendant and judgment debtor, GITIC, and a garnishee order *nisi* against GITIC HK.[58] There were two applications in the case. First, CCIC applied to make the garnishee order absolute. Second, GITIC applied for a stay of all proceedings including the garnishee application.[59] A brief factual snapshot can be summarized as follows.

On 27 March 1997, CCIC, as agent and arranger of a syndicated loan, lent to GITIC HK US$35 million. GITIC itself was not a party to this loan agreement but provided CCIC with a Letter of Support in respect of GITIC HK's obligation to repay the loan on 3 April 1997. GITIC HK then defaulted in repaying its debt owed to CCIC. On 12 October 1998, GITIC HK went into voluntary liquidation in Hong Kong. It was also in debt to its parent GITIC at the date of adjudication.[60]

GITIC was also declared bankrupt by the Guangdong People's High Court (GPHC) on 16 January 1999.[61] GPHC appointed a liquidation committee to take complete control of GITIC[62] under the EBL 1986. In the course of conducting

55 See further Shi (2002), pp. 129-33.

56 Hong Kong High Court Case No. HCA 15651/1999. Date of Judgment: 31 July 2001.

57 CCIC is a bank incorporated and carrying on business in Hong Kong.

58 GITIC HK was incorporated in Hong Kong as a wholly owned subsidiary of GITIC in 1986.

59 Judgment of 31 July 2001, supra note 56, at para.1.

60 Ibid., paras 3-6.

61 *Public Announcement for Bankruptcy* (1999) *Yue Fa Jing – Po Zi* No. 1-7, made by the People's Higher Court of Guangdong Province, 16 January 1999.

62 *Directions for the Appointment of the Liquidation Committee* (1999) *Yue Fa Jing – Po Zi* No. 1-9, made by the People's Higher Court of Guangdong Province, 16 January 1999.

its duties, the liquidation committee filed a proof of debt with the liquidators of GITIC HK for the amount claimed to be due to GITIC: about HK$819 million with the prospect of a dividend of 54 per cent of proved claims.[63]

In December 1998, CCIC lodged a proof of debt in the GITIC bankruptcy based on the Letter of Support, for the amount owed by GITIC HK.[64] However the liquidation committee rejected this claim on the ground that the Letter of Support was a mere non-binding letter of comfort and was unable to constitute a legally binding guarantee recognized by the PRC law.[65] CCIC raised objections to the liquidation committee.[66] Then without waiting for a further response, CCIC chose another way to realize its claim. On 2 October 1999, it commenced a proceeding before the Hong Kong High Court and obtained a default judgment against GITIC, with GITIC taking no steps. CCIC then sought to attach the debt owed by GITIC HK to GITIC.[67] On 29 November 1999, the Hong Kong High Court, on CCIC's application, granted a garnishee order *nisi* attaching 'all debts due or accruing due from [GITIC HK] to [GITIC]' to answer the judgment debt.[68] GITIC finally decided to defend the proceeding in Hong Kong.[69]

By the letter of 9 June 2000, CCIC supplemented its objection to the liquidation committee, citing the Hong Kong proceeding and the garnishee order it obtained. But the liquidation committee again rejected the CCIC's claim, placing no value on the garnishee order based on the GITIC's bankruptcy.[70] In November 2000, an interim dividend of 3.38 per cent was struck and paid out to the creditors whose claims had been processed and admitted in the GITIC bankruptcy proceeding. It provided no priority or other distinction between domestic and overseas creditors.[71]

### *Issues and Orders*

An initial important factor considered by Judge Gill in the *GITIC* case was whether there was a debt due by GITIC HK to GITIC giving the court jurisdiction to make a garnishee order under Order 49 Rule 1 Rules of High Court. Judge Gill thought the answer should be in the affirmative. He formed the view that a debt remains,

---

63 Supra note 56, at para. 9.

64 Ibid., at para. 10.

65 *Notice of Rejection*, Liquidation Committee of GITIC, dated on 11 August 1999.

66 *Notice of Objection to Non-Recognition of Claim*, CCIC Finance Limited, dated on 26 August 1999.

67 The rationale behind this strategy was that if CCIC attached that debt, then the dividend which would be declared by the liquidator of GITIC HK in favour of GITIC would be subject to the attachment. Accordingly, as GITIC was an extremely large creditor (over HK$800 million), it would receive a large dividend, which would be subject to the attachment and would be paid to CCIC.

68 Supra note 56, at paras 13-14.

69 Ibid., at para. 29.

70 Ibid., at para. 24.

71 Ibid., at para. 26.

until satisfied or otherwise provided for, a debt. Liquidation cannot change the nature and status of a debt, although liquidation brings into existence a liquidation appointment.[72]

This first point having been answered in the affirmative, a second issue was how the court should exercise its discretion, having regard to the liquidation of GITIC HK, the bankruptcy of GITIC in the PRC, the conduct of CCIC, and any other matters, since the exercise of the power was a discretionary one. In the opinion of Judge Gill, the most important consideration in this regard was that a garnishee order should probably not be granted if the effect would be to prefer one creditor of the judgment debtor over others.[73] It was therefore necessary to examine the nature of the bankruptcy of GITIC in the PRC, particularly whether or not that proceeding had, or purported to have, extra-territorial effect.[74]

Much of the trial was taken up in adducing the evidence given by four scholars in PRC bankruptcy law on this topic. These four expert witnesses held different viewpoints and were searchingly cross-examined in the trial.[75] However, Judge Gill considered that the approach that was being taken by the liquidation committee, as directed by the GPHC, was of the greatest concern for his decision.[76] On the basis of the factual summaries of the GITIC proceeding,[77] he deduced that the GITIC bankruptcy proceedings conducted in the PRC were being pursued, without challenge, on the basis of a universal collection and distribution of assets and that the paramount principle of *pari passu* distribution was strictly being adhered to. As a consequence, making absolute the garnishee order would interfere with that process.[78]

Based on the above considerations, Judge Gill made his order on 27 October 1999 and dismissed the judgment creditor's application that the garnishee pay to the judgment creditor the debt due from the garnishee to the judgment debtor, or so much thereof as may be sufficient to satisfy the judgment recovered by the judgment creditor against the judgment debtor.[79] The judgment debtor's application

72 Ibid., at para. 43.

73 Ibid., at para. 48.

74 Ibid., at para. 60.

75 The difficulties in this regard stem from the legislative lacuna and the issues arising therefrom. For the various opinions of four scholars, see the summaries by Judge Gill, Judgment of 31 July 2001, supra note 56, paras 62-78.

76 Supra note 56, para. 79.

77 The relevant factual summary is reflected in the Judgment of 31 July 2001, supra note 56, para. 80.

78 Ibid., paras 84-5. Among other matters covered by Judge Gill, he gave particular attention to international comity, a key concern regarding the exercise of judicial discretion. He drew a conclusion that there is an even stronger case for leaving the issue of CCIC's claim to be presented to and decided by the PHC, ibid., paras 93-5.

79 Ibid., para. 104.

that all further proceedings in this action, including the execution of any judgment therein, be stayed was granted.[80]

*Observations and Remarks*

The observations and remarks here are based on the judgment made by Judge Gill in the Court of First Instance of the Hong Kong High Court and the related theoretical background on cross-border bankruptcy. This case deserves much attention in the sense that it might bring positive implications into Chinese bankruptcy practice. The core issue in this case concerns the extraterritorial effects of China's bankruptcy law, at that time the EBL 1986. The fact was that there was a GITIC bankruptcy proceeding commenced in Mainland China. The liquidation committee, in accordance with the EBL 1986, was in charge of recovering all assets that belonged to GITIC and bringing them back to the bankruptcy distribution. Given that the disputed asset in this case (the debts due to GITIC by GITIC HK) were situated in Hong Kong, whether the liquidation committee was able to recover this asset largely depended on the recognition of the GITIC proceeding by the Hong Kong Court.

The orders made by Judge Gill showed that the GITIC proceeding opened by GPHC was recognized. The underlying reason for the orders mainly lies in his appreciation that the bankruptcy liquidation of GITIC was pursuing a universal collection and distribution of the GITIC's whole assets. And all creditors of the same rank, whether Chinese or foreign, obtained first dividend under the *pari passu* principle. Furthermore, the rejection by the liquidation committee of CCIC's proof of debt was based on the merits of the claim, and not the fact that it came from outside the territorial boundaries of the Mainland.[81] The above deliberations led to the conclusion that making the garnishee order absolute on the CCIC's application would prefer CCIC over other creditors of GITIC and breach the paramount principle of equitable treatment for all creditors.

There is a consensus that bankruptcy proceeding should be a collective legal device that operates in each case to protect and adjudicate the interests of all creditors. The individual enforcement of any creditor ought to be prohibited worldwide for this purpose. Otherwise, those 'diligent' creditors might be motivated through multiform channels to grab the debtor's assets dispersed in various jurisdictions.[82] Such behaviour would hinder the progress of bankruptcy proceedings and might even cause the proceedings to cease. If every court went its own way and gave little or no regard to foreign proceedings, creditors would be encouraged to engage in forum shopping, which would damage the interests of creditors as a whole. Notwithstanding the disadvantages of doing so, however

80 Ibid., para. 105.

81 Ibid., at para. 80.

82 See Matsushita (1998), p. 75; Unger (1985); Honsberger (1980), pp. 634-5.

there still exists protectionism more or less with respect to recognition and enforcement of foreign bankruptcy proceedings.[83]

In this case, the recognition of the bankruptcy proceeding opened in Mainland China (a socialist country with a strong civil law tradition) by the Hong Kong High Court, which traditionally conforms to the common law tradition, displayed an open attitude on the part of Judge Gill towards resolving cross-border bankruptcy issues. Second, the recognition of foreign bankruptcy proceedings largely falls into the ambit of exercising the judge's discretion. The problem is, if such discretion is to be appropriately exercised, which factors should be stressed? In this case, the EBL 1986 gave no guidance as to its extraterritorial effect and four expert witnesses held different opinions in this regard. The factors taken into consideration by Judge Gill mainly reflected the principle of creditors' equality.

It is fair to state that the *GITIC* case might not be an authority in Hong Kong for the proposition that the EBL 1986 had extraterritorial effect, nor does it establish that a Hong Kong Court will recognize any Mainland China bankruptcy proceeding. Rather it should be restricted to its limited facts.[84] But in any sense, the primary reason for Judge Gill's orders was a finding that the GITIC liquidation was being pursued on the basis of a universal collection and distribution of assets and that the creditors worldwide were to be paid *pari passu*.[85]

Further, in considering whether the GITIC proceeding treated all creditors equally, Judge Gill took account of such aspects as the transparency of the proceeding, the *pari passu* distribution, the reasons for recognizing or rejecting a claim, granting the right of objection to those creditors whose claims are rejected, etc. Despite many different considerations in respect of the recognition of foreign bankruptcy judgments among various jurisdictions, it seems that the equitable treatment of all creditors is always given priority. Then, how should a court carry out this principle in its bankruptcy practice? As the first case of recognition of a bankruptcy proceeding opened in Mainland China, the *GITIC* case may have a positive bearing on China's future cross-border bankruptcy judicial practice, particularly requiring Chinese courts to treat all creditors in a fair way. In this sense, the GITIC proceeding as conducted by GPHC may serve as an example in this field.

## Article 5 of the EBL 2006: Additional Comments and Critiques

Little attention was paid to cross-border bankruptcy in drafting the EBL 2006 prior to 2000.[86] For one reason, the provisions on foreign-related proceedings in the

83 See Shi (2001), pp. 75-7.

84 See Mitchell (2002), p. 3.

85 Ibid., p. 4.

86 There was only one very short sentence addressing this issue in previous drafts prior to 2000. This sentence simply mentioned that the bankruptcy proceedings initiated

1991 CPL (as amended in 2007) were thought to be able to handle these cases and therefore it was not considered necessary to enact specific legislation. For another reason, there was a poor theoretical and practical understanding of cross-border bankruptcy issues. The *GITIC* case and the emphasis from relevant international organizations, such as the World Bank, OECD and ADB on the cross-border aspects of the new law, ultimately gave significance and urgency to this issue and brought it to the attention of the drafting committee. As a consequence, the 2000 Draft for the first time included an article on cross-border bankruptcy, as did subsequent drafts.[87]

Article 5 is the only article concerning cross-border aspects in the EBL 2006. Basically, keeping to a revised universality principle, this article has two paragraphs which respectively deal with the effects of outbound proceedings and inbound proceedings and are to be discussed here.

### *The Outbound Effect of Chinese Bankruptcy Proceedings*

Article 5 of the EBL 2006 stipulates that bankruptcy proceedings initiated in accordance with the EBL 2006 shall be binding upon the debtors' estates situated outside the territory of China.[88] This provision adopts a universality approach as to the effect of China's outbound proceedings. The assertion of the extraterritorial effect of bankruptcy proceeding opened by Chinese courts is a significant step, which furnishes the bankruptcy administrator with a legal foundation to pursue the debtor's assets located outside the territory of China. However, it should be borne in mind that the final realization or enforcement of this extraterritorial effect relies largely, if not completely, upon co-operation from pertinent foreign courts. In addition, further details must be fleshed out in order to facilitate co-operation between Chinese courts and foreign counterparts in pursuing the debtor's assets located in different jurisdictions.[89]

### *The Inbound Effect of Foreign Bankruptcy Proceedings in China*

Paragraph 2 of Article 5 provides that, if an application is filed on the basis of a bankruptcy judgment or decision legally made by a foreign court requesting from

in foreign jurisdictions shall have no effect on the debtor's assets located in China, while keeping silent on the effect of bankruptcy proceedings commenced by Chinese courts on the debtor's assets located outside the territory of China.

87 The author originally contributed this article. While the author frequently suggested that one article was far from being sufficient to deal with complex cross-border issues and a specific chapter shall be allowed in order to devise a framework under which the Chinese courts and foreign counterparts could cooperate on cross-border cases, the advice was turned down due to various considerations.

88 Article 5(1), EBL 2006.

89 For example, the issue of whether avoidance powers should apply extraterritorially is a separate issue from whether property worldwide is part of the estate. See Booth and Smart (2000), p. 255.

Chinese courts recognition and enforcement with respect to the debtor's assets located within the territory of China, the requested Chinese courts shall scrutinize the case in accordance with international treaties to which China is a party or the reciprocity principle. The Chinese court shall adjudicate to recognize and enforce the foreign judgment or decision if it finds that the judgment or decision is not contrary to the basic principles of Chinese laws; and it does not impair sovereignty, national security, social public interests and the legitimate rights and interests of Chinese creditors.[90]

Paragraph 2 concerns the effect of foreign bankruptcy proceedings in China. The primary idea is that the Chinese court, subject to the listed conditions, can assist a foreign bankruptcy proceeding in collecting the debtor's assets located in China. While this clause does not subscribe to a clear-cut universality approach, it moves away from the territoriality approach and its approach can be termed as one of 'revised universality'. Accordingly, if a debtor is subject to a foreign bankruptcy proceeding, and the eligibly appointed administrator, or its equivalent in that proceeding, has difficulty in locating and disposing of the debtor's assets in China, he may file a petition to a Chinese court asking for recognition and assistance. Once such a petition is granted, the administrator appointed in the foreign proceeding may locate, collect, manage the debtor's assets, and control the sale proceeds. In contrast, if a foreign proceeding is denied recognition and assistance by a Chinese court, the administrator must consider filing a separate claim before the Chinese court in order to collect the debtor's assets in China. This duplicate proceeding is less economical and efficient.

## Comments and Critiques on Article 5

Article 5 can be hailed as a welcome progression in Chinese bankruptcy law, given the previous legal blank in this important topic. This article is a stride towards international cooperation between Chinese courts and foreign counterparts when a cross-border bankruptcy case is initiated. However, in order to have a realistic perspective on the practical impact of this article, there are several points to be emphasized here.

First, the article reflects a modified universality notion, which conforms to the general trend of resolving cross-border bankruptcy cases. Yet the most significant defect of this article is attributable to its brevity and lack of operability in judicial practice. When a complex cross-border case involves many different jurisdictions which have very diverse legal systems, the means to establish communication and facilitate cooperation remain unclear. This may hinder the progress of case hearing, especially for less experienced Chinese courts.

Second, the conditions for the recognition of foreign proceedings are faintly listed in Article 5. As far as international treaties are concerned, China has not

90 Article 5(2), EBL 2006.

concluded any specific cross-border bankruptcy treaty to date. Not even China and Hong Kong could have entered into a bi-lateral arrangement on this topic despite long-standing initiatives from academic circles.[91] In the above *B & T* case, the bi-lateral treaty between China and Italy on judicial assistance in civil and commercial matters and the 1991 CPL (as amended in 2007) jointly constituted the basis on which the Foshan Court recognized the Italian bankruptcy judgments. Therefore, the term 'international treaty' in Article 5 might be understood as referring to the treaties relating to judicial assistance in civil and commercial matters. If so understood, China has concluded over 30 such bilateral treaties.

In the event that there is no existing treaty relationship between China and another jurisdiction, nor is there a case in which a court in this jurisdiction has recognized a Chinese bankruptcy proceeding, the interpretation of the term 'reciprocity' becomes a crucial factor for the Chinese courts in deciding whether to grant recognition. As mentioned before, there is only one case, *GITIC*, in which a Chinese bankruptcy proceeding has been recognized by a Hong Kong court. Does this mean that there is reciprocity between Mainland China and Hong Kong? As a matter of fact, given that the reciprocity requirement often hampers judicial cooperation, Article 5 renders the assistance from Chinese courts by and large unpredictable and subject to great discretion of a Court or judge. In addition, China does not follow a common law tradition and the judges generally exercise their discretion on a case-by-case basis, which increases the uncertainty of cross-border bankruptcy cases.

Third, when it comes to other conditions for recognition, the brevity of Article 5 introduces more uncharted variables. For instance, the definition and scope of terms such as 'basic principles of Chinese laws', 'social public interest', and the 'legitimate rights and interests of domestic creditors', require further clarification. It is also essential to spell out the jurisdiction; the status and treatment of foreign creditors; the comity available to foreign proceedings and rulings; the treatment of concurrent and parallel cases; the means of communication and cooperation with foreign courts; and the documents which must be submitted by the foreign representative to obtain recognition, and so on.

In conclusion, one article is far from adequate to regulate cross-border bankruptcy issues. China, sooner or later, should hammer out more detailed rules for its courts to effectively participate in international co-operation. To this end, it is strongly recommended that consideration should be given to the UNCITRAL Model Law on Cross-Border Insolvency and the European Union Regulation on Insolvency Proceedings, the two most salient achievements in this field.[92]

---

91 See e.g. Zhang and Booth (2002), p. 17.

92 The Model Law and the EU Regulation provide the substantive detail and the practice and procedural aspects of applications for recognition and enforcement that would enable the courts in different jurisdictions to deal more effectively with cross-border cases. For more details of these two instruments, see respectively, <http://www.uncitral.org/uncitral/en/uncitral_texts/insolvency/1997Model.html> (last accessed 15 September 2007), <http://europa.eu/scadplus/leg/en/lvb/133110.htm> (last accessed 15 September 2007).

China should use internationally-recognized rules and practices reflected in these international instruments as reference to clarify the implementation of Article 5.

## References

AsiaPulse News (2000), 'Analysis – China Plans Public Fund Injection for ITICs', *Asia Pulse* (11 January), available at 2000 WL 2676073.

Blom-Cooper, L.J. (1954), *Bankruptcy in Private International Law* (London: Sweet and Maxwell).

Booth, C.D. (1995), 'The Transnational Aspects of Hong Kong Insolvency Law' 2 *Southwestern Journal of Law and Trade in the Americas* 1.

Booth, C.D. and Smart, P.S. (2000), 'The New Avoidance Powers under Hong Kong Insolvency Law: A Move From Territoriality to Extraterritoriality' 34 *International Lawyer* 255.

Boshkoff, D. (1994), 'Some Gloomy Thoughts Concerning Cross-Border Insolvencies' 72 *Washington University Law Quarterly* 933.

Boshkoff, D.G. and Song, Y. (1987), 'China's New Bankruptcy Law: A Translation and Brief Introduction' 61 *American Bankruptcy Law Journal* 359.

Burton, L.A. (1999), 'Toward An International Bankruptcy Policy in Europe: Four Decades in Search of A Treaty' 5 *Annual Survey of International and Comparative Law* 205.

Chang, G.G. (1999), 'Bankruptcy Law in China: Too Much or Too Little?' 5 *China Law and Practice* 22.

Chang, T.K. (1999), 'The East Is in the Red' *International Financial Law Review* 43.

Chinaonline (1999), 'The Spectacular Rise and Fall of GITIC' (published online 18 May, 1999), available at <http://www.chinaonline.com/top_stories/breakingnews_b2_99051423.html>.

Cho, S.S. (1996), 'Continuing Economic Reform in the People's Republic of China: Bankruptcy Legislation Leads the Way' 19 *Hastings International and Comparative Law Review* 739.

Fletcher, I.F. (1999), *Insolvency in Private International Law* (Oxford University Press).

Grieson, C.K. (1994), 'Shareholder Liability, Consolidation and Pooling', in Leonard, E.B. and Besant, C.W. (eds), *Current Issues in Cross Border Insolvency and Reorganization* (London: Kluwer).

Grieson, C.K. (1996), 'Insolvency of Financial Institutions' 5 *International Business Lawyer* 212.

Honsberger, J.D. (1980), 'Conflict of Laws and the Bankruptcy Reform Act of 1978' 30 *Case Western Reserve Law Review* 631.

Lewis, D.J. and Booth, C.D. (1990), 'Case Comment, *Liwan District Construction Co. v. Euro-American China Property Ltd*' 6 *China Law and Practice* 27.

Matsushita, J. (1998), 'Present and Future of Japanese International Insolvency Law' 33 *Texas International Law Journal* 71.

Mitchell, P. (2002), 'Recent Cross-border Insolvency Developments in Hong Kong', unpublished paper presented at *Recent Developments in Corporate Insolvency*, Hong Kong (18-19 April), on file with author.

Powers, T.E. and Mears, R.R. (1985), 'Protecting a Debtor's Assets in International Bankruptcy: A Survey and Proposal for Reciprocity', *North Carolina Journal of International Law and Commercial Regulation* 10, 298.

Seebach, S.L. (1995), 'Bankruptcy behind the Great Wall: Should U.S. Business Seeking to Invest in the Emerging Chinese Market Be Wary?' *Transnational Law* 8, 351.

Shi, J. (1999), *Legal Issues in Cross Border Bankruptcy* (Wuhan: Wuhan University Press) (in Chinese).

Shi, J. (2001), 'Chinese Cross-Border Insolvencies: Current Issues and Future Developments' *INSOL International Insolvency Review* No. 1, 36-40.

Shi, J. (2002), 'Recent Developments in Chinese Cross-Border Insolvencies' 15 *Australian Journal of Corporate Law* 122.

Toronto, S.L (1990), 'Bankruptcy of Foreign Enterprises in the PRC: An Interpretation of the "Rules Concerning Bankruptcy of Foreign Related Companies in the Shenzhen Special Economic Zone"' 4 *Journal of Chinese Law* 277.

Unger, B.K. (1985), 'United States' Recognition of Foreign Bankruptcies' 19 *International Lawyer* 1153.

Westbrook, J.L and Gaillard, E. (1994), 'Four Models for International Bankruptcy' 41 *American Journal of Comparative Law* 559.

Westbrook, J.L. (1991), 'Choice of Avoidance Law in Global Insolvency' 17 *Brooklyn Journal of International Law* 498.

Wouters, N. and Tang Liangyuan (2008), 'A Passage to China: A Cross Border Insolvency Between Belgium and the People's Republic of China' *INSOL World, The Quarterly Journal of INSOL International*, Second Quarter, 36.

Xu H. (1995), *International Judicial Assistance in Civil Matters* (Wuhan: Wuhan University Press) (in Chinese).

Xu, L. (1997), *Trial Procedures of Bankruptcy Cases* (Beijing: People's Court Press) (in Chinese).

Zhang, X. and Booth, C.D. (2002), 'Beijing's Initiative on Cross-Border Insolvency: Reflections on A Recent Visit of Hong Kong Professionals to Beijing' 10 *American Bankruptcy Institute Law Review* 29.

Zheng, H.R. (1987), 'Bankruptcy Law of the People's Republic of China: Principles, Procedure and Practice' 19 *Vanderbilt Journal of Transnational Law* 683.

# PART V
# Conclusion

# Chapter 18
# Conclusion

Rebecca Parry and Haizheng Zhang

As discussed in this book, China has established an advanced and viable bankruptcy legal framework following a difficult 12-year legislative process. We have seen the achievements of the drafters of the new law, in drawing upon systems of insolvency laws in other countries, but also in avoiding the mere transplantation of laws that might not be suitable for China. The replacement of the previous scrappy system of bankruptcy laws contained in different laws for application in relation to different types of businesses in different situations must be regarded as an impressive achievement and it is safe to say that this new law will be indispensable to the Chinese emerging market economy. The EBL 2006 provides not only easy and effective access for insolvent enterprises to its liquidation procedure, but also it provides a legal ground for financially ailing enterprises to be rescued through reorganization.

It is however unrealistic to expect that every aspect of a complex new law will work fully effectively from the start. It might have been anticipated that when the EBL 2006 came into force there would be a sharp rise in the number of bankruptcy cases recorded. However, although the new bankruptcy law has been effective since 1 June 2007, the number of cases that were brought in the first year appears to have been low,[1] as illustrated in Figure 18.1, probably owing to tight government controls.

Several factors may explain this surprisingly low rate of usage. The first factor is that loose drafting problems may have led to the uncertainty and ambiguity of provisions. The EBL 2006 is, by comparison with bankruptcy laws in many other jurisdictions, notable for its brevity and there are several areas that need to be fleshed out by the Supreme People's Court. In consequence of this lack of clarity, judges will have encountered difficulties in hearing bankruptcy cases.

Second, although no provision is made for administrative intervention under the EBL 2006, it is unlikely that such intervention will have been eliminated in reality. The state may easily exert influence upon the judiciary in the trial of a bankruptcy or reorganization case, and the state may provide financial aid to ailing SOEs because there is no state aid restricting law in China's legal system. The role of the state in working behind the scenes to resolve the difficulties of struggling companies may be important in practice for many years to come.

---

1 Available at <http://www.caosy.com/view.asp?id=82>, provided by Beijing Siyuan Merger and Bankruptcy Consultancy Firm.

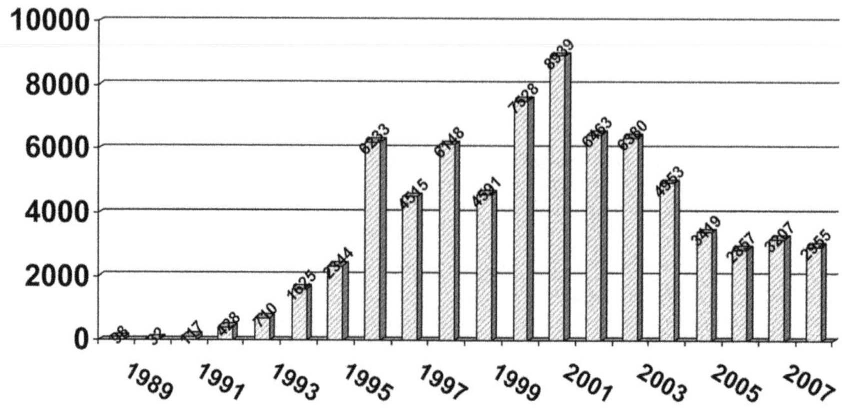


**Figure 18.1 Unofficial bankruptcy statistics**

Third, the sound implementation of a bankruptcy law needs a developed social security system. Although China has made great achievements in the reforms of social welfare during the process of economic transition, the infrastructure does not yet approach the level to be found in Western countries. The special measures taken to provide payments to employees in the Shanghai T & E Limited Company case, discussed at pp. 266-8, provide evidence that the treatment of employees may be the most difficult issue to be encountered, at least in the initial stages of the law's operation. Evidence of the inadequacies of the social security system is provided by the example of the Guiyang Refractory Materials Factory, which was declared bankrupt on 29 December 2005, under the old law. Employees (approx. 1,871) who had been made redundant failed to receive adequate sums from the social security fund, receiving only RMB 200 per month and retired workers (approx. 1,384) did not receive adequate pensions. The potential for social unrest to arise in such cases is demonstrated by a protest march held in the city on 8 July 2008. The state may therefore remain inclined to carefully control the level of redundancies for the avoidance of future disputes.

Fourth, owing to decades of government controls on corporate insolvencies, there is a huge shortage of skilled and experienced insolvency professionals, including office holders and judges. In consequence, China needs to continue to hold training programmes to develop the judges' abilities to deal with bankruptcy-related cases and to foster insolvency professionals who possess financial, accounting, valuation and bankruptcy law expertise. In view of this skills gap it may be observed that the implementation of the new bankruptcy law provides a potential market for Western insolvency practitioners who can make contributions to China's bankruptcy law reforms.

A few teething problems will inevitably be encountered in the operation of any major law. To address problems that were encountered during the first year of operation of the EBL 2006, and in order to enable the new bankruptcy law to be enforced more effectively, the Supreme People's Court has organized a committee constituted of judges and scholars to review the operation of the law and to produce a judicial interpretation, addressing weaknesses and problems that have been encountered since the new law came into force. The promulgation of this judicial interpretation in the near future will certainly further promote the establishment of an advanced and efficient bankruptcy legal framework, building on the impressive achievements to date.

# Index

www.ingramcontent.com/pod-product-compliance
Ingram Content Group UK Ltd.
Pitfield, Milton Keynes, MK11 3LW, UK
UKHW022008180926
475701UK00003B/255
*9780367602932*